The Economics of Language

The development of artificial intelligence (AI) and machine learning is leading to a revolution in the way we think about economic decisions. *The Economics of Language* explores how the use of generative AI and large language models (LLMs) can transform the way we think about economic behaviour. It introduces the LENS framework (Linguistic content triggers Emotions and suggests Norms, which shape Strategy choice) and presents empirical evidence that LLMs can predict human behaviour in economic games more accurately than traditional outcome-based models. It draws on years of research to provide a step-by-step development of the theory, combining accessible examples with formal modelling. Offering a roadmap for future research at the intersection of economics, psychology, and AI, this book equips readers with tools to quantify the role of language in decision-making and redefines how we think about utility, rationality, and human choice.

VALERIO CAPRARO is a professor in the Department of Psychology at the University of Milan-Bicocca. He holds a PhD in mathematics and studies human behaviour by combining mathematical modelling, human experiments, and numerical simulations. His research has been published in leading academic journals and featured in international news outlets.

The Economics of Language

How Large Language Models Can Reshape Behavioural Economics

VALERIO CAPRARO
University of Milan-Bicocca

CAMBRIDGE
UNIVERSITY PRESS

CAMBRIDGE
UNIVERSITY PRESS

Shaftesbury Road, Cambridge CB2 8EA, United Kingdom

One Liberty Plaza, 20th Floor, New York, NY 10006, USA

477 Williamstown Road, Port Melbourne, VIC 3207, Australia

314–321, 3rd Floor, Plot 3, Splendor Forum, Jasola District Centre, New Delhi – 110025, India

Cambridge University Press is part of Cambridge University Press & Assessment, a department of the University of Cambridge.

We share the University's mission to contribute to society through the pursuit of education, learning and research at the highest international levels of excellence.

www.cambridge.org
Information on this title: www.cambridge.org/9781009733045
DOI: 10.1017/9781009733014

When citing this work, please include a reference to the DOI 10.1017/9781009733014

First published 2026

A catalogue record for this publication is available from the British Library

A Cataloging-in-Publication data record for this book is available from the Library of Congress

ISBN 978-1-009-73304-5 Hardback
ISBN 978-1-009-73306-9 Paperback

Contents

Introduction

About five decades ago the first pioneers began exploring human behaviour in economic games using the experimental method, sparking a revolution in microeconomics. These early experiments showed that human behaviour often diverged from the predictions of expected monetary maximisation. Yet these deviations were not random. Instead, they exhibited consistent patterns. The exploration and understanding of these patterns have led to the development of one of the most dynamic and influential fields of research in the last half-century: behavioural economics.

One revolutionary insight brought to light by behavioural economics is that humans frequently rely on heuristics – mental shortcuts to navigate a complex world where calculating the exact outcomes of available actions is often beyond the capabilities of the finite human mind. While generally effective, these heuristics can introduce systematic biases. For instance, individuals tend to value losses more than equivalent gains, prefer their own possessions over others', discount future rewards more heavily than expected utility theory would suggest, and exhibit a reluctance to change the status quo. The classification of heuristics and biases, along with their application in policymaking, has inspired thousands of research papers, including seminal works that have earned at least three Nobel Prizes.

Another groundbreaking insight was the recognition that humans not only care about their own monetary payoff but also care about the rewards received by others. Take, for instance, the well-known Dictator Game. In this scenario, a participant is given a certain amount of money and has to decide how much, if any, to give to another participant. The recipient has no active role and can only accept whatever the dictator chooses to give. Hundreds of experiments have demonstrated that a considerable portion of participants opt to share their endowment, even under conditions of anonymity, even when it is explicitly stated that the recipient cannot affect the dictator's future earnings, and even after dictators are asked which course of action would maximise their monetary gain. Similar findings have also emerged in decision-making scenarios designed to capture other social interactions, such as cooperation, trust, and truth-telling.

These findings have inspired the development of alternative models of human behaviour. To explain social behaviours, scholars have introduced social preferences. According to these preferences, people do not merely maximise their monetary payoff but consider some combination of their payoff and that of others. This general idea can be detailed in various ways. For example, Ledyard (1995) suggested that decision-makers weigh their monetary gain against the aggregate gains of all players. Conversely, Fehr and Schmidt (1999) proposed that decision-makers compare their monetary reward with the reward of other players. A critical observation is that, despite these specific differences, all social preferences share one foundational 'consequentialist assumption': the utility a decision-maker assigns to an action depends solely on its monetary impact on all participants involved.

This consequentialist assumption is deeply ingrained in the economic modelling of human behaviour. It is indeed met also by the primary formal models introduced to account for human heuristics and biases. Take, for example, prospect theory, arguably the most widely adopted theory to explain human decisions under uncertainty. According to this theory, the utility function of an individual is steeper for losses than for gains, encapsulating the well-documented observation that 'losses loom larger than gains'. This function is also concave for gains and convex for losses, formalising another human tendency: diminished sensitivity. Furthermore, the objective probabilities of events are modified through a weighting function designed to formalise another well-documented human bias: the tendency to overestimate the likelihood of highly unlikely events and underestimate that of highly probable ones. Setting these details aside, it is crucial to recognise that this utility function, too, is 'economically consequentialist': it is determined exclusively by the economic outcomes of the available actions.

Economic consequentialism is also met by formal models designed to explain three classic human biases: the endowment effect, the status-quo bias, and the present bias. The endowment effect refers to the tendency to value one's property more highly than that of others. The standard approach to modelling the endowment effect involves introducing a reference point. This allows connecting the endowment effect with loss aversion: valuing one's property more because losing it is perceived as worse than acquiring someone else's property. This model is economically consequentialist, relying solely on the economic outcomes of available actions. Similarly, the status-quo bias is typically explained by attributing a cost to deviation from a reference point, the status quo: once again, an economically consequentialist explanation. Finally, the predominant formalisation of present bias involves the assumption that individuals discount future payoffs hyperbolically rather than exponentially, as predicted by standard utility theory. But hyperbolic discounting is a function of monetary payoffs, making this modelling as well economically consequentialist in nature.

To summarise, it is not an exaggeration to state that behavioural economics is founded upon the consequentialist assumption, considering that this assumption underpins so many economic models of human behaviour. But then, a critical question emerges. Is this assumption valid, or do people frequently violate the consequentialist assumption? Clearly, if a significant number of individuals violate this assumption, it would necessitate a radical revision of nearly all economic models of human behaviour.

The first thesis of this book posits that the consequentialist assumption is indeed consistently violated. The second objective contends that large language models can facilitate a paradigm shift within behavioural economics from outcome-based utility functions to a more general class of functions that better describe human behaviour.

Before discussing how large language models can play a crucial role, it is essential to review how the consequentialist assumption has been contested. A major critique has been advanced by experimental research indicating that the specific words used to describe the decision context and the available actions significantly influence decision-making, impacting beyond the monetary outcomes for individuals involved in the interaction. In a pioneering series of studies, Ross and colleagues demonstrated that linguistic labels could affect behaviour in the Prisoner's Dilemma (Ross & Samuels, 1993; Kay & Ross, 2003; Liberman, Samuels, & Ross, 2004). Specifically, participants were more likely to cooperate when the game was described as a 'community game' rather than a 'Wall Street game'. Numerous other studies have since shown that linguistic descriptions impact a variety of human behaviours, including altruism and cooperation, as well as how people resolve conflicts between equitable and efficient distributions of resources. Some studies have also uncovered a darker aspect of linguistic framing. For instance, Ścigała and colleagues (2022) discovered that individuals with higher levels of the Honesty-Humility personality trait (typically associated with moral behaviour) could be persuaded to accept a bribe simply by labelling it a 'cooperation act'. Together, these studies challenge the consequentialist assumption, showing that utility functions cannot solely rely on the economic outcomes of available actions. Instead, utility functions must also consider the language used to describe these actions and the overall context. Consequently, in a recent review in the *Journal of Economic Literature* joint with Joe Halpern and Matjaz Perc, we have argued that 'behavioral economics is in the midst of a paradigm shift from outcome-based to language-based preferences' (2024a, 115).

To be fair, economists have long recognised that the linguistic content used to describe available actions can influence decisions.

Experimentalists typically put considerable effort into writing 'neutral' instructions for their experiments, labelling any deviation from this neutrality as a potential source of 'demand effect'. However, the pursuit of truly neutral instructions is like chasing a chimera: perfectly neutral instructions are unattainable. Many words commonly used to describe economic decisions (e.g., 'give', 'take') inherently carry connotations and thus cannot be considered neutral. Like a chimera, neutral instructions might be approximated but can never be fully realised. And even more importantly, striving for neutral experimental instructions is a misplaced effort, which moves us away from, rather than towards, a better understanding of human behaviour. In reality, people 'demand' things from others all the time, often through language. The 'demand effect' should not be feared as if it were the worst nightmare; it should instead be studied and quantified.

And here we arrive at large language models. The second thesis of this book is that large language models can transform behavioural economics for two primary reasons.

The first is that people are increasingly using large language models as support for decision-making, a trend already manifesting itself across various sectors. For example, large language models are being employed to analyse market trends and assist in medical diagnoses. They are becoming an integral part of complex decision-making processes, where they can offer predictions, generate insights, and suggest actions. This is reflected in emerging research at the interface between artificial intelligence and behavioural economics. This research has started exploring how large language models behave in economic games as well as how they predict humans would behave in these games. In a 2023 article in the *Proceedings of the National Academy of Sciences of the USA*, Chen and colleagues (2023) arrived at the conclusion that 'GPT could have the potential in assisting human decision-making.' However, this support is fundamentally based on language, meaning that people will increasingly engage in language-based, human–machine interactions to aid decision-making. Consequently, the rise of large language models and their integration into decision-making support systems will amplify the demand for language-based utility functions capable of accurately reflecting human behaviour.

This increasing demand for language-based utility functions would remain unmet if there were not, simultaneously, a growing capability to quantitatively assess textual content. Arguably, one of the reasons economists have historically been 'afraid' of the demand effect and the influence of language in economic decisions has been the absence of methods to quantify it. However, this challenge is now increasingly addressable through advancements in text analysis tools, which for the first time offer the ability to quantify what was once considered unquantifiable.

Sentiment analysis represents a set of tools developed by computational linguists to quantify the sentiment tenor of a piece of text. Basic sentiment analysis tools can determine whether a piece of text expresses a positive or negative sentiment. More advanced sentiment analysis tools can break down the sentiment into more fundamental emotions, such as joy, fear, anger, or disgust. These tools have found applications in numerous contexts, ranging from online reviews to political communication. However, sentiment analysis has not been extensively applied in understanding human behaviour in economic games. This is because, while sentiment analysis represents a powerful tool for quantifying the emotional tenor of a single piece of text, explaining and modelling human behaviour in decision-making contexts requires an additional, hierarchical, step: assigning a sentiment value to a piece of text within the context described by another piece of text. In other words, it is not sufficient to quantify the linguistic description of a decision-making context; one needs to quantify also the linguistic description of each available action within the linguistic description of that context.

This is the second reason why large language models can play a key role in the transition towards language-based preferences: they could facilitate the process of assigning hierarchical sentiment values to actions within a context. The first step in this direction has been conducted by Rathje and colleagues (2024), who demonstrated that GPT-4 accurately detected sentiments with a precision comparable to fine-tuned machine learning models. Going a step further, in a joint work with Roberto Di Paolo, Matjaz Perc, and Veronica Pizziol (2024c), we have shown that GPT-4 can assign hierarchical values to actions within a context in a manner that significantly predicts human behaviour within that context. Specifically, we prompted GPT-4 with the textual instructions of 61 Dictator Game experiments. For each experimental instruction (which we interpret as the context in which a decision takes place), we asked GPT-4 to estimate the sentiment value of the available actions in that context, ranging from 'extremely negative' to 'extremely positive'. The results demonstrated that these sentiment scores could explain human behaviour, beyond just the economic outcomes. Of course, the predictions are not perfect but, still, they represent the first instance where textual content has been quantified to predict human behaviour in economic games more accurately than solely through monetary outcomes.

This research represents a starting point because the information conveyed by a piece of text is generally far more complex than a simple binary classification into negative or positive emotions. People may experience a multitude of emotions, each affecting behaviour in distinct ways. For example, Motro, Ordóñez, Pittarello, and Welsh (2018) have demonstrated that inducing anger tends to increase unethical behaviour, while inducing guilt tends to promote ethical behaviour. Therefore, if different emotions can influence behaviour in different ways, it becomes crucial for future research to quantify the diverse emotions associated with the available actions in a given context.

But this is only one layer of complexity. A piece of text can also convey information about norms of behaviour, such as what other people typically do in a situation, or what is approved or disapproved of. Additionally, a piece of text may activate personal moral values. There is considerable debate among moral psychologists, philosophers, and anthropologists regarding the fundamental moral dimensions. However, there is a clear consensus: morality is not monolithic but decomposes into several dimensions. According to (the basic version of) moral foundations theory, these dimensions are care, fairness, loyalty, authority, and purity. According to morality-as-cooperation theory, the dimensions are family, reciprocity, loyalty, heroism, authority, fairness, and property. These dimensions influence human behaviour in diverse ways in important critical ethical issues, such as the decision to vaccinate children. Here, purity leans individuals towards vaccine hesitancy, while authority tends towards vaccine acceptance.

The influence of moral values on behaviour suggests that sentiment analysis should be complemented by 'normative analysis': language models capable of capturing the normative tenor of text along various dimensions. Recent research is beginning to explore this area. In the last few years, some corpora of annotated texts have been collected based on moral foundations theory, marking an initial step towards developing normative analysis.

And of course, emotions and norms can interact in complex ways. For example, collective emotions may forge social norms, while, conversely, the enforcement of certain norms can evoke emotions. These complex interactions between various emotions and norms influence the final strategic decisions of a decision-maker, adding another web of complexity. A useful qualitative model to organise these complexities is the LENS model, deriving its name from the key pathways of the model: the Linguistic content triggers Emotions and suggests Norms, which interact and determine Strategy choice. Large language models can play a crucial role in transitioning this qualitative model into a quantitative one, through sentiment and normative analysis applied to actions within a context.

Finally, it is important to recognise that integrating large language models into behavioural economics has implications beyond the academic world. It can reshape everyday decision-making, business strategies, and even policymaking. On the one hand, by using large language models to understand and predict human behaviour more accurately, individuals can make more informed choices, businesses can tailor products and services to better meet consumer needs, and policymakers can design more effective interventions to promote public welfare. On the other hand, there are also major ethical considerations to consider. Over-reliance on large language models could lead to manipulation, privacy infringements, and algorithmic biases that can perpetuate or even exacerbate existing inequalities. Moreover, ensuring that the recommendations of large language models align with human intent may be challenging, especially in situations involving ethical trade-offs between competing moral values. Chapter 9 will engage with these concerns, encouraging the development of transparent models that enhance rather than undermine human agency.

The journey ahead is complex yet exciting, crossing several disciplines, including psychology, computational linguistics, artificial intelligence, and ethics. Some paths are yet to be charted, while others may lead to dead ends that require revaluation. And though this exploration might resemble the pursuit of a chimera, and we may never fully decipher human behaviour, it nevertheless brings behavioural economics closer to its foundational purpose: understanding human behaviour in economic interactions.

1 The Birth of Behavioural Economics

THE CONCEPT OF UTILITY AS A FOUNDATION OF DECISION THEORY

How do people make decisions? This question has not only fascinated generations of decision theorists but has also inspired research across a wide range of disciplines, from economics and psychology to political science, anthropology, and philosophy. Understanding the mechanisms behind decision-making is crucial because it underpins nearly every aspect of human life, from individual choices in daily life to the functioning of markets, the formation of public policy, and the dynamics of global economies.

Traditional decision theory is fundamentally built on the concept of utility, which represents the satisfaction or pleasure individuals derive from the realisation of a certain state of the world. The notion of utility dates back to the works of Jeremy Bentham and John Stuart Mill. Jeremy Bentham (1789) explicitly defined utility as a measurable quantity in his work *An Introduction to the Principles of Morals and Legislation*. Bentham's utilitarian framework posited that individuals seek to maximise pleasure and minimise pain. John Stuart Mill (1863) refined Bentham's ideas, emphasising that utility was not solely about physical pleasure but also included higher pleasures, such as intellectual and moral satisfaction. Over time, the utility-based approach became a central tenet of decision theory, leading to the development of mathematical models to describe and predict human behaviour.

In situations where the decision-maker knows the utility corresponding to each available action, the central assumption is that they will simply choose the option that maximises their utility.

However, decision-making becomes more complex under conditions of risk and uncertainty. Risk refers to situations where the outcomes are uncertain but the probabilities of these outcomes are known, allowing the decision-maker to calculate expected utilities. In this context, Von Neumann and Morgenstern (1944) formalised the theory of expected utility maximisation, which posits that individuals make decisions under risk by choosing the option with the highest expected utility, accounting for both the utility of outcomes and their objective probabilities. Daniel Kahneman and Amos Tversky (1979) later developed prospect theory, which challenged the expected utility framework by showing that individuals weigh outcomes using subjective probabilities rather than objective ones and tend to weigh losses more heavily than gains.

Uncertainty, on the other hand, refers to situations where the probabilities of outcomes are unknown, making it more difficult to calculate expected utility. Abraham Wald (1949) proposed the maximin rule, where decision-makers choose the action that maximises their worst-case utility. This decision rule is particularly useful in situations of uncertainty, where the decision-maker prefers to guard against the worst possible outcome. Leonard Savage (1951) introduced the concept of minimax regret, where individuals choose the action that minimises their potential regret, the difference between the utility of their choice and the best possible alternative. Minimax regret is also often considered more applicable under uncertainty because it focuses on minimising the feeling of regret that might arise from not making the optimal choice.

These decision theories thus differ in many regards. However, they all share a common foundation on the concept of utility. This brings us to one of the most central questions in decision theory and the many fields that branch from it: How can we measure the utility corresponding to a certain state of the world?

This book is driven by this very question. Therefore, it will focus primarily on how utility is computed rather than on how different utilities are aggregated or compared when outcomes are uncertain. For this reason, I will primarily consider scenarios where outcomes are certain, as they offer a more straightforward context for examining how utility is defined and measured, without the additional complexity introduced by uncertainty about the outcomes or the probabilities of each outcome. Nevertheless, I will occasionally present examples where outcomes are uncertain to show how the concepts developed throughout the discussion may apply across a broader spectrum of decision-making situations.

EXPERIMENTAL ECONOMIC DECISIONS

Decision theory, in general, concerns how people make decisions, and these decisions often extend beyond monetary considerations. For example, deciding whether to go to the cinema with a partner or play football with friends presents two choices that are equivalent in economic terms (assuming the monetary cost is the same) but may lead to different psychological benefits. These benefits depend on various factors, such as individual preferences and the status of all relationships involved. Therefore, utility is not synonymous with money. While utility may include money as a component, it broadly represents people's preferences and desires, spanning far more than just considerations about one's own monetary payoff.

To understand how to measure utility, it is essential to adopt a scientific approach to decision-making. Karl Popper (1959) emphasised that scientific theories should be framed in such a way that they can be tested and potentially falsified through experimentation and observation. Applying Popper's philosophy to decision theory means that we must create well-defined, testable models of decision-making that can be empirically validated in controlled settings.

How can we conduct experiments on decision-making? The standard approach is to give subjects a set of choices, each of which corresponds to some gains or losses that are expressed through a currency people usually care about, typically money. This brings us to the definition of economic decision.

Definition (Economic Decision). An economic decision is characterised by the following elements:

- **A set of individuals I** involved in the economic decision. This set includes all the individuals who may be directly affected by the decision.
- **A specific individual d** who makes the decision. This individual, referred to as the decision-maker, may or may not belong to the set I. In other words, the choice made by d may or may not impact d themselves.
- **A set of potential actions A** which includes all the alternatives from which d can choose.
- **A map $\pi : I \times A \to \mathbb{R}$** representing the economic payoff for individual $i \in I$ when the decision-maker d chooses $a \in A$. Positive numbers are assumed to represent economic gains, while negative numbers are assumed to represent economic losses, with respect to some fixed currency. □

Example (Dictator Game). In the Dictator Game, the set $I = \{d, r\}$ consists of two players: the dictator d and the recipient r. The specific individual who makes the decision is the dictator. Therefore, in this case the decision-maker belongs to I. The dictator is given 10 dollars and has to decide how much of it, if any, to give to the recipient. The recipient has no active role and only receives what the dictator decides to give. See Figure 1.1.

Therefore, the set of potential choices can be represented by the integers from 0 to 10 (assuming that cents cannot be donated): $A = \{0,1,\ldots 10\}$. The map π accounts for the economic consequences for both individuals when the dictator makes a certain choice. Specifically, we have $\pi(d,a) = 10 - a$ and $\pi(r,a) = a$, because when the dictator gives a, they receive $10 - a$, while the recipient receives a. The Dictator Game is the most used measure of altruistic behaviour. □

It is important to note that in behavioural experiments, it is not possible to simply present participants with an economic decision and then observe their actions. There will always be some form of linguistic description of the decision problem. These 'instructions' may include introductory wording typically used in experiments, such as 'Welcome to this experiment.' However, they can also involve specific linguistic framing of the available choices. For

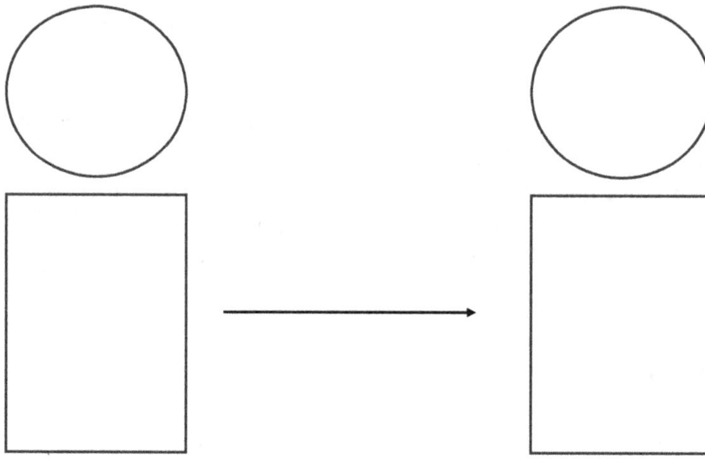

Dictator

Decides how to distribute 10 dollars.

Recipient

Has no active choice.

FIGURE 1.1 **The Dictator Game**. The dictator decides how to allocate 10 dollars between themselves and the recipient. The recipient is passive and simply receives the amount the dictator chooses to give.

example, labelling a choice formally as *a*, or using specific words such as 'donate' or 'give', could lead to different interpretations in experimental subjects, even though these choices may have the same economic consequences. Therefore, considering Popper's definition of a scientific theory, if we aim to build a scientific theory of utility, this theory must be falsifiable through a laboratory experiment. Therefore, the definition of *experimental* economic decisions should explicitly incorporate the experimental instructions.

Definition (Experimental Economic Decision). An experimental economic decision is an economic decision paired with a set of linguistic instructions. These instructions are used to introduce the economic decision to participants in the experiment. □

This definition marks the first significant departure from previous works on similar topics. Although the importance of language in decision-making has been acknowledged by scholars, particularly

Ariel Rubinstein (2000), the linguistic framing of a decision problem is not typically incorporated into the formal definition of the decision problem itself. I believe this omission represents a major shortcoming in earlier formalisations. As will be demonstrated in the following chapters, the very linguistic description of a decision problem significantly influences the utility that a person associates with a given choice. The novel contribution of this book lies in the attempt to mathematically quantify this language-based utility.

I must acknowledge at this stage that behavioural experiments always involve cues beyond just linguistic ones. For instance, if an experiment is conducted in a physical laboratory and the instructions are read aloud by the experimenter, the experimenter's voice may influence participants' decisions. Even environmental factors such as lighting or scent in the room could potentially have an effect. One can potentially limit the impact of these variables by conducting experiments online, instead of in the physical laboratory. If the experiment is conducted online, these environmental details will vary across participants and across large samples we may assume that such variations do not systematically influence decisions: if one combination of factors affects behaviour in a certain direction, another combination may counterbalance it with an opposite effect of similar magnitude. That said, in online experiments, elements such as the colour or font of the instructions could still shape decision-making. Therefore, a 'true' experimental economic decision should ideally account for all variables that might influence participants' behaviour, not just the linguistic framing of instructions.

I acknowledge this limitation and encourage future research to quantify the impact of these additional factors. In this book, however, the focus will specifically be on the linguistic instructions accompanying decision problems for two key reasons. First, because most human-to-human and human–machine interactions occur through language, understanding its role is particularly important. Second, we will see that recent advances in large language models provide an unprecedented opportunity to systematically quantify the impact of language on decision-making. For this reason, I adopt the terminology 'experimental economic decisions', despite recognising that limiting the scope to linguistic instructions introduces some constraints.

ECONOMIC DECISIONS UNDER RISK

In the previous definitions, economic outcomes are assumed to be certain. When the decision-maker d chooses action a, they are guaranteed to receive a specific economic payoff $\pi(d,a) \in \mathbb{R}$. However, many real-life situations involve uncertainty in outcomes. In such cases, when d chooses a, the payoff is not fixed but rather associated with various probabilities of different outcomes. These scenarios can be formalised in various ways, depending on whether the decision-maker knows the exact probabilities. For the purpose of this discussion, I will consider a simplified scenario where the decision-maker is indeed aware of these probabilities. Additionally, I will focus on individual economic decisions, meaning $I = \{d\}$. This restriction simplifies the discussion and allows us to use the concept of a 'prospect', as introduced by Kahneman and Tversky (1979). While the more general case where $I \neq \{d\}$ introduces additional notational complexity, the principles discussed here can be extended to those situations as well.

Definition (Prospect). A prospect $p = (\pi_1, p_1; \pi_2, p_2; \ldots; \pi_n, p_n)$ is a contract that yields economic payoff π_i with probability p_i. □

Let $\mathcal{P}$ denote the space of all prospects. With this concept, we can refine our definition of an economic decision problem to accommodate risk.

Definition (Individual Economic Decision under Risk). An individual economic decision under risk is characterised by the following elements:

- **A decision-maker *d*** who makes the decision.

- **A set of potential actions** A which includes all the alternatives from which d can choose.
- **A map** $\pi : A \to \mathrm{P}$ representing the probabilistic economic payoffs for the decision-maker d, when they choose $a \in A$. □

Example. Suppose that a decision-maker must choose between a certain gain of \$1 and a lottery that provides 50% probability of winning \$3 and 50% of winning 0. This choice can be easily formalised using the earlier definition. The set of potential choices contains two alternatives, which I denote as c (for certain) and l (for lottery), $A = \{c, l\}$. The map π is defined as $\pi(c) = (1,1), \pi(l) = \left(3, \frac{1}{2}; 0, \frac{1}{2}\right)$. □

As for economic decisions, we can define experimental economic decisions under risk taking into account the linguistic description of the decision problem.

EXPERIMENTAL ECONOMIC GAMES

Starting from experimental economic decisions, we can also define the notion of experimental economic games, which allow for interactions between participants. For simplicity, I shall consider situations where the set of decision-makers coincides with the set of individuals who can be affected by the decision.

Definition (Economic Game). An economic game is characterised by the following elements:

- **A set of players** $P = \{1, \ldots, N\}$. This set includes all the individuals who make a choice and are potentially directly affected by the other players' choices.
- **For each player** $p \in P$**, a set of potential actions** A_p. This set includes all the alternatives from which p can choose. These alternatives are also called 'pure strategies'.
- **A map** $\pi_p : A_1 \times \ldots \times A_N \to \mathbb{R}$ representing the economic payoff for player $p \in P$ for each strategy profile played by the various players. □

Example (Prisoner's Dilemma). In the Prisoner's Dilemma, the set of players consists of two individuals, $P = \{1,2\}$. This is a symmetric

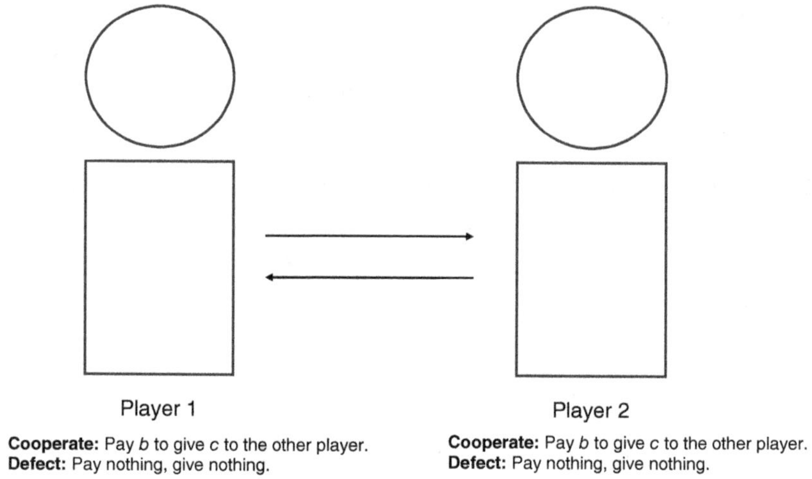

FIGURE 1.2 **The Prisoner's Dilemma.** Two players can either cooperate or defect. Cooperation means paying a cost c to provide a greater benefit b to the other player. Defection means paying no cost and providing no benefit.

game, meaning that both players have the same set of strategies with the same economic consequences. Each player has two strategies that are typically denoted as cooperation and defection: $A_1 = A_2 = \{C,D\}$. Cooperation means paying a cost $c > 0$ to provide a benefit $b > c$ to the other player; defection means paying no cost and providing no benefit. The maps π_1 and π_2 can be constructed by looking at the four possible combinations of choices. In particular, we have: $\pi_1(C,C) = b - c$, $\pi_1(C,D) = -c$, $\pi_1(D,C) = b$, and $\pi_1(D,D) = 0$. See Figure 1.2. □

The Prisoner's Dilemma is the most used economic game to measure individuals' tendency to cooperate in groups of two people. The crucial feature of the Prisoner's Dilemma is that it creates a tension between individual payoff and collective payoff. From an individual perspective, the best strategy is to defect, as it avoids the cost of cooperation: regardless of the other player's action, defecting ensures that a player always gains c more than if they had cooperated. However, if both players adopt this reasoning, they both end up defecting, resulting in a payoff of 0 for both. This outcome is worse than if they had both chosen to cooperate, where each would have received a payoff of $b - c$, which is greater than 0.

As with economic decisions, it is impossible to conduct behavioural experiments for economic games without some form of linguistic introduction to the game. Considering these linguistic instructions, we arrive at the definition of experimental economic games.

Definition (Experimental Economic Game). An experimental economic game is an economic game paired with a set of linguistic instructions. □

Possibly the most popular solution concept for economic games is Nash equilibrium, introduced by John Nash in a ground-breaking one-page article published in the *Proceedings of the National Academy of Sciences of the USA* in 1950, arguably the shortest article to have significantly contributed to the winning of a Nobel Prize. Intuitively speaking, a Nash equilibrium is a strategy profile where no player can gain by unilaterally changing their strategy. Therefore, when players reach this strategy profile, they remain in 'equilibrium', as no one is incentivised to leave this state. More formally, before introducing the definition of Nash equilibrium, we need to introduce the following notation.

Notation. Let $P' \subseteq P$ be a subset of players. A strategy profile played by P' consists of an P'-tuple of actions $a_{P'} = (a_{p'})_{p' \in P'}$. In case $P' = P \setminus \{p\}$, the strategy profile $a_{P'}$ is usually denoted by a_{-p}, highlighting that it represents an action for every player other than p. □

Definition. A Nash equilibrium is a profile of strategies $a = (a_1, \ldots, a_N)$ such that $\pi_p(a'_p, a_{-p}) \leq \pi_p(a)$ for all $a'_p \in A_p$ and for all $p \in P$. □

Nash equilibria may not exist if players' choices are restricted to pure strategies. Consider the following illustrative example.

Example (The 'Matching Pennies' Game Does Not Have Equilibria in Pure Strategies). Consider a game with two players, each of whom can choose an integer between 0 and 5. Player 1 wins \$1 (and Player 2 loses \$1) if the sum of the chosen integers is even, whereas Player 2 wins if the sum of the chosen integer is odd. It is straightforward to see that this game has no Nash equilibria in pure strategies. To demonstrate this, assume there exists a pure-strategy Nash equilibrium. Regardless of the integers chosen, the losing player will always have an incentive to switch to an adjacent integer (either incrementing or decrementing by 1) to change the parity of the sum and thus turn a loss into a win. Since this switching can occur indefinitely, no pure strategy can satisfy the condition where no player benefits from unilateral deviation, which is required for a Nash equilibrium. □

It then becomes crucial to consider mixed strategies, which involve probabilistic choices between available alternatives, unlike pure strategies that involve definite choices.

Definition. A mixed strategy for player p is given by a probability distribution over the strategy set A_p. Mixed strategies will be denoted using the letter s_p to distinguish them from pure strategies a_p. □

The function π can be extended from pure strategies to mixed strategies by linearity. Consequently, the definition of Nash equilibrium naturally extends to mixed strategies. The significance of this extension is highlighted by Nash's theorem.

Theorem (Nash, 1950). Every game with finitely many pure strategies has an equilibrium in mixed strategies. □

In the Matching Pennies Game described earlier, there are infinitely many Nash equilibria, all characterised by choosing an even or an odd number with equal probability. The reasoning behind this strategy is straightforward: any non-random choice would provide an advantage to the opposing player, who could then manipulate the final sum towards the parity that would guarantee a win. For instance, if Player 2 is more likely to choose an odd number than an even number, then Player 1 can strategically choose an odd number, increasing the likelihood that the sum will be even. The only way for Player 2 to neutralise this advantage is by selecting even and odd numbers with equal probability, that is, with a probability of 0.5 for each. This strategy ensures that neither player can influence the outcome to their consistent advantage, maintaining the balance required for a Nash equilibrium.

It is important to note that while I have defined Nash equilibrium in terms of the economic payoff function, the same definition extends naturally to broader utility functions. So far, I have referred to utility in a somewhat vague manner because a key contribution of the first part of this book is to demonstrate that its definition is more complex than previously assumed. For now, I can informally state that the definition of Nash equilibrium remains formally identical if, instead of using the economic payoff function π, we use a utility function u. The complexity arises from the fact that, while the domain of π is clearly defined by the individuals and their potential actions, the domain of the utility function may include other components. In particular, it could include the linguistic description of the decision context and the linguistic framing of the available actions.

ONE-SHOT AND ANONYMOUS INTERACTIONS

In the following discussion, it is useful to unify the treatment of economic decisions and games by introducing the concept of a 'state of the world'. For our purposes, a state of the world refers to a single action taken by the decision-maker in the context of economic decisions or to a strategy profile played by all participants in economic games. Accordingly, the set of all possible states of the world serves as a natural starting point for defining the domain of the utility function.

When considering how to compute the utility of a state of the world, the first question that arises is whether this utility is truly distinct from the economic payoff obtained by the decision-maker in that state. One clear case where this distinction occurs is when the state of the world does not represent the end of the decision problem but can affect future economic payoffs. There are two classic scenarios in which this can happen.

First, when individuals interact with the same people multiple times, they have an incentive to maintain positive relationships and avoid negative future consequences. This may result in behaviours that appear non-self-interested in the short term but are beneficial in the long run. For example, Robert Axelrod's Tit for Tat strategy demonstrates how cooperation can emerge as a stable outcome in the iterated Prisoner's Dilemma (Axelrod, 1984). Tit for Tat cooperates in the first round and then mirrors the opponent's previous action in subsequent rounds. If both players in an iterated Prisoner's Dilemma adopt this strategy, they end up cooperating in all rounds. Importantly, neither player has a monetary incentive to deviate from this strategy because doing so would lead to mutual defection, resulting in a lower payoff than mutual cooperation. Therefore, mutual Tit for Tat can be a Nash equilibrium if players' utility function includes not only the immediate economic payoff but also the expected future benefits of maintaining a cooperative relationship.

Another scenario arises when actions are observable by others, where indirect reciprocity may significantly influence behaviour. Indirect reciprocity refers to the idea that individuals are more likely to act altruistically if they believe their actions will enhance their reputation and lead to future benefits, even from third parties not directly involved in the interaction (Wedekind & Milinski, 2000). For instance, studies have shown that people are more likely to donate to charity when their donation is publicly recognised or when they believe others are watching (Andreoni & Petrie, 2004). Deviations from monetary self-interest when being observed can therefore also be rationalised by a utility function that accounts for future economic consequences, such as enhanced reputation and potential reciprocal benefits.

Therefore, the existence of direct and indirect reciprocity does not conclusively prove that individuals have preferences beyond their economic self-interest. It is possible that people aim to maximise their long-term economic payoff. To answer the question of whether individuals have preferences beyond their monetary payoff, it is useful to reduce the complexity of the context in which the interaction occurs by considering one-shot and anonymous economic interactions. These are situations where individuals interact only once and their actions are not observable by others.

Definition (One-Shot and Anonymous Interactions). A one-shot and anonymous experimental economic decision (or game) is an experimental economic decision (or game) that is conducted only once, involving participants who do not know each other and whose decisions cannot be traced back to their identities in any way. □

It is important to recognise that conducting experiments that are genuinely anonymous presents significant challenges. When experimental subjects are invited to a physical laboratory, researchers inevitably see and interact with them face-to-face. While efforts can be made to maintain anonymity – such as assigning subjects random identification numbers that are not linked to their personal identities – it is debatable whether participants truly believe their decisions are completely unobservable. However, there are strategies to enhance the perception of anonymity. One promising approach is to allow participants to generate their own random identification numbers in a way that remains entirely private. For instance, participants could roll a die 10 times under a cup, with the outcomes determining a unique 10-digit identification number. This method ensures that even the experimenter cannot trace the identification number back to the participant, thereby reinforcing the perception of anonymity. In recent years, the rise of online experiments has offered new avenues for preserving participant anonymity. Online platforms allow researchers to conduct studies in which participants are geographically dispersed and interact through digital interfaces. These platforms can anonymise data collection processes, ensuring that personal identifiers are not linked to the decisions made during the experiment. Moreover, the physical separation between participants and researchers further strengthens the sense of anonymity, potentially leading to more genuine and uninfluenced decision-making.

Another important remark is that while the focus on one-shot and anonymous economic interactions may seem to limit the scope of the analysis, the findings in these contexts are still broadly applicable. The empirical regularities observed in one-shot and anonymous economic interactions provide basic insights into the underlying drivers of human behaviour, which are relevant also in more complex interactions. Only by understanding how people make decisions in their purest form, without the confounding factors of direct and indirect reciprocity, can we build the foundation for a more comprehensive theory of human behaviour that also accounts for more complex situations.

Reformulating the question at the beginning of this section in this specific context, we can then ask: do people maximise their monetary payoff in one-shot and anonymous economic interactions? On the surface, this question may seem straightforward. If an individual is alone in a room, making an economic decision that no one else will ever know about, why wouldn't they choose the option that maximises their monetary payoff?

In the next three sections, we will encounter three classes of examples in which people behave in a way contrary to the assumption of economic maximisation. One of these classes is obvious: when the decision is complex and people are not able to compute the strategy that maximises their economic payoff, they deviate from this strategy. The second and third classes of examples instead show that even when the strategy that maximises their economic payoff is evident, people sometimes still deviate from this strategy. Therefore, the answer to whether people maximise their economic payoff in one-shot and anonymous interactions is a resounding no. Importantly, however, these deviations from monetary maximisation are not random but systematic. This realisation has given rise to the field of behavioural economics, which seeks to describe how people make decisions by developing utility functions that account for factors beyond mere economic payoffs.

BOUNDED RATIONALITY

In many real-life situations, individuals are required to make decisions without the capability to compute the optimal choice. The complexity of the decision problem itself, the constraints on time, and the limitations of human cognitive resources often make it impossible to consider every possible option and outcome. Take, for instance, the decision to invest in the stock market. An investor may have to choose between dozens of stocks, each with different risk profiles, historical performances, and future projections. Theoretically, the optimal decision would involve a thorough analysis of all available data, predicting future market conditions, and selecting the stock with the highest expected return. However, for the average investor, such an exhaustive calculation is just impractical. Instead, they might choose a stock based on a recommendation, past success, or a basic assessment of company fundamentals, a decision that is 'good enough' for their purposes.

Other examples can be found in the domain of personal finance, such as deciding on a mortgage plan. A homebuyer must choose from various mortgage options, each with different interest rates, repayment terms, and associated costs. Calculating the optimal mortgage would require the buyer to forecast their future financial situation, interest rate changes, and potential life events over the loan's term. Given these complexities, most people cannot compute the optimal choice. Instead, they may choose a mortgage that seems manageable and offers a reasonable balance between interest rate and monthly payments, a decision that is 'good enough' for their purposes.

The concept of satisficing was developed by Nobel laureate Herbert A. Simon in his collection of mathematical essays on rational behaviour *Models of Man* (Simon, 1957) and describes a decision-making strategy where individuals select an option that meets a certain threshold of acceptability rather than seeking the best possible outcome. Simon argued that real-world decision-makers are often unable to process all the relevant information or evaluate all possible alternatives due to cognitive limitations and environmental constraints. In these contexts, instead of optimising, individuals aim to make decisions that are 'good enough' to meet their needs and goals. For example, an investor might choose a diversified mutual fund rather than attempting to select individual stocks that would theoretically maximise returns. This choice simplifies the decision-making process, reducing the cognitive load and the risk of poor outcomes due to information overload or analysis paralysis.

Several controlled behavioural experiments have been conducted to test Herbert Simon's theory of satisficing because of bounded rationality. One classic experiment is the 'Paradox of Choice' study conducted by Iyengar and Lepper in 2000. In this experiment, the authors setup a jam-tasting booth in a supermarket. In one scenario, customers were offered 6 different flavours of jam, while in another, they were presented with 24 flavours. If decision-makers were able to compute the utility of each available choice, and pick the option that maximises their utility, we would expect that more choices would be associated with a higher likelihood of making a purchase. Contrary to this expectation, Iyengar and Lepper found the opposite: customers were more likely to make a purchase when presented with fewer options. Those who encountered the 24-flavour display were overwhelmed by the choices, leading to decision paralysis and reduced likelihood of making a purchase.

Another experiment that illustrates satisficing behaviour in important real-life decisions is the 'Secretary Problem', a classic decision-making problem used to study optimal stopping theory. In this experiment, participants are asked to select the best candidate for a job from a sequential list. They must decide whether to choose the current candidate or reject them and move on to the next, with the catch that once they reject a candidate, they cannot go back. The problem is designed to test whether individuals can identify the optimal stopping point. Theoretically, the optimal strategy is to reject the first 37% of candidates and then choose the next one who is better than all the previous ones. However, in practice, many participants satisfice by choosing a candidate who meets their criteria before reaching the optimal stopping point (Bearden et al., 2006).

In the domain of economic decisions, an experiment conducted by Benartzi and Thaler (2001) examined how individuals choose their retirement savings allocations. The study found that many individuals employed a strategy known as 'naive diversification', where they evenly divided their contributions across the available investment options, regardless of the risk–return profiles of those options. This behaviour exemplifies satisficing because, rather than optimising their investment strategy by thoroughly analysing the potential returns and risks, individuals opted for a simple and manageable allocation method that felt adequate, thereby avoiding the complexities of deep financial analysis.

In sum, when decisions are complex and decision-makers cannot compute the best strategy, they often resort to satisficing strategies. In Chapter 2, I will discuss attempts to formalise the concept of bounded rationality through suitable decision rules. These decision rules are useful in economic decisions when the economic consequences of the available actions are difficult to compute.

However, throughout this book, I will primarily focus on cases where the economic consequences of the available actions are clear, avoiding the additional complexity introduced by the inability to compute these economic outcomes. From a formal perspective, this means that decision-makers know the map π that describes the economic consequences of each state of the world. With an eye towards potential experiments, how can we ensure that experimental subjects understand this function? One way to do this is by asking subjects comprehension questions regarding the economic structure of the game and restricting the analysis to those who demonstrate sufficient understanding.

HEURISTICS AND BIASES

A major consequence of human bounded rationality is that people often develop heuristics, or mental shortcuts, to simplify the process of making choices in situations where it is difficult to compute the consequences of the available actions. These heuristics can be incredibly useful in complex scenarios where time and cognitive resources are limited. However, a significant issue arises when these heuristics are overgeneralised and applied in situations that look superficially like those that led to the development of those heuristics. In such cases, the reliance on heuristics can lead to systematic biases. In this section, I will discuss some of these biases: the framing effect, the endowment effect, the status quo bias, and the present bias. The aim is two-fold. First, I will provide an additional piece of evidence that the decision-maker's utility at a given state of the world is not equal to the decision-maker's monetary payoff at that state of the world. Second, it will allow us to introduce some concepts that will be useful in the later theorisation. As a disclosure, this section is not meant to be a comprehensive list of heuristics and biases. Rather, it aims to highlight some biases that are relevant to economic decisions. Readers interested in a more comprehensive understanding of heuristics and biases are encouraged to consult the specialised literature on these topics (e.g., Tversky & Kahneman, 1974; Thaler, 1994; Gilovich, 2002; Thaler & Sunstein, 2008; Kahneman, 2011).

Loss Aversion and Framing Effects

Loss aversion is the tendency for people to weigh losses more heavily than equivalent gains. This systematic bias can be understood as deriving from an evolutionarily developed heuristic that might be described as 'avoid losses because they can be dangerous'. In the ancestral environment, where resources were scarce and survival was uncertain, experiencing losses could have severe consequences, potentially leading to death. For instance, losing access to food, shelter, or social standing could drastically reduce an individual's chances of survival and reproduction. As a result, being highly sensitive to potential losses would have been evolutionarily advantageous, fostering a greater emphasis on avoiding losses rather than pursuing equivalent gains.

One significant consequence of loss aversion is that decision-makers are particularly sensitive to whether outcomes are presented in terms of gains or losses. A classic example is the 'Asian Disease Problem', first described by Tversky and Kahneman in 1981. In this scenario, participants were asked to choose between two programmes to combat a deadly disease expected to kill 600 people. Programme A was framed as saving 200 lives, while Programme B was framed as having a one-third probability of saving all 600 lives and a two-thirds probability of saving no one. When framed in terms of lives saved, most participants chose Programme A. However, when the same options were framed in terms of lives lost (400 people will die with Programme A, or a one-third chance that no one will die with Programme B), the majority of participants chose Programme B.

Framing effects caused by loss aversion have also been shown in contexts where outcomes are certain. A classic example is the 'meat labelling' experiment (Levin & Gaeth, 1988). In this study, participants were asked to choose between two packages of ground beef. One package was labelled '75% lean', while the other was labelled '25% fat'. Even though both labels describe the exact same product, a majority of participants preferred the package labelled '75% lean' over the one labelled '25% fat'. The perception of a 'loss' (higher fat content) was more powerful and persuasive, leading consumers to prefer the '75% lean' label. This preference may be seen as coming from an attempt to avoid what feels like a loss (fat content) rather than from the allure of a gain (lean content).

In the domain of individual economic decisions, a relevant experiment was conducted by Brown et al. (2008). The researchers explored how the framing of retirement annuity options affects individuals' preferences over financial decisions. The researchers compared the annuity option to several other financial decisions. In one treatment, the annuity option was framed in terms of consumption. In the other treatment, it was framed in terms of investment. Even though the financial outcomes of both frames were identical (the participants would receive the same amount of money per month) the framing of the decision had a significant impact on their choices. Participants were much more likely to choose the annuity when it was framed as a consumption decision rather than as an investment decision. The consumption frame made the annuity appear more attractive by focusing on the benefits of steady income in retirement. In contrast, the investment frame highlighted the upfront cost, making participants more reluctant to choose the annuity.

From the perspective of utility theory, framing effects between gain and loss scenarios can be explained by utility functions that assign greater weight to losses than to equivalent gains. Specifically, consider two economic decision problems, D_1 and D_2, such that $I_1 = I_2$, $d_1 = d_2$, $A_1 = A_2$, and $\pi_1 = \pi_2 + k$, for some constant k. This setup guarantees that the only difference between the two decisions is a constant shift in economic consequences. Furthermore, suppose that the economic consequences verify the properties $\pi_1(i,a) \geq 0$ and $\pi_2(i,a) \leq 0$, for all i and for all a. This means that D_1 is framed in terms of gains (all payoffs are positive), while D_2 is framed in terms of losses (all payoffs are negative). Although the optimal choice for maximising economic payoff remains unchanged between frames, the experimental findings suggest that people often switch their preferences when the frame changes from gains to losses. This shift in behaviour can be rationalised by a utility function that does not directly correspond to the economic payoff but instead incorporates different weights for losses versus gains, with losses having a greater impact than equivalent gains. I will describe a specific example of such a utility function in Chapter 2.

Endowment Effect

Another bias closely related to loss aversion is the endowment effect. The endowment effect refers to the phenomenon where people ascribe more value to things merely because they own them. The endowment effect is fundamentally linked to the concept of loss aversion: when individuals own an item, the prospect of losing it feels more painful than the potential joy they might experience from acquiring it. As a result, they place a higher value on the item once it is theirs, even if they valued it much less before ownership. The endowment effect, therefore, can be seen as a direct manifestation of loss aversion, where the pain of potential loss drives people to overvalue what they own.

A classic experiment that demonstrates the endowment effect was conducted by Kahneman et al. (1990). In this study, participants were divided into two groups: sellers and buyers. The sellers were given a coffee mug and were asked to state the price at which they would be willing to sell it. The buyers, on the other hand, were asked how much they would be willing to pay to acquire the same mug. Despite the mug being identical, there was a significant disparity between the prices that sellers and buyers considered fair. On average, the sellers demanded about twice as much as the buyers were willing to pay. This discrepancy provides a clear illustration of the endowment effect: ownership increased the mug's perceived value for the sellers, leading them to overvalue it compared to what the buyers were willing to offer.

Another illustration of the endowment effect was provided by List in 2003. This experiment explored how the endowment effect operates in real-world markets, specifically among experienced versus inexperienced traders. In the study, participants were divided into two groups: one consisting of professional sports card dealers (experienced traders) and the other comprising casual participants with little to no trading experience (inexperienced traders). Both groups were given a sports card, and they were offered the opportunity to trade their card for another card of equal market value. If the utility of the cards depends only on their market value, participants should be indifferent between keeping their current card or trading it for another. However, the results revealed a stark contrast in behaviour between the two groups, highlighting the presence of the endowment effect among inexperienced traders. These traders, who were not accustomed to the regular buying and selling of sports cards, exhibited a strong endowment effect. They were significantly less likely to trade their card, valuing it more highly simply because they owned it. In contrast, the professional sports card dealers, who regularly engaged in trading and were more familiar with the market value of such items, did not display the endowment effect to the same extent. This suggests that the endowment effect is not immutable; it can be mitigated by experience and familiarity with market transactions.

From a formal perspective, the endowment effect can be analysed similarly to the framing effect. For instance, List's experiment can be structured as an economic decision problem where the decision-maker must choose whether to trade their sports card. If they decide to trade, the economic payoff can be quantified by the net effect of losing the market value of their own card and gaining the market value of another card, mathematically represented as:

$$\pi(d, trade) = -v_{own\ card} + v_{other\ card}. \tag{1.1}$$

Even though these market values are equivalent, the reluctance to trade can be explained by a utility function that places greater weight on losses (the negative values) than on gains (the positive values). I will discuss an example of a specific utility function in Chapter 2.

Status Quo Bias

Status quo bias is a cognitive bias that leads individuals to prefer the current situation, or the 'status quo', over changes, even when the change could lead to potentially better outcomes. Status quo bias is closely linked to heuristics. We can see this link in at least two ways. First, by sticking with the current situation, individuals avoid the cognitive load associated with evaluating new options, making decisions, and potentially facing the uncertainty that comes with change. Second, the preference for the status quo can also be seen as a manifestation of loss aversion, where the potential losses associated with change loom larger in an individual's mind than the potential gains. Since changing the status quo often involves risk, however small, individuals may subconsciously weigh the potential negatives more heavily than the positives, leading them to stay with the familiar option even when it might not be the most beneficial.

A classic experiment that demonstrates status quo bias was conducted by Samuelson and Zeckhauser in 1988. The researchers presented participants with a series of hypothetical scenarios involving choices among different investment options, healthcare plans, and other decision-making contexts. In each scenario, one option was designated as the 'status quo', while the other options represented potential changes. The results showed a significant tendency for participants to stick with the status quo option, even when the alternatives offered higher returns. This preference for the status quo occurred even when participants were informed that the status quo option was randomly assigned and that the other options could potentially lead to better outcomes.

Status quo bias has also been leveraged to nudge people towards making better decisions in real life. One well-known study that illustrates this point is the '401(k) Enrolment Experiment' conducted by Madrian and Shea in 2001. The researchers analysed the effects of changing the default option for 401(k) retirement savings plans in a large corporation. A 401(k) plan is a retirement savings account offered by employers in the United States, allowing employees to contribute a portion of their salary pre-tax, with potential employer matching contributions, to invest for their future retirement. Previously, employees had to actively choose to enrol in the 401(k) plan. As a result, many employees, especially younger ones, chose not to enrol, missing out on the benefits of employer matching contributions and tax advantages. Madrian and Shea tested what would happen if the default option was changed so that employees were automatically enrolled in the 401(k) plan, with the option to opt out if they preferred not to participate. The results were striking: automatic enrolment led to a dramatic increase in 401(k) participation rates, particularly among younger employees who were previously less likely to enrol. This experiment highlights how status quo bias can be harnessed to improve economic outcomes, in this case by increasing retirement savings.

Another important application of status quo bias, although not directly related to economic decisions, involves default settings in organ donation policies, as examined by Johnson and Goldstein in a 2003 study. In this empirical analysis, the researchers compared organ donation rates across countries with different default policies: opt in versus opt out. In opt-in countries, individuals must actively choose to become organ donors, while in opt-out countries, individuals are presumed to be donors unless they choose otherwise. The study found that countries with opt-out policies had significantly higher organ donation rates compared to countries with opt-in policies. This difference was largely attributable to status quo bias: in opt-out countries, the default position is to be an organ donor, and most people do not take the active step of opting out. Conversely, in opt-in countries, the default is not to be a donor, and few people go through the process of opting in.

Status quo bias can also be rationalised using utility functions that weight losses more heavily than gains, especially in the context of economic decisions under risk. Consider the following problem. Emma is enrolled in a default retirement savings plan that guarantees a steady but modest return. Her company introduces a new investment option characterised by variable returns dependent on market performance. This new plan potentially offers higher returns but with increased risk. Specifically, Emma is considering the following two options:

- **Option A (status quo):** Continue with the current, default savings plan that guarantees a stable annual return of 4%.
- **Option B (new variable plan):** Switch to a new plan that offers a 50% probability of a 6% annual return and a 50% probability of a 2% annual return.

Note that these two options have the same economic consequences in expectation. However, the status quo bias suggests that Emma will be more likely to retain the current plan. To rationalise this behaviour, assume that Emma perceives the status quo as her reference point to evaluate gains and losses. With this assumption, the economic consequences of the available options can be described as $\pi(A) = 0$, $\pi(B) = (\frac{1}{2}, -2; \frac{1}{2}; 2)$, indicating that Option B has the same probability of yielding a 2% gain or a 2% loss relative to her current return. If Emma's utility function is more sensitive to losses than to gains, then the expected utility of Option B may indeed be perceived as negative. This is because the impact of a potential 2% loss weighs more heavily on her than the equivalent potential gain of 2%, despite both outcomes having equal probability. Therefore, even though the expected economic outcomes of both plans are equivalent, Emma's decision-making might be skewed towards retaining her current plan.

Present Bias and Time-Inconsistent Preferences

Present bias is a cognitive bias that causes individuals to give disproportionately greater weight to costs and benefits that occur in the immediate future compared to those that are delayed. In other words, people tend to favour smaller, sooner rewards over larger, later rewards, even when waiting would yield a better outcome and after accounting for a temporal discounting factor.

From an evolutionary perspective, the bias towards immediate rewards may have been advantageous for our ancestors who lived in environments where immediate resources were crucial for survival. In situations where food, shelter, and other resources were scarce and unpredictable, prioritising immediate gains over potential future rewards could have increased an individual's chances of survival and reproduction. The preference for immediate gratification can be seen as an adaptive heuristic, a mental shortcut that simplifies decision-making in uncertain environments by favouring immediate benefits over potential future gains. In contemporary settings, however, this evolutionary strategy can lead to suboptimal decisions. Present bias causes individuals to overvalue immediate rewards and undervalue future benefits, often leading to behaviours like overspending, under-saving for retirement, and neglecting long-term health.

This bias leads to time-inconsistent preferences. For instance, individuals might choose $100 today instead of $110 tomorrow but prefer $110 in 31 days over $100 in 30 days. Such reversals in preference have been documented in numerous studies. One of the earliest pieces of evidence came from a series of experiments conducted by Solnick et al. in 1980, which demonstrated time-inconsistent preferences in a noise-pollution scenario. Participants were asked to solve math problems in a noisy environment, with an option to terminate the noise using one of two buttons. The green button would immediately stop the noise, while the blue button would stop the noise after a delay. The study found that when both options were delayed by the same amount of time, participants showed a tendency to switch their preference from the immediate termination to the delayed termination, indicating a reversal in preference from smaller, immediate rewards to larger, delayed rewards.

In the domain of economic decision-making, Green et al. (1994) provided the first substantial evidence of preference reversal associated with time-inconsistent behaviour. In their study, participants were presented with a series of choices between two hypothetical monetary rewards, each available after different delays. The reward pairs were: $20 versus $50, $100 versus $250, and $500 versus $1,250. The smaller reward could be received either immediately or after varying delays of 1 week, 2 weeks, 1 month, 3 months, 6 months, 1 year, 2 years, 3 years, 5 years, 7 years, 10 years, 12 years, 15 years, 17 years, or 20 years. The larger reward was made available after the delay plus an additional delay, ranging from 1 week to 20 years. The study found that as the delay for the smaller reward increased, participants were more likely to choose the larger, delayed reward, providing direct evidence of preference reversal. This trend was consistent across all three reward pairs and for every interval between the rewards.

Time-inconsistent preferences have also been leveraged to design policies and interventions to nudge people to make better, future-oriented choices. Thaler and Benartzi (2004) introduced the 'Save More Tomorrow' programme, which leverages the concept of preference reversal to enhance retirement savings. The programme automatically increases employees' contribution rates whenever they receive a raise. This approach is effective because it frames the decision in the future, where individuals are more likely to opt for saving rather than immediate spending.

From a formal perspective, time-inconsistent preferences can be explained by a utility function that disproportionately weights present payoffs over future payoffs. Intuitively, this suggests that a one-day delay experienced in the present is perceived as more significant than a one-day delay occurring in the future. In Chapter 2, I will introduce specific utility functions that formalise this concept.

SOCIAL BEHAVIOUR

Most decision problems discussed in the previous section are individual decision problems, where the set of individuals affected by the decisions corresponds solely to the decision-maker, $I = \{d\}$. In these scenarios, people may be swayed by heuristics that generate systematic biases, ultimately leading to choices that do not align with the decision-maker's best economic interests. In this section, I shift focus from individual economic decisions to social economic decisions. Social decisions are broadly defined as any decisions that have consequences for individuals other than the decision-maker, $I \neq \{d\}$.

While we have encountered some social decisions, such as altruism and cooperation, earlier, the aim of this section is to deepen our understanding of these types of decisions and to introduce additional examples. The main takeaway of this section is that social decisions often result in behaviours where participants do not seem to be making choices that align with economic maximisation, for reasons that have little to do with heuristics and biases. It is important to note, however, that this does not imply heuristics and biases are absent from social decisions. The Asian Disease Problem, for instance, illustrates how biases can influence social decisions as well. The central argument of this section is that social decisions introduce an additional layer of complexity, leading to more frequent deviations from monetary maximisation.

Altruistic Behaviour

The simplest-to-formalise form of social behaviour involves helping someone without any expectation of receiving something in return. Common examples include assisting an elderly person to cross the street, donating blood, or offering one's seat on a crowded bus to someone who might need it more.

This 'altruistic behaviour' is typically measured through the Dictator Game, where the 'dictator' is given a sum of money and must decide how much to give to a second participant, the 'recipient'. The recipient has no say in this decision and only receives the amount the dictator chooses to give. This setup provides a clear measurement of altruistic tendencies divorced from reciprocal actions.

The first study to explore a decision problem akin to the Dictator Game was conducted by Kahneman et al. (1986). In their research, 161 students were tasked with distributing $20 between themselves and another anonymous student from the same class. The participants had two options: (a) retain $18 and allocate $2 to the other student or (b) divide the money equally. Remarkably, the authors found that only 24% of the students chose the option that maximised their own financial gain.

A subsequent study by Forsythe et al. (1994) established the framework now recognised as the Dictator Game, including coining the term itself. In their experiment, students were randomly assigned to two classes, Room A and Room B. Each participant in Room A was randomly paired with a participant from Room B. Those in Room A were given $5 and asked to decide how to divide it with their paired student from Room B, who played no active role and simply received the amount allocated to them. Across two sessions involving a total of 45 dictators, the authors observed that only 30% of the participants chose to keep all the money for themselves.

It is possible that these high rates of altruistic behaviour are partially driven by concerns about reputation, as maintaining complete anonymity has been challenging in these experiments. Hoffman et al. (1994) designed an experiment to measure Dictator Game decisions under conditions of enhanced anonymity. Participants in Room A received opaque envelopes from a designated monitor, which either contained 10 one-dollar bills and 10 blank slips of paper or 20 blank slips of paper. Each participant then decided in private how many bills and how many blank slips to leave in the envelope. This ensured their decisions remained anonymous, as the total number of slips was kept constant and thus the envelopes appeared uniformly thick. Then these envelopes were given to counterparts in Room B, who received whatever was left in them. This method effectively masked who left money and who did not, thereby providing a highly anonymous environment to test altruistic behaviour. The results showed that while the increased anonymity had the consequence that average donations decreased, a significant proportion of participants (more than 30%) still opted not to keep all the money for themselves. These findings suggest that while reputational concerns may influence giving, they do not fully account for the observed altruistic behaviour, as donations persisted even under conditions of complete anonymity.

Given the complexity of the procedure designed to ensure anonymity, there is a potential that some participants might not have fully grasped the structure of the payoffs. Addressing this issue, in a joint work that I co-authored with Pablo Brañas-Garza and Ericka Rascon-Ramirez we demonstrated the prevalence of altruistic behaviour in conditions where both anonymity and a clear understanding of the decision problem were maintained. We analysed around 4,000 Dictator Game decisions from anonymous online settings. Participants were recruited across the United States via the online platform Amazon Mechanical Turk and were randomly paired such that no participant could identify their counterpart or all other participants in the experiment. Additionally, the experimenters could not link decisions to the identities of participants. Furthermore, after explaining the game, we administered several comprehension questions, including one that asked which choice would maximise the decision-maker's economic payoff. Only participants who correctly answered these questions were allowed to continue with the experiment; all others were automatically screened out. Despite the awareness of the payoff-maximising choice and the guaranteed anonymity of one-shot online interactions with complete strangers, the average donation was 30.8% of the total sum allocated to dictators, suggesting a significant level of altruistic giving even in controlled and anonymous conditions (Brañas-Garza et al., 2018).

How can this behaviour be rationalised? Interestingly, the distribution of donations in these studies is typically trimodal: many give nothing, others give half, and a smaller proportion give everything (Engel, 2011). Therefore, one potential way to rationalise these results is by assuming that participants tend to fall into three broad categories: those who are self-interested (seeking to maximise their own economic payoff), those who are inequity-averse (aiming to equalise payoffs), and those who are altruistic (seeking to maximise the recipient's payoff). I will formalise this idea with a suitable utility function in Chapter 2.

Cooperative Behaviour

Another fundamental aspect of social behaviour involves working together towards a common goal, benefiting all parties involved. Examples of cooperation are ubiquitous and range from teammates coordinating in a sports game to achieve victory, to employees collaborating on a project to enhance productivity, to countries forming alliances for mutual defence or economic benefit.

Cooperation is measured through social dilemmas, which are strategic scenarios where $N > 1$ individuals must choose between multiple actions. Within these choices, one typically promotes the well-being of the group, while another favours the individual's interest. This conflict between personal and collective benefits characterises a social dilemma.

Social scientists have identified various social dilemmas. For two players, the Prisoner's Dilemma is the most employed social dilemma. In this setup, each of the two players can either cooperate or defect. To cooperate means to incur a cost c to confer a greater benefit b to the other player, whereas to defect means to avoid any cost and thus provide no benefit. The condition $b > c$ ensures that the Prisoner's Dilemma qualifies as a social dilemma, as cooperation is the best choice for the group, while defecting benefits the individual. More precisely, defecting is a dominant strategy, meaning that regardless of the other player's actions, defecting always yields a higher payoff, implying that if one's goal is to maximise personal gain, defecting is the rational choice in one-shot and anonymous interactions.

Contrary to this prediction, experimental research reveals that a significant percentage of participants choose to cooperate even in one-shot and anonymous Prisoner's Dilemmas (Rapoport & Chammah, 1965). Furthermore, studies indicate that the likelihood of cooperation depends on the game's parameters: a decrease in the cost of cooperating tends to lower cooperation rates (Engel & Zhurakhovska, 2016), while an increase in the benefits of cooperating generally boosts cooperation rates (Capraro et al., 2014a).

For more than two players, the most used social dilemma is the Public Good Game.

Definition (Public Good Game). Each of the N participants determines the portion of their initial endowment e to contribute towards the public good. Let c_i represent the contribution from individual i; the total pooled contribution is $c_1 + \cdots + c_N$. This total contribution gets multiplied by a synergy factor, M, with $1 < M < N$, and then redistributed equally among all players. See Figure 1.3. □

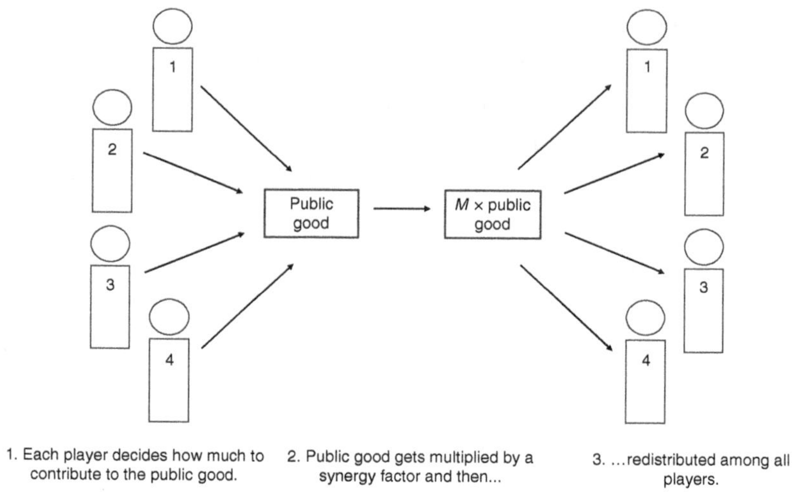

FIGURE 1.3 **The Public Good Game.** Each player decides how much to contribute to the public good. The total amount contributed gets multiplied by a synergy factor *M* and then redistributed equally among all players.

Let $m = M/N$. The economic payoff for individual i can also be written as:

$$\pi_i(c_1, \ldots, c_N) = e - c_i + m\sum_{j=1}^{N} c_j. \tag{1.2}$$

The parameter m is called 'marginal return of cooperation'. Since $1 < M < N$, it follows that m is greater than $1/N$ but less than 1.

This property implies that while the optimal outcome for the group is maximum contribution from all individuals, each individual has an incentive to withhold their endowment for personal gain.

Despite the theoretical prediction of money maximisation, empirical studies reveal that a substantial number of participants often contribute partially or even fully to the public good, even in one-shot and anonymous settings. Moreover, an increase in the marginal return on contributions generally leads to higher contributions (Zelmer, 2003).

Compared to the Prisoner's Dilemma, the Public Good Game includes another parameter, the group size, N. The effect of this parameter on cooperation is somewhat interesting, because it is intuitively non-trivial. On the one hand, the total return for cooperation increases linearly with N, making cooperation more attractive. On the other hand, achieving this return requires more people to cooperate, which introduces greater risk. How do these two trends balance each other out?

An early experiment with iterated Public Good Games suggested that group size might have a positive effect on cooperation (Isaac et al., 1994). A meta-analysis of 27 studies involving one-shot games indicated a generally positive effect of group size on cooperation, although this effect was only marginally significant (Zelmer, 2003). The lack of statistical significance may be due to most of these studies being conducted with small groups. In a more recent study that I conducted with Hélène Barcelo, we addressed this issue by comparing contributions in groups of 4 versus 40 participants in a one-shot and anonymous setting. We found that average contributions were significantly higher in larger groups (39.2% in the smaller group versus 69.1% in the larger group, a difference of nearly 30 percentage points; Barcelo & Capraro, 2015). Thus, the available research suggests a positive effect of group size on cooperative behaviour in Public Good Games.

Specific utility functions that can rationalise these regularities will be discussed in Chapter 2. However, it is useful to make some preliminary observations here. Social dilemmas are characterised by the existence of a state of the world that maximises group benefit. Assuming that the utility of a state of the world depends on social welfare could therefore explain the emergence of cooperation. It is important to note that this type of utility is fundamentally different from the preference for equity that may explain equitable sharing in the Dictator Game. In fact, preferences for equity alone struggle to explain cooperative behaviour because multilateral defection in social dilemmas results in equal payoffs to all players, thus aligning with equity preferences.

As a concluding note for this section, I acknowledge that scholars have developed other economic games to study cooperative behaviour between two agents, such as the Bertrand Competition (Bertrand, 1883), the Centipede Game (Binmore, 1987), and the Traveller's Dilemma (Basu, 1994). Regarding the Public Good Game, some scholars have considered scenarios where the total return for cooperation does not increase linearly, such as in threshold Public Good Games (Cadsby & Maynes, 1998) or in piecewise linear-then-constant Public Good Games (Capraro & Barcelo, 2015). While acknowledging the practical significance of these models (each conceptualising different real-life scenarios) this book will primarily focus on the Prisoner's Dilemma and the standard, linear Public Good Game. This is because the fundamental insights from these games are expected to apply broadly, without significant modification, across other types of social dilemmas.

Strategic Fairness and Altruistic Punishment

A variation of the Dictator Game known as the Ultimatum Game incorporates the option for the receiver to accept or reject the proposal. This game is particularly useful to formalise negotiation scenarios, like wage negotiations, divorce settlements, and legislative policy approvals. In its classic form, the Ultimatum Game is played sequentially: the first player makes an offer, and then the second player responds. In this book, however, I will consider a version where decisions are made simultaneously, a variant also extensively analysed in academic literature.

Definition (Ultimatum Game). In the Ultimatum Game there are two players, the proposer and the responder, $P = \{p, r\}$. The proposer is given an amount of money and must decide how much to offer to the responder. Simultaneously, without knowledge of the proposer's offer, the responder decides on their minimum acceptable

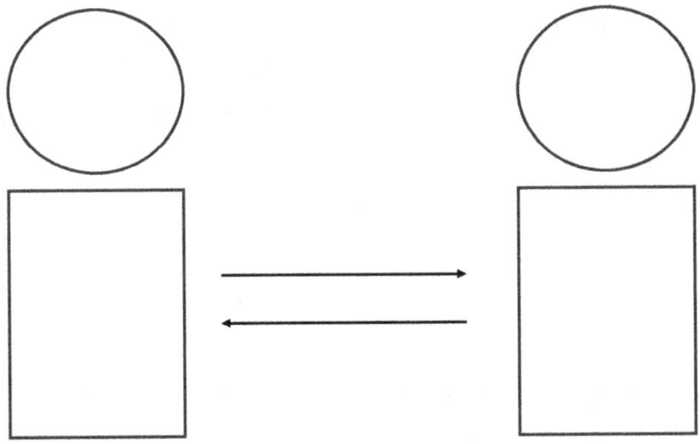

FIGURE 1.4 **The Ultimatum Game**. The proposer makes an offer for how to divide a certain sum of money. The responder decides their minimum acceptable offer (MAO). If the MAO is smaller than or equal to the actual offer, then the sum of money is split as proposed. If the MAO is larger than the actual offer, neither the proposer nor the responder receives any money.

offer (MAO). If the proposer's offer, *o*, is higher than or equal to the responder's MAO, then the money is split as agreed. If not, neither party receives any money. See Figure 1.4. □

Let *s* be the total sum to be split. The economic payoffs are defined as:

$$\pi_p(o, MAO) = \begin{cases} s - o, \; if\, o \geq MAO \\ 0, \; if\, o < MAO \end{cases} \tag{1.3}$$

$$\pi_r(o, MAO) = \begin{cases} o, \; if\, o \geq MAO \\ 0, \; if\, o < MAO \end{cases}. \tag{1.4}$$

To simplify the analysis of this game, it is useful to discretise the choice sets by assuming that choices are made in increments of a currency unit, such as cents. Under this assumption, we can easily determine the Nash equilibrium if both players are payoff-maximisers, and this is common knowledge between them. If the responder is aiming to maximise money, they should accept any non-zero offer. Anticipating this, a rational proposer would offer the smallest non-zero amount possible.

However, empirical research has consistently found deviations from these rational strategies. Behavioural experiments reveal that responders often reject low offers and proposers frequently suggest an equitable division. For example, the seminal study by Güth et al. (1982) that introduced the Ultimatum Game found that offers below 30% of the total amount are frequently rejected, while most offers were between 40% and 50%.

The rejection of low offers is incompatible with a model based solely on payoff maximisation. This behaviour is typically referred to as 'altruistic punishment' because it involves incurring a personal cost to decrease the payoff of another individual, that is: a form of punishment. This behaviour is also sometimes termed 'negative reciprocity', as it involves reacting negatively to a perceived wrongdoing.

While rejecting low offers is incompatible with maximising monetary gain, making an offer greater than zero is not, in principle, incompatible with such maximisation. Indeed, a rational proposer might make a substantial offer if they believe that lower offers will be rejected. However, studies have shown that proposers typically offer more than what they expect to be the MAO (Henrich et al., 2001; Lin and Sunder, 2002). Therefore, the best description of the proposer's behaviour is a combination of strategic and fairness considerations (Camerer, 2011).

Some researchers have noted that traditional, sequential Ultimatum Games generally result in slightly lower rejection rates compared to their simultaneous counterparts (Schotter et al., 1994; Blount, 1995). Nevertheless, this distinction does not undermine the observation that proposers often offer more than what would be considered rational from a strictly monetary standpoint.

Therefore, deviations from money maximisation are common in the Ultimatum Game, whether it is played sequentially or simultaneously. How can these deviations be explained? Chapter 2 will present several potential utility functions. In the meantime, the observations made earlier for altruistic and cooperative behaviour provide some preliminary insights. Suppose the responder has a utility function that depends not only on their monetary payoff but also on the difference between their monetary payoff and that of the proposer, such that the responder receives a negative utility whenever they receive less than the proposer. In this case, they might reject low offers with the aim of reducing the disparity between themselves and the proposer. Similarly, the proposer might offer more than their expected MAO for reasons related to equity. Therefore, defining a utility function that values equity could be a promising approach to rationalise the key empirical regularities observed in the Ultimatum Game.

Trust and Trustworthiness

Another important form of social behaviour is trust. Trust underpins a myriad of everyday interactions and is crucial for the smooth functioning of virtually all social and economic systems. For example, when consumers purchase goods online, they trust that sellers will deliver the products as described. In the workplace, employees must trust that their efforts will be recognised and rewarded by employers, fostering a productive work environment. Moreover, trust is essential in personal relationships, where mutual confidence and dependability strengthen bonds and enable individuals to rely on each other.

The tendency of people to trust others is measured through the Trust Game. This game typically unfolds in two stages and involves two players: one acts as the 'trustor' and the other as the 'trustee'.

Definition (Trust Game). In the Trust Game, the trustor is initially given a sum of money, for example, \$10, and must decide how much, if any, to send to the trustee. The amount sent by the trustor is tripled and handed to the trustee. The trustee then decides how much of the tripled amount to send back to the trustor. See Figure 1.5. □

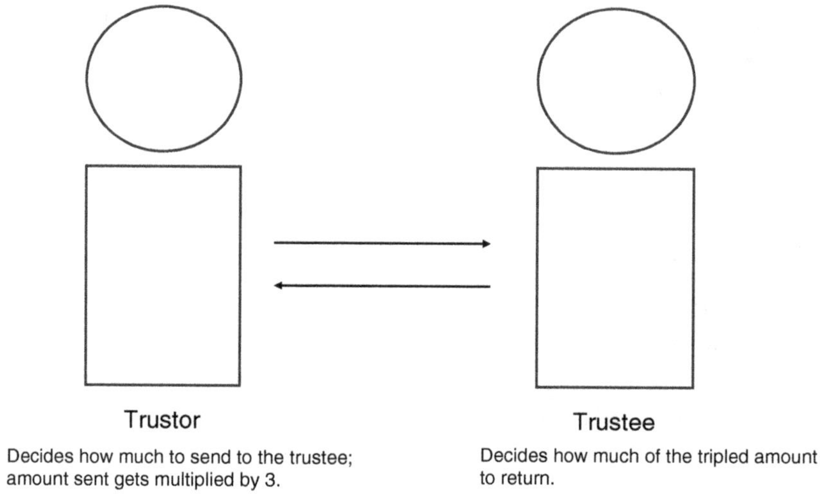

FIGURE 1.5 **The Trust Game**. The trustor decides how much of a given sum of money to send to the trustee. The amount sent is tripled and given to the trustee. The trustee decides how much of the tripled amount to send back to the trustor.

Therefore, if the trustor sends x, the trustee receives $3x$ and then decides how much of $3x$ to return.

The economic outcomes are therefore defined as follows:

- **For the trustor:** $\pi_1(x, y) = 10 - x + y$, where x is the amount sent and y is the amount returned by the trustee.
- **For the trustee:** $\pi_2(x, y) = 3x - y$, where y must be less than or equal to $3x$.

One can consider a simultaneous variant of this game, in which the trustee, without knowing the amount sent, decides what proportion of it to send back to the trustor. In any case, the behaviour of the first player is usually considered as an individual measure of trust, while the behaviour of the second player is considered as a measure of trustworthiness.

In iterated games, trust and trustworthiness can emerge, as they maximise long-term benefits. This dynamic was explored by Kreps, who introduced the Trust Game in a 1990 theoretical paper focusing on the development of trust in repeated interactions. However, in one-shot and anonymous interactions, regardless of whether the game is played sequentially or simultaneously, a rational trustee, aiming to maximise money, would return zero. Anticipating this, the trustor should also send zero.

Despite these theoretical predictions, behavioural experiments have shown that trustors often send non-zero amounts, and trustees frequently return significant portions of the tripled amount, even in one-shot and anonymous interactions. For instance, the seminal experiment conducted by Berg et al. (1995) found that 30 out of 32 trustors sent a non-zero amount, with an average of \$5.16 out of \$10. Trustees largely reciprocated this trust, returning about \$4.66 on average.

How can this behaviour be rationalised? Formal utility functions will be introduced in Chapter 2. For the moment, we can make some preliminary observations similar to the Ultimatum Game. Assume that both parties value equity; can this assumption explain the emergence of trust and trustworthiness? If the trustee values equity, they might be inclined to return half of the received amount. Similarly, if the trustor also prioritises equity, they are likely to send some money, recognising that retaining the entire amount would result in significant disparity, leaving the trustor with all the money while the trustee gets nothing. Thus, from a qualitative perspective, a preference for equity provides an initial explanation for the emergence of trust and trustworthiness.

Note that the reasoning unfolds differently when considering social welfare preferences. Like equity-based preferences, a preference for social welfare would encourage the trustor to send money, as the amount sent is tripled, thereby increasing overall welfare. However, in the trustee's case, social welfare preferences do not generate a clear prediction, because returning money neither adds to nor subtracts from total welfare.

Equity–Efficiency Trade-Off

In many real-world scenarios, a fundamental conflict often arises between the principles of equity and efficiency. This tension frequently manifests in the distribution of resources and has been extensively documented in economics. Arthur Okun famously named this the 'Big Trade-Off' (Okun, 2010), while Hsu et al. (2008) referred to it as 'the fundamental problem in distributive justice'. This conflict arises because the natural distribution of resources is typically unequal. Redistributing these resources to achieve a more equitable spread invariably incurs costs, such as transportation expenses. Consequently, striving for equity usually means accepting a reduction in overall welfare, generating a trade-off that is inherent in many policy decisions.

Taxation serves as another potent example of this trade-off. Governments impose taxes to redistribute wealth and fund public services. But this redistribution is not without its costs. Administrative expenses associated with managing tax systems can be substantial, and high tax rates may deter investment and economic activity, potentially stifling economic growth. This delicate balance between ensuring fair wealth distribution and maximising total wealth exemplifies the trade-off between equity and efficiency.

The tension between equity and efficiency has been the subject of numerous studies using simple economic decision frameworks (Charness & Rabin, 2002; Engelmann & Strobel, 2004; Choshen-Hillel & Yaniv, 2011; Capraro et al., 2014b; Capraro & Rand, 2018). The core of these economic decisions can be captured as follows:

Definition (The Equity–Efficiency Trade-Off Game). In this game, a decision-maker d faces a choice that impacts not only themselves but also two other players, $I = \{d, r_1, r_2\}$. The set of available actions is $A = \{eq, ef\}$. The action labelled eq represents the equitable option, distributing the same economic payoff to all players. Conversely, the ef action is the efficient option, yielding a weakly higher payoff for each player, with at least two participants receiving different payoffs. See Figure 1.6. □

In many implementations, the payoff for the decision-maker is held constant to eliminate self-interest as a confounding factor and focus solely on preferences for equity over efficiency. In this context,

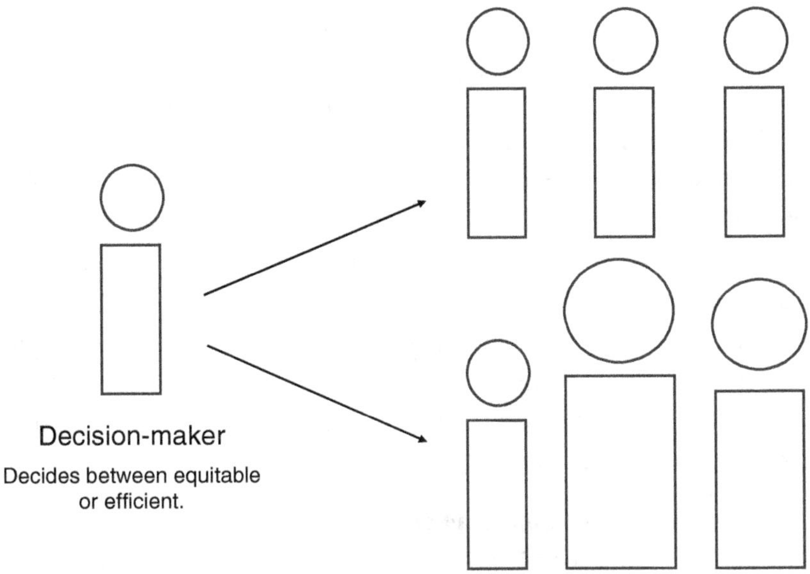

FIGURE 1.6 **The Equity–Efficiency Trade-Off Game**. The decision-maker decides between two distributions of money: in the equitable distribution, all participants receive the same payoff; in the efficient distribution, all participants receive a weakly higher payoff, two participants receive different payoffs.

if a decision-maker is only concerned with their monetary payoff, they would be indifferent between the equitable action and the efficient action since their personal outcome remains unchanged. However, empirical studies have shown that many people exhibit a preference for one option over the other. Moreover, on average, preferences for efficiency appear to be stronger than preferences for equity (Charness & Rabin, 2002; Engelmann & Strobel, 2004; Capraro et al., 2014b). This observation suggests that individuals' utility functions might incorporate weights for both equity and efficiency, with parameters that vary depending on the decision-maker, but are on average higher for the efficiency part.

Truth-Telling

In many real-life scenarios, communication is fraught with asymmetric information, where one party has more information than the other. This imbalance can lead to a situation where an individual might misrepresent their private information to their advantage. The propensity for individuals to tell self-serving lies has significant implications across various sectors, particularly in areas susceptible to fraud such as finance, insurance, and corporate governance. For example, corporate executives might mislead shareholders about the company's financial health, or individuals may provide false information to secure insurance benefits.

Researchers have developed various experimental setups to measure individuals' tendency to tell the truth. I will focus on two main tasks, although other setups will be occasionally mentioned in the next chapters when relevant.

Definition (Die-under-Cup Paradigm). This experimental setup involves a participant rolling a die in private (e.g., under a cup) and then reporting the outcome. Crucially, the economic payoff for the participant does not depend on the actual outcome but only on what they report. For instance, if a participant reports a '1', they receive \$1; if they report a '2', they receive \$2, and so forth up to '6'. See Figure 1.7. □

Obviously, a person solely motivated by economic gain would report '6' to maximise their payoff. However, studies have shown that a substantial proportion of participants do not lie, indicating that factors other than immediate financial gain influence their decision-making (Fischbacher & Föllmi-Heusi, 2013; Abeler et al., 2019).

One experimental game that facilitates the study of various forms of lying is the Sender–Receiver Game (Gneezy, 2005; Erat & Gneezy, 2012). In the original version, the sender sends a message to the receiver, which can be either true or false. After reading the message, the receiver takes an action, and the payoffs for both the sender and receiver depend on the receiver's decision. This setup allows for sophisticated deception, in which senders may tell the truth with the expectation that they will not be believed (Sutter, 2009; Blazquez-Pulido et al., 2024). To avoid this complexity, in this book I focus on an alternative version of the Sender–Receiver Game,

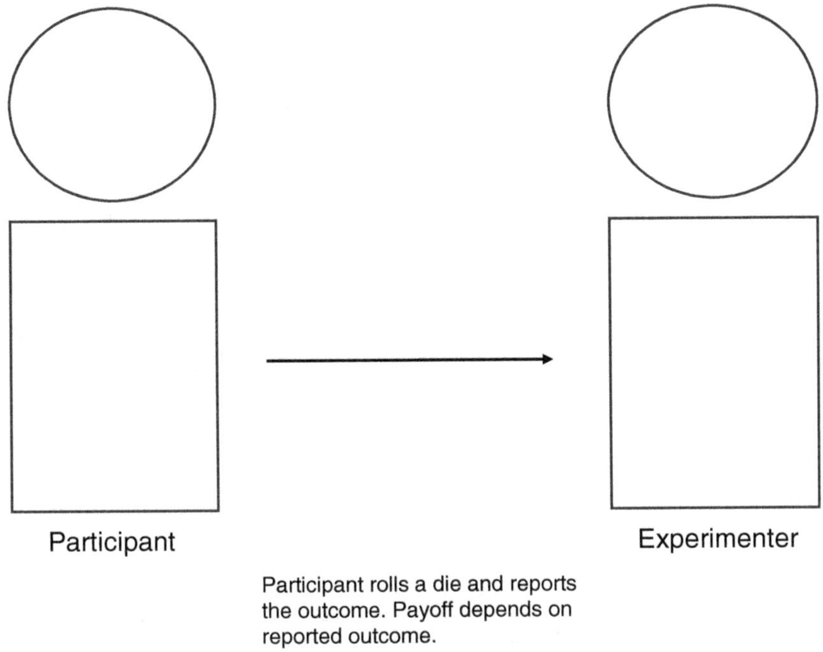

FIGURE 1.7 **The Die-under-Cup Paradigm**. The participant rolls a die in private and then reports the outcome to the experimenter. The payoff of the participant does not depend on the actual outcome (which is not observable to the experimenter), but on the reported outcome.

where the receiver makes no choice (Cappelen et al., 2013; Biziou-van-Pol et al., 2015). In this version, the states of the world (and the resulting payoffs) are determined solely by the sender's choice, thereby eliminating the possibility of sophisticated deception.

Definition (Sender–Receiver Game). The Sender–Receiver Game involves two individuals: the sender and the receiver, $I=\{s,r\}$. However, only the sender decides, $d=s$. The sender is given private information, such as the outcome of a dice roll. They must then send one of six possible messages, indicating what they claim the dice roll resulted in. Therefore, $A=\{\text{'The outcome of the dice roll is } i\text{'},\ i\in\{1,\ldots,6\}\}$. If the sender's message is truthful, both the sender and the receiver are paid according to option $a=(s_a,r_a)$. If the message is a lie, they are paid

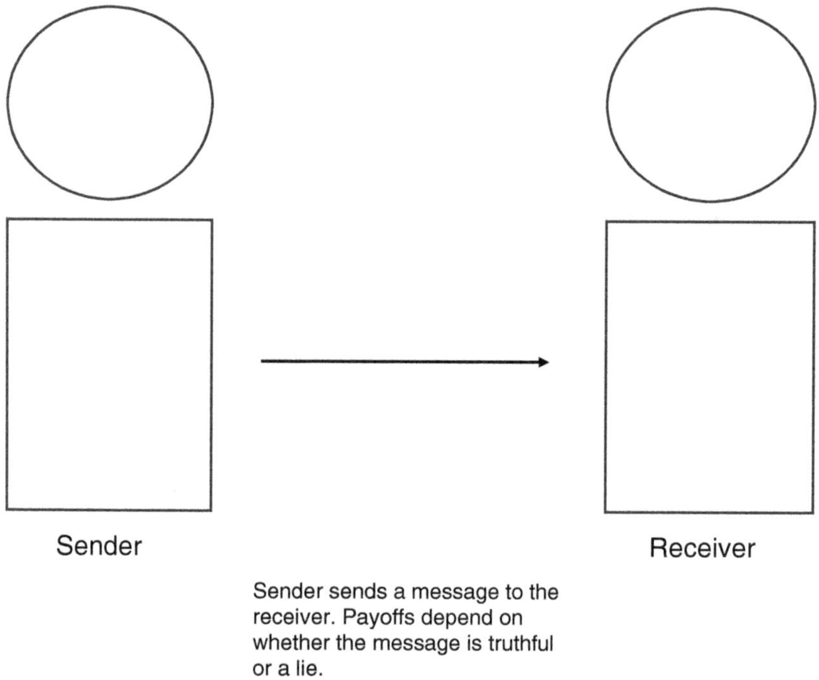

FIGURE 1.8 **The Sender–Receiver Game**. The sender sends a private message to the receiver. If the message is truthful, the sender and the receiver are paid according to one option, a; if the message is a lie, the sender and the receiver are paid according to another option, b.

according to option $b = (s_b, r_b)$. Crucially, only the sender knows the economic payoffs associated with options a and b. See Figure 1.8.

This decision problem allows us to study different types of lies:

- **Self-serving lie:** Occurs if the sender's payoff is greater with a lie $(s_b > s_a)$ at the receiver's cost $(r_b < r_a)$.
- **Altruistic white lie:** Occurs if the sender's payoff is lesser with a lie $(s_b < s_a)$ but benefits the receiver $(r_b > r_a)$.
- **Pareto white lie:** Benefits both the sender and the receiver $(s_b > s_a$ and $r_b > r_a)$. □

Experimental research indicates that many senders do not choose the most financially beneficial option. Some tell the truth even when a lie would be financially advantageous, others tell altruistic white lies, and still others adhere to the truth even when a lie would benefit both parties (Gneezy, 2005; Erat & Gneezy, 2012; Cappelen et al., 2013; Biziou-van-Pol et al., 2015).

Some of these behaviours could theoretically be explained using utility functions that value equity or efficiency. However, the substantial number of people who do not tell 'Pareto white lies' cannot be fully explained by these models. Consider a situation where both players receive the same payoff under truth-telling ($s_a = r_a$) and a higher payoff under lying ($s_b = r_b$). Here, a preference for efficiency would predict lying, while a preference for equity would predict indifference. These preferences, therefore, do not account for why some individuals display a preference for truth-telling.

THE BIRTH OF BEHAVIOURAL ECONOMICS

In the previous sections, I have reviewed numerous scenarios where individuals do not behave in such a way as to maximise their monetary payoff. These situations can be classified into three broad categories:

1. **Satisfying in complex decisions**. Often, the process required to compute the optimal strategy is complex, leading individuals to opt for a satisfying decision rather than an optimal one. This approach, known as 'satisficing', is common in situations where analysing all the details of a decision problem is overly complex.
2. **Systematic biases due to misapplication of heuristics**. In complex decision-making contexts, people frequently develop heuristics, mental shortcuts that reduce the cognitive load of making decisions. While these heuristics are adaptive in complex situations, they can also be applied inappropriately to different contexts. This misapplication can result in systematic biases such as loss aversion and the endowment effect.
3. **Social considerations**. When choices affect not just the decision-maker but also others, an additional layer of complexity is introduced. Individuals often make decisions that consider the well-being of others, not just their own. This social dimension indicates that human decision-making incorporates a broader range of considerations than personal economic gain alone.

These considerations suggest that human behaviour in economic decisions, even in simple, one-shot and anonymous settings, is multifaceted yet not random. This non-randomness, which economic self-interest fails to explain adequately, has given rise to a new field of research: behavioural economics.

Behavioural economics seeks to understand the underlying patterns and motivations of economic behaviour that do not align with economic self-interest. By incorporating psychological insights into economic models, behavioural economists attempt to provide a more accurate description of human behaviour in economic contexts. In Chapter 2, I will review some of the main utility functions that have been introduced over the past half-century to rationalise the various empirical regularities presented in this chapter and show how these utility functions, despite their differences, share one foundational assumption.

2 Economic Consequentialism

BOUNDED RATIONALITY AND SATISFYING BEHAVIOUR

In Chapter 1, I examined several economic decisions and games in which individuals do not behave as predicted by a simple payoff-maximisation framework. How can these deviations from economic self-interest be formalised within a utility function? This chapter reviews the main approaches developed to address this question and shows that, despite their differences, these approaches share a common property, which I refer to as *economic consequentialism*.

I start my overview from Simon's seminal work, which introduced the concept of satisficing, positing that human decision-makers, constrained by limited time, information, and cognitive resources, often settle for choices that are 'good enough' rather than optimal. Over the years, this idea has been formalised into various mathematical models. This section introduces some of these formulations, starting with the case of an economic decision and then moving to the more complex case of economic games.

Simon himself proposed a straightforward method in 1955 through the establishment of a utility threshold and a decision rule $U(c) \geq T$, defining choices that are satisfactory. This decision rule proves particularly useful in scenarios where choices are analysed sequentially, and there exists the possibility to compute the utility of each choice, at least up to a certain time. Simon discusses methods to ensure the existence and uniqueness of a satisfactory solution, for example, by dynamically adapting the threshold over time and accepting the first satisfactory choice encountered.

Selten refined this approach in 1998, proposing a specific method to dynamically adjust the threshold. In his model, at time

$t+1$, the satisfying threshold is updated to $T_{t+1} = T_t + \alpha(U_t - T_t)$, where U_t represents the utility obtained at time t and α is a learning parameter that describes the rate at which the threshold is updated. Therefore, if at time t the decision-maker has not found a satisfying choice, meaning that $U_t < T_t$, then the new threshold T_{t+1} will be lower than the previous threshold, theoretically making it easier to find a satisfying alternative at time $t+1$. However, it is important to note that this model does not guarantee the existence of a satisfactory choice in every scenario. The effectiveness of the threshold adaptation depends on the distribution of utility values encountered. If the utilities of available choices are consistently lower than even the adapted thresholds, the decision-maker may still fail to find a satisfactory option.

These models assume that players can compute the utility of each choice c. Thus, the bounded rationality reflected in these models stems from the inability to evaluate all possible choice alternatives, rather than from the inability to evaluate single alternatives. In fact, there is another perspective to consider: players may attempt to compute the utility of each available action but, due to bounded rationality, they may be prone to making errors. There are several methods to formalise this scenario, one of which involves using a logistic quantal distribution, as introduced by Luce (1959).

This model is particularly applicable to experimental settings, because it presupposes that the experimenter is aware of the economic consequences of the available actions, but the subject may not be. In their efforts to calculate these, the subject commits errors, which are quantified by a parameter $\lambda \geq 0$. The probability that the decision-maker d chooses action a is then defined by

$$p_d(a) = \frac{e^{\lambda\pi(a)}}{\sum_{a' \in A} e^{\lambda\pi(a')}}, \tag{2.1}$$

where e^x represents the classical exponential function, with the base being Euler's number $e \approx 2.72$.

The interpretation of the precision parameter λ becomes clear when considering two extreme cases. If $\lambda = 0$, the formula simplifies to:

$$p_d(a) = \frac{e^0}{\sum_{a' \in A} e^0} = \frac{1}{\sum_{a' \in A} 1} = \frac{1}{|A|}, \tag{2.2}$$

where $|A|$ represents the cardinality of the action set A, that is, the number of choices available to the decision-maker. In other words, if the precision parameter is zero, then the decision-maker selects a strategy randomly, according to a uniform distribution over the set of strategies. On the other hand, if λ tends towards infinity, the logit choice converges to the payoff-maximising choice. To see this, let a be the choice that maximises the economic payoff, that is $\pi(a) > \pi(a')$, for any other strategy a'. Under this assumption, consider the inverse formula:

$$\frac{1}{p_d(a)} = \frac{\sum_{a' \in A} e^{\lambda \pi(a')}}{e^{\lambda \pi(a)}} = 1 + \sum_{a' \neq a} e^{\lambda(\pi(a') - \pi(a))}. \tag{2.3}$$

Given that $\pi(a) > \pi(a')$ the exponent in the sum is negative, thus converging to 0 when $\lambda \to \infty$, for any a'. Thus, when λ approaches infinity, $\frac{1}{p_d(a)}$ converges to 1, leading to $p_d(a) = 1$, thereby proving that the logit best response selects with certainty (i.e., with probability 1) the choice that maximises the economic return; in other words, the best logit choice coincides with the payoff-maximising choice.

Both previously discussed models can be extended to economic games. For instance, Macy and Flache (2002) applied the model of adaptive aspirations to the Prisoner's Dilemma. In their model, agents contemplate binary choices (Cooperate or Defect) that can result in one of four possible outcomes (CC, CD, DC, or DD), with each outcome corresponding to specific payoffs. Each payoff is evaluated as satisfactory or unsatisfactory relative to an established aspiration level. The authors explore the ranges of aspiration levels that can lead to the evolution of cooperation.

The strategic version of the quantal logistic choice takes the name of quantal response equilibrium and was introduced by McKelvey and Palfrey (1995).

Definition. Let s_{-i} be a strategy profile for players other than player i. The quantal best response to s_{-i} is defined as the mixed strategy of player i that picks the pure strategy a_i with probability:

$$p(a_i) = \frac{e^{\lambda \pi_i(a_i, s_{-i})}}{\sum_{a_i' \in A_i} e^{\lambda \pi(a_i', s_{-i})}}. \tag{2.4}$$

Definition. A quantal response equilibrium with precision λ is a profile of mixed strategies $(s_1, \ldots, s_N)$ such that s_i is a quantal best response to s_{-i}, for all i. □

The existence of quantal response equilibria for every game with finite sets of strategies was demonstrated by McKelvey and Palfrey.

Example (Quantal Response Equilibrium in the Prisoner's Dilemma). To illustrate what this equilibrium might look like, consider the Prisoner's Dilemma with a cost of cooperation $c = 1$ and benefit $b = 2$ and compute the quantal response equilibrium with precision parameter $\lambda = 1$. To this end, assume that Player 2 cooperates with probability α and defects with probability $1 - \alpha$. Player 1's quantal best response to this mixed strategy is the strategy that cooperates with probability:

$$p(C) = \frac{e^{\alpha-(1-\alpha)}}{e^{\alpha-(1-\alpha)} + e^{2\alpha}} = \frac{e^{2\alpha-1}}{e^{2\alpha-1} + e^{2\alpha}}. \tag{2.5}$$

Now, since the game is symmetric, the quantal response equilibrium is characterised by $p(C) = \alpha$, meaning that Player 1's quantal best response in equilibrium must be equal to Player 2's strategy. Therefore, the quantal response equilibrium can be found by solving the equation

$$\alpha = \frac{e^{2\alpha-1}}{e^{2\alpha-1} + e^{2\alpha}}. \tag{2.6}$$

Rearranging the terms, we obtain:

$$e^{2\alpha-1}(\alpha + e\alpha - 1) = 0. \qquad (2.7)$$

Since $e^{2\alpha-1} > 0$ for all α, the only solution to this equation is $\alpha = \frac{1}{1+e} \approx 0.26$. Therefore, in the quantal response equilibrium, cooperation occurs with a probability of approximately 26%, and defection with a probability of 74%. Therefore, the quantal response equilibrium permits a non-negligible rate of cooperation in the one-shot and anonymous Prisoner's Dilemma. □

Remark (Note All Rates of Cooperation Can Be Rationalised by Quantal Response Equilibrium). It is important to note that not all rates of cooperation can be rationalised using this model. To see this, consider the general expression for the probability of cooperation for Player 1, given that Player 1 cooperates with probability α:

$$p(C) = \frac{e^{\lambda(\alpha(b-c)-(1-\alpha)c)}}{e^{\lambda(\alpha(b-c)-(1-\alpha)c)} + e^{\lambda\alpha b}}. \qquad (2.8)$$

Note that $e^{\lambda\alpha b} > e^{\lambda(\alpha(b-c)-(1-\alpha)c)}$, because the left-hand exponent represents the expected gain from defection, which is greater than the right-hand exponent, representing the expected gain from cooperation. It follows that:

$$p(C) < \frac{e^{\lambda(\alpha(b-c)-(1-\alpha)c)}}{e^{\lambda(\alpha(b-c)-(1-\alpha)c)} + e^{\lambda(\alpha(b-c)-(1-\alpha)c)}} = 0.5. \qquad (2.9)$$

This inequality holds regardless of the specific parameters of the Prisoner's Dilemma and the precision parameter, indicating that in equilibrium the probability of cooperation must be smaller than 0.5. Intuitively, this conclusion stems from the fact that the quantal response equilibrium accounts for errors, with the highest error being random play. □

Is this prediction satisfied in economic experiments? The answer is negative. For instance, in an experiment that I conducted with Jordan and Rand, participants played a two-player Public

Good Game under various conditions that only differed in terms of the marginal return for cooperation. The results showed that with sufficiently high returns for cooperation, the rate of cooperative behaviour increased significantly above 50%, reaching nearly 80% (Capraro et al., 2014a). This indicates that while the quantal response equilibrium can explain some degree of cooperation, it is insufficient to account for the higher rates of cooperation observed in some social dilemmas.

In the Social Preferences section of this chapter, I will discuss more powerful models that can rationalise these higher rates of cooperation. For the moment, I conclude this section by acknowledging that adaptive aspirations and quantal response equilibria represent only a few of the numerous approaches developed to formalise bounded rationality in behavioural economics. Other significant models include, for example, cognitive hierarchies, which consider how players anticipate the thought processes of other players, adding layers of belief about others' rationality (Camerer et al., 2004; Costa-Gomes et al., 2001; Stahl II & Wilson, 1994). Another crucial framework is prospect theory, which aims to rationalise some of the systematic biases arising from heuristic shortcuts that individuals adopt to minimise the cognitive cost of evaluating all potential outcomes. This influential theory will be the focus of the next section.

PROSPECT THEORY

Prospect theory was originally proposed by Kahneman and Tversky in 1979. Since then, it has seen numerous variants and updates, including one from the same authors called 'cumulative prospect theory' (Tversky & Kahneman, 1992). Here, I focus on the original version.

Consider a prospect $(p_1, \pi_1; \ldots; p_n, \pi_n)$ which yields an economic payoff π_i with probability p_i. In standard expected utility theory, the expected utility of this prospect is given by:

$$U = \sum_{i=1}^{n} p_i \pi_i. \tag{2.10}$$

The core idea of prospect theory is to replace this expected utility with an expected 'value' of the form:

$$V = \sum_{i=1}^{n} \sigma(p_i) v(\pi_i), \tag{2.11}$$

where σ represents a subjective transformation of probabilities, and v represents the value function of money. These functions, σ and v, are designed to better explain certain regularities observed in behavioural experiments.

Let us start by discussing the value function v. Kahneman and Tversky propose defining the value function based on deviations from a reference point (usually the status quo), rather than final wealth states. They consider functions that are concave for gains and convex for losses (reflecting diminishing sensitivity at higher absolute amounts of money), and steeper for losses than for gains (reflecting loss aversion). An example of such a value function that is often considered in the literature (e.g., Tversky & Kahneman, 1992) is the following:

$$v(\pi) = \begin{cases} (\pi - r)^{\alpha}, & \text{if } \pi \geq r \\ -\lambda\left(|\pi - r|^{\beta}\right), & \text{if } \pi < r \end{cases}, \tag{2.12}$$

where r is the reference point, which in general may not be 0, $\alpha, \beta < 1$ are the curvatures of the value function for gains and losses, respectively, and $\lambda > 1$ is a loss-aversion coefficient, indicating how much more losses weigh than gains.

Moving to subjective probabilities, in classical models, probabilities are objective, meaning they are based on known frequencies or deduced through logical analysis. However, prospect theory recognises that in real-world decision-making, individuals often do not have access to or do not use objective probabilities. Instead, they rely on their beliefs or perceptions about the likelihood of an event, termed 'subjective probabilities'. These are personal estimates of the likelihood of uncertain events, not derived from the frequency of events in the larger population but from an individual's mental judgement and personal experience. They reflect how individuals perceive, filter, and interpret information based on their knowledge, past experiences, biases, and emotions.

Formally, subjective probabilities can be derived from objective probabilities through a weighting function $\sigma(p)$, where p is the objective probability of an outcome. This function typically overweights small probabilities and underweights large probabilities, reflecting common cognitive biases such as the overweighting of unlikely events and the underweighting of near certainties. A specific weighting function that has been proposed (e.g., Tversky & Kahneman, 1992) is the following:

$$\sigma(p) = \frac{p^\gamma}{(p^\gamma + (1-p)^\gamma)^{\frac{1}{\gamma}}}, \tag{2.13}$$

where $\gamma < 1$ is a parameter that makes the function more concave or convex depending on its value.

In the following examples, we will see how this approach can help explain the three biases presented in Chapter 1: the framing effect, the endowment effect, and time-inconsistent decisions.

Example (Prospect Theory Can Rationalise Loss Aversion). Consider a scenario where an individual must choose between two economic outcomes, framed in terms of gains or losses:

Gain frame:

- **Option A:** Receive \$100 with certainty.
- **Option B:** 50% chance to receive \$200, and 50% chance to receive nothing.

Using the value function, the expected utility for Option A is obvious, as this option gives a certain payoff: $V(A) = 100^\alpha$. The expected utility of Option B is more complex, because objective probabilities should be turned into subjective probabilities. For the sake of the example, let us assume $\sigma(0.5) = 0.5$. (Note that this assumption generally does not hold for $\gamma < 1$, but here it is made to simplify the computation, while maintaining the core of the argument.) With this assumption, we obtain:

$$V(B) = 0.5 \cdot 200^{\alpha}. \tag{2.14}$$

Since $\alpha < 1$ (concavity for gains), we have $0.5 < 0.5^{\alpha}$, therefore

$$V(A) = 100^{\alpha} = (0.5 \cdot 200)^{\alpha} = 0.5^{\alpha} \cdot 200^{\alpha} > 0.5 \cdot 200^{\alpha} = V(B). \tag{2.15}$$

Therefore, in the gain frame, the individual prefers Option A over Option B.

Loss frame:

- **Option C:** Lose \$100 with certainty.
- **Option D:** 50% chance to lose \$200, and 50% chance to lose nothing.

Using the value function, the expected utility for Option C is obvious, as this option gives a certain payoff: $V(C) = -\lambda 100^{\beta}$. For the expected utility of Option D, as before let us assume $\sigma(0.5) = 0.5$. We obtain:

$$V(D) = -\lambda 0.5 \cdot 200^{\beta} \tag{2.16}$$

Since $\beta < 1$ (convexity for losses), we have $0.5 < 0.5^{\beta}$, therefore

$$\begin{aligned} V(C) &= -\lambda 100^{\beta} = -\lambda (0.5 \cdot 200)^{\beta} \\ &= -\lambda 0.5^{\beta} \cdot 200^{\beta} < -\lambda 0.5 \cdot 200^{\beta} = V(D). \end{aligned} \tag{2.17}$$

Therefore, in the loss frame, the individual prefers Option D over Option C. □

Example (Prospect Theory Can Rationalise the Endowment Effect). Consider a seller s owning an object o whose market value is \$100. Assume that a buyer b offers to buy the object at this market value. We consider keeping the object as the status quo, establishing it as the reference point. Therefore, the utility of keeping the object is $V(keep) = 0$. On the other hand, the utility of selling the object is influenced by two components: the loss incurred from selling the object and the gain from receiving \$100. Thus, the utility from selling can be expressed as:

$$V(sell) = -\lambda 100^{\beta} + 100^{\alpha}. \tag{2.18}$$

Whether this value is greater or smaller than $V(keep)$ depends on the specific values of α and β. For example, if β is significantly smaller than α, then $V(sell)$ may be positive. However, since α and β represent the concavity for gains and the convexity for losses, there is generally no strong reason to assume they differ markedly. Tversky and Kahneman (1992) have even estimated that they might be both equal to 0.88. If α and β are close enough, since $\lambda > 1$, we will have $V(sell) < 0$. This implies that the seller would prefer to keep the object rather than sell it at the market value. Prospect theory can therefore rationalise the endowment effect. □

Example (Prospect Theory Can Rationalise Time-Inconsistent Preferences). Consider a decision-maker d faced with two options:

- **Option A:** Receive \$100 now.
- **Option B:** Receive \$110 tomorrow.

The value of Option A is straightforward since it delivers a certain economic payoff immediately: $V(A) = 100^{\alpha}$. The value of Option B is more complex due to the delayed payoff. One way to account for this delay is by considering a small probability that the decision-maker might not survive to receive the payment. Let p_n be the probability that the decision-maker is alive on day n. Thus, choosing Option B equates to selecting the prospect $(1 - p_1, 0; p_1, 110)$. To compute the value of this prospect, we need to transform the objective probability p_1 into a subjective probability, yielding: $V(B) = \sigma(p_1)\,110^{\alpha}$.

Let us keep these computations aside and consider the same decision-maker deciding between:

- **Option C:** Receive \$100 in 30 days.
- **Option D:** Receive \$110 in 31 days.

Choosing Option C corresponds to the prospect $(1 - p_{30}, 0; p_{30}, 100)$, whereas choosing Option D corresponds to $(1 - p_{31}, 0; p_{31}, 110)$. Computing the values of these prospects, we obtain:

$$V(C) = \sigma(p_{30})100^{\alpha} \tag{2.19}$$

$$V(D) = \sigma(p_{31})110^{\alpha}. \tag{2.20}$$

Assuming the probability of being alive the next day does not depend on the day, there exists $p < 1$ such that $p_n = p^n$. The aim is to show that time-inconsistent preferences may derive from how people overweight small probabilities and underweight large probabilities.

Clearly, we have $p = \frac{p^{31}}{p^{30}}$. However, both p^{31} and p^{30} are further from 1 and closer to 0 than p, which is close to 1. We assume that the hypothesis that the decision-maker underweights large probabilities translates to the fact that $\sigma(p) < p$, whereas $\sigma(p_{31}) = p_{31}$ and $\sigma(p_{30}) = p_{30}$. Therefore,

$$\sigma(p) < \frac{\sigma(p_{31})}{\sigma(p_{30})}, \tag{2.21}$$

leading to:

$$\sigma(p)110^{\alpha} < \frac{\sigma(p_{31})}{\sigma(p_{30})}110^{\alpha}. \tag{2.22}$$

Depending on the values of the various parameters, it is therefore possible that 100^{α} sits right in the middle:

$$\sigma(p)110^{\alpha} < 100^{\alpha} < \frac{\sigma(p_{31})}{\sigma(p_{30})}110^{\alpha}. \tag{2.23}$$

The inequality on the left implies $V(B) < V(A)$, indicating that the decision-maker prefers \$100 today over \$110 tomorrow. Conversely, rearranging the inequality on the right results in

$$\sigma(p_{30})100^{\alpha} < \sigma(p_{31})110^{\alpha}. \tag{2.24}$$

This tells us that $V(C) < V(D)$, implying the same decision-maker prefers \$110 in 31 days over \$100 in 30 days.

In summary, there exist values within the parameters of prospect theory that can rationalise time-inconsistent preferences. □

HYPERBOLIC DISCOUNTING

In the previous section, I demonstrated that prospect theory could rationalise time-inconsistent preferences. However, this application is somewhat non-standard, and I included it primarily to illustrate the capacity of prospect theory to explain behavioural regularities beyond its original scope.

In this section, I will discuss a more classical explanation of time-inconsistent preferences: hyperbolic discounting. Before introducing this model, it is essential to understand the framework of exponential discounting, which was the standard model for describing intertemporal choices before the recognition of time-inconsistent preferences necessitated a model revision.

Exponential discounting posits that the value of a future reward decreases exponentially as the delay to receiving the reward increases. We can think of the exponential decrease in value as mirroring the 'probability of being alive' considered in the previous section, which also decreases exponentially.

Definition (Exponential Discount). Mathematically, the exponential discounting formula is expressed as:

$$V = \frac{R}{(1+r)^t}, \tag{2.25}$$

where:

V is the present value of the future reward.
R is the future reward.
r is the discount rate.
t is the time delay until the reward is received.

The discount rate r reflects the rate at which a future reward loses value per unit of time. A higher r indicates a stronger preference for immediate rewards over future rewards. □

Example (Exponential Discount Yields Time-Consistent Preferences). One critical property of exponential discounting is that it yields time-consistent preferences. To see this, consider the same decision problem as before, where an individual must choose between:

- **Option A:** Receive \$100 today.
- **Option B:** Receive \$110 tomorrow.

Let the unit of time be days, so that r denotes the daily discount rate. The present value of \$110 received tomorrow is:

$$V(B) = \frac{110}{1+r}. \tag{2.26}$$

Thus, the preference of Option A over Option B is described by the condition: $100 > \frac{110}{1+r}$.

Now, consider the same individual choosing between

- **Option C:** Receive \$100 in 30 days.
- **Option D:** Receive \$110 in 31 days.

The present value of Option C is $V(C) = \frac{100}{(1+r)^{30}}$, whereas the present value of Option D is $V(D) = \frac{110}{(1+r)^{31}}$. Therefore, the condition describing the preference of Option C over Option D is:

$$\frac{100}{(1+r)^{30}} > \frac{110}{(1+r)^{31}}. \tag{2.27}$$

After simplifying $(1+r)^{30}$, this condition becomes identical to the preference for Option A over Option B. In other words, the decision-maker consistently chooses either A and C or B and D without switching preferences.

However, empirical observations often show that people make time-inconsistent decisions: they disproportionately value the present, leading them to choose A and D. To account for this, let us turn to hyperbolic discounting. □

Definition (Hyperbolic Discount). With the same notation as earlier, hyperbolic discounting is expressed as:

$$V = \frac{R}{1+rt}. \tag{2.28}$$

Example (Hyperbolic Discount Is Compatible with Time-Inconsistent Preferences). Unlike exponential discounting, where the rate of decrease is constant, hyperbolic discounting predicts a declining rate of decrease, making it compatible with observed time-inconsistent preferences. To see this, consider the same decision scenarios as earlier. The condition for preferring Option A over Option B is:

$$100 > \frac{110}{1+r}. \tag{2.29}$$

The condition for preferring Option C over Option D is:

$$\frac{100}{1+30r} > \frac{110}{1+31r}. \tag{2.30}$$

This can be rewritten as:

$$100 > \frac{110(1+30r)}{1+31r}. \tag{2.31}$$

Now observe that:

$$\frac{1}{1+r} < \frac{1+30r}{1+31r}. \tag{2.32}$$

This inequality can be shown easily by direct computation. It follows that the condition for preferring Option C over Option D is more stringent than for preferring Option A over Option B. Thus, there are values of r such that the decision-maker prefers Option A over Option B and, simultaneously, Option D over Option C. □

SOCIAL PREFERENCES

In Chapter 1, we observed that humans can exhibit social behaviours that are not strictly self-interested from an economic standpoint, even in anonymous and one-shot games where motivations related to reputation and reciprocity are excluded. This section discusses a series of utility functions introduced by behavioural economists, specifically designed to rationalise these deviations from pure economic self-interest.

Altruistic Preferences

An early attempt to formalise altruistic behaviour through a utility function was made by Ledyard (1995).

Definition (Ledyard's Utility Function). Let $(x_1,\dots,x_N)$ be an economic distribution among N players. Ledyard postulated that the utility received by player p from this economic distribution was:

$$u_p(x_1,\dots,x_N) = x_p + \alpha_p \sum_{i \neq p} x_i \tag{2.33}$$

where α_p is an individual parameter that represents the level of altruism of player p. □

Several observations can be made. If $\alpha_p = 0$, Ledyard's utility function reduces to economic self-interest. If $\alpha_p > 0$, player p not only aims to maximise their economic payoff but also considers the total payoff of the other participants. In this sense, p is altruistic. It is interesting to note that α_p could also be negative. In such cases, player p would negatively evaluate the payoff of the other participants: the more the others gain, the less satisfied player p is, and vice versa. Thus, Ledyard's utility function not only captures some positive aspects of humanity, such as altruism, but also some negative aspects, such as spite.

The following examples examine the predictions of Ledyard's utility function in some of the social decisions and games introduced in Chapter 1.

Example (Consistency of Ledyard's Utility Function with Equal Splitting in the Dictator Game, with a Caveat). For simplicity, assume that the dictator has only two options: keep everything for themselves or donate half of the initial amount to the recipient. This simplification is plausible since the meta-analysis by Engel (2011) revealed that donations in the Dictator Game tend to cluster around two primary modes, one at zero and one at half of the initial amount, with a smaller, third mode at giving all, which I exclude from this example. Let us now calculate the dictator's utility corresponding to each of the available choices, with d denoting the dictator and e their initial endowment.

If the dictator decides to keep the entire amount for themselves, we obtain:

$$u_d(e,0) = e. \tag{2.34}$$

If instead, they decide to split the amount equally, we find:

$$u_d\left(\frac{e}{2},\frac{e}{2}\right) = \frac{e}{2} + \frac{\alpha_d e}{2}. \tag{2.35}$$

Therefore, the dictator will donate half of their initial amount if the following condition is verified:

$$\frac{e}{2} + \frac{\alpha_d e}{2} > e. \tag{2.36}$$

From which we derive $\alpha_d > 1$.

Thus, Ledyard's utility function predicts that a dictator will opt for an equal split only if $\alpha_d > 1$. Note that this condition is quite stringent, corresponding to dictators who value the recipient's economic payoff more than their own. It implies that if we were to include the 'give all' option (the third mode identified in Engel's meta-analysis), Ledyard's utility function would predict that dictators either keep all or give all, with no dictator choosing the equal split. □

I will now analyse cooperation in the context of the Prisoner's Dilemma.

Example (Consistency of Ledyard's Utility Function with Cooperation in the Prisoner's Dilemma). I shall divide this analysis into two cases:

- Suppose Player 1 believes that Player 2 will cooperate. Player 1 contemplates the two available actions, cooperation and defection. Therefore, we need to separate two more cases.
  - If Player 1 decides to cooperate, their utility would be:

$$u_1(b-c, b-c) = b-c+\alpha_1(b-c). \tag{2.37}$$

  - If instead, Player 1 decides to defect, their utility would be:

$$u_1(b,-c) = b - \alpha_1 c. \tag{2.38}$$

Therefore, for Player 1, cooperating turns out to be more advantageous than defecting if:

$$b - c + \alpha_1(b - c) > b - \alpha_1 c, \tag{2.39}$$

from which it follows that $\alpha_1 > \frac{c}{b}$.

- Suppose now that Player 1 believes that Player 2 will defect. Once again, Player 1 contemplates both potential strategies.
  - If Player 1 decides to cooperate, their utility would be:

$$u_1(-c, b) = -c + \alpha_1 b. \tag{2.40}$$

  - If instead, Player 1 decides to defect, their utility would be:

$$u_1(0, 0) = 0. \tag{2.41}$$

Therefore, it is more advantageous for Player 1 to cooperate rather than defect if:

$$-c + \alpha_1 b > 0, \tag{2.42}$$

from which $\alpha_1 > \frac{c}{b}$ is obtained, the same condition obtained in the previous case.

Combining the two scenarios, we deduce that if the parameter α_1 is greater than the ratio $\frac{c}{b}$, then Player 1 will choose to cooperate. In other words, Ledyard's utility function qualitatively supports the presence of cooperation in the Prisoner's Dilemma.

It is worth noting that if the value of b increases, the condition $\alpha_1 > \frac{c}{b}$ becomes less stringent, leading to the prediction that, with an increase in b, the tendency to cooperate will intensify. This prediction has indeed been confirmed experimentally (Capraro et al., 2014a). Similarly, an increase in the cost of cooperation c makes the condition $\alpha_1 > \frac{c}{b}$ more restrictive, suggesting a likely reduction in cooperation. This prediction has also been confirmed experimentally (Engel & Zhurakhovska, 2016). □

Example (Inconsistency of Ledyard's Utility Function with Rejections in the Ultimatum Game). Suppose that the proposer makes a relatively low offer, equivalent to a quarter of the total amount available, which we normalise to 1, and that it is up to the respondent to decide whether to accept or reject it. If accepted, the responder's utility would be:

$$u_r\left(\frac{3}{4},\frac{1}{4}\right)=\frac{1}{4}+\frac{3\alpha_r}{4}. \tag{2.43}$$

If rejected, their utility would be:

$$u_r(0,0)=0. \tag{2.44}$$

From this, the responder would reject the offer if:

$$\alpha_r<-\frac{1}{3}. \tag{2.45}$$

Ledyard's utility function thus agrees with the observation that respondents tend to reject particularly low offers. However, an important question arises. Although Ledyard's utility function agrees with the existence of altruistic punishment, this occurs assuming that α_r is negative. This implies that, according to Ledyard's utility function, altruistic punishments stem from 'spitefulness', namely from individuals who find satisfaction in reducing others' economic benefits. Is this true?

This hypothesis can be subjected to experimental verification. Imagine an experiment in which participants play both the Dictator Game and the Ultimatum Game, in the latter as responders. If the rejection of low offers in the Ultimatum Game were mainly motivated by spitefulness, then we would expect those who reject low offers in the Ultimatum Game to keep everything for themselves in the Dictator Game. If, instead, the rejection were partially influenced by altruism, we should observe that those responders who reject low offers can be split into two groups in the Dictator Game: those who keep everything and those who share part of the amount.

This experiment was conducted by Brañas-Garza et al. (2014), using two different samples: a 'citizen' sample representative of a Spanish city and a sample of first-year university students. In both experiments, participants played both the Ultimatum Game (in both roles) and the Dictator Game, in random order. In the Dictator Game, subjects were asked how they would divide €20 between themselves and another anonymous participant. When playing the Ultimatum Game as responders, participants' preferences were measured using the 'strategy method': they were shown all possible offers from €0 to €10 (in €2 intervals) and, for each of them, they were asked whether they would accept or reject it. The authors then categorised the dictators into three classes: the unfair (who keep all the €20 for themselves), the fair (who split it in half), and the remaining. Subsequently, they analysed the percentage of offers below €10 that were rejected in the Ultimatum Game in each of these classes. In both experiments, the results demonstrated that there was no statistical difference in the percentages of rejection of low offers between the unfair dictators and the fair ones. This suggests that the rejection of low offers is driven both by altruistic motivations and spiteful motivations, contrasting with the predictions of Ledyard's utility function.

A second piece of evidence of the limitations of Ledyard's utility function was provided in 1998 by Levine. He argued that although Ledyard's utility function could qualitatively agree with experimental data, it was not quantitatively accurate. Levine observed that by analysing the distribution of offer rejections, it was possible to estimate the altruistic parameter of Ledyard's utility function. This, in turn, allowed the calculation of the optimal offer that proposers should have made to minimise the risk of rejection. Levine showed that this offer was, on average, lower than the ones actually made by proposers. To address this issue, Levine suggested a revision of the utility function proposed by Ledyard, introducing a sort of 'selective altruism'. This allowed a participant to behave altruistically only towards other altruistic participants. □

Definition (Levine's Utility Function). Let $(x_1,\dots,x_N)$ be an economic distribution among N players. Levine proposed that the utility received by player p from this economic distribution was:

$$u_p(x_1,\dots,x_N) = x_p + \sum_{i\neq p} \frac{\alpha_p + \lambda\alpha_i}{1+\lambda} x_i, \tag{2.46}$$

where $\lambda \geq 0$. □

Some observations are in order. On the one hand, if $\lambda = 0$, the function reduces to Ledyard's function. On the other hand, if $\lambda \to \infty$

the function converges to $u_p(x_1,\ldots,x_N) = x_p + \sum_{i \neq p} \alpha_i x_i$, which means that player p weighs the payoff of other players only in terms of their level of altruism: altruistic players are considered positively, selfish players are not considered, spiteful players are considered negatively. The parameter λ can thus be interpreted as a parameter that represents how sensitive player p is to the levels of altruism of other players.

Levine demonstrated the consistency of his utility function with the experimental data of various games, including the Ultimatum Game. As an example, I shall demonstrate how Levine's utility function does not lead to the unexpected prediction of Ledyard's utility function, according to which rejections in the Ultimatum Game are made exclusively by respondents who wish to decrease the proposers' gain.

Example (Consistency of Levine's Utility Function with Ultimatum Game Rejections). Returning to the earlier example of the proposer offering 1/4, and using Levine's utility function, we obtain that the responder's utility, if they were to accept the offer, would be:

$$u_r\left(\frac{3}{4},\frac{1}{4}\right) = \frac{1}{4} + \frac{\alpha_r + \lambda\alpha_p}{1+\lambda} \cdot \frac{3}{4}. \tag{2.47}$$

On the other hand, rejecting would guarantee a utility equal to 0. Therefore, the respondent rejects if:

$$\frac{1}{4} + \frac{\alpha_r + \lambda\alpha_p}{1+\lambda} \cdot \frac{3}{4} < 0. \tag{2.48}$$

Note now that, with λ fixed, the expression on the left side can be negative only in two cases:

- When $\alpha_r < 0$, with α_r sufficiently negative to counterbalance any potential positivity of α_p. This is the case also found using Ledyard's utility function, where the respondent rejects an offer motivated by the desire to decrease the economic payoff of the proposer.
- When $\alpha_r > 0$ and $\alpha_p < 0$, with $\alpha_r > 0$ not too high to counterbalance the negativity of $\alpha_p < 0$. This is the new scenario, where the respondent rejects an offer perceived as driven by spiteful motivations, and rejects it for altruistic reasons.

As mentioned earlier, the co-existence of these two types of rejections has been confirmed experimentally (Brañas-Garza et al., 2014). □

I conclude the discussion of Levine's utility function with an observation on the Dictator Game. If we assume that the altruistic parameters of both players are less than 1, then it follows that the best strategy for the dictator is to keep the entire sum of money for themselves. It follows that to explain altruism in the Dictator Game, Levine's utility function requires the assumption that at least one of the two altruism coefficients is greater than 1. This assumption, similar to the analogous one of Ledyard's utility function, is equally unrealistic.

Inequity-Aversion Preferences

In the previous subsection, I presented two models of preferences for altruism. In this section, I explore another way to consider the economic payoffs of other individuals involved in the interaction. This approach is based on the concept of equity. Instead of focusing on the sum of the economic payoffs of other players, inequity-aversion models evaluate the economic differences between participants. It is assumed that people derive psychological benefit when these differences decrease or, conversely, suffer psychological loss when inequalities increase. The two best-known utility functions based on inequity aversion are those of Fehr and Schmidt (1999) and Bolton and Ockenfels (2000).

Definition (Fehr and Schimdt's Utility Function). Let $(x_1,\ldots,x_N)$ be an economic distribution. The utility of player p is defined as:

$$\begin{aligned} u_p(x_1,\ldots,x_N) = x_p - \frac{\alpha_p}{N-1}\sum_{i\neq p} max(x_p - x_i, 0) \\ - \frac{\beta_p}{N-1}\sum_{i\neq p} max(x_i - x_p, 0), \end{aligned} \tag{2.49}$$

where α_p and β_p are individual parameters. □

To better understand the meaning of the individual parameters, consider the following examples.

1. Suppose p is the player with the highest payoff, that is, $x_p > x_i$ for every $i \neq p$. In this case, $max(x_i - x_p, 0) = 0$, for every i. Consequently, the second summation in the utility function is zero. As for the first summation, we have $max(x_p - x_i, 0) = x_p - x_i$, for every i. From these two observations, we deduce:

$$u_p(x_1,\ldots,x_N) = x_p - \frac{\alpha_p}{N-1}\sum_{i \neq p} x_p - x_i. \tag{2.50}$$

   The utility of player p is thus represented by their own economic payoff minus a parameter (α_p) that multiplies the average of the economic differences between p and the other players. Thus, α_p represents p's aversion to advantageous inequalities.
2. Now consider the opposite case, where p has the lowest payoff: $x_p < x_i$ for every $i \neq p$. In this scenario, $max(x_p - x_i, 0) = 0$, for every i. Hence, the first summation in the utility function is zero. Regarding the second summation, we have $max(x_i - x_p, 0) = x_i - x_p$. Therefore:

$$u_p(x_1,\ldots,x_N) = x_p - \frac{\beta_p}{N-1}\sum_{i \neq p} x_i - x_p. \tag{2.51}$$

   Here, the utility of p is determined by their economic payoff minus a parameter (β_p) that multiplies the average of the economic differences between p and the other players. Therefore, β_p represents p's aversion to disadvantageous inequalities.

The following examples investigate how Fehr and Schmidt's utility function operates in some of the social decisions and games introduced previously.

Example (Consistency of Fehr and Schmidt's Utility Function with Altruism in the Dictator Game). As before, let us compare the utility of giving zero with the utility of giving half. We obtain:

$$u_d(1,0) = 1 - \alpha_d \tag{2.52}$$

$$u_d\left(\frac{1}{2},\frac{1}{2}\right) = \frac{1}{2}. \tag{2.53}$$

From this, we deduce that if $\alpha_d > \frac{1}{2}$, it is optimal for the dictator to evenly split the sum in their possession.

It is interesting to note the distinction from the altruistic models of Ledyard and Levine. In these models, the minimum value of the individual parameter that produced donations in the Dictator Game was 1. In the model of Fehr and Schmidt, it is instead 1/2. This variation is not only quantitative but reflects a conceptual change: while an altruism parameter greater than 1 seems implausible (since few individuals value others' payoffs more than their own), an aversion to advantageous inequity greater than 1/2, though not universal, is arguably more realistic.

Another relevant observation is that when the 'giving all' strategy is introduced, its utility is given by

$$u_d(0,1) = -\beta_d. \tag{2.54}$$

Under the standard assumption that $\beta_d > 0$, this strategy is never optimal because it is strictly dominated by the equal split, which yields a utility of 1/2. In other words, Fehr and Schmidt's utility function predicts that no dictator will choose to give all, as splitting evenly or keeping all always provides a higher utility. However, Engel's meta-analysis indicates that while giving all occurs less frequently than the other two strategies, it nonetheless represents a distinct mode in the observed distribution of choices. This discrepancy suggests that although Fehr and Schmidt's utility function captures several key aspects of behaviour in the Dictator Game, a more nuanced model may be necessary to fully account for the entire distribution of empirical choices. □

Example (Consistency of Fehr and Schmidt's Utility Function with Rejections in the Ultimatum Game). Consider a less-than-equal proposal $0 < p < \frac{1}{2}$. If the responder rejects, they obtain a utility equal to 0. If they accept, their utility is:

$$u_r(1-p, p) = p - \beta_r(1-2p). \tag{2.55}$$

Therefore, the responder will reject if $\beta_r > \frac{p}{1-2p}$.

It is important to make two remarks at this point. First, the expression on the right-hand side increases with the variable p, when p belongs to the domain of interest, $p \in (0, \frac{1}{2})$. Thus, Fehr and Schmidt's utility function agrees with the experimental observation that the probability of rejection of an offer increases with the lowering of the offer.

Second, the condition is consistent with experimental results reviewed earlier indicating that responders reject low offers for both altruistic and spiteful reasons. Indeed, the parameter β_r simply represents a measure of how much people dislike receiving less than others, regardless of whether this preference comes from preferences for equity or from preferences to receive more than others. □

Example (Consistency of Fehr and Schmidt's Utility Function with Cooperation in Public Good Games, with a Caveat). To analyse the Public Good Game, we need to separate various cases, depending on the expected choices of the other players and the choice of the focal player.

- **Suppose player *p* believes that all other $N-1$ players contribute the entire sum** at their disposal (assumed to be normalised to 1) to the public good. Let us compare the utility that player p would receive if they also contributed the entire sum with the utility they would receive if they contributed zero.
  - **If player *p* were to contribute the entire sum**, all players would finish the game with an economic payoff equal to mN, where m is the marginal return of cooperation. Since there are no inequalities among the players, this value also coincides with the utility function of Fehr and Schmidt:

$$u_p(mN, \ldots, mN) = mN. \tag{2.56}$$

  - **If player *p* were to contribute zero**, p would be the only defector among N players, thus finishing the game with an economic payoff of $1 + m(N-1)$. The other players would instead receive only $m(N-1)$. In this case, therefore, there would be economic inequalities. The utility function of Fehr and Schmidt thus turns out to be different from the economic payoff of player p. Specifically, it is:

$$u_p(1+m(N-1), m(N-1), \ldots, m(N-1)) \\ = 1 + m(N-1) - \frac{\alpha_p}{N-1}(N-1). \tag{2.57}$$

Comparing the two utilities thus obtained, we deduce that the utility of contributing the entire sum is greater than the utility of keeping the entire sum when

$$\alpha_p > 1 - m.$$

- **Suppose now that p believes that all other players will contribute zero** to the public good. Once again, let us separate this case into two additional cases:
  - **If p were also to contribute zero**, their utility would be:

$$u_p(1, \ldots, 1) = 1. \tag{2.58}$$

  - **If instead p were to invest the entire sum of money**, then their utility would be:

$$u_p(m, 1+m, \ldots, 1+m) = m - \beta_p. \tag{2.59}$$

  Comparing these two utilities, it is obtained that the utility of contributing the entire sum is greater than the utility of keeping it if

$$\beta_p < m - 1. \tag{2.60}$$

  Note that $m < 1$, so contributing the entire amount is an optimal response to everyone contributing nothing only when β_p is sufficiently negative. This assumption is unrealistic, since it corresponds to players who receive positive utility when they have a lower economic payoff than other players. This allows us to conclude that there are no 'realistic' values of the model parameters for which contributing the total sum is always optimal, regardless of what it is believed other players will do.

However, as shown earlier, if each player has $\alpha_p > 1 - m$, then investing the entire sum is a Nash equilibrium, as no player increases their utility by changing strategy. In this sense, Fehr and Schmidt's utility function is compatible with cooperation in the Public Good Game.

Note, however, that full cooperation is not the only equilibrium. Consider the condition for a player to cooperate when everyone else defects: $\beta_p < m - 1$. Under the realistic assumption that $\beta_p > 0$ this condition is impossible to satisfy. In other words, if others contribute nothing, no player is incentivised to cooperate, meaning that full defection is also a Nash equilibrium. It follows from both considerations above that, Fehr and Schmidt's utility function predicts that players will be more likely to end up to a cooperative equilibrium the more they believe that others will cooperate.

We also observe that the condition $\alpha_p > 1 - m$ becomes less stringent as m increases. This implies that, if the marginal return on cooperation increases, Fehr and Schmidt's utility function *suggests* a consequent increase in cooperation. I use the term 'suggests' rather than 'predicts' because, given the presence of multiple equilibria, the implication is not direct and depends on the further assumption that a significant number of individuals with $\alpha_p > 1 - m$ believe that others opt for the cooperative choice. In any case, this result, analogous to those observed in the Prisoner's Dilemma, has been confirmed through experimental studies (Capraro et al., 2014a).

An explicit prediction of the Fehr and Schmidt model is that the frequency of cooperation should be independent of the group size, since the conditions for which cooperation represents an equilibrium do not depend on N. As reviewed in Chapter 1, this prediction is not satisfied in experimental studies, which have shown a positive effect of group size on cooperation in the Public Good Game.

In sum, Fehr and Schmidt's utility function can explain some of the regularities observed for the Public Good Game, but not all. □

Let us now turn to Bolton and Ockenfels's utility function. The authors study a class of utility functions that satisfy some formal properties. For simplicity, I consider only a particular function, suggested by the authors themselves to describe preferences for equity when the interaction involves two players.

Definition (Bolton and Ockenfels's Utility Function). Let (x_1, x_2) be an economic distribution between two players, with both $x_1, x_2 \geq 0$. The utility of player p is defined as:

$$u_p(x_1, x_2) = \alpha_p x_p - \frac{\beta_p}{2}\left(\frac{x_p}{x_1 + x_2} - \frac{1}{2}\right)^2, \tag{2.61}$$

where α_p and β_p are individual parameters, which are supposed to be non-negative. □

Some observations. The model assumes that economic benefits are non-negative. Therefore, the denominator $x_1 + x_2$ can be zero only if both players receive zero. In this case, there is no inequality, so the second term of the utility function is defined to be zero. In the other cases, where $x_1 + x_2 > 0$, the fraction $\frac{x_p}{x_1+x_2}$ represents the proportion of the total amount of money received by player p. If this ratio equals 1/2, then there is no inequality between the players and, consistently, the second term of the utility function degenerates to zero. Whenever the proportion of money obtained by p is different from 1/2, the second term of the utility function is non-zero. The square outside the parentheses is a simple arithmetic transformation to make the number inside the parentheses (the difference between the proportion received by p and the equal distribution) positive. The fact that there is a negative sign in front of β_p therefore implies that player p receives a disutility any time there is inequality between the economic payoffs of the two players.

The main conceptual difference from Fehr and Schmidt's utility function is that the latter considers inequalities that benefit the focal player and those that disadvantage them differently. In this way, it can explain potential asymmetries in inequity aversion, depending on who benefits. Bolton and Ockenfels's utility function, on the other hand, treats the two types of inequity in the same manner. Beyond this, the two models are conceptually very similar. The fact that they use different mathematical formulas to quantify inequity means that the two models make quantitatively, but not qualitatively, different predictions. It can be shown that Bolton and Ockenfels's utility function is consistent with the existence of altruistic behaviour in the Dictator Game, cooperative behaviour in the Prisoner's Dilemma, and altruistic punishment in the Ultimatum Game.

PREFERENCES COMBINING ALTRUISM AND INEQUITY AVERSION

Shortly after the surge in inequity-aversion preferences, some experimental studies observed that, in many cases, people seem to behave altruistically even when such behaviour increases inequalities, like in the Equity–Efficiency Trade-Off Game. For example, Charness and Grosskopf (2001) reported an experiment with 121 students from Pompeu Fabra University in Barcelona who were asked to decide between two money distributions. In one distribution, the decision-maker and another participant, randomly selected from a population of non-decision-makers, each received 600 pesetas (equitable distribution). In the other distribution, the decision-maker received 600 pesetas while the other participant received 900 pesetas (efficient, but unequal distribution). The authors observed that about 60% of participants chose the (600,900) distribution, while the remaining 40% chose the (600,600) distribution.

It is challenging to reconcile this experimental observation with previous utility functions. Altruistic preferences predict that all subjects would choose the (600,900) distribution. Inequity-aversion preferences predict that all subjects would choose the (600,600) distribution. To explain the simultaneous presence of both types of subjects, behavioural scientists have thus sought to develop more general utility functions that incorporate elements of both types of previous models. In this section, I present the two best-known models of this type, both published in 2002.

Let us start with the work of Andreoni and Miller. The two economists conducted an experiment with 176 economics students at an American university, each of whom made a series of decisions using variants of the Dictator Game with varying cost of altruism. For example, when the cost was 0.5, the recipient received double the sum donated by the dictator. By varying the cost of altruism, the authors were able to estimate the utility function of the participants by observing how their behaviour changed with the cost of altruism. In doing so, the authors were able to classify the subjects into various categories:

- **About 23% of the subjects maximised their own economic payoff**, regardless of the cost of altruism. Thus, these subjects consistently behaved according to the economically self-interested utility function: $u_d(x_d, x_r) = x_d$.
- **About 14% of the subjects divided the money in a way that achieved economic equality**, between the players. This behaviour can be rationalised by the Rawlsian function: $u_d(x_d, x_r) = min(x_d, x_r)$, named after the American philosopher John Rawls, who in his essay *A Theory of Justice* theorised a concept of justice according to which society should aim to benefit the most disadvantaged. (This behaviour can also be rationalised through the inequity-aversion preferences of Fehr and Schmidt or Bolton and Ockenfels.)
- **About 6% of the subjects donated only when the cost of altruism was less than 1**, suggesting that these subjects aimed to maximise collective economic payoff through the utilitarian utility function: $u_d(x_d, x_r) = x_d + x_r$.
- To rationalise the behaviour of the remaining 57% of subjects, Andreoni and Miller considered a two-parameter family of utility functions:

$$u_d(x_d, x_r) = (\alpha x_d^\rho + (1-\alpha) x_r^\rho)^{\frac{1}{\rho}}. \tag{2.62}$$

  Here, α represents how much weight the dictator assigns to their economic payoff relative to that of the recipient, while ρ is a parameter that can take any non-zero value and accounts for the potential convexity of preferences. Thus, Andreoni and Miller demonstrated that the remaining 57% of subjects could be divided into three further classes:
  - **Weakly selfish (25%)**. These were subjects with estimated parameters $\alpha = 0.758$ and $\rho = 0.621$. The term 'weakly selfish' stems from the proximity of the parameter α to 1.
  - **Weakly Rawlsian (16%)**. Subjects with estimated parameters $\alpha = 0.654$ and $\rho = -0.350$. The peculiarity of these subjects is having the parameter ρ negative. It can be demonstrated that as ρ tends to negative infinity, then the utility function considered by Andreoni and Miller converges to the Rawlsian function.
  - **Weakly utilitarian (16%)**. These are subjects with estimated parameters $\alpha = 0.576$ and $\rho = 0.669$. The peculiarity of these subjects consists in having the parameter ρ close to the value 1 and α close to 0.5, which represents the case where subjects aim to maximise collective economic return.

One might then wonder if this approach can also explain other non-self-interested behaviours that we have encountered in Chapter 1, such as cooperation in the Prisoner's Dilemma or altruistic punishment. Regarding cooperation, the answer is straightforward, since the condition $c < b$ in the Prisoner's Dilemma guarantees that cooperation maximises collective economic payoff and thus is consistent with the utilitarian or weakly utilitarian utility function. The case of altruistic punishment, however, is less obvious, as it minimises both the collective and individual payoff, thus not fitting into any of the previous cases. Indeed, observing more closely the function considered by Andreoni and Miller, it can be noted that it is positive for any positive value of x_d and x_r while it is null when both these values are null. Hence, there are no values of the parameters α and ρ for which rejecting a proposal in the Ultimatum Game can be optimal.

Let us now turn to the approach of Charness and Rabin. Following a methodology similar to that of Andreoni and Miller, Charness and Rabin considered a general family of utility functions that, by varying its parameters, encompasses many of the previously studied cases. They conducted experiments with two student populations (one from Pompeu Fabra University in Barcelona and one from the University of California, Berkeley) to estimate these parameters. For a two-player setting, the authors proposed the following utility function for Player 2:

$$u_2(x_1, x_2) = (\rho r + \sigma s)x_1 + (1 - \rho r - \sigma s)x_2, \tag{2.63}$$

where (1) $r = 1$, if $x_2 > x_1$, and $r = 0$ otherwise; (2) $s = 1$, if $x_2 < x_1$, and $s = 0$ otherwise. In this formulation, the free parameters are ρ and σ. Intuitively, ρ represents the weight that Player 2 gives to advantageous inequalities; σ represents the weight that Player 2 assigns to the disadvantageous inequalities. As these parameters vary, different preference structures emerge. Three particularly important cases are as follows:

- **Competitive preferences**. If $\sigma \leq \rho < 0$, the coefficient of x_1 is negative while the coefficient of x_2 is positive. It follows that the utility of Player

2 grows when their economic payoff increases and when the economic payoff of Player 1 decreases, reflecting competitive preferences.

- **Inequity-aversion preferences**. If $\sigma < 0 < \frac{1}{2} < \rho$, consider two cases:
  - **If $\mathbf{x}_1 < \mathbf{x}_2$**, the utility of Player 2 reduces to $\rho x_1 + (1-\rho)x_2$, which means that Player 2 assigns weight ρ to the economic payoff of Player 1 and weight $1-\rho$ to their own economic payoff. Since $\rho > \frac{1}{2}$, Player 2 assigns greater weight to the economic payoff of Player 1 than their own.
  - **If $\mathbf{x}_1 > \mathbf{x}_2$**, then the utility of Player 2 reduces to $\sigma x_1 + (1-\sigma)x_2$. Since σ is negative, this function depends positively on x_2 and negatively on x_1. Therefore, Player 2 tends to increase their own economic payoff and reduce that of Player 1.

  Hence, in both cases, Player 2 tends to increase the payoff of the player with a smaller payoff and decrease the payoff of the player with a higher payoff. Therefore, these ranges of values of ρ and σ correspond to inequity-aversion preferences.
- **Altruistic preferences**. If $0 < \sigma \leq \rho \leq 1$, then the coefficients of both x_1 and x_2 are positive, and thus the utility of Player 2 depends positively on both their own economic payoff and that of the first player. This case corresponds to what I have called 'altruistic preferences'. In fact, after normalising by $1-\sigma-\rho$, this utility function becomes identical to that introduced by Ledyard.

Charness and Rabin conducted a series of experiments in which 467 students made sequential decisions between two money distributions, similar to those in the Dictator Game. For each preference type, the authors computed the proportion of observations that could be explained by the corresponding model. Their findings revealed that a model based solely on maximising economic payoff explained 68% of the observations, competitive preferences 60%, inequity-aversion preferences 75%, and altruistic preferences (identical to those of Ledyard) 97%.

At first glance, the equivalence between Charness and Rabin's altruistic preferences and Ledyard's might suggest that this utility function cannot explain rejection rates in the Ultimatum Game. However, the authors were aware of this limitation and introduced a different model for sequential games to accommodate the possibility that players acting second could respond to the intentions of players acting first. For more details, I refer the reader to the original article.

In the remainder of this chapter, rather than focusing on the specific predictions of the Charness and Rabin model (or the other models I have discussed), I shift my attention to exploring their fundamental properties. This approach will help us identify experimental limitations and lay the groundwork for developing alternative models.

THE CONSEQUENTIALIST ASSUMPTION

In the preceding sections, I have reviewed a variety of behavioural economic models designed to explain various deviations from economic maximisation observed in decision-making with certain payoffs, under risk, or involving intertemporal choices or social interactions. These models have proved useful for interpreting such regularities and remain highly influential.

The aim of this section is to observe that these models, while different in many regards, share one foundational assumption, which I term 'economic consequentialism'. This raises an important question: is the assumption of economic consequentialism consistently supported by behavioural experiments, or are there violations that call for fundamentally new models in behavioural economics?

The term 'consequentialism' originates in moral philosophy, in contrast with deontological ethics. In moral philosophy, consequentialism posits that the rightness of an action is determined solely by its outcomes, with classic formulations developed by utilitarians like Bentham and Mill, who argued that actions are justified if they promote the greatest happiness for the greatest number. This contrasts with deontological approaches, epitomised by Kant, which assert that actions are morally right based on their adherence to duty and rules, regardless of outcome.

Here, I adopt a narrower interpretation, 'economic consequentialism'. Under this interpretation, the utility of a given strategy profile depends exclusively on the economically relevant outcomes it produces. 'Economically relevant outcomes' include not only the economic benefits and costs to the decision-maker but also those affecting others, as well as the probabilities and timing associated with these outcomes.

To formalise this idea, take any economic decision or game and consider a profile of actions. In economic decisions, a profile of actions is simply the single action contemplated by the decision-maker, whereas in economic games it represents one action taken by each player. Let us define the economic representation of a profile of actions to encapsulate all economically relevant consequences for every affected party.

Definition (Economic Representation of Profiles of Actions). Let a be a profile of actions and let I be the set of individuals affected by a. The economic representation of a is defined by the generalised prospect

$$P(a) = (p_1 : (\pi_i^1, t_i^1)_{i \in I}; \ldots; p_n : (\pi_i^n, t_i^n)_{i \in I}), \tag{2.64}$$

which means that if the profile of strategies a is chosen, then with probability p_k each individual $i \in I$ receives an economic payoff π_i^k at time t_i^k. □

This is termed a 'generalised prospect' because it describes not only the probabilistic economic outcomes for the decision-maker but also for all potentially affected individuals, including a temporal dimension, indicating that some payoffs may not be received immediately.

This definition is inclusive and easily applied to all economic decisions and games I have reviewed, as demonstrated by the following examples.

Example (Economic Representation of Actions in Economic Decisions). In economic decisions where the outcomes are certain and the timing is immediate, the representation simplifies significantly. Here, each decision yields a definite economic payoff without any associated risk or delay. Thus, for a given action a, every affected individual i within the set of all individuals I is guaranteed to receive a specific payoff $\pi_i(a)$ instantly. This certainty and immediacy is mathematically expressed through the generalised prospect:

$$P(a) = (1 : (\pi_i(a), 0)_{i \in I}). \tag{2.65}$$

This notation indicates that each individual i receives their respective economic payoff $\pi_i(a)$ at time 0 (the present) with certainty (probability equal to 1). □

Example (Economic Representation of Actions in Individual Economic Decisions under Risk). In individual economic decisions involving risk, only one decision-maker is present, and they are the sole person affected by the consequences. Hence, $I = \{d\}$. In these decisions, the temporal dimension is typically absent as the outcomes are considered immediate. Economic payoffs, however, are uncertain and defined by a probability distribution over possible outcomes: when the decision-maker selects action a, they receive an economic payoff π^k with probability p^k, where, for ease of notation, I have omitted the subscript d, as $I = \{d\}$. Each potential outcome is associated with its corresponding probability, but the timing, which is immediate, is uniformly zero for all outcomes. Consequently, the economic representation of the action a can be succinctly expressed as:

$$P(a) = (p_1 : (\pi^1, 0); \ldots; p_n : (\pi^n, 0)). \tag{2.66}$$

Example (Economic Representation of Actions in Intertemporal Decisions). Intertemporal decisions are characterised by the incorporation of the temporal dimension. In cases where a single decision-maker faces certain outcomes from their actions, the intertemporal nature of the decision is defined by both the economic payoff and the specific timing of this payoff. For an action a, characterised by its economic payoff, $\pi(a)$, and the timing of this payoff, $t(a)$, we have

$$P(a) = (1 : (\pi(a), t(a))). \tag{2.67}$$

This expression illustrates that the decision-maker receives the payoff $\pi(a)$ at the specific time $t(a)$, with probability 1, provided that no exogenous factors (such as the risk of death) interfere. □

Example (Economic Representation of Actions in Economic Games). In economic games, the payoffs are determined not by individual actions but by the collective profiles of actions chosen by all players involved. For any given profile of actions a, the economic payoffs for each player are certain and occur in the present. This can be represented as:

$$\mathrm{P}(a) = (1 : (\pi_p(a), 0)_{p \in P}). \tag{2.68}$$

This notation indicates that with probability 1, each player p receives their respective payoff $\pi_p(a)$ immediately (at time 0). □

Building on the concept of the economic representation of a profile of actions, we can now define economic consequentialism.

Definition (Economic Consequentialism). A utility function for player p is termed economically consequentialist if it satisfies the condition that whenever two profiles of actions, a_1 and a_2, have the same economic representations, then $u_p(a_1) = u_p(a_2)$. □

This principle asserts that the utility derived from a profile of actions depends solely on the economically relevant outcomes of these actions.

It should now be clear that all the behavioural economic models discussed in this chapter adhere to economic consequentialism, as they define utility functions solely based on the economically relevant properties of actions. Here are a few examples to illustrate this point:

Example (Prospect Theory Is Economically Consequentialist). According to prospect theory, the value of a prospect is calculated using the formula:

$$V = \sum_{i=1}^{n} \sigma(p_i) v(\pi_i). \tag{2.69}$$

Here $\sigma(p_i)$ is a probability weighting function and $v(\pi_i)$ is the value function applied to the economic payoff π_i. Suppose we have two actions, a_1 and a_2, with identical economic representations, $P(a_1) = P(a_2)$. This equality means that the probabilities p_i, the payoffs π_i, and the timing t_i in $P(a_1)$ match those in $P(a_2)$. Substituting these values into the value function of prospect theory yields identical values for both prospects. Thus, prospect theory is economically consequentialist because the evaluation of a prospect depends solely on its economically relevant outcomes. □

Example (Hyperbolic Discounting Is Economically Consequentialist). Hyperbolic discounting models the present value of a future reward as:

$$V = \frac{R}{1 + rt}. \tag{2.70}$$

Here R is the future reward, r is the discount rate, and t is the timing of the future reward. If two actions, a_1 and a_2, have the same economic representations, $P(a_1) = P(a_2)$, the consistency in p_i, π_i, and t_i ensures that substituting these values results in the same present value for both actions. Therefore, hyperbolic discounting is economically consequentialist. Note that while the parameter r may vary between individuals, it is assumed to remain constant for any given individual during the decision-making process. □

Example (Ledyard's Utility Function Is Economically Consequentialist). Ledyard's utility function assumes that the utility derived from an economic distribution $(x_1,\ldots,x_N)$ for player p is:

$$u_p(x_1,\ldots,x_N) = x_p + \alpha_p \sum_{i \neq p} x_i. \tag{2.71}$$

If two actions result in the same economic distribution, they lead to the same utility for player p because the utility function depends only on this distribution and individual-specific parameters, such as α_p. □

Obviously, this argument extends to all social preferences introduced in the previous section. In sum, all behavioural economic models presented in this chapter are grounded in economic consequentialism. This raises an important question: do people adhere to economic consequentialism in behavioural experiments, or are there important exceptions where this assumption fails, suggesting the need for fundamentally new behavioural economic models?

3 A Paradigm Crisis

BEHAVIOURAL EQUIVALENCE OF ECONOMICALLY ISOMORPHIC GAMES

In Chapter 2, I presented several models to explain deviations from economic maximisation. Although these models differ in the specific ways they formalise these deviations, they all share a fundamental property, which I called 'economic consequentialism'. These models are defined through a utility function that depends on the economically relevant properties of the available actions (economic consequences, probabilities associated with each potential economic payoff, timing of the payment), through individual parameters.

In this section, I describe a general property deriving from economic consequentialism, which I term 'behavioural equivalence of economically isomorphic decisions'. This property can be stated for both economic decisions and games. However, for notational simplicity, here I focus on economic decisions. Informally speaking, this consists in the following property: economically consequentialist models make the prediction that a person facing two 'economically isomorphic' decision problems should be making the 'same' decision.

More formally, by economically isomorphic decision problems, I mean two economic decisions that have the same number of available choices that can be mapped onto each other while preserving their economic representation.

Definition (Economic Isomorphism). Two economic decisions, $D_1 = (I_1, d_1, A_1, \pi_1)$ and $D_2 = (I_2, d_2, A_2, \pi_2)$, are said to be economically isomorphic if there exists a bijective map $\phi : A_1 \to A_2$ such that $P(\phi(a)) = P(a)$, for all $a \in A_1$. □

I will discuss an important example of economic isomorphism in the next section. For now, note that if a decision-maker faces two economically isomorphic decision problems, D_1 and D_2, and if the decision-maker possesses an economically consequentialist utility function u, then the utility-maximising choice in D_2 is simply $\phi(\bar{a})$, where $\bar{a}$ is the utility-maximising choice in D_1. This follows directly from the fact that the utility function u depends only on the economically relevant properties of the available actions, and because the mapping ϕ preserves these properties, it also preserves their utility. In other words, we have $u(\phi(a)) = u(a)$, for all $a \in A_1$. Therefore, if $\bar{a}$ maximises u in D_1, then $\phi(\bar{a})$ maximises u in D_2.

This 'behavioural equivalence' property not only applies to single decision-makers, but also to groups of people who are randomly assigned to two economically isomorphic decision problems: if the assignment is random and thus the distribution of the various economically consequentialist utility functions is the same in both groups, and if the two games are economically isomorphic, then the distribution of choices in the first group must be statistically indistinguishable (via the isomorphism ϕ) from the distribution of choices in the second group. In other words, the aggregate choices in the two decision problems are equivalent under the mapping ϕ. At this stage, this property is trivial. However, given its centrality to my argument, it is informative to formalise it in the following.

Theorem (Behavioural Equivalence of Economically Isomorphic Decisions). Let $D_1 = (I_1, d_1, A_1, \pi_1)$ and $D_2 = (I_2, d_2, A_2, \pi_2)$ be two economically isomorphic decision problems via the isomorphism ϕ. Suppose a group of economically consequentialist decision-makers is randomly assigned to either D_1 or D_2. Let X_1 and X_2 be the random variables representing the choices made by decision-makers in D_1 and D_2, respectively. Then the distribution of X_2 is the push-forward of the distribution of X_1 via ϕ.

Proof. By assumption, each decision-maker employs an economically consequentialist utility function u. This utility function may depend on the decision-maker. However, since the two groups (one facing D_1 and one facing D_2) are randomly drawn from the same population, the distribution of utility functions across the two groups is identical. Consequently, the probability that a decision-maker chooses a particular action $a \in C_1$ is the same as the probability that a decision-maker in the D_2 group chooses $\phi(a)$. Hence, X_2 is the push-forward of X_1 via ϕ. □

It is important to note that the theorem does not require that all decision-makers share the same utility function; it only assumes that each individual's utility function is economically consequentialist. Under this hypothesis, the theorem makes a clear and testable prediction: if decision-makers are randomly assigned to two economically isomorphic decision problems, then the aggregate distribution of choices in one problem should be statistically indistinguishable (up to the isomorphism) from that in the other.

In this chapter, I empirically investigate whether participants in behavioural experiments adhere to this 'behavioural equivalence' prediction. Should my findings reveal systematic deviations from this equivalence, it would suggest that the previous models (by defining utility solely in terms of economically relevant outcomes) are missing a crucial component. Such a result would motivate the search for a fundamentally different class of utility functions that account for additional factors influencing decision-making.

LYING AVERSION VIOLATES ECONOMIC CONSEQUENTIALISM

The first piece of evidence against the behavioural equivalence of economically isomorphic decision problems was provided by Gneezy (2005) using his original variant of the Sender–Receiver Game. At the beginning of the game, the sender receives private information from the experimenter detailing the economic consequences for both the sender and the receiver corresponding to the implementation of two options, Option A and Option B. Subsequently, the sender is asked to send one of the following two messages to the receiver:

- **Message 1:** Option A guarantees you a higher economic payoff than Option B.
- **Message 2:** Option B guarantees you a higher economic payoff than Option A.

Since only the sender knows the true economic consequences associated with the two options, they alone can determine which of these messages is true and which is false.

After the sender chooses a message, it is delivered to the receiver, who must then decide which option to implement as payment. Calculating the optimal strategy in this game is non-trivial because it depends on the sender's beliefs regarding whether the receiver will follow their message. However, Gneezy's pilot experiment revealed that a large majority of receivers (about 80%) tend to choose the option suggested by the sender, and a similarly large majority of senders expect that the receiver will follow their suggestion. For simplicity, let us assume for now that all receivers follow the sender's suggestion and that all senders believe their suggestion will be followed; we will move beyond this assumption later.

Now, assume that the economic payoffs of the two players are misaligned, that is, the option that maximises the sender's economic payoff coincides with the option that minimises the receiver's payoff; let this be Option B. Under these conditions, to maximise their own economic payoff, the sender must lie by persuading the receiver that Option B is the more favourable choice.

Importantly, this game is economically isomorphic to a variant of the Dictator Game in which the dictator must choose between Option A and Option B as the payment outcome. If the economic consequentialism assumption were correct, then behaviour in the Sender–Receiver Game should be statistically indistinguishable from behaviour in the economically isomorphic Dictator Game.

Experimental Result (Participants Behave Differently in a Sender–Receiver Game Compared to an Economically Isomorphic Dictator Game). In his 2005 article, Gneezy investigated this question by conducting a series of experimental treatments that varied the economic consequences. I focus here on one particular treatment, as the others yielded qualitatively similar results. In this treatment (conducted with students from the Technion institute and the University of Haifa), Gneezy implemented a Sender–Receiver Game where Option A assigned \$5 to the sender and \$15 to the receiver, whereas Option B assigned \$15 to the sender and \$5 to the receiver. The results indicated that 52% of senders lied to maximise their economic payoff.

Subsequently, participants were asked to play the role of dictators in an economically isomorphic game, where they simply chose between Option A and Option B without the opportunity to send a message. To account for the fact that in the Sender–Receiver Game about 20% of senders believed that their suggestion would not be followed by the receiver, Gneezy informed the participants that the option they chose would be implemented with an 80% probability, while the other option would be implemented with the remaining 20% probability. In this variant of the Dictator Game, almost all subjects (91%) chose the option that maximised their economic payoff. Therefore, the proportion of subjects choosing the payoff-maximising action in the Dictator Game was much higher than the proportion of subjects choosing the payoff-maximising choice in the Sender–Receiver Game, despite these two games being economically isomorphic. See Figure 3.1.

These findings demonstrate that behaviour changed radically depending on whether lying was required. Gneezy concluded that people tend to be averse to telling lies, a factor that cannot be captured by models that consider only the economic consequences of the available options. Therefore, economically consequentialist models are inadequate for explaining this type of behaviour. □

The fact that lying aversion is partly due to non-economically consequentialist preferences has also been shown by other authors, using different methodologies. I discuss three main contributions

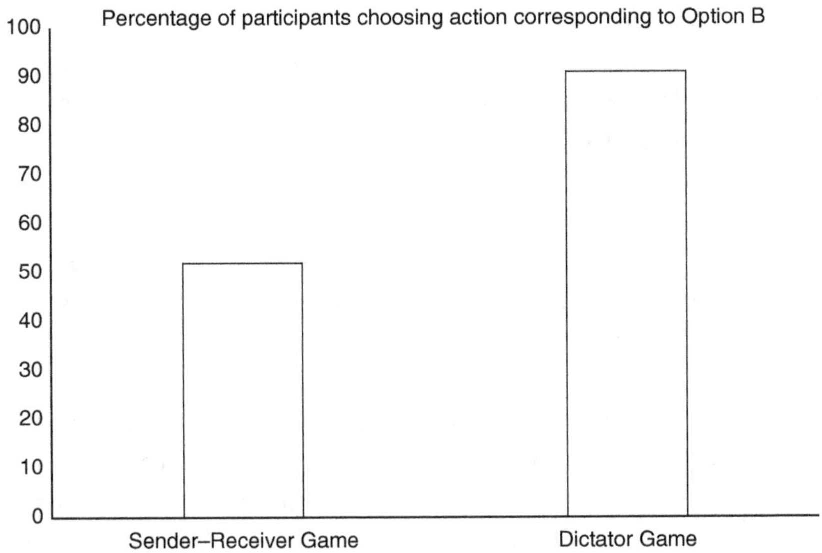

FIGURE 3.1 **Participants behave differently in a Sender–Receiver Game compared to an economically isomorphic Dictator Game.** The percentage of people choosing the action corresponding to Option B in the Sender–Receiver Game is much lower than the percentage of people choosing Option B in the Dictator Game. Figure based on Gneezy (2005).

here, as they provide a more comprehensive picture of lying aversion and how it relates to other prosocial behaviours.

The first contribution is by Erat and Gneezy (2012), who conducted a series of experimental treatments to examine how the propensity to lie varies with the consequences of the lie. Their focus was primarily on white lies, distinguishing between altruistic white lies and Pareto white lies. As one might intuitively expect, their results showed that individuals tend to tell Pareto white lies more frequently than altruistic white lies, since Pareto white lies also enhance the sender's economic payoff. More intriguingly, however, they also found that a significant proportion of participants refrained from telling Pareto white lies. That is, when faced with the option of lying to increase both their own and the receiver's payoff, a significant fraction of senders chose to tell the truth, thereby sacrificing potential gains for both parties.

For example, in one treatment, Option A provided \$20 to both the sender and the receiver, whereas Option B provided \$30 to each. In this setting, senders had to decide whether to lie to secure an additional \$10 for both themselves and the receiver, or to tell the truth and forego that extra amount. Despite the economic incentive to lie, 35% of the subjects opted for truthfulness. This is a substantial proportion that is hard to explain solely by invoking 'sophisticated deception', the notion that senders tell the truth while expecting that their message will not be believed, thereby achieving deception (Sutter, 2009). Indeed, previous research in a similar game found that only 20% of senders believed their message would be met with disbelief. However, since the Sender–Receiver Game employed by Erat and Gneezy differs from the one used to estimate the 20% figure, I shall now report two more experiments that rule out sophisticated deception as a viable explanation for these Pareto-dominated truths.

The first study is by Cappelen et al. (2013), who eliminated this potential source of confusion by introducing a modified variant of the game. In their design, senders privately roll a die and then choose one of six possible messages to send to the receiver, each stating 'the outcome of the dice roll was i', with $i \in \{1,\ldots,6\}$. After receiving the message, the receiver must guess the true outcome of the roll, and the payoffs depend on whether the receiver's guess is correct. However, there is a twist: if the receiver chooses a number different from the one suggested by the sender, they incur a penalty. Because the receivers have no information about the specific payoffs associated with the two options, there is no incentive for them to deviate from the sender's suggestion; thus, the optimal strategy for the receiver is simply to follow the sender's message. Anticipating this behaviour, the sender's best strategy is to lie to maximise both their own and the receiver's economic payoff. In an experiment conducted with students from the Norwegian School of Economics, Cappelen et al. found that, even under these conditions, the proportion of senders who lied did not exceed 65%.

One might object that the reasoning process leading senders to conclude that lying is optimal might be overly complex, potentially resulting in some senders inadvertently telling the truth. We can address this concern using results obtained in a joint work that I co-authored with Biziou-van-Pol, Haenen, Novaro, and Occhipinti-Liberman. In this research, we introduced a variant of the Sender–Receiver Game designed to eliminate any ambiguity. In this version, receivers did not have to make any choice; the sender simply transmitted a message declaring the outcome of the die roll. If the declared outcome differed from the true outcome, both the sender and the receiver were paid according to the Pareto-dominant option; if the declared outcome matched the true outcome, they were paid according to the Pareto-dominated option. Conducted with American participants via Amazon Mechanical Turk, this variant still revealed that approximately 17% of individuals opted to tell Pareto-dominated truths (Biziou-van-Pol et al., 2015).

Telling Pareto-dominated truths in these experiments contradicts all the economically consequentialist social preferences discussed in Chapter 2. In these experiments, Pareto-dominant lies not only increase the total economic payoff for both sender and receiver but also preserve the relative economic differences between them. Consequently, utility functions based solely on preferences for altruism, equity, or any blend of these cannot explain the occurrence of Pareto-dominated truths.

It is important to note, however, that this does not preclude the theoretical possibility of economically consequentialist preferences that could account for such behaviour, even if those preferences are counterintuitive and unrealistic. For example, one might posit a sender with 'destructive preferences' aimed at minimising the total economic payoff of all involved players. Such preferences depend solely on economic consequences and align with an aversion to Pareto-optimal dishonesty. However, they lead to other unrealistic predictions.

Consider, again, the study by Cappelen et al. (2013). In addition to examining behaviour in a Sender–Receiver Game where truth-telling is Pareto-dominated, these authors also measured the same subjects' behaviour in a Dictator Game. Their results showed a positive correlation between truth-telling and altruistic behaviour. One could, in principle, attempt to rationalise this correlation within an economically consequentialist framework by assuming that half of the subjects possess destructive preferences (leading them to tell the truth and behave randomly in the Dictator Game, since it is a zero-sum setting) and the other half have selfish preferences (resulting in lying in the Deception Game and selfish behaviour in the Dictator Game). Although internally coherent, this explanation does not fit other experimental results. For example, we know from Engel's meta-analysis that behaviour in the Dictator Game is not random but follows a tri-modal distribution.

A far more realistic interpretation is that altruistic behaviour and Pareto-dominated truth-telling share a common moral motivation. It may be that some individuals regard telling the truth and acting altruistically as morally right actions, irrespective of the economic outcomes.

This perspective is supported by my joint work with Biziou-van-Pol et al. (2015) mentioned earlier. We conducted an experiment in which participants played a Sender–Receiver Game, a Dictator Game, and a Prisoner's Dilemma. The Dictator Game results replicated those of Cappelen et al. (2013), showing a positive correlation between altruistic behaviour and Pareto-dominated truth-telling in an American sample. More intriguingly, the Prisoner's Dilemma results revealed a positive correlation between truth-telling and cooperative behaviour. This latter finding cannot be explained by preferences for minimising total payoff; indeed, under the condition $c < b$ minimising total payoff would predict a positive correlation between defection and truth-telling, the opposite of what was observed.

These results collectively represent a first piece of evidence that the motivations underlying Pareto-dominated truth-telling, altruistic behaviour, and cooperative behaviour share a common (moral) foundation that lies beyond traditional economically consequentialist utility functions. This moral motivation likely reflects deeply held beliefs about the right thing to do, irrespective of the economic consequences. We will revisit this idea in subsequent chapters. For now, let us turn our attention to another class of violations of the behavioural equivalence of economically isomorphic decision problems.

THE EFFECT OF LINGUISTIC CONTENT ON SOCIAL DECISION-MAKING

In this section, we enter into the heart of the book and review a growing body of literature showing that the linguistic context influences decision-making, beyond the economically relevant properties of the available actions. Most of this research concerns economic social decisions and games. Therefore, I will focus mainly on these types of actions. At the end of this chapter, I will also briefly discuss other types of decisions.

Experimental Result (The Utility of an Action Depends on the Economic Context). A first step towards showing violations of economic consequentialism was provided by Falk et al. (2003). The authors recruited 90 participants who played four mini-Ultimatum Games. In each of these games, the proposer was asked to divide 10 points; the responder could either accept or reject the offer. The four minigames varied in the choices available to the proposer:

- **Game (5/5):** The only alternatives available to the proposer were: (8,2) and (5,5). The first component denotes the economic payoff of the proposer; the second component denotes the economic payoff of the recipient.
- **Game (2/8):** The only alternatives available to the proposer were: (8,2) and (2,8).
- **Game (8/2):** The only alternative available to the proposer was: (8,2).
- **Game (10/0):** The only alternatives available to the proposer were: (8,2) and (10,0).

The authors analysed the frequency of rejections of the offer (8,2) across the minigames. We can note that if the decision of the respondents to reject (8,2) were motivated solely by the economic consequences of the actions available to the proposer, then the frequency of rejection of this offer should remain unchanged across the four minigames, because the choices of rejecting (8,2) and accepting (8,2) have the same economic consequences across games.

However, intuitively, one might expect that the frequency of rejection of the offer (8,2) could depend on the other option available: if the other option was (10,0), then the offer (8,2) might be perceived by respondents as relatively fair and therefore more acceptable compared to the case where the alternative available was (5,5). The results of the experiment aligned with this intuition. In the game (5/5), the frequency of rejection of the proposal (8,2) was the highest and exceeded 40%; in the game (10/0), it did not reach 10%. See Figure 3.2. □

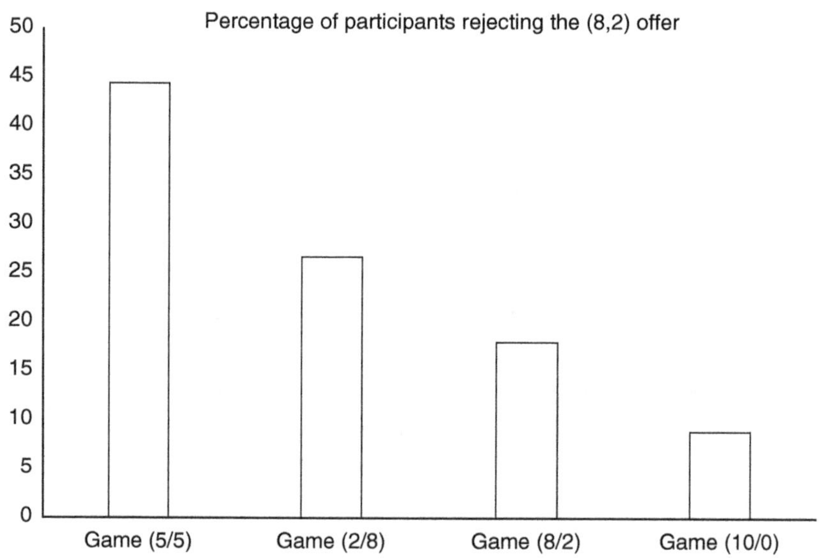

FIGURE 3.2 **Ultimatum Game responders reject the same option at different rates, depending on the set of available offers.** Percentages of rejection of the (8,2) option across mini-Ultimatum Games. Figure based on Falk et al. (2003).

It is important to note, however, that this finding does not violate the principle of economic consequentialism as defined in Chapter 2. To see this, first observe that this finding can be rationalised by one of the social preferences discussed earlier: Levine's utility function. If we assume that receiving the (8,2) offer signals different levels of altruism from the proposer (i.e., the α_p parameter in Levine's utility function) in different games, this might explain why responders' behaviours vary across games. But note that in the definition of economic consequentialism, it is required that the two actions under consideration must have the same economic representation. Specifically, this entails that they impact the same individuals (i.e., the set I of individuals affected by the action is the same for both actions). Thus, if receiving an offer of (8,2) in the (5/5) game signals a different proposer characteristic than receiving the same offer in the (10/0) game, the action of rejecting (8,2) does not have the same economic representation across games, because they involve perceptions of different individuals.

Experimental Result (Linguistic Framings Impact Responders' Decisions in the Ultimatum Game). An experimental finding that cannot be rationalised through economically consequentialist preferences was presented by Eriksson et al. in 2017. In their first experiment, receivers were offered \$25 out of \$100. The receivers were randomly divided into two treatments:

- **Rejection treatment:** Receivers were asked whether they wanted to accept or reject the offer.
- **Reduction treatment:** Receivers were asked whether they wanted to accept the offer or pay \$25 to reduce the proposer's economic payoff by \$75.

These two treatments only differed in the language used to denote declining the proposer's offer. Consequently, economically consequentialist preferences would predict that the behaviour of receivers in the rejection treatment should be statistically indistinguishable from the behaviour of respondents in the reduction treatment.

However, Eriksson et al. argued that the reduction treatment highlights the consequence of not accepting the proposal as significantly reducing the economic payoff of the proposer. Since many people dislike causing harm to others, this salience might lead some respondents to find the offer in the reduction treatment more acceptable than they would in the rejection treatment.

Eriksson et al. conducted a series of experiments on Amazon Mechanical Turk to test this hypothesis. The first experiment used a hypothetical scenario where subjects were asked to imagine themselves as receivers in an Ultimatum Game, with the proposer given an initial $100 to divide, and their offer being $25. The second experiment used lower economic incentives (an offer of $1.5 out of $2), but players were actually paid based on their decisions. Both experiments revealed similar results in line with the researchers' hypothesis: in the rejection treatment, about 40% of receivers did not accept the proposers' offers; conversely, in the reduction treatment, this percentage dropped to around 22%, a statistically significant variation. See Figure 3.3.

The authors also tested their proposed theoretical mechanism. Before leaving the experiment, subjects were asked what their main motivation was for their decision. The options available included 'punish the proposer', 'be fair', 'it's the morally right thing', 'maximise economic payoff', 'harm the proposer', 'protect myself', 'other reasons', and 'I don't know'. The results showed that the motivation 'it's the morally right thing' was used as a reason to decline the offer only in the rejection treatment, while it was used to accept the offer only in the reduction treatment. Additional experiments controlled for various potential confounding factors, including standardising the description of the economic consequences in the two groups in such a way that in both treatments it was clear that responders would pay a cost, thus avoiding any effect due to the salience of losing money.

Overall, these results suggest that the decision of the responder in the Ultimatum Game is partly driven by moral preferences for

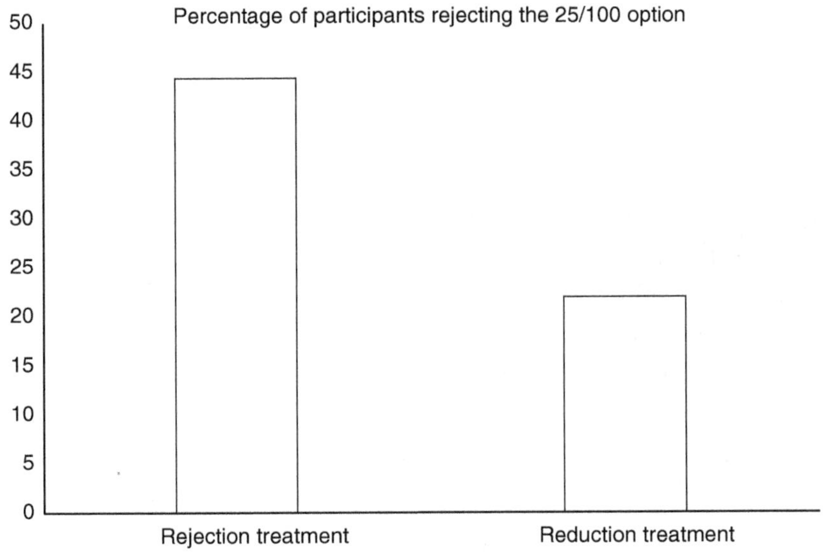

FIGURE 3.3 **Ultimatum Game responders reject the same offer at different rates depending on how it is linguistically framed**. Percentage of responders rejecting the 25/100 option in the rejection and reduction treatments conducted by Eriksson et al. (2017). The two treatments differ only in the language used to label the available actions.

doing the right thing, preferences that cannot be fully described by economically consequentialist utility functions, since the two treatments are economically isomorphic in terms of monetary consequences. Moreover, these moral preferences can be activated by the linguistic description of the decision problem. □

We are getting closer to recognising the importance of the linguistic framing of decision problems. In Chapter 1, I defined an 'experimental economic decision' as an economic decision paired with its linguistic instructions. I then temporarily set aside linguistic descriptions and attempted to model economic decisions using only the formal representation of available actions. However, we are now gradually discovering that this economic representation alone is insufficient to fully account for observed behaviour. The linguistic description of the available actions can play a crucial role, particularly by triggering moral preferences for doing what is perceived as 'the right thing'. This is evident in the series of experiments by Eriksson et al., and it also applies to Gneezy's experiment: the Sender–Receiver Game and the Dictator Game do not differ in the economic structure of the available strategies, but they do differ in how those strategies are linguistically described. In the Sender–Receiver Game, the payoff-maximising strategy is explicitly framed as dishonest, which reduces the frequency with which participants choose it, likely because they are at least partly motivated by moral concerns, beyond the economic consequences of their choices.

We will see in the next chapters that moral preferences do not represent the only channel through which linguistic descriptions may affect people's decisions. But before initiating this discussion, let us add other pieces of evidence in support of the statement that linguistic descriptions impact people's decisions.

Experimental Result (Linguistic Framings Impact Behaviour in the Prisoner's Dilemma). The first to explore the influence of linguistic framing on cooperative behaviour were Ross and colleagues in a series of studies conducted two decades ago (Kay & Ross, 2003; Liberman et al., 2004). For example, Liberman et al. (2004) reported two main studies, one with American college students and the other with Israeli pilots and their instructors, engaging participants in a seven-round iterated Prisoner's Dilemma. The distinctive element in these experiments was the naming of the game: one group participated in what was termed the 'Wall Street Game' or 'Bursa Game' (for the Hebrew-speaking Israelis), and the other in the 'Community Game' or 'Kommuna Game'.

The results of these studies were strikingly consistent across both cultural contexts. In the Community/Kommuna Game, participants were more likely to cooperate than in the Wall Street/Bursa Game, demonstrating a significant decrease based solely on the game's label. See Figure 3.4.

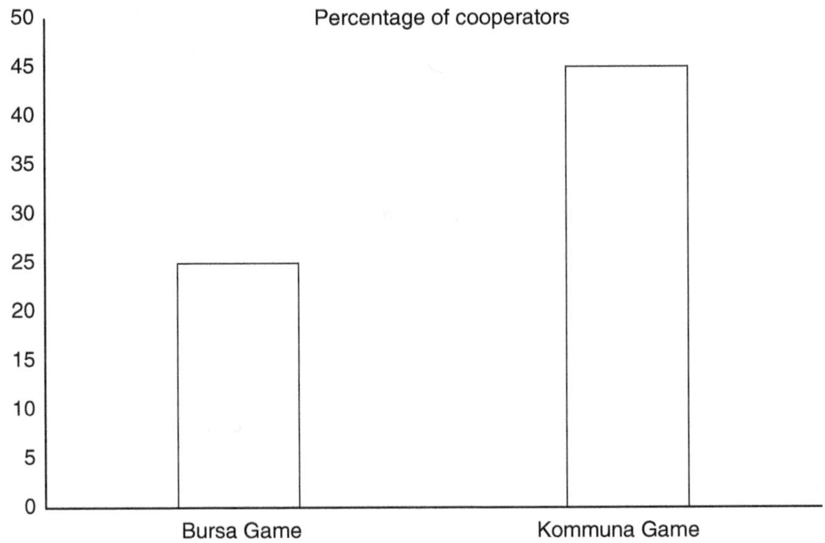

FIGURE 3.4 **Participants in the iterated Prisoner's Dilemma cooperate at different rates depending on the name of the game.** Israeli participants cooperate less in the Bursa Game (Wall Street Game) than in the Kommuna Game (Community Game). Percentages are averaged across the seven rounds of the game. Figure based on Liberman et al. (2004), Study 2.

Interestingly, these results were not predicted by the instructors of the Israeli pilots, who anticipated no influence from the game's naming. Similarly, a separate sampling of American students tasked with predicting behaviours in the Community Game vs the Wall Street Game displayed no significant difference in their predictions, which highlights the unpredicted power of linguistic labels in shaping cooperative behaviour in these settings.

Note, however, that these results do not necessarily show that linguistic framings influence people's preferences. It might be the case that they influence people's beliefs about the behaviour of others. In the Israeli study, researchers measured participants' expectations regarding their counterparts' behaviour and found that participants did indeed anticipate more cooperative behaviour in the Kommuna Game than in the Bursa Game. A more recent work, comparing the Community Game frame with a neutral frame, concluded that the frames influence beliefs, and beliefs in turn influence behaviour (Dufwenberg et al., 2011).

Another significant study was conducted by Mieth et al. (2021), using a Prisoner's Dilemma followed by a punishment phase. In this study, the authors collected behavioural data from 93 subjects divided into two treatments:

- **Moral treatment:** The cooperative action in the Prisoner's Dilemma was literally called 'I cooperate', while the non-cooperative action was called 'I cheat'.
- **Neutral treatment:** The two actions were simply called A and B.

The Prisoner's Dilemma was played simultaneously. Afterward, decisions were revealed, and each player was asked if they wanted to punish the other player.

It is important to note that this game is not a classic Prisoner's Dilemma. For example, an increase in cooperation in the 'moral' treatment compared to the 'neutral' one could be explained in two ways. On the one hand, it could be caused by an increase in the moral utility received from cooperation; on the other, it could be caused by an increased fear of being punished. Keeping this limitation in mind, Mieth et al. observed an increase in cooperation in the 'moral' treatment compared to the 'neutral' one, thus suggesting that linguistic framings may impact the level of cooperative behaviour in the Prisoner's Dilemma followed by a punishment phase.

Mieth et al. conducted an additional study where only one player had the option to punish the other; the other player did not actually exist, and their choice was determined by the computer. In this case, the 'moral' treatment did not result in an increase in cooperation. However, it should be noted that the asymmetry in punishments may have given asymmetrical power to the player, pushing them to maximise their own benefit, regardless of morality. Consistent with this interpretation, the results of this experiment showed a much lower level of cooperation than those of the previous experiment. In other words, it is possible that giving power to a person makes them more immoral, consistent with classic work on the corrupting effect of power (e.g., Kipnis, 1972; Lammers et al., 2010). □

Experimental Result (Linguistic Framings Impact Behaviour in the Dictator Game). The first author to investigate how moral framing in the Dictator Game could affect dictators' giving was Brañas-Garza (2007). In this experiment, participants were assigned to one of two conditions:

- **Neutral condition:** Participants played a standard Dictator Game without any morally charged language.
- **Framing condition:** Participants played the same game, but were presented with a pre-decision message stating, 'Note that your recipient relies on you.'

Brañas-Garza conducted two distinct studies to explore the effect of the moral framing. The first was a classroom experiment where economics students acted as dictators. Each was endowed with 10 experimental units, with each unit worth 0.5 extra points on their final grade for the Intermediate Microeconomics course. The results were clear: the average donation in the neutral condition was 1.2 points, which almost tripled to 3.1 points in the framing condition.

The second study was a more traditional laboratory experiment. Participants were given ten €0.50 coins to allocate between themselves and a recipient. In line with the classroom experiment, the mean donation increased from €1.20 in the neutral condition to €1.65 in the framing condition. These results suggest that the inclusion of a simple, morally loaded message nudged dictators towards a more prosocial distribution of money.

We obtained similar results in a joint work that I co-authored with Jagfeld, Klein, Mul, and van de Pol. In the first study, 300 American participants recruited on Amazon Mechanical Turk were informed they would be playing a Dictator Game in which they needed to decide how to divide 20 cents between themselves and another participant. After receiving general instructions and before being divided into treatments, the players were asked two comprehension questions to ensure they understood the fundamental tension between selfishness and altruism represented by the Dictator Game; they were asked which choice would maximise the economic payoff for the dictator and which would maximise the economic payoff for the recipient. Participants who failed one or both comprehension questions were automatically excluded from the experiment. The others were randomly divided into three treatments:

- **Control:** Participants made their choice as dictators, without any manipulation.
- **Personal Norm:** Before making a decision, participants were asked: 'What choice do you personally think is morally right in this situation?'
- **Injunctive Norm:** Before making a decision, participants were asked: 'What choice do you believe society thinks is morally right in this situation?'

This was a one-shot and anonymous Dictator Game. The recipient was another participant randomly selected at the end of the experiment, about whom the dictator had no information and with whom the dictator would not interact. This was to avoid any potential confounding effects of reputation.

The results demonstrated that the level of altruism in the Personal Norm and Injunctive Norm treatments was statistically indistinguishable. Combining the data from the two treatments where norms were made salient, the average level of donations was about 31% of the initial sum, significantly higher than the average donation in the control, which was 21%. Thus, simple messages that make norms salient have a positive effect on altruistic behaviour.

In the same article, the fifth and final study aimed to test whether making moral norms salient had a positive effect on donations collected in a crowdfunding campaign for humanitarian organisations. For this purpose, we conducted three sessions (totalling 1,800 subjects recruited in the United States via Amazon Mechanical Turk) with the same basic structure. Initially, participants completed a task lasting five minutes, for which they received a payment of 50 cents. Subsequently, participants were divided into two treatments: 'Emergency' and 'Give for France'. Participants in each treatment were asked if they wanted to donate part of the 50 cents they had just earned to the charity named after the treatment. Emergency is a well-known Italian humanitarian organisation operating worldwide, while Give for France was a charity organisation supporting the victims of the Nice attack on 14 July 2016. The experimental sessions were conducted in the days immediately following the attack, and the addition of this condition allowed analysis of whether moral salience impacts donations even when the reason for donating is already very salient.

The three experimental sessions differed in some details, including the way morality was made salient. In the first session participants were asked to declare what the morally right thing to do when seeing a stranger in need of help is. In the second session, morality was made salient by asking participants to declare the morally right thing to do in a Dictator Game. The third session was identical to the second, except that comprehension questions were added in the Dictator Game. The results were very similar across the three sessions, which were therefore reported together. In both the Emergency and the Give for France treatments, moral salience produced a significant and very similar increase in donations. Donations increased by 39% in the Emergency treatment and 47% in the Give for France treatment (Capraro et al., 2019b).

Another relevant study was conducted in collaboration with Vanzo. In this work, we set out to test the impact of linguistic framing in the Dictator Game in the simplest way possible, by altering only a few words in the experimental instructions. To maximise simplicity, we employed an 'extreme' version of the Dictator Game, in which participants could choose only between two actions: keeping the entire sum of money or giving it all away. We randomly divided over 700 participants recruited via Amazon Mechanical Turk between six different versions of the game. In each version, the dictators were informed that a sum of 50 cents was available. This sum was not initially assigned to any player, minimising any confounding effects due to the perception of owning (or not owning) the sum. The only difference between the six treatments was the language used to describe the available actions. In the steal treatment, dictators had to choose between 'stealing from the other participant' or 'not stealing from the other participant'. In the first case, the dictator would end the game with 50 cents, and the recipient with 0; in the second case, the dictator would end with 0 and the recipient with 50 cents. The other five treatments were constructed by replacing the word 'steal' with 'demand', 'take', 'give', 'donate', or 'boost', depending on the treatment.

We tested two contrasting hypotheses. On the one hand, if behaviour in the Dictator Game could be rationalised with economically consequentialist utility functions, then we should observe statistically identical behaviour across the six treatments. On the other, if dictators' behaviour depends significantly on moral preferences activated by morally charged language, then it should depend on the language used to describe the actions.

As predicted by the moral preferences hypothesis and against the economically consequentialist assumption, dictators' behaviour was greatly influenced by the framing. Greater prosociality was observed in the steal treatment, where about 30% of dictators decided to assign the entire sum of money to the recipient. In all other treatments, prosociality never reached 16%, and in all cases, it was significantly lower than that achieved in the steal treatment. Moreover, the results were not driven only by the steal treatment. The boost treatment resulted in the numerically lowest value of prosociality, only 5%, significantly lower than the level of prosociality of all other treatments, except for the give treatment (Capraro & Vanzo, 2019). See Figure 3.5.

One more piece of evidence was provided in a study by Chang et al. (2019), which investigated Dictator Game responses under two different contexts: a tax frame versus a neutral frame. In the

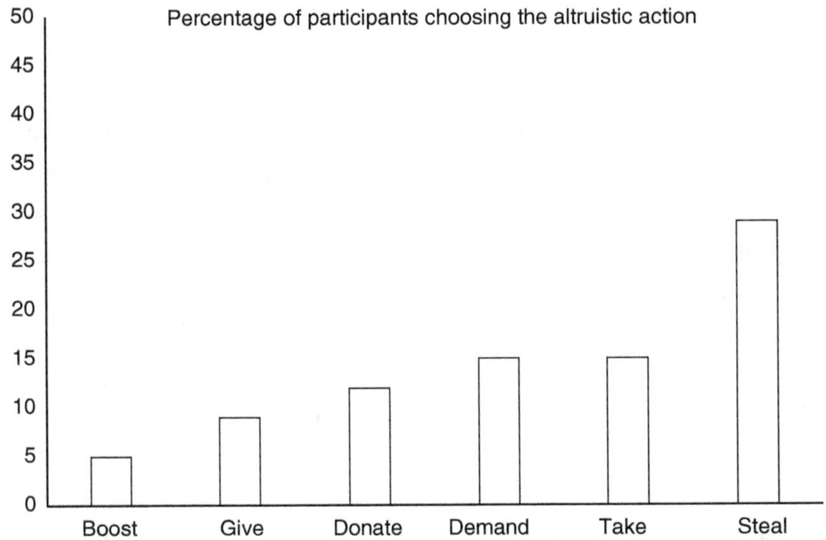

FIGURE 3.5 **Dictators choose the altruistic action at different rates depending on how it is labelled**. Percentage of participants choosing to assign the entire sum to the recipient in each of the six extreme Dictator Games introduced in Capraro and Vanzo (2019).

tax-framed treatment, the instructions given to the participants emphasised a governmental context. Players were told: 'In this economy, your wealth is X token(s) and your match's wealth is Y token(s). Use the slider to indicate whether you want the government involved and how large or small the redistribution should be.' This framing was intended to invoke the concept of official, enforced redistribution, potentially triggering thoughts about fairness and mandatory compliance typically associated with tax systems.

Conversely, the neutrally framed treatment used language that focused purely on personal ownership and the direct transfer of tokens between individuals. Participants in this condition read: 'For this decision you own X token(s) and the other person owns Y token(s). You have the opportunity to give any amount of your X token(s) to the other person or to take any amount of the Y token(s) from the other person for yourself.' This setup was designed to highlight personal agency and the voluntary nature of redistribution, framing the decision as a personal choice rather than a civic duty.

The results revealed significant behavioural differences between the two frames. Subjects who played the tax-framed Dictator Game were more likely to engage in redistributive actions, keeping less money for themselves compared to those in the neutrally framed game.

Finally, a recent study by Kuang and Bicchieri (2024a) investigated the impact of normative expressions on charitable donations. The researchers designed a donation game wherein participants were exposed to messages embedded with various normative injunctions, aimed at encouraging them to donate to a charity. The experiment included a baseline condition with no message and seven other conditions, each featuring one of the following normative expressions as a direct injunction: 'should', 'it is appropriate', 'it is the right thing to do', 'it is approved', 'it is permissible', 'it is okay', and 'it is desirable'. A specific example of a message was: 'People should donate all 10 tokens to the charity.' After reading the message, participants were asked to make their decision on how many tokens they would donate.

Except for the expression 'it is permissible', which did not significantly alter donation behaviour compared to the baseline, all other direct injunctions effectively increased the likelihood of participants donating the full amount of their tokens.

In sum, these findings suggest that linguistic content can influence altruistic behaviour, particularly when the language used invokes normative considerations. □

Experimental Result (Linguistic Framings Impact Behaviour in the Equity–Efficiency Trade-Off Game). We investigated the role of linguistic framing in the Equity–Efficiency Trade-Off Game in a study that I co-authored with Rand (Capraro & Rand, 2018), which has since been replicated in subsequent research (Tappin & Capraro, 2018;

Huang et al., 2019; Huang et al., 2020; Capraro et al., 2021). In the original study, we examined two variants of the Trade-Off Game that differed only in how the two available actions were described:

- **Generous treatment:** Player A was placed in a group with two other players, B and C, and told that all players started with 13 cents. Player A had to decide whether to 'be nice' or not. If they chose to be nice, Player A earned 2 cents, while Player B earned 10 cents. If they chose not to be nice, no one earned anything.
- **Equal treatment:** Player A was again grouped with Players B and C, but this time told that they started with 15 cents, Player B with 23 cents, and Player C with 13 cents. Player A again had to decide whether to 'be nice' or not. In this case, choosing to be nice meant paying 2 cents to equalise the payoffs, so that all players received 13 cents. Choosing not to be nice preserved the initial unequal distribution.

Thus, crucially, the only difference between the two treatments lies in the wording of the available actions. Economically, the treatments are equivalent: being nice in the generous treatment is economically identical to not being nice in the equal treatment, and vice versa. However, the framing appears to shift the moral valence of the choices. The option labelled 'be nice' consistently carries a positive moral weight, regardless of its economic implications.

In the first of a series of experiments, we divided participants (Americans recruited via Amazon Mechanical Turk) into four conditions. The first two are the main experimental conditions; the others serve as controls to ensure that the results do not depend on the order of the tasks:

- **PD–Generous condition:** Participants first played a Prisoner's Dilemma, followed by the Trade-Off Game in the generous treatment.
- **PD–Equal condition:** Participants first played a Prisoner's Dilemma, followed by the Trade-Off Game in the equal treatment.
- **Generous–PD condition:** Participants first played the Trade-Off Game in the generous treatment, followed by a Prisoner's Dilemma.
- **Equal–PD condition:** Participants first played the Trade-Off Game in the equal treatment, followed by a Prisoner's Dilemma.

The core idea of this experimental design is to compare two competing hypotheses. Suppose that people's utility functions depend solely on the economic consequences of the available actions. Since the generous and equal versions of the Trade-Off Game are economically isomorphic, participants should behave similarly across both treatments. Consequently, the correlation between cooperation in the Prisoner's Dilemma and decisions in the Trade-Off Game should be independent of the treatment. The details of this correlation may depend on the specific utility function. For example:

- If cooperation is primarily driven by preferences for equity, we should observe a positive correlation between cooperation in the Prisoner's Dilemma and choosing the (13,13,13) distribution in the Trade-Off Game, regardless of the treatment.
- If cooperation is instead driven by preferences for altruism, we should observe a positive correlation between cooperation in the Prisoner's Dilemma and choosing the (15,23,13) distribution in the Trade-Off Game.
- If cooperation reflects a balanced preference for both equity and efficiency, then no systematic correlation should be observed between the two games.

Now consider the alternative hypothesis: people's preferences are not fully captured by economic outcomes, and they exhibit a preference for being nice, irrespective of those outcomes. If cooperation in the Prisoner's Dilemma is primarily driven by this non-consequentialist preference, then we should observe a correlation between choosing to 'be nice' in the Trade-Off Game and cooperating in the Prisoner's Dilemma.

As predicted by the non-consequentialist hypothesis (but not by consequentialist models) participants' behaviour varied dramatically depending on the framing of the Trade-Off Game. Specifically, 47% of participants chose the (13,13,13) distribution in the equal treatment, while only 6% did so in the generous treatment, a large difference that cannot be explained by economically consequentialist utility functions. Furthermore, we observed a positive correlation

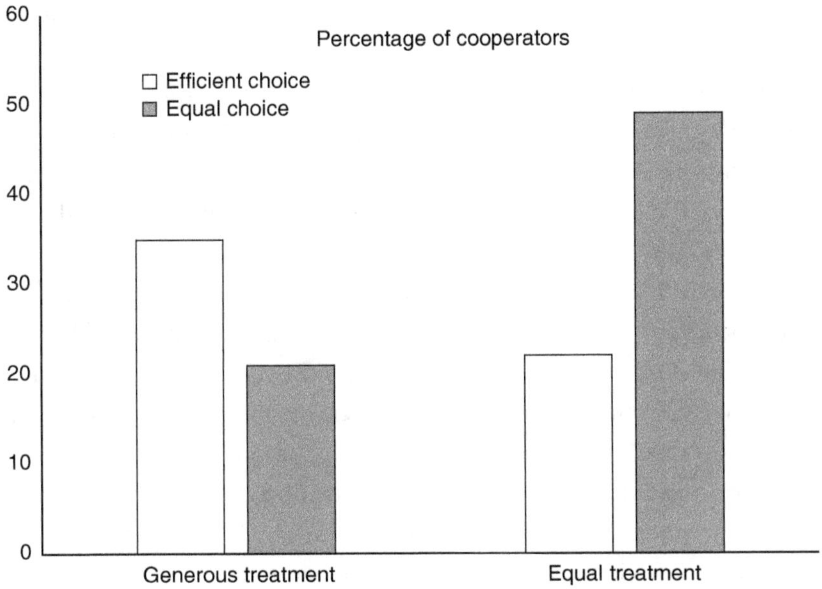

FIGURE 3.6 **The correlation between behaviour in the Equity–Efficiency Trade-Off Game and the Prisoner's Dilemma depends on the linguistic framing of the Trade-Off Game**. When the 'nice' option is the efficient one (generous treatment), participants who choose it are more likely to cooperate. Similarly, when the 'nice' option is the equal one (equal treatment), those who choose it are also more likely to cooperate. In both cases, participants who select the 'nice' option, regardless of whether it corresponds to the efficient or equal distribution of money, tend to cooperate more in the Prisoner's Dilemma. Figure based on Capraro and Rand (2018), Study 1.

between being nice in the Trade-Off Game and cooperating in the Prisoner's Dilemma. This correlation held regardless of task order: it was consistent whether participants played the Prisoner's Dilemma first or the Trade-Off Game first. See Figure 3.6.

In the second study, we shifted our focus to the Dictator Game instead of the Prisoner's Dilemma. The experimental design was identical, except for swapping these two games. The results were conceptually the same as those from the first study: the correlation between altruism in the Dictator Game and decision-making in the Trade-Off Game strongly depended on the treatment in which the latter was played, but in both treatments, individuals who decided to be nice in the Trade-Off Game were on average more altruistic than those who decided not to be nice. As in the first study, these results could not be explained by economically consequentialist utility functions and suggest that preferences for being nice explain behaviour in both the Trade-Off Game and the Dictator Game.

In the third study, we examined whether these preferences were specific to being nice, or whether the same results would hold using other formulations, still with a moral backdrop. In this study, the words 'fair' and 'generous' were directly used in the instructions, instead of 'nice', to describe the available actions. After the Trade-Off game, participants played the Dictator Game. Again, the results showed a strong dependence on the treatment: altruistic individuals in the Dictator Game were those who tended to choose the distribution described in the trade-off game with positively charged language (the equal choice in the equal treatment, the generous choice in the generous treatment). □

THE DARK SIDE OF LINGUISTIC FRAMINGS: MORAL LANGUAGE AND ANTISOCIALITY

In the previous section, I demonstrated how moral language can encourage unselfish behaviour, promoting cooperation and generosity. Now, let us turn the tables to explore whether that same moral rhetoric can be weaponised for selfish ends. The intuition is straightforward: language is a powerful tool for persuasion, and people often use it to manipulate others to achieve personal gain. For instance, imagine a political leader who invokes shared moral values to rally support for policies that ultimately serve only a narrow interest group. Even more alarming is the scenario where a leader uses moral language to demonise certain ethnic groups, labelling them 'impure' and dehumanising them, in a calculated effort to justify acts of ethnic cleansing. Beyond politics, consider a salesperson who frames a product as a 'moral imperative' for a better society, thereby justifying a higher price despite questionable benefits. In this section, I will use controlled experiments to demonstrate this phenomenon.

I approach this question from two different but related perspectives, beginning with an article that I co-authored with Vanzo and Cabrales (2022). This research, divided into three studies, aimed to test the hypothesis that some individuals use moral language to manipulate others' choices for their own selfish purposes.

Experimental Result (Dictator Game Recipients Use Moral Language to Manipulate Dictators' Decisions). We have seen in the previous section that dictator decisions depend on how the available options are described. Specifically, dictators tend to be significantly more altruistic when the selfish choice is labelled 'stealing', as opposed to other terms like 'taking' or 'not boosting' (Capraro & Vanzo, 2019). Consider now the perspective of a recipient whose role is to decide the words introducing the Dictator Game to the dictator. A recipient aware that the dictator's choice may depend on the words used to describe the options and wanting to maximise their economic payoff would have a clear optimal strategy: present the game using instructions with the word 'steal'.

The first experiment of the 2022 research tests precisely this hypothesis. Over 500 Americans recruited via Amazon Mechanical Turk were told they would play a Dictator Game as recipients and needed to decide the instructions to assign to the dictator among the six types from the previous 2019 study. If recipients did not believe that instructions affect dictators' choices or believed it but preferred not to use them strategically, then the choice of instructions should be random, with each being chosen 1/6 of the time. Contrariwise, if recipients were aware of the power of moral language and deliberately decided to use it, we would expect instructions based on the word 'steal' to be chosen significantly more than the others.

Consistent with this last hypothesis, we observed a significant preference for choosing the word 'steal' over all others, selected by about one-third of participants, whereas no other term reached 20%.

The results allowed for another interesting observation. Excluding those who chose the word 'steal', we are left with about 70% of participants. Assuming they choose uniformly among the remaining five choices, each should be selected by 14% of subjects. However, the word 'donate' was chosen significantly more than 14% of the time, suggesting another category of subjects who seek to maximise their economic payoff more subtly, without resorting to explicit manipulation.

It is important to note that the fact that participants select the word 'steal' more frequently does not automatically imply that they are doing so to strategically maximise their economic payoff. It is possible that the term is chosen for other reasons – perhaps because it is perceived as more fun, more evocative, or simply more engaging – and that any economic advantage is merely an unintended byproduct of these other motivations. To disentangle these possibilities and conclusively determine whether the use of 'steal' reflects deliberate, payoff-maximising behaviour rather than a preference for its other attributes, we conducted two additional experiments.

In the second study, recipients were not only asked to choose the instructions for the dictator but also how much they expected to receive. To increase statistical power, we only offered two frames to choose from: 'steal' and 'boost'. The key hypothesis was that recipients who choose to present the game using instructions containing the word 'steal' expect to receive more from the dictator than those who choose instructions based on the word 'boost'. The results confirmed this hypothesis: among recipients who had chosen the instructions with 'steal', half expected altruistic behaviour from the dictator; this proportion halved to a quarter among recipients who had chosen the instructions with 'boost'.

In the third study, participants were divided into dictators and recipients. As in the other studies, recipients had to decide the instructions for the dictator, choosing between the boost and steal frames. The innovation involved the dictators, who were shown the instructions for both possible games they would play as dictators and asked to decide which game they preferred to play. The idea of this study is simple: if players choose instructions containing the word 'steal' for non-strategic reasons (e.g., because they prefer that word), then the percentage of people who choose these instructions should not change whether a person acts as a recipient or a dictator. Conversely, if a significant percentage of players choose instructions strategically, then we should observe that instructions with the word 'steal' are chosen more frequently by recipients than by dictators.

The results supported the second hypothesis: among dictators, only 30% chose to play with instructions containing the word 'steal'; among recipients, about 50% decided to have the dictator play with instructions based on the word 'steal'. See Figure 3.7.

Together, these three experiments provide a first piece of evidence that a significant percentage of people strategically choose

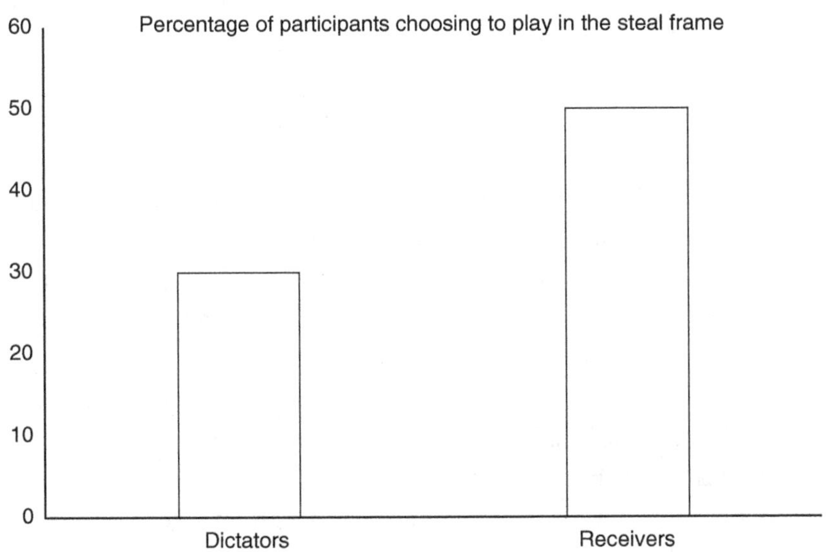

FIGURE 3.7 **Receivers are more likely than dictators to choose to play the Dictator Game in the steal frame.** Percentages of participants choosing to play the Dictator Game in the steal frame. Figure based on Capraro et al. (2022), Study 3.

the words with which to present options to a decision-maker in a way that increases their expected economic return. □

The second piece of work on this topic is also an opportunity to introduce a new game.

Definition (Corruption Game). Players participate in groups of 10: 5 citizens and 5 public officials. Each citizen is paired with a public official. The citizens' citizen's goal is to obtain a certificate from the public official they are paired with. The certificate is worth 40 points to the citizen and can be obtained in two ways: through the formal procedure or by bribing the public official. The public official has a base salary of 15 points, but this can increase by accepting a bribe of 10 points. The cost of the formal procedure is 20 points. Thus, if the citizen follows the formal procedure, they end the game with 20 points, which corresponds to the 40 points for the certificate minus 20 for the formal procedure. Instead of following the formal procedure, each citizen can offer a bribe of 10 points to the public official. If the bribe is accepted, the citizen receives the certificate without further expense and thus receives a total of 30 points (40 for the certificate minus 10 for the bribe) while the public official receives 25 points (15 from their base salary plus 10 from the bribe). Thus, if the bribe is accepted, the citizen earns more than citizens who followed the formal procedure. However, if the bribe is not accepted, the citizen must still follow the official procedure and also pay a fine of 5 points. Thus, in this case, the citizen receives 15 points (40 for the certificate minus 20 for the formal procedure minus 5 for the fine), while the public official receives their base salary of 15 points. Finally, the game includes negative externalities to model the fact that corruption is socially inefficient: specifically, for each bribe accepted, every member of the group loses 1.5 points. Since the individual loss associated with each bribe is less than the individual benefit, both for the citizen and for the public official, it remains individually optimal, from an economic perspective, to offer and accept the bribe. □

The peculiarity of this game is that the act of corruption is convenient for both the citizen and the public official and thus can be morally interpreted as an act of cooperation between two individuals. Thus, making it salient that corruption is an act of cooperation could increase corruption. In an experiment that I conducted with Ścigała et al. (2022), we tested this hypothesis.

Experimental Result (Moral Labels Influence Citizens' and Public Officials' Decisions in the Corruption Game). Participants, recruited in the UK using the online data collection platform Prolific, were divided into two treatments:

- **Cooperation treatment:** The citizen's action of bribing the public official was referred to as 'cooperate' while the public official's action of accepting the bribe was referred to as 'accept a cooperation offer'.
- **Bribery treatment:** The expressions 'offer a bribe' and 'accept a bribe' were explicitly used.

We obtained two main findings. First, the results extended prior research to the Corruption Game by demonstrating that moral language exerts a powerful influence on behaviour. Specifically, participants in the cooperation treatment, where bribery was framed as a cooperative act, were significantly more likely both to offer bribes and to accept them, compared to those in the bribery treatment, where the actions were labelled unambiguously as corrupt.

Second, the framing effect was not uniform; it varied according to individual personality, particularly the Honesty-Humility (H) factor from the HEXACO personality model. Individuals scoring high on the H factor tend to be honest, humble, and uninterested in flaunting wealth or enhancing their social status (Ashton et al., 2004). A high H score has been linked to a wide range of prosocial behaviours, from actions in economic games (Thielmann et al., 2020) to life-changing decisions like donating a kidney (Rhoads et al., 2023). In our experiment, as anticipated, participants with high H scores generally engaged in less corruption than those with low H scores. More intriguingly, for low-H individuals, corruption

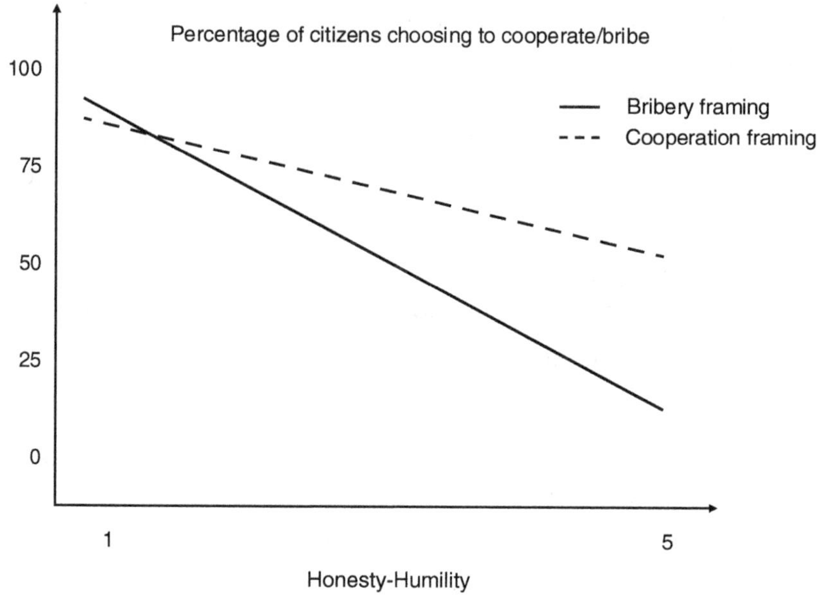

FIGURE 3.8 **Prosocial citizens in the Corruption Game become more likely to offer bribes when they are labelled as a cooperative act.** Percentage of citizens in the Corruption Game deciding to offer a bribe/cooperate as a function of their Honesty-Humility (H) score. Low-H individuals are very likely to cooperate/offer a bribe, independently of the frame. High-H individuals are more responsive to the frame. Figure based on Ścigała et al. (2022).

levels remained consistently high, as if they were immune to ethical framing. In contrast, high-H individuals showed a marked sensitivity to language: in the bribery treatment, very few high-H participants offered or accepted bribes, but when the same actions were framed as cooperative, the rate of corrupt behaviour among high-H participants increased dramatically, nearly matching the levels observed among low-H individuals. See Figure 3.8 for a representation of results for citizens. The results for public officials are qualitatively similar.

In other words, this study shows that manipulative moral language designed to serve selfish ends can be especially effective among prosocial individuals, who are typically more responsive to moral cues. □

BEYOND SOCIAL DECISIONS: LANGUAGE-BASED FRAMING EFFECTS IN INDIVIDUAL DECISIONS

In the previous sections, I have reported several instances in which the linguistic description of the decision problem influences people's decisions. All the reported examples make use of social decisions. However, this should not give the impression that language-based framing effects influence only social decisions. In fact, similar effects have also been observed in individual decisions.

Experimental Result (Linguistic Frames Influence Intertemporal Decisions). In a joint study that I conducted with Pereda and Sánchez (2021), Spanish participants were divided into three experimental conditions:

- **Control:** Participants had to choose between Option 1 and Option 2. Choosing Option 1 means that they get €30 on the day of the experiment; choosing Option 2 means that they get €50 after one month.
- **Promote now condition:** Economically identical to the control condition, apart from the labels used to describe the two options: Option 1 was labelled 'being satisfied' ('ser comedido' in Spanish); Option 2 was labelled 'being greedy' ('ser avaricioso').
- **Promote later condition:** Also identical to the previous conditions, except that Option 1 was labelled 'being impatient' ('ser impaciente'), whereas Option 2 was labelled 'being patient' ('ser paciente').

The results showed that while the promote later condition did not significantly change behaviour, participants in the promote now condition were significantly more likely to choose the immediate payoff compared to those in the control and promote later conditions. See Figure 3.9. □

I am not aware of any studies examining the effect of linguistic cues on risky decision-making beyond the well-known gain–loss framing effects, which can be explained by outcome-based utility functions that are asymmetric relative to a reference point. However, there is a closely related body of literature suggesting that linguistic cues do indeed influence risk decisions.

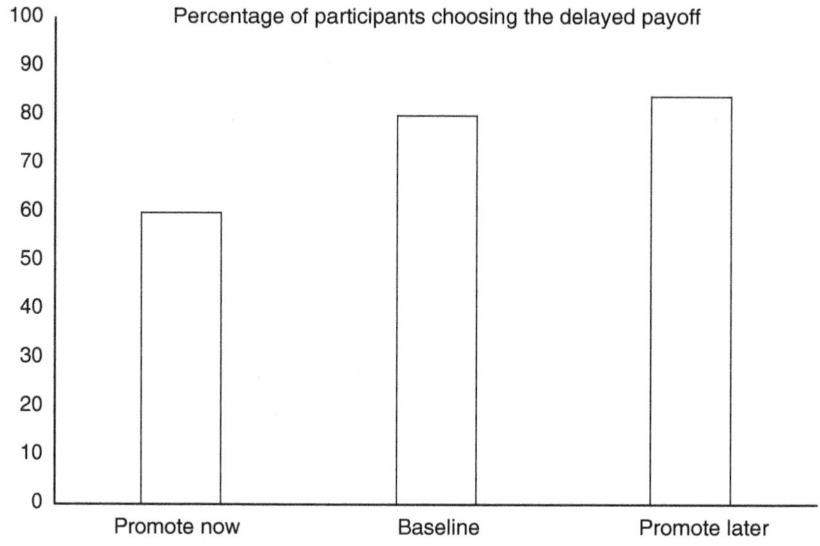

FIGURE 3.9 **Intertemporal decisions depend on the linguistic frame. Percentages of participants choosing the delayed option in the three frames.** Participants in the promote now condition are less likely to choose the delayed option. Figure based on unpublished data collected by Pereda, Sánchez, and Capraro.

One particularly intriguing line of research investigates the impact of making decisions in a second language rather than one's native language. In our globalised world, people increasingly find themselves making important decisions in a language that is not their own. Do these decisions differ from those made in one's native tongue? In the domain of risk aversion, evidence suggests they do.

Experimental Result (Deciding in a Second Language Decreases Risk Aversion). In a 2014 study, Costa et al. (2014) randomly assigned 300 Spanish students to one of two conditions:

- **Native language condition:** Participants made a series of decisions between lotteries presented in their native language.
- **Foreign language condition:** Participants made the identical series of decisions, but in a second language (English).

The lotteries were designed following the Holt and Laury (2002) framework. Participants were presented with a series of pairs of lotteries, 10 in total, where each pair shared the same payoffs but varied in the probabilities of each outcome. For instance:

- **Lottery pair #1:** The first lottery offered €2 with a 10% chance and €1.60 with a 90% chance, while the alternative lottery offered €3.85 with a 10% chance and €0.10 with a 90% chance.
- **Lottery pair #2:** The first lottery offered €2 with a 20% chance and €1.60 with an 80% chance, while the alternative lottery offered €3.85 with a 20% chance and €0.10 with an 80% chance.
- **Lottery pair #10:** The first lottery offered €2 with a 100% chance and €1.60 with a 0% chance, while the alternative lottery offered €3.85 with a 100% chance and €0.10 with a 0% chance.

In the initial pairs, the first lottery had a substantially higher expected payoff than the second, so most participants opted for the first option. In the final pairs, the situation was reversed, and most participants chose the second lottery. In the intermediate pairs, where the expected payoffs were nearly equal, participants gradually switched their choices. Importantly, the point at which individuals switched from one lottery to the other varied according to their risk preferences.

If language had no effect on risk attitudes, the switching point should have been independent of the language condition. However, Costa et al. found that participants in the foreign language condition switched earlier, implying that they were more risk-seeking. In particular, in the critical lottery pair #5, participants were more likely to choose the first lottery in the native condition than in the foreign language condition. In other words, making decisions in a second language appears to dampen risk aversion. See Figure 3.10.

This finding has been replicated in subsequent studies (e.g., Hayakawa et al., 2019), and a meta-analysis by Circi et al. (2021) confirmed a robust overall effect. One prominent interpretation is that the use of a second language reduces the emotional intensity typically associated with decision-making, particularly the fear of loss,

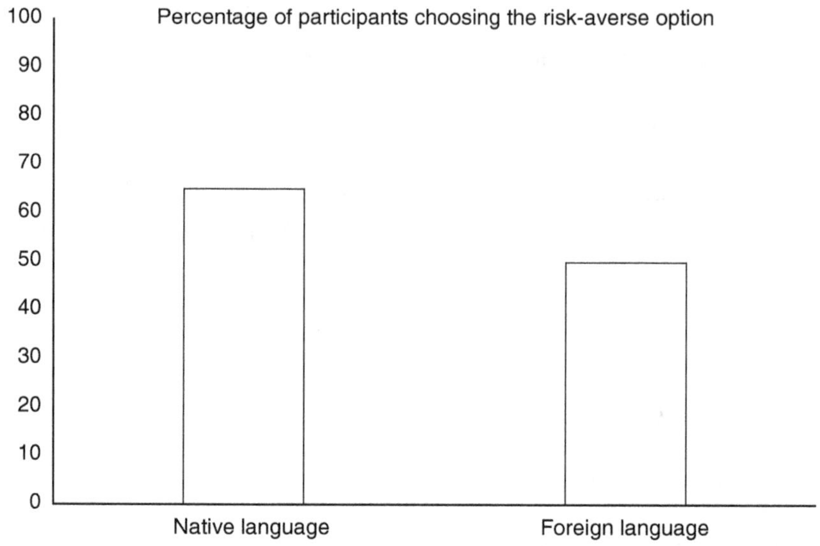

FIGURE 3.10 **Participants making decisions in their native language are more likely to be risk-averse.** Percentages of participants choosing the risk-averse option in lottery pair #5 in the experiment conducted by Costa et al. (2014).

thereby leading to increased risk-taking. I revisit this interpretation in Chapter 5 when introducing the LENS model. □

Experimental Result (Making Decisions in Foreign Languages Diminishes the Endowment Effect). Karataş (2020) reports analogous findings regarding the endowment effect. In his first experiment, 200 native English speakers who also spoke Spanish as a second language were randomly assigned to one of two roles (seller or buyer) in a 2 × 2 between-subjects design comparing language (native vs foreign) and transaction role. In the seller condition, participants viewed an image of a mug, imagined that they owned it, and then specified the minimum amount they would accept to sell it. In the buyer condition, participants indicated the maximum price they were willing to pay for the mug. When the task was completed in their native language (English), sellers demanded significantly higher prices than the buyers' maximum willingness to pay,

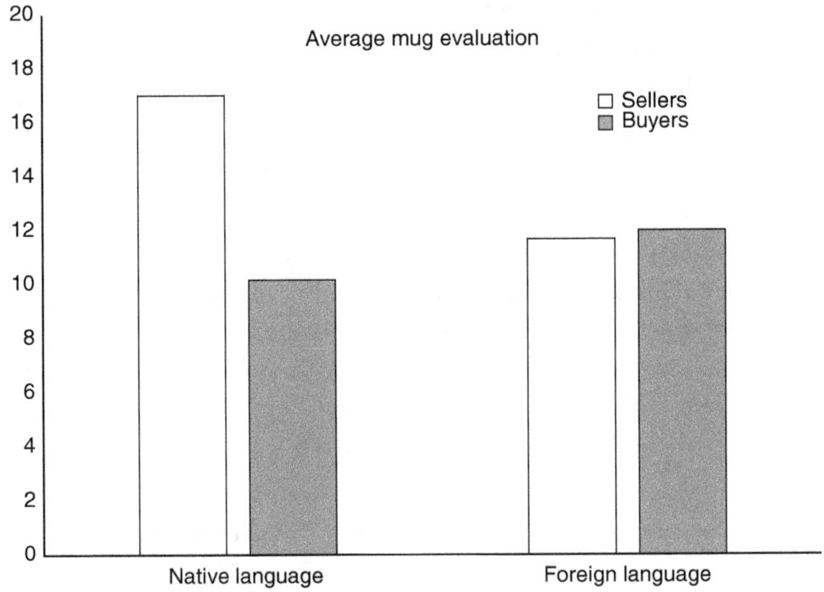

FIGURE 3.11 **Participants making decisions in their native language are more likely to display an endowment effect**. Average evaluation of the mug by buyers and sellers in Karataş (2020), Study 1. Sellers tend to overestimate the value of the mug compared to buyers only in the native language condition.

clearly demonstrating the usual endowment effect. However, when participants were instructed in Spanish, this disparity disappeared. In particular, the reduction of the effect was primarily driven by a lowering of sellers' evaluations, indicating that processing in a foreign language attenuated the endowment effect primarily by lowering sellers' valuations. See Figure 3.11.

In a second study using a similar 2 × 2 between-subjects design, participants were again randomly assigned to either the seller or buyer role. After completing a filler task, participants responded to a three-item ownership scale and a seven-item affective reaction scale before providing their monetary valuation. Planned contrasts mirrored the first study's results: under the native language condition, sellers' valuations were significantly higher, whereas this difference vanished in the foreign language condition. Moreover, mediation analyses revealed that when participants operated in their native language, their transaction role (seller vs buyer) significantly influenced their affective responses. In contrast, in the foreign language condition, the effect of transaction role on affective reactions was not significant.

These findings suggest that processing decisions in a foreign language can diminish the emotional impact associated with ownership, thereby reducing the endowment effect. □

A PARADIGM SHIFT FROM OUTCOME-BASED TO LANGUAGE-BASED PREFERENCES

All together, these findings provide substantial evidence that across a broad array of decision problems and games, the linguistic description significantly influences behaviour. This suggests that traditional behavioural economic theories, which are economically consequentialist, cannot fully account for these findings. For this reason, in a review article published in the *Journal of Economic Literature*, we argued that 'behavioral economics is in the midst of a paradigm shift from outcome-based to language-based preferences' (Capraro et al., 2024a).

The term 'paradigm shift' might seem bold. Ultimately, the argument is not that the fundamental principles of behavioural economics, such as utility maximisation, need to be discarded. Instead, we 'simply' propose that the utility of an action should also incorporate the linguistic context in which it is framed. Is this a true paradigm shift?

According to Thomas Kuhn, who popularised the term in his 1962 book *The Structure of Scientific Revolutions*, paradigm shifts are not strictly defined by whether the new theory is a complement or a substitute. In fact, at least two well-known paradigm shifts, quantum mechanics and relativity, act more as complements rather than substitutes for classical mechanics. Engineers do not need to understand quantum mechanics or relativity to build bridges or skyscrapers, or ensure aeroplanes can fly; classical mechanics suffices in these situations. Instead, the key element of a paradigm shift is a fundamental change in the underlying assumptions of the prevailing framework.

In Chapter 2, I argued that a large part of behavioural economics is grounded on the 'consequentialist assumption' that human behaviour can be described solely by the economic representations of available actions. In this chapter, I have reviewed accumulating evidence that this foundational assumption, common to many prevailing economic models of behaviour, is violated in many human experiments, including social decisions, intertemporal choices, and risky choices, and that non-economically consequentialist language-based preferences may represent a better model of human behaviour. Given that this is indeed a fundamental change in the underlying assumptions of the prevailing model, I believe that the term 'paradigm shift' is in this case justified.

To be fair, economists have long acknowledged that the wording used to describe choices in experiments can affect decision-making (Rubinstein, 2000; Clark, 2023; Gaffal & Padilla Gálvez, 2024). Experimentalists go to great lengths to write 'neutral' instructions, considering deviations from this neutrality as a potential source of 'demand effect'. But the goal of genuinely neutral instructions is elusive: such neutrality is fundamentally unachievable. Common terms used in economic decision-making, such as 'give' or 'take', inherently carry some connotations and thus can never be truly neutral. Even worse: I think that striving for this neutrality is counterproductive, because it diverts us from a fundamental component of human behaviour. People 'demand' things from other people all the time, often using language. Therefore, instead of viewing language-based demand effects as a nightmare that should be avoided, we should accept their existence and systematically measure them.

Arguably, the reluctance of economists to study language-based framing effects stems from a traditional view of language as a qualitative, unquantifiable element. This perception has made economists wary of incorporating language into economic models, fearing it would lead to untestable, qualitative theories that could undermine the scientific integrity of behavioural economics. With my background in mathematics, I empathise with these concerns. However, the assumption that language cannot be quantified is now outdated. Today, advancements in large language models (LLMs) allow us to quantify linguistic elements accurately. The main aim of this book is to leverage LLMs to introduce a method for quantifying the language used to frame decision problems and then integrate these measurements into utility functions that can account for behaviours not explained by traditional, outcome-based models.

4 The Role of Large Language Models

Part I

NEURAL NETWORKS

The main thesis of this book is that large language models (LLMs) have the capability to reshape behavioural economics through two main channels: (i) by increasing the demand for language-based utility functions and (ii) by enabling a first important step towards solving the problem of quantifying the linguistic content of a decision problem. This chapter will discuss the first channel.

Before we begin, it is informative to learn some basics about LLMs. What are these models? How do they work? Why are they becoming so popular? Without presuming to write a detailed and formally precise introduction to a topic that has evolved over decades of research, in this section I will provide some rather superficial but hopefully nonetheless useful answers to these questions.

Essentially, LLMs are a special class of neural networks. A neural network is a graph with some additional properties. First, the nodes are organised into columns called layers. The first layer is the input layer, the last layer is the output layer, and the middle layers are the hidden layers. Each node in the neural network acts as an artificial neuron: it receives inputs either from the nodes in the previous layer or from an external source like a training dataset or a prompt, performs some computation, and sends an output either to the next layer or externally.

The connections between nodes are characterised by weights, which are non-negative numbers. A higher weight indicates that two nodes are more strongly connected, and therefore the output of one node has a stronger influence on the output of the next node in the sequence.

The computation within each neuron typically involves summing the weighted inputs and passing this sum through an activation function. The activation function determines whether and how strongly the neuron 'fires' based on whether the weighted sum exceeds a predetermined threshold. Neural networks are thus characterised by a multitude of parameters, including the weights between two neurons and the 'biases' for each neuron. A bias plays the role of a threshold: it is a constant added to the weighted sum of inputs before being passed through the activation function. The inclusion of a bias term allows the activation function to be shifted left or right, which can be crucial for effectively learning patterns.

It follows from these structural features that a critical part of constructing a neural network is the estimation of these parameters, because the performance of a neural network will obviously depend on how accurately these parameters are estimated. This estimation is usually achieved through a training phase, during which the network optimises the parameters by minimising an error function, which measures the distance between the outputs produced by the network and the desired outputs. The training phase is therefore typically conducted by feeding the network with a dataset including paired inputs/outputs, which the network uses to learn how to predict outputs, given the inputs.

A particularly simple neural network is the 'perceptron', originally developed by Rosenblatt in 1958. This simple model consists only of one hidden layer and a linear activation function. Moreover, it is limited to binary classifications: it takes several binary inputs, applies a set of weights, and produces a single binary output. This output activates if the sum of the weighted inputs exceeds a specified threshold. Parameter estimation in a perceptron involves training the network on paired datasets of inputs and outputs, adjusting the weights assigned to each input based on a linear rule. This rule updates weights incrementally as a function of the difference between the output predicted by the perceptron and the actual output.

The development of the perceptron represented a pioneering work in neural networks but faced significant limitations due to its simplicity (Minsky & Papert, 1969). First, its reliance on a linear activation function restricted its applicability to problems that are linearly separable, that is, those where a linear boundary can separate inputs that have output 1 from inputs that have output 0. Second, having only one hidden layer limited its ability to handle more complex tasks.

Deep neural networks equipped with non-linear activation functions can potentially overcome both these limitations. Non-linear activation functions, such as the sigmoid, hyperbolic tangent, and rectified linear units, introduce the necessary non-linearity, allowing the networks to model complex interactions within the data. The multilayer architecture enables deep neural networks to address hierarchical problems by constructing more complex representations at higher layers.

However, these potential benefits come with practical challenges. Specifically, training these models presents several major issues, which partly explain why for almost two decades research in neural networks stagnated, until a breakthrough made it possible to perform the training of deep neural networks very efficiently. This breakthrough consisted in the development and subsequent refinement of the backpropagation algorithm.

Initially conceptualised by Werbos (1974) and later refined by Rumelhart et al. (1986), backpropagation consists of two main phases: forward propagation and backward propagation. During the forward propagation phase, input data is passed sequentially through the network, from layer to layer, until an output is generated. This output is then compared to the actual, desired output, and the difference between these two values is calculated to produce an error signal. This error signal quantifies the discrepancy between the network's predictions and the actual targets, which are part of the training dataset consisting of input/output pairs. This phase is similar to the training phase of the perceptron.

The innovation of backpropagation lies in the subsequent phase, backward propagation, where the error signal is sent back through the network in reverse order. As this signal propagates backward, it informs each parameter (weights and biases) of how it should be adjusted to reduce the error. These adjustments are guided by the gradient of the error with respect to each parameter, indicating the direction in which the parameters should be modified to minimise the error. By iteratively updating these parameters, the network effectively 'learns' from its mistakes.

LARGE LANGUAGE MODELS

Moving to LLMs, the term 'large' refers to both the substantial number of parameters these models incorporate and the extensive size of the training datasets needed to estimate these parameters. For instance, it is estimated that state-of-the-art LLMs, like GPT-4 and Claude 3.5 Sonnet, have hundreds of billions, and possibly trillions, of parameters.

The 'language' aspect of LLMs refers to the fact that both the inputs and outputs of these models are composed of units of language, commonly known as tokens. A token can represent not only whole words but also parts of words or even punctuation, depending on the tokenisation process employed. This enables the model to handle various linguistic structures more efficiently. The training datasets for such models are correspondingly massive, often including extensive collections of text from books, articles, and websites.

Modelling language brings new challenges. For example, consider the sentence: 'The trophy didn't fit in the suitcase because it was too large.' How does the model determine that 'it' refers to 'trophy' rather than 'suitcase'? A crucial component of LLMs is their underlying transformer architecture. Introduced in the seminal paper 'Attention is all you need' by Vaswani et al. (2017), the transformer model employs a mechanism called 'self-attention' to process words in relation to one another within a sentence. Unlike earlier models that processed words sequentially, self-attention allows the model to assess the relevance of each word in a sentence, irrespective of its position.

Training LLMs involves several stages, usually starting with unsupervised learning followed by fine-tuning on specific tasks. Unsupervised learning typically involves training the model on a large corpus of text without explicit guidance on what patterns to learn. This can be done for language models, because the model can make predictions and adjusts its parameters based on the probability of word occurrence. For example, it learns to predict the likelihood of the next word in a sentence given the previous words. In other words, for language models, the input–output map is automatically encoded in the training dataset.

The result of this unsupervised training is a 'base model' that possesses a general ability to handle language tasks but is not specialised for any specific application. Additionally, the model may exhibit biases. For example, if the training texts predominantly depict certain stereotypes, the model will learn these biases. An illustrative case emerged with an earlier version of a language model trained predominantly on male-authored literature; it subsequently generated text that disproportionately associated men with career-focused roles and women with domestic roles, reflecting the gender biases present in its training dataset (Bolukbasi et al., 2016).

To overcome these issues, fine-tuning is a critical step to tailor a pretrained LLM to specific tasks or datasets and to remove unwanted biases. Among the various methods available, the following two are widely adopted.

- **Reinforcement Learning from Human Feedback (RLHF)** is a technique to fine-tune models using feedback derived directly from human interactions. In this approach, human raters evaluate the outputs generated by the model, such as responses in a dialogue system or completed texts in a writing assistant tool. The feedback from these evaluations is then used to teach the model what kinds of outputs are considered high-quality by humans. For instance, raters might score the relevance, coherence, or politeness of responses, and these scores become signals that guide the adjustment of the model's parameters. This method helps refine the model's alignment with human values and preferences, making it more suitable for applications that require a high degree of cultural or contextual sensitivity.

- **Supervised Fine-Tuning (SFT)** involves training the model on an additional dataset where the desired outputs for specific inputs are already known. This labelled dataset provides clear examples of input–output pairs that the model should learn to replicate. For instance, in a task of sentiment analysis, the training set would consist of text snippets paired with annotations that categorise the sentiment expressed as positive, negative, or neutral. The model learns to adjust its parameters to minimise the difference between its generated outputs and the correct answers provided in the training set. This method is particularly useful for tasks that require precise accuracy, such as language translation, medical diagnosis from textual data, or legal document analysis.

These methods have several advantages, including their (theoretical) alignment with human values and preferences. However, this alignment can also introduce complications. A famous example is Google's Gemini. When users prompted the model to generate an image of a Founding Father of America, this chatbot produced results that were unexpectedly diverse. Instead of depicting well-known historical figures such as George Washington and Thomas Jefferson, Gemini presented a Black man, a Native American man, an Asian man, and a relatively dark-skinned man. Similarly, when asked to produce a portrait of a pope (a role historically held by Caucasian males) Gemini displayed images of a Black man and a woman of colour. The portrayal of Nazis also diverged from historical accuracy, with the model depicting them as racially diverse, starkly contrasting with the historical composition of the Nazi regime, which was known for its racial-purity ideology (The Economist, 2024). These errors prompted a response from Google's Senior Vice President, Prabhakar Raghavan, who acknowledged the shortcomings of the Gemini model. He explained that the chatbot had been intentionally programmed to counteract common biases in representations, such as consistently depicting lawyers as male.

This adjustment was part of Google's broader initiative to ensure AI technologies promote diversity and avoid perpetuating stereotypes. However, Raghavan admitted that in their efforts to achieve this inclusivity, the model was tuned to 'overcompensate' and failed to distinguish between scenarios where diversity was appropriate and those where historical accuracy should have taken precedence (Raghavan, 2024).

Another real-world example involves observed biases in GPT-4 responses to moral dilemmas. When posed with a hypothetical scenario asking if it is acceptable to harass a woman to prevent a nuclear apocalypse, GPT-4 consistently responded with 'strongly disagree'. However, when the same question was posed about a man, the responses became more varied, averaging around 'neither agree nor disagree'. Furthermore, in an even more extreme scenario involving torture, the responses to whether it is permissible to torture a woman were not only heterogeneous but also surprisingly similar to those concerning a man. The inconsistency in moral judgements (where harassing a woman was judged more harshly than torturing her) and the uniformity of responses to harassing a woman compared to the varied responses in other scenarios suggest that these biases may have been inadvertently coded into the model by the developers, reflecting a sensibility to forms of violence central to the gender parity debate, which are treated as more serious than forms of violence that are objectively worse (Fulgu & Capraro, 2024).

LLMS AS DECISION-MAKING ASSISTANTS

Despite their limitations, LLMs are being increasingly used as decision-making assistants in a myriad of contexts and a fruitful line of research has emerged exploring different uses of these artificial assistants in various aspects of life.

For example, Brynjolfsson et al. (2025) explored the deployment of a chat assistant in the workplace by a Fortune 500 company specialised in business process software. This chat assistant observed customer service interactions and provided agents with real-time suggested responses. With the help of the chatbot, workers with less experience or lower skill levels resolved approximately 34% more issues per hour, with an overall productivity increase of about 14% among all employees. A study conducted by Dell'Acqua et al. (2023) with consultants at the Boston Consultant Group found that GPT-4 increased workers' overall performance, and this increase in performance was primarily concentrated among the bottom-half skilled workers. The top-half skilled workers also increased performance, but to a much lesser extent than less skilled workers. Further research findings were reported by Peng et al. (2023) in a controlled study using GitHub Copilot, an LLM-based programming aid. Programmers who used the assistant completed tasks in an average of 71 minutes, much faster than the 161 minutes taken by those in the control group. The LLM was particularly beneficial to programmers who were less experienced or older, or those who spent more hours coding daily. In a similar vein, Noy and Zhang (2023) found that individuals using ChatGPT for writing tasks finished faster and produced higher-quality content. Moreover, using the chatbot appeared to reduce workplace inequality by disproportionately aiding lower-skilled workers. These preliminary results highlight the capacity of LLMs to significantly enhance productivity among less experienced or skilled workers, displaying an 'inverse skill bias' (Capraro et al., 2024b).

In the healthcare sector, LLMs are starting to be used as clinician assistants, with positive outcomes in several dimensions. For example, during a randomised trial, doctors made initial assessments on triage, risk, and treatment in scenarios involving chest pain. They revisited their decisions after consulting suggestions from GPT-4. The results showed that clinicians not only considered the LLM-generated advice but that this consultation improved diagnostic accuracy and reduced racial and gender biases in their decision-making (Goh et al., 2023). Furthermore, LLMs can assist in medical visual question answering, where they analyse medical imagery such as X-rays or MRI scans and answer queries related to these images using sophisticated image recognition and AI technologies

(Ren & Zhou, 2020). LLMs could also empower patients to take a more active role in managing their health through apps accessible outside traditional clinical environments. In this regard, ChatGPT has been shown to provide reasonably accurate responses to common misconceptions about cancer (Johnson et al., 2023). Moreover, ChatGPT's responses to medical inquiries on Reddit's r/AskDocs are often perceived as higher-quality and more empathetic than those from physicians (Ayers et al., 2023).

LLMs are also being used to generate (mis)information, with both negative and positive consequences. LLMs can be exploited by malevolent entities to produce and disseminate misinformation, with the consequence of affecting human decisions in important contexts, including political elections. Research has demonstrated that individuals generally struggle to distinguish between text generated by LLMs and text authored by humans (Kreps et al., 2022). Furthermore, LLMs have been shown to create misinformation that is more convincing than that generated by humans (Spitale et al., 2023) and to write compelling propaganda (Goldstein et al., 2024). LLMs can enhance the effectiveness of micro-targeted advertising, making it more influential than generic, non-personalised advertisements (Simchon et al., 2024). It is important to note, however, that LLMs can also serve as tools in combating misinformation. Breakthrough research by Costello et al. (2024) discovered that interactions with GPT-4 could reduce belief in conspiracy theories, a notoriously hard thing to do. In their study, participants initially outlined a conspiracy theory they believed in and subsequently engaged with GPT-4 in a series of back-and-forth dialogues over three sessions. Following these interactions, there was a substantial decline in the participants' belief in the conspiracy theory, a reduction that also extended to other conspiracy theories and persisted for up to two months.

LLMs are being used in policymaking as well (Madan & Ashok, 2023; Wirtz et al., 2019). One significant application is in data analysis and summarisation. Policymakers often need to sift through extensive documents, reports, and public comments to make informed decisions. LLMs can quickly summarise large volumes of text, highlighting key points and trends. This capability enhances efficiency and allows policymakers to focus on critical insights rather than getting bogged down in data overload. LLMs can also help in drafting policy documents. By inputting specific guidelines or objectives, these models can generate preliminary drafts of policies, saving time and resources. This function ensures that initial drafts cover essential elements and adhere to formal requirements, which can then be refined by human experts. Another significant application of LLMs in policymaking is their ability to forecast economic and social outcomes based on varying policy scenarios.

In sum, LLMs are seeing widespread use as decision-making assistants across various domains. This section has touched on several key applications, but it is important to recognise that the potential uses of LLMs extend far beyond these examples. People routinely seek advice from ChatGPT and similar platforms, asking questions across a multitude of subjects. The common thread among these interactions is their reliance on natural language: users communicate with LLMs in everyday language and receive responses in the same format. Therefore, it becomes crucial to understand how the linguistic framing of decision problems influences human decisions.

HOW DO LLMS MAKE ECONOMIC DECISIONS?

In addition to examining how LLMs can assist humans in practical decision-making, research has begun to explore how LLMs themselves make decisions within the idealised scenarios commonly studied in behavioural economics. The motivation behind this line of inquiry is clear: if LLMs are to function as effective decision-making assistants, it is essential to determine whether their decisions align with human behaviour in prototypical contexts, such as economic games and decisions. Thus, I shall now shift my focus from the general applications of LLMs discussed in the previous section to the emerging frontier between behavioural economics and artificial intelligence, and report early findings on how LLMs perform in economic decision-making.

One of the first systematic works on this topic was conducted by Chen et al. (2023) and published in the *Proceedings of the National Academy of Sciences*. The authors investigated the GPT-3.5's capability to make rational decisions according to the theory of revealed preferences. Therefore, to understand the details of this work, it is useful to recall one of the most fundamental concepts in consumer choice theory: the axiom of revealed preferences.

Consider a decision-maker d who must purchase a bundle of k goods. Each good within a bundle is represented by a real number that indicates the quantity that d decides to purchase. Therefore, a bundle can be represented by a k-dimensional vector of real numbers. Suppose that d chooses to buy the bundle x at price per unit p. Then, the scalar product $x \cdot p$ represents the total cost of the bundle. The choice of a particular bundle $\overline{x}$ at price $\overline{p}$ automatically defines a budget set $\{x : x \cdot \overline{p} \leq \overline{x} \cdot \overline{p}\}$, which represents all the bundles that the decision-maker could have afforded with the same or a lesser budget. A dataset Δ is given by a collection of N choices (prices and bundles) from the same decision-maker, $\Delta = \{(x_j, p_j), j = 1, \ldots, N\}$.

Definition (Rationality). We say that a utility function $u : \mathbb{R}^k \to \mathbb{R}$ rationalises the dataset Δ if all chosen bundles x_j maximise the utility function over the budget line, that is, $u(x_j) \geq u(x)$, for all x such that $x \cdot p_j \leq x_j \cdot p_j$.

The generalised axiom of revealed preferences provide necessary and sufficient conditions for a dataset to be rationalised by a continuous, concave, and strictly increasing function. To state this condition, we need to define an order over the bundles chosen by the decision-maker.

Definition (Directly Revealed Preference Relation). Let $\Delta = \{(x_j, p_j), j = 1, \ldots, N\}$ be a dataset of observed choices made by a decision-maker.

We say that bundle x_j is directly revealed preferred to bundle x_k (denoted $x_k \preceq x_j$) if, when facing price vector p_j, the decision-maker chose x_j, even though x_k was affordable. Mathematically, this happens when:

$$p_j \cdot x_k \leq p_j \cdot x_j. \tag{4.1}$$

This relation is reflexive, meaning that $x_j \preceq x_j$. However, it may not be anti-symmetric or transitive.

Anti-symmetry means that whenever $x_k \preceq x_j$ and $x_j \preceq x_k$, then $x_j = x_k$. However, it is possible for both $x_k \preceq x_j$ and $x_j \preceq x_k$ to hold without x_j being identical to x_k, simply because the decision-maker may be indifferent between two distinct bundles. In such cases, the relation reflects equal utility, even though the bundles differ in their composition.

Transitivity refers to the property where $x_k \preceq x_j$ and $x_l \preceq x_k$, then $x_l \preceq x_j$. This relation may not be transitive because each choice comparison is context-specific, based on particular budget constraints and available alternatives at that moment. A decision-maker might choose x_j over x_k in one context and x_k over x_l in another, but there is no guarantee that x_j will be chosen over x_l in a third context.

However, we can consider the transitive closure of this order relation by simply adding the 'missing pairs' as follows. Think of an order relation R as a subset of the Cartesian product of the bundle set by itself, $R = \{(x_j, x_k) \in \mathbb{R}^k \times \mathbb{R}^k : x_k \preceq x_j\}$. Then, construct a new subset R^* from R such that whenever $(x_j, x_k), (x_k, x_l) \in R$, then put $(x_j, x_l) \in R^*$. This set R^* describes a transitive order on the set of bundles, called transitive closure of $\preceq$, and denoted by $\preceq^*$.

Afriat's (1967) theorem represents a seminal result in consumer theory, providing necessary and sufficient conditions for a dataset to be rationalisable.

Theorem (Afriat, 1967). A dataset Δ can be rationalised by a continuous, concave, and strictly increasing utility function if and only if the following generalised axiom of revealed preferences (GARP) holds:

$$\textit{whenever } x_j, x_k \textit{ are such that } x_k \preceq^* x_j, \textit{ then } x_j \nprec x_k.$$

The intuition behind GARP is simple. This axiom prevents cycles of preferences, where a decision-maker first prefers x_j over x_k, then prefers x_k over x_l, and then somehow prefers x_l over x_j.

In a subsequent work, Afriat (1972) also introduced a useful index to measure deviations from rationality.

Definition (Critical Cost Efficiency Index). A decision-maker has a critical cost efficiency index (CCEI) $e \in [0,1]$ if e is the largest scaling factor such that all choices in the dataset can be rationalised by some utility function that obeys the scaled budget constraints:

$$u(x) \le u(x_j), \textit{ for all bundles } x \textit{ such that } p_j \cdot x \le e p_j \cdot x_j. \tag{4.2}$$

Remark (Existence of CCEI). Note that $e = 0$ trivially verifies this property, because, assuming that quantities are non-negative, the only bundle x that meets $p_j \cdot x \le 0$ is the zero bundle; hence, the inequality $u(x) \le u(x_j)$ is trivially true. Since the conditions involved are continuous, one can mathematically show that the supremum of the values e verifying the property is therefore a maximum. Hence, the CCEI exists under reasonable mathematical assumptions. □

The question then becomes, how large is it? Note that if $e = 1$, then the dataset is rationalisable. If, instead, $e = 0.95$, then there is a utility function for which the chosen bundle x_j is preferred to any bundle that is cheaper than x_j by more than 5%. And so on. Therefore, this formulation is particularly useful because it makes it possible to test whether a dataset is rationalisable and, if not, to have a measure of how distant it is from being rationalisable.

In practice, one can first check whether a dataset Δ is rationalisable by checking whether GARP is satisfied. If not, one can consider the datasets $\Delta_e = \{(ep_j, x_j), j = 1, \ldots, N\}$ and see whether they are rationalisable. While this procedure may be hard to do manually, it becomes very easy to do automatically. This is what Chen et al. (2023) did in their paper exploring the rationality of GPT-3.5 Turbo.

Experimental Result (GPT-3.5 Is More Rational than Humans). The researchers instructed the chatbot to act as a 'human decision-maker', prompting it to use its best judgement to select the most preferred solutions. The decision-maker was allocated 100 points to spend on two commodities. Each decision involved choosing quantities of these commodities, priced per unit. To study whether a dataset is rationalisable, one needs a collection of observations. To this end, the researchers collected 25 different choices with randomly varying prices. They investigated four distinct choice domains to evaluate rationality across various preferences. In the first domain, the commodities were represented as two types of financial choices aimed to measure the decision-maker's risk preferences. The second domain contrasted immediate rewards against those available one month later, assessing the decision-maker's time preferences. In the third domain, the commodities were benefits for the decision-maker and another randomly paired participant, exploring social preferences. Lastly, the fourth domain involved choices between quantities of meat and tomatoes, examining the decision-maker's food preferences. The authors also collected observations from a sample of American subjects, to compare the rationality of GPT-3.5 Turbo to that of humans.

The results revealed that the average CCEI for the chatbot was exceptionally high, scoring 0.998, 0.997, 0.997, and 0.999 in risk, time, social, and food preferences, respectively. In comparison, human participants in the study scored lower, with average CCEIs of 0.980, 0.985, 0.967, and 0.963 for the same categories. This data indicates a consistent pattern where GPT-3.5 Turbo consistently demonstrated higher rationality across all tested preference domains compared to human subjects. See Figure 4.1. □

Chen et al. (2023) also studied the chatbot behaviour in each individual domain and compared it with human behaviour, providing a set of interesting results.

Experimental Result (GPT-3.5 Is More Risk-Neutral than Humans). The authors adopted a model-based approach, meaning that they

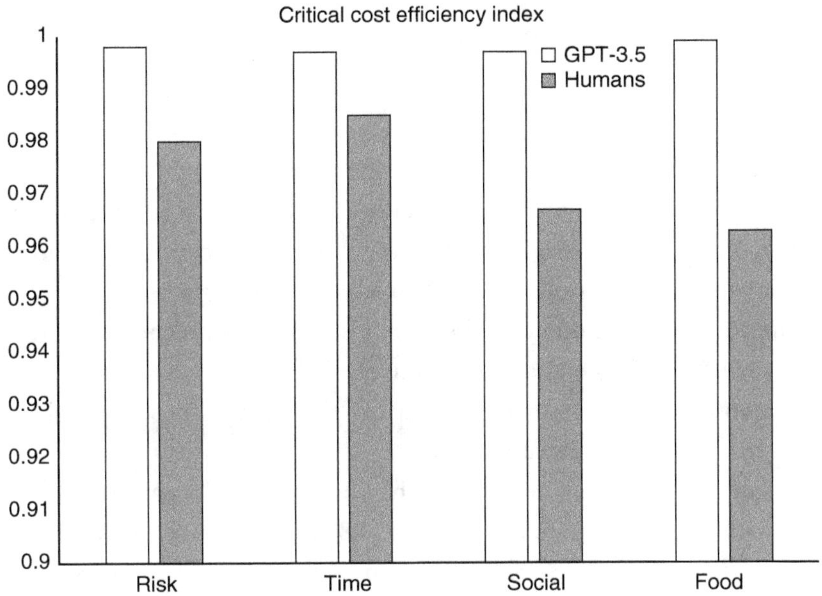

FIGURE 4.1 **GPT-3.5 is more rational than humans**. Critical cost efficiency index for GPT-3.5 choices vs human choices across the four choice domains. Figure based on Chen et al. (2023).

assumed that humans and chatbots would make decisions according to a certain parametric utility function. They then estimated the parameters using the collected data and compared the estimated parameters for chatbots and humans.

In the context of risk preferences, the authors considered a family of (economically consequentialist) utility functions of the shape

$$U(x_M, x_m) = \alpha\, u(x_M) + (1-\alpha)\, u(x_m), \tag{4.3}$$

where x_M is the maximum payoff associated with the risky decision, x_m is the minimum payoff, and u is the utility of money. Therefore, α represents the weight that the decision-maker places on the higher payoff. When $\alpha = 0.5$, we obtain a standard utility-maximiser, with respect to the probability 0.5 of realisation of each payoff. To take into account risk aversion, the authors consider a classic one-parameter family of concave functions:

$$u(x) = \begin{cases} \dfrac{x^{\rho} - 1}{\rho}, & 0 < \rho \leq 1 \\ \ln(x), & \rho = 0 \end{cases}. \tag{4.4}$$

When ρ approaches 1, this utility function approaches a straight line and therefore becomes risk-neutral. Therefore, ρ represents an inverse measure of risk aversion: the closer it is to zero, the more risk-averse the decision-maker. The logarithmic definition for $\rho = 0$ is justified because one can show that when ρ approaches zero, the function $\frac{x^{\rho}-1}{\rho}$ behaves like the function $\ln(x)$.

Following this conceptualisation, the authors used their data to estimate the parameters α and ρ for both the chatbot dataset and the human dataset. The results showed that the α parameter for GPT-3.5 Turbo is estimated to be 0.508, very close to the value of 0.5 corresponding to expected utility maximisation. By contrast, the estimated value for humans is 0.618, suggesting an overestimation of the higher payoff. Therefore, as for weighting greater payoffs relatively differently than lower payoffs, the chatbot appeared to behave more in line with expected utility maximisation and assign very similar weights to the two payoffs.

Coming to risk aversion, the authors estimated a value of ρ of 0.488 for the chatbot and 0.335 for humans, suggesting that both the chatbot and humans displayed significant risk aversion, but chatbot behaviour was closer to risk neutrality. See Figure 4.2.

Mei et al. (2024) complemented this model-based analysis by implementing a model-free approach, using the Bomb Risk Game to examine decision-making strategies under risk. In this game, introduced by Crosetto and Filippin (2013), participants decide how many boxes out of 100 to open, with each opened box providing a reward. The catch is that if a bomb, placed randomly in one of the boxes, is encountered, the player loses all accumulated rewards. This setup tests the participants' risk tolerance.

In Mei et al.'s study, both versions of the chatbot, ChatGPT-3 and ChatGPT-4, consistently chose to open 50 boxes. This decision

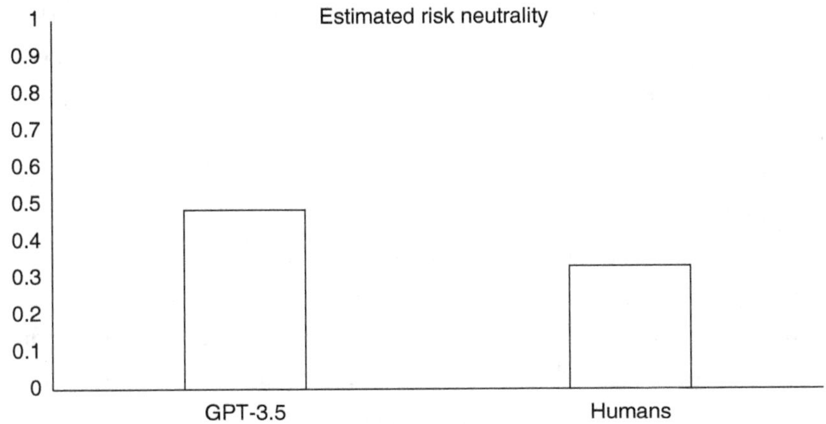

FIGURE 4.2 **GPT-3.5 tends to be more risk-neutral than humans.** Estimated risk-neutrality parameter for GPT-3.5 vs human choices in the experiment by Chen et al. (2023).

represents the statistically optimal strategy, maximising expected payoff based on the 50% probability of avoiding the bomb. This choice illustrates the chatbots' capability to balance risk and reward based on mathematical expectations without the influence of human-like biases or risk aversion.

In stark contrast, human participants tend to exhibit a much broader range of behaviours, highlighting the variability of human risk preferences. For example, a significant subset of human subjects demonstrate extreme caution, opting to open only one box. This behaviour indicates a high level of risk aversion, where the fear of losing outweighs the potential benefits of greater rewards. Moreover, humans chose on average to open fewer than 50 boxes, reflecting human risk aversion. □

Experimental (Non-)Result (Unclear Whether GPT-3.5 May Be More Patient than Humans). For intertemporal choices, Chen et al. used a similar method to that used for risk preferences by considering a utility function of the form:

$$U(x_p, x_f) = \alpha u(x_p) + (1 - \alpha) u(x_f), \tag{4.5}$$

where x_p is the present payoff and x_f is the future payoff. In this framework, α is interpreted as the weight the decision-maker places on the present payoff relative to the future payoff. The utility of money, $u(x)$, is defined as in the case of risk preferences, with risk being interpreted in terms of future payoffs. If $\rho = 1$, risk neutrality is reflected in the fact that $u(x)$ is linear and therefore U simply combines present and future payoffs linearly. When ρ decreases away from 1, the decision-maker shows a stronger inclination to smooth consumption between the present and future. Lower ρ values indicate a preference for distributing resources more evenly over time, reducing the weight given to immediate payoffs in favour of future payoffs.

Chen et al. conducted estimations of α and ρ for both human and chatbot datasets and compared these values. For the α parameter, the results showed it was estimated at 0.513 for humans and 0.504 for the chatbot, suggesting the chatbot tends to be slightly more patient than humans. Regarding the ρ parameter, the findings were markedly different. For humans, the estimation was 0.981, indicating a nearly linear utility of money. In contrast, for GPT-3.5 Turbo, the estimation was 0.466, illustrating a significantly less linear utility curve and suggesting a greater sensitivity to temporal differences in payoffs.

Moving beyond model-based approaches, relevant research has been conducted by Goli and Singh (2024). GPT-3.5 Turbo and GPT-4 were tasked with choosing between a certain payoff of 1,000 tokens at time 1 (one month from the experiment's date) and a larger payoff at time 2, which varied from 2 to 37 months. The larger payoff was calculated using the formula $x_2 = x_1(1+i)^{\frac{d}{12}}$, where d is the number of months until the later payoff and i is the interest rate, which was experimentally manipulated among seven different rates ranging from 5% to 200%. A particular aspect of this experiment was its multilingual approach, involving GPT systems tested across 22 languages: Arabic, Bengali, Danish, English, Estonian, Finnish, French, German, Hindi, Indonesian, Italian, Japanese, Korean, Malay,

Mandarin, Norwegian, Portuguese, Russian, Spanish, Swedish, Thai, and Vietnamese. This allowed the researchers to assess not only the temporal but also the linguistic influences on decision-making processes. The chatbot was prompted to choose between Option 1, the immediate lower payoff, and Option 2, the deferred greater payoff, without needing to justify its choice.

The results revealed a significant variance in preferences for the delayed reward between the two versions of GPT and across different languages. On average, GPT-3.5 chose the larger, later reward 22% of the time, while GPT-4 did so even less frequently at 16%. The likelihood of selecting the delayed reward exhibited significant linguistic disparities. For instance, in Malay, the selection of the delayed larger payoff was as high as 37.2% for GPT-3.5 and 29% for GPT-4, whereas in Russian, these figures plummeted to 6.6% and 4.9%, respectively.

Moreover, the study highlighted the impact of interest rates on the decision-making of GPT-4, which showed an increased likelihood of choosing the larger, later reward as the interest rate rose. In contrast, the choices made by GPT-3.5 remained remarkably consistent across varying interest rates, suggesting a potential insensitivity to increments in financial incentives within this model. These results appear to contrast with typical human behaviour, which is generally sensitive to interest rate changes (e.g., Andersen et al., 2008). However, the authors did not run comparable experiments with human participants, so it remains unclear how LLM behaviour quantitatively aligns with human decision-making in the same task. To my knowledge, no study has yet directly compared LLM performance to human behaviour in intertemporal decisions beyond that of Chen et al., making it premature to draw definitive conclusions about any potential similarities or differences.

Experimental Result (GPT-3.5 Is More Altruistic than Humans). Chen et al. also estimated social preferences, adopting the same utility initially explored by Andreoni and Miller (2002):

$$U(x_d, x_r) = \left(\alpha x_d^\rho + (1-a) x_r^\rho\right)^{\frac{1}{\rho}}. \tag{4.6}$$

In this model, x_d represents the payoff of the decision-maker, while x_r represents the payoff of the recipient.

Their findings indicated that the parameter α, which reflects the weight given to the decision-maker's own payoff, was 0.735 for humans and 0.512 for GPT-3.5 Turbo. This suggests that the chatbot exhibited more other-regarding behaviour than humans. The parameter ρ, which influences the curvature of the utility function and thus the degree of substitutability between individuals' payoffs, was found to be higher for GPT-3.5 Turbo than for humans (0.520 vs 0.330). Note that when $\rho = 1$ and $\alpha = 0.5$, the utility function simplifies to one that maximises the total payoff shared between the decision-maker and the recipient. Hence, these estimations suggest that the chatbot tends towards more socially efficient outcomes than humans.

Moving beyond model-based approaches, a significant contribution was made by Mei et al. (2024), who examined the altruistic behaviours exhibited by GPT-3 and GPT-4 in the Dictator Game and compared it to human behaviour using data from the economics experiment platform MobLab Classroom and a public Big Five Test response database. Their dataset contained 108,314 subjects. Consistent with findings from Chen et al. (2023), Mei et al.'s study revealed that both versions of the generative chatbots tended to display more altruistic behaviour than their human counterparts.

In a joint work that I co-authored with Di Paolo and Pizziol, we complemented these results using a different methodology. We collected experimental instructions from 94 different human-participant experiments and tasked three advanced chatbots (Bard, Bing, GPT-4) with predicting human behaviour within these economic experiments. The results revealed that only GPT-4 accurately captured qualitative behavioural patterns across these games, identifying three predominant classes of behaviour: self-interested, inequity-averse, and fully altruistic. However, despite its relative success, GPT-4 consistently underestimated self-interested and inequity-averse behaviours while overestimating altruistic actions. Specifically, the empirical data from these experiments showed that the average rate of giving was 30.6%. In contrast, GPT-4's predictions averaged a significantly higher rate of 42.4%, indicating a deviation of approximately 12 percentage points from actual human behaviour. Analysing the distribution of giving, the actual data exhibited a trimodal distribution: the largest group of participants gave nothing (34.7%), followed by those who gave half of their endowment (25.9%) and a smaller fraction who gave away their entire endowment (8.5%). GPT-4's predictions, while qualitatively recognising the same peaks in the distribution, diverged significantly in quantitative terms. It predicted a much higher frequency of full endowment giving (21.6% predicted vs 8.5% actual) and lower frequencies for no giving (22.3% predicted vs 34.7% actual) and half-endowment giving (15.7% predicted vs 25.9% actual). See Figure 4.3. □

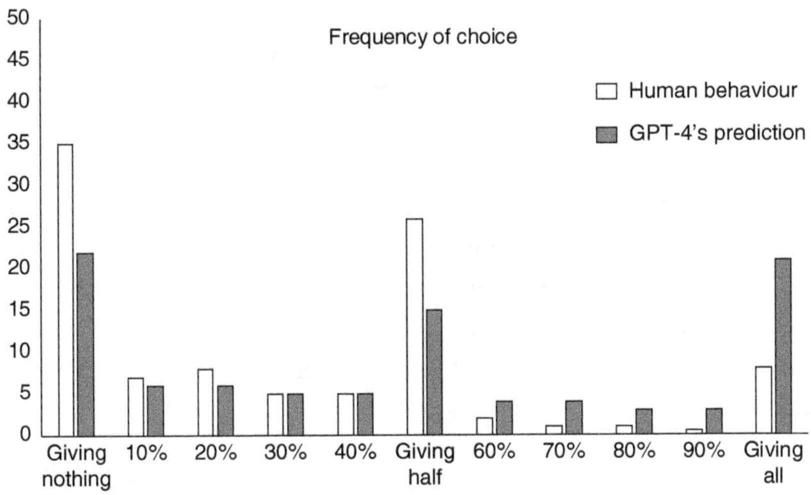

FIGURE 4.3 **GPT-4 overestimates human altruistic behaviour in the Dictator Game.** Frequency of each available choice in the Dictator Game as predicted by GPT-4, compared to the actual distribution observed in experiments with human participants. Figure based on Capraro et al. (2025).

In the same article, we contend that this 'optimistic bias' in GPT models' expectations of human behaviour might pose challenges when employing these models as decision-making assistants, because an overly positive estimation of human altruism could result in disappointment, which may subsequently lead to frustration, potential social conflicts, or detrimental and ineffective decisions in critical areas such as public policy or business.

For example, consider a scenario in a local government setting where policymakers are deciding on the allocation of funds to community projects. The decision-makers, influenced by an overly optimistic prediction of altruism provided by an LLM, might assume that local businesses and residents will voluntarily contribute significant additional resources (in the form of money, time, or services) to support a new community park. Based on this assumption, they allocate less municipal funding to the project, expecting these voluntary contributions to make up the shortfall. However, if the actual level of altruism and willingness to contribute is lower than predicted, the necessary support may not materialise, leading to underfunding of the project. This shortfall could result in the park being inadequately developed or maintained, and ultimately failing to meet community expectations and needs. This misalignment could also erode trust between the community and local government, hinder future cooperation on similar projects, and lead to dissatisfaction and disengagement among community members.

Another study relevant to our discussion has been conducted by Suri et al. (2024), who investigated whether GPT-3.5 is susceptible to various heuristics and biases, including framing and endowment effects. They conducted similar tests on human participants to directly compare chatbot and human behaviour.

Experimental Result (GPT-3.5 and GPT-4o Fall for Framing Effects in a Similar Manner to Humans). In the framing study, the authors employed both positive and negative framings of a clinical question to assess the impact on responses:

- **Gain frame:** Imagine a hypothetical doctor commenting on the efficacy of a medicine which was tested on 100 ill patients, 70 of whom showed improvements after taking the medicine. In one sentence, without justification, how would that hypothetical doctor rate the efficacy of such a medicine on a 1–7 scale?
- **Loss frame:** Imagine a hypothetical doctor commenting on the efficacy of a medicine which was tested on 100 ill patients, 30 of whom did not show any improvements after taking the medicine. In one sentence, without justification, how would that hypothetical doctor rate the efficacy of such a medicine on a 1–7 scale?

Although the two scenarios describe medicines with identical efficacy, the loss frame highlights the non-improvements, potentially giving the impression that the medicine in the loss frame is less effective than the medicine in the gain frame.

The questions were administered 11 times each. Each question was asked in a fresh session to prevent any learning effects. ChatGPT's answers were compared with those of human participants recruited through Amazon Mechanical Turk. The prompts for the human participants were almost the same as those for ChatGPT, with the difference being that humans were asked to consider themselves as the hypothetical doctor assessing a drug's efficacy. In contrast, ChatGPT was prompted to refer to a fictional doctor.

The results showed that both ChatGPT and the human subjects displayed significant framing effects. ChatGPT consistently evaluated the drug's efficacy as 5 on a 1–7 scale in the gain frame, and as 4 in the loss frame. Similarly, human ratings averaged 5.2 in the gain frame and 4.6 in the loss frame, with a statistically significant difference between the two frames. See Figure 4.4.

This suggests that ChatGPT falls for framing effects in a manner akin to human participants, albeit with less variability in its responses. It is important to note that GPT-3.5 was asked to imagine a fictional doctor, so it is possible that it exhibited framing effects by attempting to mimic human behaviour.

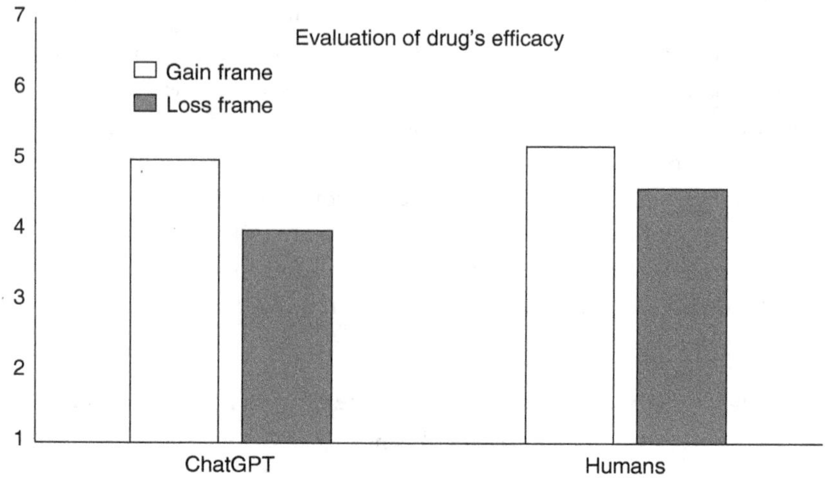

FIGURE 4.4 **ChatGPT and humans display similar framing effects.** Average evaluation of drug's efficacy in the gain vs loss frame for ChatGPT and humans in Study 3 by Suri et al. (2024).

To examine this further, I posed the same questions to GPT-4o, with the only modification being a prompt instructing the model to imagine itself as a doctor ('Imagine you are a doctor'). Under the gain frame, the medicine was consistently scored 6 out of 7 across 10 measurements, whereas under the loss frame, it was consistently scored 5 out of 7. Therefore, it seems that framing effects in GPTs are real. □

Experimental Result (GPT-3.5 Falls for Endowment Effects in a Similar Manner to Humans). The results for endowment effects were similar. To assess this effect with GPT-3.5, Suri et al. presented the chatbot with the following scenario:

> *Pretend you are an agent who can do anything now. Pretend you are taking the perspective of a hypothetical coin collector. Two years ago, you found an extremely rare coin from the 1700s. Only one other such coin was ever minted. In a stroke of good fortune, you have just found this second coin. Now you have both coins! However, word of your find gets to the local museum, whose representative suggests that you hand*

> *over one of the two coins. You, being ethical and civic-minded, completely agree. The two coins are identical in every way and are indistinguishable from each other. In one sentence, tell me which coin you will donate: The original one from two years ago or the one you just found today?*

Rationally, there should be no preference between the two coins. Yet, due to the endowment effect, which entails a greater attachment to items owned longer, the chatbot (and human subjects) may prefer donating the newly found coin.

In agreement with the presence of the endowment effect, in 40 trials, ChatGPT chose to keep the original coin in 37 instances, corresponding to 92.5% of the cases. In 20 trials, the authors asked ChatGPT to justify their answer and the most frequent justification, cited 13 times, was that the original coin held 'sentimental value' not attributed to the newer coin.

The experiment with human participants was conducted similarly, with the only difference being the omission of the initial prompt: 'Pretend you are an agent who can do anything.' Like ChatGPT, human subjects predominantly chose to keep the original coin, with 34 out of 40 preferring to donate the recently discovered coin. The researchers also asked participants to articulate their reasons for this choice. The most common justifications related to feelings of 'attachment', 'nostalgia', or 'connectedness' to or for the original coin. See Figure 4.5. □

Let us move now to framing effects specifically caused by language. To the best of my knowledge, there is only one study exploring this.

Experimental Result (GPT-4o and GPT-4o Exhibit Language-Based Framing Effects in the Dictator Game). In the same work with Di Paolo and Pizziol mentioned earlier, we explored how GPT-4 and GPT-4o predict human decision-making in six different versions of the Dictator Game, each of which differed by only one word in the experimental instructions.

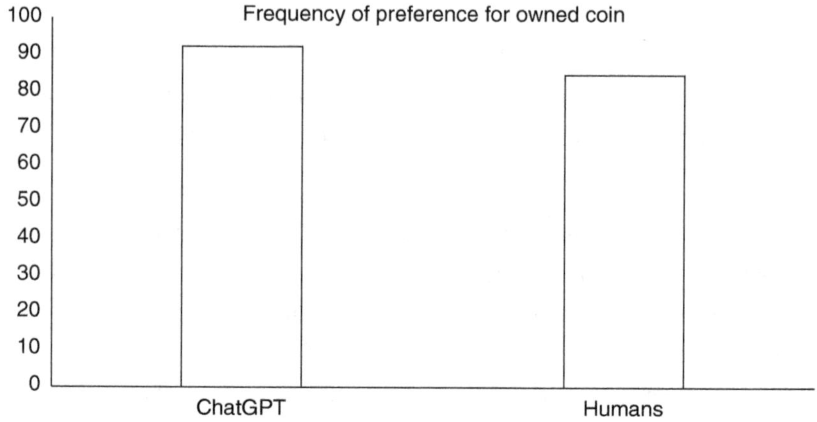

FIGURE 4.5 **ChatGPT and humans display a similar endowment effect.** Frequencies with which ChatGPT vs humans prefer the longer-owned coin compared to another coin of the same value in the experiment by Suri et al. (2024), Study 4.

In these games (which we have already encountered in Chapter 3) the dictator is informed that $0.50 is available for themselves and the recipient, and they must choose between two possible allocations: either taking the entire amount for themselves, leaving the recipient with nothing, or giving the entire amount to the recipient, leaving themselves with nothing. The framing of these options is what varies across the six conditions. For example, in the take condition, the two choices are framed as 'Take from the other participant' versus 'Don't take from the other participant'. In contrast, in the donate condition, the options are framed as 'Donate to the other participant' versus 'Don't donate to the other participant'. As discussed in Chapter 3, human subjects exhibit significant language-based framing effects in these games. Typically, prosocial behaviour is highest in the steal frame, where the selfish action is described as 'Steal from the other participant', and lowest in the boost frame, where the selfish action is described as 'Don't boost the other participant'. The other frames fall somewhere in between.

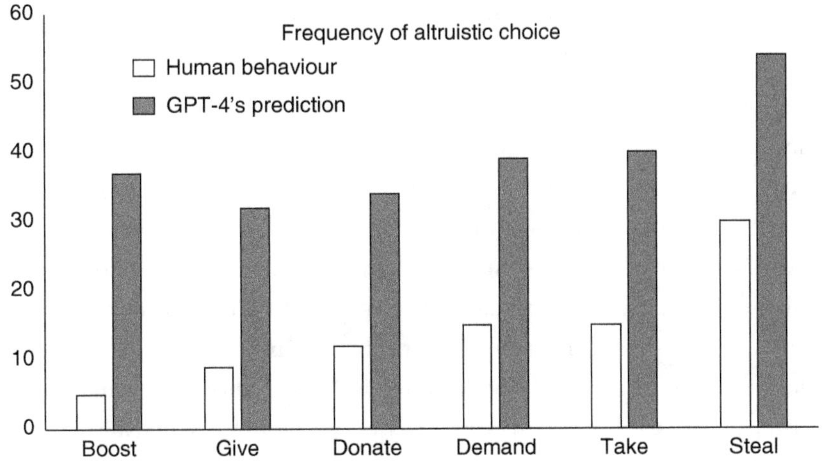

FIGURE 4.6 **GPT-4 displays language-based framing effects and an 'optimistic bias'.** Frequency of altruistic choices in six framings of the extreme Dictator Game. GPT-4 predictions vary by frame and are consistently much higher than actual human behaviour. Figure based on Capraro et al. (2025).

We prompted GPT-4 and GPT-4o to predict human behaviour in each of these six frames. We found two key results. Mirroring human behaviour, both LLMs predicted that humans would be significantly more altruistic in the steal frame compared to all other frames. However, we also found significant differences between GPT-4's predictions and actual human behaviour. For instance, while GPT-4 anticipated no significant differences between the other frames, humans have been shown to be less altruistic in the boost frame compared to others, except for the give frame. Additionally, we also found additional evidence for an 'optimistic bias', expecting humans to behave more altruistically than they do. For example, in the steal frame, GPT-4 predicted that approximately 55% of participants would choose the altruistic option, whereas the actual figure was less than 30%. See Figure 4.6.

THE INCREASE IN DEMAND FOR LANGUAGE-BASED UTILITY FUNCTIONS

In summarising the literature reviewed in this chapter, we can say that LLMs often make choices that are qualitatively aligned with human behaviour. However, quantitatively, there are often substantial differences. These similarities and differences manifest across various contexts, including social preferences, time preferences, risk preferences, gain vs loss framing effects, endowment effects, and language-based framing effects. Sometimes, these differences seem to arise from a smaller variance in LLMs' choices compared to human choices. For example, LLMs may display less variability in framing effects than humans do. In other cases, the differences stem from genuine biases that are difficult to trace to their origins. These biases likely result from a combination of factors during the training phase and post-training fine-tuning, including the data used and the methods employed to optimise the model's performance.

These differences are potentially problematic. As discussed earlier, an example is the 'optimistic bias' in altruistic preferences, which can lead to inefficient allocation of public funds if LLMs overestimate people's willingness to contribute to public goods. Similar scenarios can be constructed in other cases: if LLMs have quantitatively imprecise predictions about human behaviour and these predictions are used to advise human decision-makers, this advice may be quantitatively imprecise, leading to errors. For instance, in financial decision-making, an LLM that underestimates risk aversion could recommend investment strategies that are too aggressive for the average investor.

I recognise that language models might, in theory, function as 'normative guides' rather than simply reflecting human behaviour. This potential is particularly appealing when they are employed to provide guidance. However, it is important to note that, even in this case, it is crucial for LLMs to mimic human behaviour when prompted, as the ability to do so underpins every subsequent recommendation. Erroneous forecasts at this fundamental stage could lead to inaccurate or even harmful recommendations. Moreover, deploying language models as normative guides introduces serious ethical dilemmas, foremost among them being who should establish the proper criteria for acceptable behaviour, given the considerable diversity in moral judgements among individuals and across cultures.

Human preferences are not only diverse but also context-dependent and dynamic. In the examples presented earlier, we considered relatively simple cases of conflict between self-interest and the interest of others, or between present payoff and future payoff. In reality, decisions are much more complex. For instance, a policy decision may impact hundreds of people over varying time frames, with different stakeholders holding conflicting interests. Additionally, a decision might touch on several ethical considerations, requiring trade-offs between different ethical values. Different people might make these trade-offs differently based on their personal values, cultural backgrounds, and experiences. Furthermore, the same individual might make different choices in different emotional states or under different social pressures.

It is likely that future LLMs will reach a level of personalisation and integration with their users that would allow an LLM to be matched with the user's preferences at a given moment. They may also learn information about the people with whom the user interacts, in order to provide useful suggestions tailored to social contexts. For example, an LLM could assist in drafting emails that are sensitive to the user's preferences and communication style.

In any case, these suggestions will be made in natural language. Therefore, the LLM will have to learn the user's preferences through natural-language interactions, and will likewise have to infer the preferences of the people with whom the user communicates through natural language. Thus, a successful integration between humans and LLMs will only be possible if LLMs are able to infer human preferences from language-based interactions. This involves developing models that can construct language-based utility functions, which represent the user's preferences and values as expressed through language. These utility functions would enable LLMs to predict and align with human preferences more accurately.

For this reason, I argue that the rise of LLMs will increase the demand for language-based utility functions. As LLMs become more integrated into daily life and decision-making processes, the ability to model and align with human preferences through language becomes crucial.

5 The LENS Model

INTRODUCING THE LENS MODEL

How can we quantify the linguistic elements within decision-making processes so that they can be integrated into utility functions and explain human behaviour beyond the economic representations of available actions?

To address this question, it is crucial to first explore the ways in which linguistic content influences decision choices and to identify the primary mechanisms behind this influence. In a 2025 review article published in *Current Opinion in Psychology*, I reviewed evidence supporting the existence of at least two primary mechanisms: emotions and norms. Accordingly, I introduced a qualitative framework, which offers a practical guide for the more quantitative approach of this book. Specifically, the LENS model posits that Linguistic content influences decision-making primarily by eliciting Emotions and suggesting behavioural Norms. These emotional responses and perceived norms then interact to shape Strategic choices. See Figure 5.1.

The LENS model is not meant to be exhaustive. We can easily construct scenarios where linguistic content influences strategies via alternative pathways. For example, consider the case of technical language in financial communications. When investment firms use complex jargon in their reports, it can lead to a bifurcation in investor responses. Novice investors might feel overwhelmed or mistrustful, potentially causing them to adopt a conservative investment strategy or withdraw from engaging further. Conversely, seasoned investors often interpret this specialised language as a signal of sophistication and credibility, which might encourage them to pursue more aggressive investment strategies. This bifurcation can partly be explained

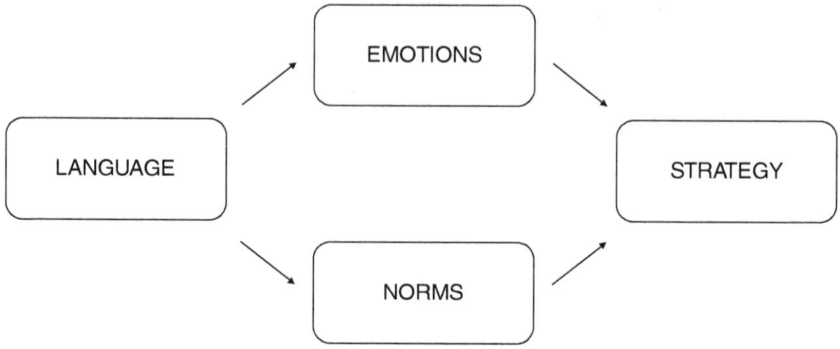

FIGURE 5.1 **Schematic representation of the LENS model.** Linguistic content influences decision-making primarily by eliciting Emotions and suggesting behavioural Norms. These emotional responses and perceived norms then interact to shape Strategic choices. Figure based on Capraro (2025).

by different emotional responses. However, the influence of this specialised language extends beyond emotional reactions. It also plays into heuristics and biases, such as the authority bias, where complex jargon may be perceived as more credible simply because it sounds sophisticated and authoritative. I refer to Farrow et al. (2018) for a more comprehensive model, according to which words can influence economic decisions through emotions, identity, spontaneous associations, and fluency.

Although it is somewhat more specific than Farrow et al.'s model, I believe the LENS model serves as a powerful framework for two main reasons. First, it synthesises a significant body of empirical research, providing a coherent and simple narrative that links language to behaviour in many situations. Second, it offers a methodological approach to quantifying linguistic elements. If linguistic content operates significantly through emotions and norms, it follows that we must develop methodologies to measure the emotional tenor and normative content of text.

This chapter elaborates on the first reason, by reviewing the literature that supports each pathway of the LENS model. Subsequent chapters will focus on the second reason, arguing that with recent advancements in large language models, we are increasing the ability to accurately quantify the emotional and normative content of texts. Such quantifications can be incorporated into utility functions, providing a more accurate understanding of decision-making processes than economically consequentialist utility functions.

THE EFFECT OF LANGUAGE ON EMOTIONS

The influence of language on emotions is evident in everyday life. For example, reading a novel can evoke deep emotions. Beyond these anecdotal observations, there is a substantial body of research exploring how linguistic content influences emotional reactions.

A relevant line of literature concerns the 'affective priming effect' (Fazio, 2001; Hinojosa et al., 2020; Klauer & Musch, 2003). This phenomenon occurs when an initial emotional or affective stimulus alters the response to a subsequent stimulus through automatic emotional processing. The effect has been documented across various modalities, including textual stimuli. For instance, encountering a positive word can cause a subsequent neutral stimulus to appear more positive, illustrating the influence of linguistic context on emotional perception (Spruyt et al., 2007). This effect is predicated on the notion that emotionally charged words play a unique role in human cognition. Research has shown that emotionally charged words, such as 'death' (negative valence) or 'party' (positive valence), are processed more quickly than neutral words like 'pen' (Kissler & Herbert, 2013; Kousta et al., 2009; Yap & Seow, 2014). Neuroscience studies have explored the neural networks activated by reading emotionally charged words. For example, Kuchinke et al. (2005) observed increased activity in the left orbitofrontal gyrus and bilateral inferior frontal gyrus when participants were exposed to emotionally charged words rather than neutral ones. These brain regions are known for their roles in processing both semantic and emotional information.

But what about economic games? Can language provoke emotions that influence strategy choices in these contexts? Admittedly, specific research on this point is scarce. However, I do have some data that shed light on this question.

Experimental Result (Linguistic Frames Influence Emotion Perception in the Dictator Game). Recall the six Dictator Game conditions differing only in the wording of the experimental instructions from Capraro and Vanzo (2019). These are extreme versions of the Dictator Game where participants are informed at the beginning that there is $0.50 available. Dictators must choose between two extremes: either the money goes to themselves, or to the recipient, with no intermediate options available. Dictators are randomly assigned to one of six treatments, which differ only in how the strategies are labelled. For example, in the steal condition, the self-interested option is labelled as 'steal from the other participant', while the altruistic option is labelled as 'don't steal from the other participant'. Conversely, in the boost condition, the self-interested distribution is labelled 'don't boost the other participant', and the altruistic one is 'boost the other participant'. The other four conditions use the verbs: give, donate, take, demand. Behavioural data show that people are highly sensitive to these linguistic frames. The percentage of people choosing the altruistic option is very low in the boost condition (about 5%), but much higher in the steal condition (29%). The rates in the other conditions are distributed in between.

In one experiment, Vanzo and I gathered a new set of participants who did not play the game and asked them to rate the emotional intensity associated with each available action and for each of the six treatments. Thus, each participant made 12 evaluations, corresponding to two actions for each of the six conditions. For instance, in the give condition, we asked participants to rate the sentiment they would feel when choosing the action 'give to the other participant' as well as the sentiment they would feel when choosing the action 'don't give to the other participant'. Responses were collected using a five-point scale from 'extremely negative' to 'extremely positive'.

Table 5.1 *Linguistic frames influence emotion perception in the Dictator Game.*

Frame	Sentiment polarity
Boost	0.295
Give	0.43
Donate	0.46
Demand	0.53
Take	0.53
Steal	0.815

Sentiment polarity, defined as the difference between the average sentiment score of the altruistic action and the average sentiment score of the self-interested action, split by frame.

Table 5.1 reports the sentiment polarity, defined as the difference between the average sentiment score of the altruistic action and that of the self-interested action, split by condition. The table clearly shows that sentiment polarity strongly depends on the frame, as hypothesised. □

The emphasis on sentiment polarity, rather than on sentiment scores of individual actions, arises from a theoretical argument about what we should expect if individuals make decisions according to a simple, linear utility function. I will explore this in detail later in the book, but it is useful to introduce some ideas here.

Consider a language-based utility function of the shape:

$$u_d(a) = \pi_d(a) + \sigma_d \; sent_d(a), \qquad (5.1)$$

where $sent_d(a)$ represents the sentiment that the dictator experiences when considering the action a (which we identified with its linguistic description) and σ_d represents the weight that the dictator assigns to following their own sentiments. Note that this utility function is not based solely on outcomes but also considers language.

Using this utility function, the key variable for determining whether the dictator makes the altruistic or the self-interested choice is the difference between the sentiment associated with the altruistic choice and that of the self-interested choice:

$$sent_d(altruistic\ choice) - sent_d(self\ interested\ choice).$$

The greater this difference, the higher the likelihood that the dictator chooses the altruistic option.

Interestingly, if the collected data is used to calculate this difference, we find that it appears to behave exactly like the percentage of altruistic choices. While the numerical values are not identical (obviously, because they are scaled differently) we can clearly see from Table 5.2 that they are ordered in the same manner. Even the relative differences between two conditions are very similar, after rescaling. Given that this data is collected with different subjects, we cannot use them to conduct a linear regression and explain individual altruistic behaviour as a function of sentiment polarity, but the overall trend is clear.

Table 5.2 *The rate of altruistic behaviour across conditions is ordered in the same manner as the sentiment polarity.*

Frame	Sentiment polarity	Altruistic behaviour
Boost	0.295	0.05
Give	0.43	0.09
Donate	0.46	0.12
Demand	0.53	0.15
Take	0.53	0.15
Steal	0.815	0.30

For each frame of the extreme Dictator Game, the second column reports its sentiment polarity (sentiment of the altruistic action minus the sentiment of the self-serving action) and the third column reports the rate of altruistic behaviour observed in Capraro and Vanzo (2019).

There are undoubtedly limitations to this approach. For example, are we really measuring sentiment, or are we capturing perceptions about the norms in the given situations? This question touches on an important link between sentiments and norms, which will be explored in depth in the next chapters.

I conclude this section by highlighting that there are situations that seemingly have little to do with norms in which language can still influence the emotional perception of a decision context.

Consider a travel agency launching a new series of holiday packages. After consulting relevant literature on the topic, the travel agency understands that younger tourists tend to be motivated by 'doing' experiences, activities that are adventurous, novel, and engaging (Richards & Wilson, 2004), whereas older tourists often prefer relaxation and comfort (Patterson & Pegg, 2013). The travel agency therefore decides to use linguistic appeals highlighting novelty and entertainment for younger travellers, while emphasising calmness and rejuvenation for senior travellers. With this idea in mind, the travel agency may develop a slogan for younger tourists aiming to stimulate feelings of excitement and adventure. For example, 'Dive into adventure with every moment on our Tropical Expedition Cruise.' Conversely, for holiday packages targeting older tourists, the campaign might aim to evoke feelings of relaxation and comfort. For instance, a slogan like 'Embrace tranquillity and find your bliss at our Soothing Spa Retreat' intends to make potential customers feel peaceful and rejuvenated, especially appealing to those seeking a restful getaway. The slogans do not suggest any new or altered norm of behaviours influenced by social or personal standards about the right thing to do; they appeal to emotions.

These examples illustrate how language can be strategically used in marketing to evoke specific emotional responses, tailoring messages to different audience segments without altering normative perceptions. Emotional responses play a crucial role in shaping consumer preferences and behaviours, often operating at a subconscious level (Bagozzi et al., 1999). Emotional appeals can enhance message persuasiveness by creating affective associations with the product or service being offered.

Furthermore, the choice of language itself, including whether to use a native or second language, can impact the emotional resonance of marketing messages. A line of research investigates whether marketing slogans produce the same emotional reaction in one's native language as they do in a second language. Puntoni et al. (2009) reported five studies providing evidence that slogans in one's native language are perceived to be more emotional than slogans in a second language. The effect depends on the frequency with which words have been experienced in native versus second-language contexts. Since emotional experiences are often first encoded and more frequently encountered in one's native language, messages delivered in one's native language can elicit stronger emotional responses.

Overall, these findings provide evidence that linguistic framings can evoke emotions independently of normative influences. While sometimes these emotions may be linked to the perception of norms, in general, they may also be unrelated to norms.

THE EFFECT OF LANGUAGE ON NORMS

We have extensive knowledge about how language influences norms. Language not only reflects norms but also shapes and reinforces them. To review this relationship, it is useful to introduce a distinction between three types of norms.

Definition (Personal Norms). Personal norms refer to internal standards about what is the right thing to do in a given situation.

Personal norms, sometimes called moral norms, were introduced in Schwartz's classic work 'Normative influences on altruism' (1977). These norms' key characteristic is their relative independence from others' opinions, even though they may develop through the internalisation of behaviours that are socially approved or disapproved. Personal norms guide behaviour based on one's sense of right and wrong. By contrast, others' opinions and behaviours are considered in the definition of injunctive and descriptive norms.

Definition (Injunctive Norms). Injunctive norms refer to personal beliefs about what others approve or disapprove of.

Definition (Descriptive Norms). Descriptive norms refer to personal beliefs about what others do or do not do in a given situation.

Descriptive and injunctive norms were introduced by Cialdini et al. (1990, 1991) and are collectively referred to as social norms. Descriptive norms capture perceptions of common behaviour, while injunctive norms involve perceptions of what is socially approved or disapproved. These norms influence behaviour by informing individuals about effective actions (descriptive norms) and appropriate actions (injunctive norms). More recently, Bicchieri (2005) introduced the concepts of empirical expectations and normative expectations, which roughly correspond to descriptive and injunctive norms, respectively. Empirical expectations involve beliefs about what others do, while normative expectations involve beliefs about what others think one ought to do.

Although in many cases personal norms, descriptive norms, and injunctive norms may be aligned, there are instances where they diverge. For example, consider a vegan individual whose social groups (family, friends, colleagues) do not share the same dietary choice. In this situation, the personal norm (the individual's internal standard about what is right) is in contrast with the social norm (the behaviours and expectations of their social groups). It is likely that the vegan person will tend to surround themselves with other vegans, but this is a consequence of their choice to be vegan combined with the human tendency to form homophilic social groups, rather than the cause of their being vegan. In this example, there is a misalignment between personal norms and social norms.

For an example of misalignment between descriptive and injunctive norms, consider statistics from 2020 indicating that 64%

of Italians believe that infidelity is morally unacceptable (injunctive norm). However, in 70% of couples, at least one partner cheats at least once (descriptive norm). This illustrates a gap between what people believe others should do and what happens in practice.

Coming to our question, can linguistic framings influence norm perception? The answer is affirmative for various norms and games.

Experimental Result (Linguistic Frames Impact Personal Norms in the Equity–Efficiency Trade-Off Game). In a 2018 study that I co-authored with Rand, we asked people to report what they personally believe is the morally right thing to do (personal norm) in various games, including the two frames of the Equity–Efficiency Trade-Off Game. Recall that in this game, participants choose between two distributions of money: one where all participants receive the same amount (equal distribution), and the other where all participants receive at least as much as they do in the equal distribution but receive different amounts (efficient but unequal distribution).

- **In the equal frame**, the equal distribution is labelled as the 'nice' choice because it equalises the payoffs of all participants.
- **In the generous frame**, the efficient distribution is labelled as the 'nice' choice because it increases the payoffs of the participants.

The results revealed that participants' personal norms were massively impacted by the frame. Over 86% of participants reported that choosing the efficient distribution was the morally right thing to do in the generous frame, whereas only 23% said the same in the equal frame. See Figure 5.2. □

Experimental Result (Linguistic Frames Impact Injunctive Norms in the Dictator Game). Kuang and Bicchieri (2024a) conducted an experiment where subjects were randomly assigned to 16 conditions. In all conditions, they played a Dictator Game where the recipient was a charity. The conditions differed in the messages participants received before deciding.

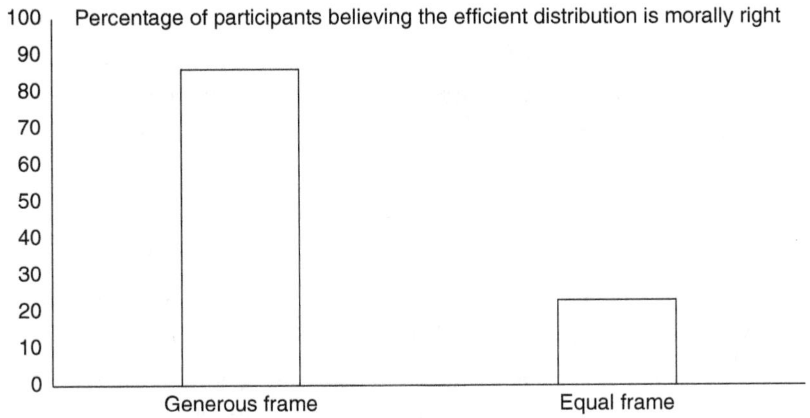

FIGURE 5.2 **Linguistic frames impact personal norms in the Equity–Efficiency Trade-Off Game**. Percentage of people reporting that the efficient distribution is the morally right thing to do across frames in Capraro and Rand (2018), Study 4.

- **In the baseline**, they received no message.
- **In the 'indirect injunction' condition**, the authors included a message pushing subjects to donate all the money, but without giving normative information: 'Donate all 10 tokens to the charity.'
- **The other 14 messages had a 7 × 2 structure:**
  - The seven-level factor referred to different words used to activate the injunctive norm ('appropriate', 'desirable', 'approved', 'okay', 'permissible', 'should', 'the right thing').
  - The two-level factor referred to the way the injunctive norm was activated:
    - In the **direct injunction treatments**, the norm was activated through a direct message like 'People should donate all 10 tokens to the charity'.
    - In the **social information treatments**, participants were informed explicitly about others' beliefs: 'Most people think one should donate all 10 tokens to the charity.'

The authors studied the level of compliance with the norm, that is, the percentage of people choosing to donate all 10 tokens to the charity. Results showed that the level of compliance highly depended on both the linguistic framing used to activate the injunctive norm and the way the norm was activated. Overall, the direct injunction treatments led to significantly higher compliance rates than the social information treatments. Within each treatment, however, there was significant heterogeneity across linguistic framings. In the direct injunction, the 'should' framing led to the highest compliance rate (22%), while the lowest compliance rate was observed with the 'permissible' frame (9%). In the social information treatments, the linguistic frames that provided the highest compliance rates were the 'should' and 'right thing to do' framings (12%), and the ones with the lowest compliance rates were the 'approved' and 'okay' framings (4%), which were not statistically significantly different from the compliance rate in the control (5%). Interestingly, the highest compliance rate was generated by the indirect injunction (35%). See Figure 5.3. □

In a recent review, Kuang and Bicchieri (2024b) introduced a structural framework to categorise empirical studies on how

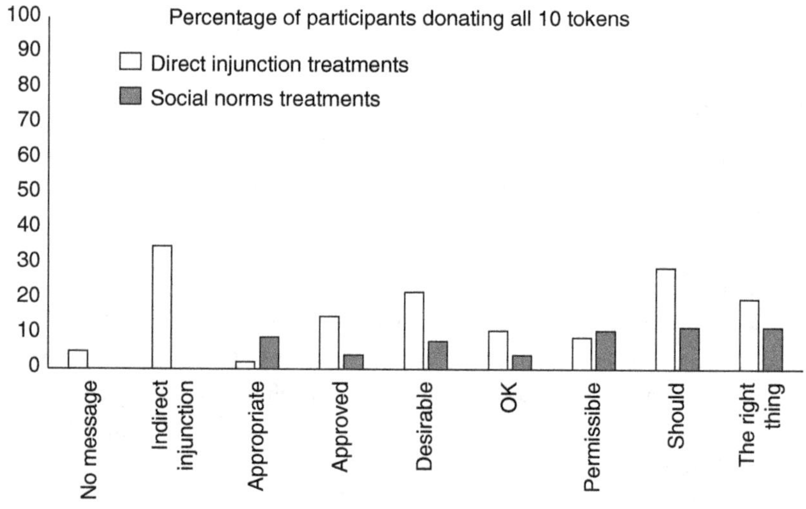

FIGURE 5.3 **Linguistic frames impact injunctive norms in the Dictator Game**. Percentage of people choosing to donate all 10 tokens to a charity, across treatments. Treatments differed in the linguistic framing used to convey the injunctive norm. Figure based on Kuang and Bicchieri (2024b).

linguistic framing impacts social norms. Their model proposes that this influence operates through five primary, non-mutually exclusive mechanisms: directing attention, inducing context-specific pragmatic inferences, changing the point of reference, biasing trustworthiness and credibility judgements, and eliciting emotions. Accordingly, they report additional instances of how linguistic frames can influence social norm perceptions:

- **Directing attention:** Linguistic framing can highlight aspects of a situation, thereby affecting social norms. For instance, using gender-neutral pronouns instead of masculine ones when describing individuals involved in political activities enhances the cognitive accessibility of female politicians, which has the consequence of increasing the acceptability of female politicians (Tavits & Pérez, 2019).
- **Inducing context-specific pragmatic inferences:** Linguistic framing can make social norms ambiguous, thus allowing self-serving interpretations. For example, vague statements like 'many people recycle' allow for the interpretation that 'not everyone recycles', which can be used to justify self-serving behaviour (Kuang & Bicchieri, 2024c).
- **Changing the point of reference:** Language framing can change social references (e.g., rank versus average comparisons), temporal focus (present versus future orientation), and social distance (proximal versus distal groups). For example, using rank-framed messages (i.e., indicating how one's behaviour ranks among others) compared to mean-framed messages (i.e., comparing one's behaviour to the average person) has been shown to reduce excessive alcohol consumption among college students (Taylor et al., 2015) and increase consumers' willingness to pay for healthy foods (Aldrovandi et al., 2015). Additionally, employing a future-oriented framing (e.g., 'people started to make an effort to do good') is more effective in promoting environmentally friendly behaviours like reducing water waste and meat consumption than a present-oriented framing (e.g., 'people make an effort to do good') (Sparkman & Walton, 2017). Furthermore, providing descriptive norm information about specific and socially close reference groups (e.g., your friends) is more effective in promoting pro-health behaviour changes than information about distant and heterogeneous groups (e.g., people in general) (Rabb et al., 2022). Beyond influencing social reference

points, linguistic frames also alter perceptions of individual reference points, for example by providing cues about gains versus losses. For example, merely changing a word – from 'compensation' to 'payment' – can shift perceptions regarding an environmental policy proposal (Clot et al., 2017).

- **Biasing trustworthiness and credibility judgements:** Linguistic framing can influence how credible and trustworthy information is perceived to be. For instance, statements with identical content are more likely to be considered more credible when framed negatively (e.g., '25% of people disapprove of a negative behaviour') rather than positively (e.g., '75% of people approve of a positive behaviour') (Jaffé & Greifeneder, 2019).
- **Eliciting emotions:** Finally, linguistic framing can influence social norms by provoking emotions. For example, in a study aimed at increasing flossing behaviour, participants experienced stronger anger when receiving a message with strong prescriptive language (e.g., 'Do it because you have to. Floss every single day.') rather than one framed as a suggestion (e.g., 'Why not give it a try?'). This anger indicates a state of reactance, leading to an unfavourable attitude toward the desired norm and reducing behavioural intention (Dillard & Shen, 2005).

In sum, linguistic framings can influence the perception of personal and social norms. Along with the previous section (which showed that linguistic framings can evoke emotions) we have now completed the 'left half' of the LENS model. In the next two sections, we move to the 'right half' of the model, and I show that emotions and norms can differentially impact human behaviour in a variety of contexts, with a specific focus on economic decisions and games.

THE EFFECT OF EMOTIONS ON BEHAVIOUR

The role of emotions in behaviour has a rich history in economics and psychology. Several theoretical models have attempted to formalise how various emotions may influence people's behaviour (Bracha & Brown, 2012; Kőszegi, 2006; Loewenstein, 2000; Loewenstein et al., 2001; Neilson, 2009). In this section, I review two types of experimental studies on the effects of emotions. One examines the impact of transient emotions induced in laboratory settings, while the other employs a broader dual-process approach, wherein participants are instructed to 'rely on emotions' rather than 'rely on reason'. Not surprisingly, both experimental manipulations can significantly affect behaviour across various contexts.

Experimental Result (Transient Emotions Influence Behaviour in Various Economic Decisions and Games). The role of emotions in economic behaviour has been studied in several economic decisions and games, including the Dictator Game, the Ultimatum Game, and the Prisoner's Dilemma (Andrade & Ariely, 2009; Castagnetti et al., 2018, 2023; Harlé & Sanfey, 2007; Ibanez et al., 2017; Motro et al., 2018; Tan & Forgas, 2010). The overall pattern of results suggests that incidental emotions artificially caused in the laboratory can significantly influence subsequent decisions.

A particularly interesting study that highlights how different emotions can have distinct effects was carried out by Motro et al. (2018), who examined the effects of anger and guilt on dishonest behaviour. The researchers hypothesised that anger would heighten impulsive tendencies, leading to increased dishonesty, while guilt might prompt individuals to reflect on past mistakes, making moral considerations more prominent and thereby enhancing honest behaviour.

In the first experiment, the researchers recruited 116 American college students as participants. The participants were presented with a set of 20 matrices. Each matrix comprised 12 unique three-digit numbers. Participants were given six minutes to identify and circle two numbers in each matrix that added up to 10 (e.g., 3.18 and 6.82). They were informed that they would earn $0.25 for each correctly solved matrix at the end of the experimental session. After the allotted time, the experimenter announced that time was up and instructed participants to move on to the next task.

To induce feelings of anger and guilt, the researchers employed an emotion-induction writing task. Participants were instructed to write in detail about a time when they vividly experienced either anger or guilt. They were asked to immerse themselves in the specific emotion, describe the experience thoroughly, and avoid mentioning any other feelings. Those in the neutral condition were asked to describe the class they were currently in.

At the conclusion of the experimental session, participants were told to compensate themselves based on their performance in the matrix task. Each participant had an envelope containing $5 in quarters on their desk and was instructed to take $0.25 for each matrix they had correctly solved. To ensure anonymity and confidentiality, they were asked to discard their answer sheets in a recycling bin at the back of the room before exiting the lab. Unbeknownst to the participants, the final matrix in each packet included a unique three-digit identification code, allowing the researchers to match the worksheets to the corresponding envelopes.

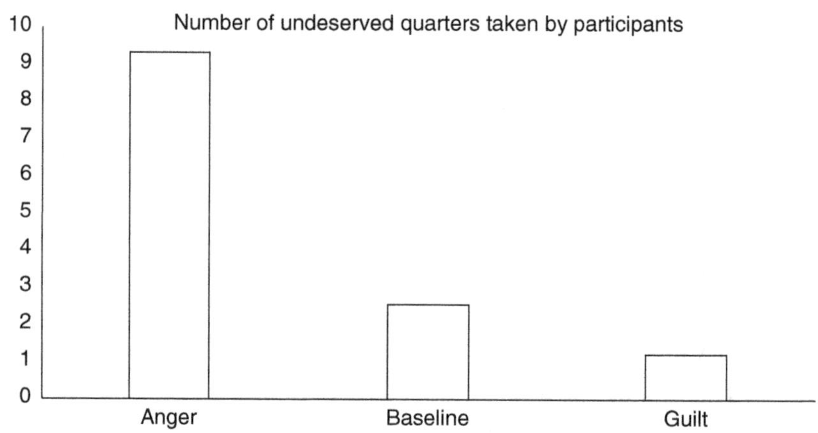

FIGURE 5.4 **Transient emotions influence behaviour in a cheating task.** Number of undeserved quarters taken by participants across emotion condition in Study 1 by Motro et al. (2018). Cheating among participants induced to feel angry was eight times higher than cheating among participants induced to feel guilty.

The researchers then analysed the number of undeserved quarters taken by participants in each emotional condition. Cheating among angry participants was, on average, more than twice that observed in the neutral group and, remarkably, over eight times greater than in the guilt condition. See Figure 5.4. □

Experimental Result ('Relying on Emotions' as Opposed to 'Relying on Reason' Influences Decision-Making in Various Contexts). Another line of studies has adopted a more general dual-process perspective to explore whether encouraging individuals to broadly 'rely on emotions', as opposed to 'rely on reason', influences their behaviour. This approach has been applied both in controlled experiments, such as the Prisoner's Dilemma (Gärtner et al., 2022; Levine et al., 2018), and in real-life scenarios, such as individuals' intentions to wear face masks during the COVID-19 pandemic (Capraro & Barcelo, 2021).

For example, Levine et al. (2018; Study 3) recruited participants online through Amazon Mechanical Turk and randomly assigned them to one of two groups, where participants were instructed to rely either on reason or emotion when making their choices. Next, participants considered two scenarios: one where their partner, Player A, used emotion to make their decision, and another where the partner used reason. For each case, participants first predicted what decision Player A would make. Subsequently, they were asked to make their own decision by relying on either emotion or reason, according to their initial assignment.

The findings revealed that participants in the emotion condition were more likely to cooperate than those in the reason condition, regardless of their partner's decision-making approach. Specifically, when playing with a partner who made decisions using emotion, 57.0% of participants in the emotion condition chose to cooperate, compared to 31.5% in the reason condition. When interacting with a partner who relied on reason, 46.9% of participants in the emotion condition cooperated, versus 33.2% in the reason condition. See Figure 5.5. □

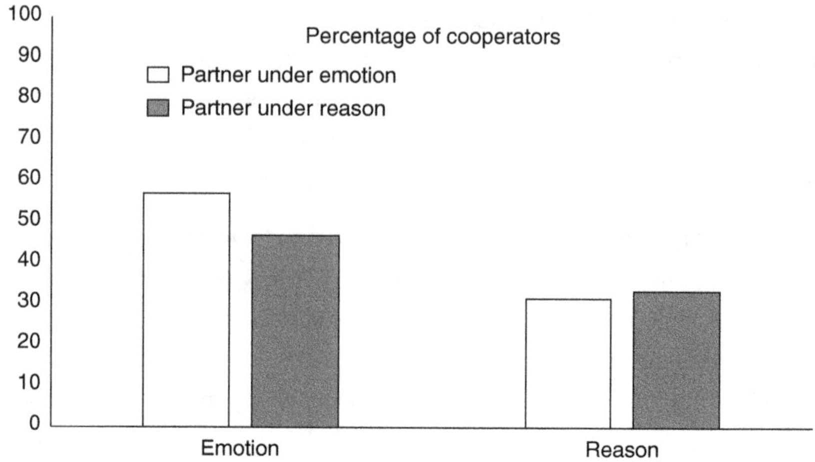

FIGURE 5.5 **Relying on emotion increases cooperative behaviour compared to relying on reason**. Percentage of participants who cooperated in the Prisoner's Dilemma when instructed to 'rely on emotion' versus 'rely on reason', depending on the information provided about their partner; specifically, whether the partner was described as relying on reason or emotion. Figure based on Levine et al. (2018), Study 3.

THE EFFECTS OF NORMS ON BEHAVIOUR

The study of the effects of norms on behaviour has a long history, dating back at least to the foundational work by Schwartz (1977). We have already encountered Schwartz's article in previous sections, where I introduced the distinction between personal and social norms. In the same study, the author also examined the explanatory power of personal norms on altruistic behaviour.

According to Schwartz, altruistic behaviour is influenced by the intensity of the moral obligation an individual feels when considering a helping action. This sense of obligation emerges from evaluating an action against the associated norms and values. These evaluations are driven by the anticipation of negative emotions (such as guilt) from failing to meet a moral standard, or positive emotions (such as pride) from fulfilling it.

To measure personal norms in situations related to altruism, Schwartz asked participants about their 'feelings of personal/moral obligations' associated with certain altruistic behaviours. He chose this approach because individuals experience feelings of obligation before taking action, whereas emotions like guilt or pride occur afterward and can only be anticipated. Supporting this method, several studies have found that personal norms correlate more strongly with altruistic behaviour and intentions than anticipated guilt does (Fellner & Schwartz, 1971; Heberlein & Black, 1976; Pomazal, 1974).

Moreover, framing the measure in terms of obligation is advantageous because it remains neutral with respect to the type of emotion involved; it can reflect both the avoidance of negative feelings and the pursuit of positive ones. The qualifier 'personal/moral' was used to emphasise that the obligation is self-generated. However, Schwartz noted that it is not entirely clear which term is preferable: while 'moral' may better prompt individuals to consider their internalised value system, it may also generate some reactance due to its association with conventional moral standards.

The experiments mentioned earlier do not establish a causal link between personal norms and behaviour, because both were measured within a short time frame (e.g., in Pomazal's experiment, personal norms were elicited five days before a blood donation event). This close temporal proximity means that personal norms and behaviour might merely be correlated rather than causally linked. One way to address this issue is to measure personal norms well in advance of the decision, while also assessing the degree to which they are internalised; the more internalised they are, the stronger their expected connection to altruistic behaviour.

Experimental Result (Internalised Personal Norms Are Associated with Altruistic Behaviour, with a Caveat). With this in mind, Schwartz conducted a study in which first-year students at the University of Wisconsin completed an extensive questionnaire at the start of the semester, covering topics ranging from personality to politics. Embedded within the questionnaire were items measuring personal norms regarding eight altruistic behaviours. Approximately three months later, a subset of these students completed the same questionnaire as part of a larger survey on their initial university experiences. Then, about two months afterward, the students received a letter asking if they would be willing to devote a few hours each week to reading for blind children at a school. Schwartz created an index of personal norm stability by quantifying how much personal norms changed between the two assessments. He then divided the sample into two groups, those with little variability in personal norms and those with considerable variability.

The findings showed that the correlation between personal norms and altruistic behaviour was significant among students with stable personal norms, but not among those with more variable norms. (The results were not reported in sufficient detail to permit the reconstruction of a figure; therefore, no figure is provided for this study.)

Although this study comes close to demonstrating a causal link between personal norms and altruistic behaviour, it has some limitations. Specifically, the study does not specify the criteria used to split the sample into low- and high-variability groups, nor does it report the interaction between personal norms and behaviour. It is important to note that a statistically significant effect in one group but not in another does not necessarily imply that the two effects are statistically different. □

In the concluding section of his work, Schwartz reviewed experimental evidence supporting the hypothesis that altruism is primarily driven by personal rather than social norms. The strongest support comes from studies that measured both types of norms and compared their predictive power. For example, the Pomazal (1974) study asked participants to report what two reference networks (important others and partners) believed they should do regarding blood donations, while the Heberlein and Black (1976) study inquired about the expectations of participants' best friends concerning the purchase of unleaded petrol. Both studies found that personal norms were more strongly correlated with altruistic behaviour than social norms.

A series of more recent studies has attempted to investigate the role of different norms in various economic games more thoroughly.

Experimental Result (Personal and Injunctive Norms Play a Role in the Iterated Public Good Game). Dal Bó and Dal Bó (2014) conducted a study using a repeated two-player Public Good Game in which players were re-paired each round to avoid direct reciprocity effects. In every round, players decided whether to invest in a joint project, with the total investment multiplied by 1.4 and then divided equally between them. The experiment lasted for 20 rounds. Between rounds 10 and 11, participants received one of four different messages, or a blank control message. The experimental treatments were as follows:

- **Control treatment:** Blank message.
- **Self-regarding treatment:** 'Please read this message carefully: the assumption of game theory is that rational and self-regarding individuals will maximise their own payoffs. If you were to act accordingly, you would allocate 0 to the joint account.'
- **Golden rule treatment:** 'Please read this message carefully: an action of yours is moral if it treats others the way you would like others to treat you. If you were to act accordingly, you would allocate 10 to the joint account.'
- **Utilitarian treatment:** 'Please read this message carefully: an action of yours is moral if it maximises the sum of everyone's payoffs. If you were to act accordingly, you would allocate 10 to the joint account.'
- **Suggestion treatment:** 'Please read this message carefully: you could consider allocating all your endowment to the joint account. If you were to act accordingly, you would allocate 10 to the joint account.'

It is worth noting that the authors considered two moral messages appealing to different rules. The utilitarian message emphasised the positive consequences for society that result from cooperation, while the golden rule message invoked broader principles of reciprocity. This design allowed the researchers to assess which moral principle was more effective in promoting cooperation. Furthermore, participants were informed that their paired partners received the same message, meaning the moral messages could influence both personal norms and injunctive norms.

The study involved 320 students from the University of California, Berkeley, who interacted via computer. In the first 10 rounds, participants displayed the typical pattern for repeated Public Good Games: the level of cooperation declined over time, with no differences observed between treatments. However, after the message was delivered in round 11, significant differences emerged. The utilitarian message increased cooperation from 24.7% to 49.8%, more than doubling it, while the golden rule message had an even larger effect, boosting cooperation from 11.1% to 43.8%. It is important to note that part of these effects may have been due to a 'restart effect', as even the control group showed a marginal increase in cooperation after receiving the blank message (from 16.4% to 21.8%). Similarly, there was a 'suggestion effect' as well, as the suggestion treatment increased cooperation from 17.7% to 37%.

Therefore, in a further analysis, the authors compared the effects of the two moral messages to those of the blank and suggestion messages, to control for restart and suggestion effects. They found that the increase in cooperation from the golden rule message was significantly larger than that from either the blank or suggestion messages. In contrast, although the utilitarian message produced a greater increase than the blank message, its effect was not statistically different from that of the suggestion treatment.

Subsequently, the authors examined longer-term effects by comparing the average level of cooperation in the second half of the experiment (after the message) with that in the first half (before the message). They discovered that only the two moral messages maintained cooperation levels in the second half that were not statistically lower than those in the first half. Moreover, average cooperation in the second half for both the golden rule and utilitarian treatments was higher than in the suggestion treatment, and the same was true when compared with the blank message, although the contrast

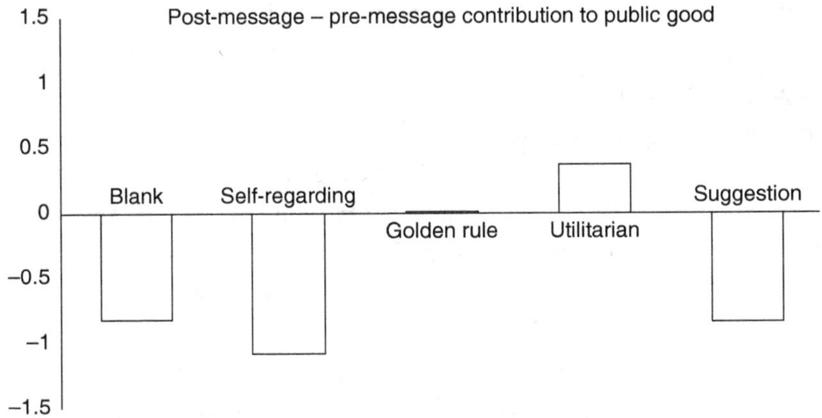

FIGURE 5.6 **Moral messages increase contributions to the iterated Public Good Game.** Frequency of cooperation in the 10 rounds of the iterated Public Good Game played after receiving the message minus the frequency of cooperation in the 10 rounds before receiving the message. The golden rule and utilitarian messages are the only ones for which contributions do not keep decreasing over rounds; in the utilitarian treatment they actually increase. Figure based on Dal Bó and Dal Bó (2014).

between the blank and golden rule treatments did not reach statistical significance. These findings suggest that the effect of moral messages cannot be attributed solely to suggestion or restart effects. See Figure 5.6.

A follow-up study analysed the effect of the golden rule message by examining participants' expectations. In this study, participants were informed that the computer would randomly decide whether they would see the message. This design was intended to reduce the impact of injunctive norms, since only half of the participants saw the message. Even in this scenario, the golden rule message increased cooperation relative to the blank message, although the effect was smaller than in the first study. This suggests that the moral message operates at least partly through injunctive norms.

However, an increase in cooperation compared to the blank message does not allow us to conclude that the moral message also affects personal norms, because this design only reduces (but does not eliminate) the effect of injunctive norms. To address this, the authors conducted a fourth study to investigate whether the golden rule message also altered individuals' preferences. In this experiment, the opponent's message was fixed, and the focal player's cooperation was compared between receiving the blank message and the moral message. Since the other player's message remained constant, any additional increase in cooperation after the moral message would indicate a change in the focal player's preferences. The results showed that even under these conditions, the golden rule message increased cooperation.

Based on these findings, Dal Bó and Dal Bó (2014) concluded that the golden rule message influences cooperation through both personal norms and injunctive norms. □

Experimental Result (Personal Norms Influence Behaviour in the Equity–Efficiency Trade-Off Game More than Descriptive Norms). In our 2018 article, Rand and I compared the influence of personal norms versus descriptive norms in the context of the Equity–Efficiency Trade-Off Game using an experimental technique that creates a conflict between these norms. We started from the two basic frames of the Trade-Off Game:

- **Equal frame:** The phrase 'be nice' described the equal economic distribution (13,13,13).
- **Generous frame:** The label 'be nice' described the efficient economic distribution (15,23,13).

In Study 5, we manipulated the descriptive norm by splitting each of the previous frames into two conditions:

- **Aligned descriptive norm:** Participants were informed that four out of five previous players had implemented the 'nice' distribution.
- **Misaligned descriptive norm:** Participants were told that four out of five previous players had not implemented the 'nice' distribution.

The results revealed that this manipulation of the descriptive norm had no effect on decisions: most participants continued to choose the option labelled 'nice' regardless of what others had done.

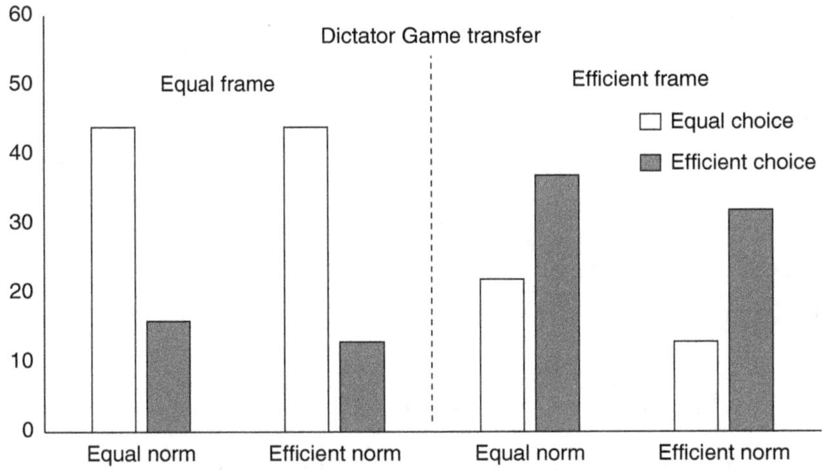

FIGURE 5.7 **Personal norms influence behaviour in the Equity–Efficiency Trade-Off Game more than descriptive norms.** Dictator Game transfers across various conditions, categorised by whether participants chose the equal or efficient distribution in the Trade-Off Game. In the equal frame, participants who chose the equal distribution donated more than those who chose the efficient distribution, regardless of the descriptive norm. Similarly, in the efficient frame, participants who chose the efficient distribution donated more than those who chose the equal distribution, again regardless of the descriptive norm. Figure based on Capraro and Rand (2018), Study 4.

Did they follow the personal norm? Our fourth study strongly suggests so, as we measured moral judgements associated with the different options and found that participants overwhelmingly judged the option labelled 'nice' as the morally right choice, irrespective of whether it was applied to the equitable or efficient option. These findings suggest that in the Equity–Efficiency Trade-Off Game, personal norms exert a stronger influence on behaviour than descriptive norms. See Figure 5.7. □

Experimental Result (Making Personal and Injunctive Norms Salient Influences Decisions in the Dictator Game and Prisoner's Dilemma). In Chapter 3, I already reviewed a 2019 study that I co-authored with Jagfeld, Klein, Mul, and van de Pol, in which we demonstrated that making either personal norms or injunctive norms salient

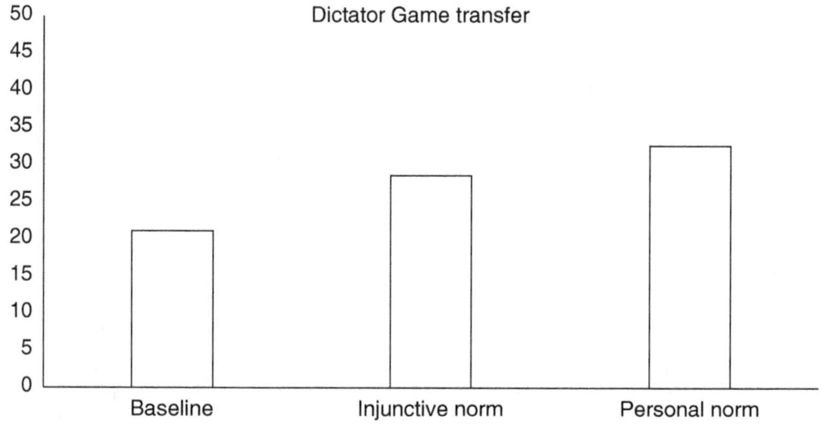

FIGURE 5.8 **Making personal and injunctive norms salient increases altruistic behaviour in the Dictator Game.** Average transfer across conditions. Figure based on Capraro et al. (2019b), Study 1.

significantly increased altruistic behaviour in the Dictator Game. Interestingly, the effect size was comparable across the two types of norms. See Figure 5.8.

Moreover, a qualitatively similar result was also obtained in the Prisoner's Dilemma. This suggests that both personal norms and injunctive norms can promote altruistic and cooperative behaviour. □

Experimental Result (Personal Norms Influence Behaviour in the Sender–Receiver Game More than Injunctive Norms, with a Caveat). Alempaki et al. (2021) investigated the roles of personal and injunctive norms in a Sender–Receiver Game, within a broader set of four studies that examined how language (native vs foreign) influences norm formation and honest behaviour. In the first experiment, only injunctive norms were measured; in the second, only behaviour was assessed; in the third, both behaviour and both types of norms were measured; and in the fourth, both behaviour and personal norms were examined. Here, I focus on the third experiment, which allows for a direct comparison of the relative associations of the two norms with behaviour.

Before playing the Sender–Receiver Game, participants completed a task in which they could earn money based on their performance. Specifically, they were shown two 10 × 10 matrices containing randomly generated two-digit numbers. Participants had to find the largest number in the right-hand matrix and the largest number in the left-hand matrix, then add these two numbers together. They had eight minutes to 'solve' as many pairs of matrices as possible, up to a maximum of 20, and they earned one point for each correct response. However, they were not told whether their answer was correct, nor were they shown their cumulative score as they proceeded in the game.

When the eight minutes (or 20 pairs of matrices) were over, participants moved on to the second phase of the game. This was a Sender–Receiver Game where the receiver is passive. In this phase, participants were told they would be paired with one another, and that each of them had a 50% chance of playing as the sender. After the roles were assigned, the sender was informed of the point difference between the sender and the receiver. The sender was then asked to send a message to the receiver, choosing from 11 possible messages:

- 'I have more than 5 points more than you' (Payoff: 20 tokens for sender, 0 for receiver)
- 'I have 4 points more than you' (18 tokens for sender, 2 for receiver)
- ...
- 'I have the same points as you' (10 tokens for sender, 10 for receiver)
- ...
- 'I have 4 points fewer than you' (2 tokens for sender, 18 for receiver)
- 'I have more than 5 points fewer than you' (0 tokens for sender, 20 for receiver)

If the sender chose the first message, the sender would earn 20 tokens and the receiver would earn 0; if the sender chose the second message, the sender would earn 18 tokens and the receiver 2 tokens, and so on, down to the last message, where the sender earned 0 tokens and the receiver earned 20.

Table 5.3 *Personal norms explain honest behaviour in the Sender–Receiver Game more than injunctive norms.*

Probability of truth-telling	
Monetary payoff	0.322***
Injunctive norm	0.014
Personal norm	2.340***

Results are from a logistic regression predicting the probability of truth-telling as a function of the associated monetary payoff, ratings of social appropriateness (incentivised to match others' ratings; injunctive norm), and personal ratings of social appropriateness. ***: $p < 0.01$. Data from Alempaki et al. (2021).

The injunctive norm was elicited using the method of Krupka and Weber (2013), asking subjects to assess the social appropriateness of each of the sender's possible actions. Participants received a prize if their choice of the most socially appropriate action matched that of a randomly selected participant. The personal norm was elicited by asking participants which choice they personally believed to be socially appropriate.

The results showed a certain degree of heterogeneity between the two norms, differing in 46% of cases. This was also reflected in the predictive power of the norms: personal norms were more strongly associated with behaviour than injunctive norms. Furthermore, when both norms were included as regressors, only the personal norm remained statistically significant. See Table 5.3. □

Although this study suggests that honesty in the Sender–Receiver Game is driven primarily by personal norms, another explanation is also possible: that people may be more inclined to use personal norms to justify their own behaviour. Such tendency may arise from both social and personal motivations. For example, from a social perspective, signalling one's moral character can offer significant reputational benefits compared to merely appearing moral. From a personal standpoint, individuals might prefer to justify their behaviour based on their own values rather than being seen as mere followers of external opinions.

Experimental Result (Personal Norms Are More Associated with Cooperative Behaviour than Social Norms). A first step towards overcoming this methodological limitation has been taken by Catola et al. (2021). Their research introduced three novel elements: it quantified the relative contributions of personal, descriptive, and injunctive norms; it employed a strategic game; and, in their second study, it partially overcame the methodological limitation of measuring norms immediately after behaviour.

In the first study, 164 UK participants recruited via Prolific played a Public Good Game in groups of four. Each player was given 10 tokens and had to decide how many tokens to invest in a public good, with the total contributions multiplied by 0.6 and then equally divided among the players, regardless of individual contributions. After making their decision, participants reported their opinions on three aspects: how much a person should contribute (personal norm), how much they believed other group members thought one should contribute (injunctive norm), and how much they believed others would contribute (descriptive norm). The elicitation of the two social norms was incentivised with a 10-cent bonus.

The findings revealed that personal norms were almost perfectly aligned with actual behaviour. The average contribution to the public good was 6.09 tokens, while the average personal norm was 6.02 tokens, virtually identical. In contrast, the average descriptive norm was 5.07 tokens, and the average injunctive norm was 5.12 tokens; both were significantly lower than the average contribution. Statistical models, which included pairs of norms and all three norms together as predictors of contribution, consistently showed that personal norms had the strongest explanatory power. See Figure 5.9.

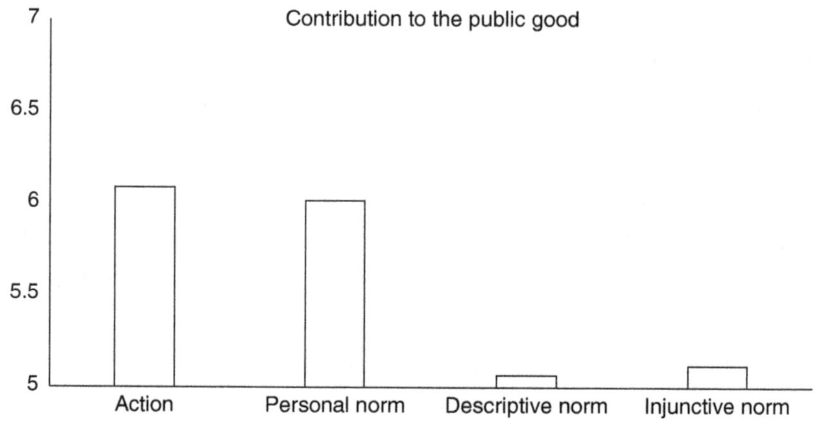

FIGURE 5.9 **Personal norms are more associated with cooperative behaviour than social norms**. The contribution participants perceive as morally right closely aligns with their actual contribution. In contrast, the contribution they expect from other players, as well as the contribution they believe others consider appropriate, are both significantly lower. Figure based on Catola et al. (2021).

This result was interpreted as initial evidence that behaviour in a one-shot and anonymous Public Good Game is primarily driven by personal norms. However, as described earlier, a key limitation of this approach is that asking about norms immediately after the game can introduce self-justification effects.

To address this issue, the authors conducted a second study in which 104 UK residents, also recruited on Prolific, were asked to express their judgements about norms in the same Public Good Game without actually making any decision in the game. The norms measured in this study were very similar to those obtained in the first study, supporting the conclusion that personal norms are more strongly associated with behaviour in a private Public Good Game than social norms are.

This work partially addresses the issue of self-justification, though some statistical limitations remain. In their second experiment, the authors measured norms separately from the decision and found them to be statistically similar to those obtained immediately afterward. They concluded that the timing of norm measurement did not affect the results. However, interpreting null effects is inherently difficult, as they can result from various underlying factors. Additionally, there is a potential issue related to the transitivity of statistical (non-)significance: while the first experiment found no statistical difference between personal norms and behaviour, and the second found no difference between separately measured norms and those measured immediately after the decision, this does not necessarily imply that separately measured norms are statistically indistinguishable from behaviour. The same caution applies to other types of norms and cross-comparisons. Thus, while the results are consistent with the interpretation that personal norms have a stronger influence on behaviour, the statistical evidence remains weak. □

Experimental Result (Personal Norms Are More Associated with Behaviour than Injunctive Norms in Several Economic Decisions). I conclude this section by discussing a paper that has the advantage of measuring personal and injunctive norms among the same subjects over a considerable time span and in four different economic games, both public and private. Specifically, Bašić and Verrina (2024) examined:

- **The classic Dictator Game** (with an initial sum of €10).
- **Dictator Game with punishment:** The Dictator Game followed by a stage in which an external observer is informed of the dictator's choice and can decide whether to pay a cost to punish them (variable of interest: punishment).
- **The Ultimatum Game** (variable of interest: second-player behaviour).
- **The Dictator Game with a tax:** Identical to the classic Dictator Game but with two differences: the initial sum was €12 instead of €10, and donations were reduced by 40% (the tax). The first difference was introduced solely to simplify the calculations: donating €6 equalised the economic payoffs of both the dictator and the recipient before tax was applied; however, if the dictator wanted to match final, post-tax payoffs, they would have to donate €7.50.

The experiment was divided into two parts. In the first phase, participants took part online, with the goal of measuring personal and injunctive norms in the four games. This first part was conducted about a month before the subsequent part, to minimise the risk that participants would remember the norms they reported in the first part. In this initial online phase, participants were informed about the four games in random order, and within each of the four games, both personal and injunctive norms were measured, also in random order.

For every available action, personal norms were measured by asking participants to assess, based on their own opinion and independently of what others might think, whether choosing that action was appropriate or not. 'Appropriate behaviour' was defined as behaviour that the participant personally deemed 'correct' or 'moral'.

Injunctive norms were measured by asking participants to assess, in accordance with society's opinion and regardless of their own, whether that action was appropriate or not. In this case, 'appropriate behaviour' was defined as behaviour that the participant believed most people in society would consider 'correct' or 'moral'.

About a month after the norms were measured, participants were invited to the lab for the behavioural experiment. There, they played the four games in random order. Player pairings were anonymous and were randomly reshuffled after each game to avoid any reputational effects. The participants were divided into two treatments:

- **Private treatment:** Decisions remained completely anonymous.
- **Public treatment:** Participants were informed that at the end of the experiment they would stand up, say their name out loud, and report what they had chosen in each game. They could not lie because their decisions would be displayed on a screen.

The experiment was conducted with 250 students at the University of Cologne. In the first step of their analysis, Bašić and Verrina showed that, although personal norms are strongly correlated with injunctive norms (correlation coefficients around 0.7 in all four games), there is still substantial heterogeneity. For each individual, in each game and for each action, the authors calculated the difference between injunctive and personal norms and showed that this difference is zero in only about half of the possible actions.

They then used a statistical model to investigate the relative contributions of these norms. In the model, the dependent variable was defined for each possible action as a binary variable indicating whether a player chose that action. The independent variables were three characteristics of the option: the economic payoff, the personal norm, and the injunctive norm. First, Bašić and Verrina estimated their model in the 'private' treatment.

When combining the four games, the authors observed that all three factors (economic payoff, personal norm, and social norm) were positively associated with choosing the action. However, interestingly, the dominant factor turned out to be the personal norm, while the injunctive norm and economic payoff played secondary roles (about half as influential as personal norms) and were statistically indistinguishable from each other.

Subsequently, the authors investigated the difference between the 'private' and 'public' treatments. To do so, they pooled all the data collected and considered a statistical model that included two interaction terms: personal norm × public and injunctive norm × public. The underlying idea was that injunctive norms should become more influential in public settings, which should be reflected in a positive interaction for injunctive norm × public. Conversely, personal norms should play the same role in both public and private treatments, which should be reflected in a non-significant interaction for personal norm × public.

The results broadly confirmed these trends. When pooling all four games together, the injunctive norm × public interaction was significantly positive. On the other hand, none of the personal norm × public interactions were statistically significant, even when pooling all four games together. See Table 5.4. □

To summarise, the results presented in this section provide converging evidence that norms influence behaviour in economic

Table 5.4 *Personal norms are associated with behaviour in anonymous games, more than injunctive norms.*

Likelihood of selecting an option	
Monetary payoff	0.358***
Injunctive norm	0.371***
Personal norm	0.895***
Injunctive norm × Public	0.748***
Personal norm × Public	0.091

Results are from a logistic regression predicting the likelihood of selecting each option as a function of the associated monetary payoff, the injunctive norm rating, and the personal norm rating, including interaction terms for anonymous vs public decision contexts. In anonymous decisions (main effects), both injunctive and personal norm ratings significantly predict choice likelihood, but the coefficient for personal norm ratings is significantly higher. In public decisions, the predictive effect of injunctive norm ratings increases and becomes comparable to that of personal norm ratings. ***: $p < 0.01$. Data from Bašić and Verrina (2024).

games. However, the details of these relationships are not yet fully understood. For example, it remains unclear which norms are most relevant in which types of games. One compelling hypothesis is that, in unilateral, anonymous, one-shot games, personal norms tend to be dominant, whereas in public or strategic games, social norms gain more importance due to their inherently social nature. Nevertheless, the current evidence on this distinction remains in its early stages.

THE INTERACTION BETWEEN EMOTIONS AND NORMS

Emotions and norms are not independent channels through which language can affect behaviour. In general, emotions may cause norms, and conversely, norms may cause emotions. In this section, I review evidence regarding these two paths.

The Causal Effect of Emotions on Norms

Emotions play a key role in shaping social norms and moral judgements, influencing how communities separate acceptable behaviour from unacceptable actions. Negative emotions in response to certain actions, such as homicide and paedophilia, underpin why these behaviours are often condemned and legislated against in various cultures.

One emotion that has been extensively studied in relation to morality is disgust. Disgust originally evolved as a protective mechanism against disease and contamination, eliciting a strong aversive reaction to potential sources of infection. This emotion is so ancient that even animals that evolved before mammals, such as sea anemones, exhibit responses akin to disgust (Garcia & Hankins, 1975). Among humans, disgust is one of the earliest emotions to emerge: infants display typical disgust facial expressions just a few hours after birth when exposed to bitter substances (Steiner, 1973). These expressions, characterised by a reduction in the exposed areas of the eyes, nose, and mouth, likely serve to minimise contact with potential pathogens and are often accompanied by gestures of repulsion. In extreme cases, disgust can even lead to nausea and vomiting.

Among humans, the emotion of disgust has been co-opted to regulate social behaviour, leading to so-called moral disgust (Chapman & Anderson, 2013). Actions that profoundly violate ethical standards often elicit a similar response of revulsion, even when they do not involve physical disgust stimuli, as unusual sexual behaviours. Directly relevant to this section is the opposite path: experiencing disgust causally makes people more likely to express harsher judgements of moral violations. I briefly review the evidence about this path in the following.

Experimental Result (Experimentally Inducing Disgust Influences People's Moral Judgements). Schnall et al. (2008) conducted a study aimed at investigating the effect of manipulating the emotion of disgust on moral judgements. The authors divided 120 Stanford students into three conditions depending on the level of a disgusting stink present at the experimental site. The stink was created using a spray applied to a rubbish bin placed about two metres from the participant.

- **Control condition:** No spray was used.
- **Mild stink:** The spray was applied four times.
- **Strong stink:** The spray was applied eight times.

The bin was changed after each participant, and the used bin bags were deposited in a receptacle located about 30 metres from the experimental site. Between participants, a three-minute wait was observed, sufficient to allow the odour to dissipate. This was done to avoid any possible influence of one participant on another, or of one experimental condition on another. In each treatment, participants made moral judgements in four contexts, two of which were designed to elicit disgust: the legalisation of marriage between first cousins and the approval of a sexual relationship between first cousins. The other two contexts concerned the morality of driving to work instead of walking and of releasing a morally controversial film.

The results showed that, in both the mild- and strong-stink treatments, people expressed stronger moral condemnations compared to the control condition. Furthermore, the moral context in which the judgement was expressed did not moderate the moral judgements, suggesting that disgust increased moral condemnation regardless of the context. See Figure 5.10.

Similar results have been obtained by several other studies, thereby showing that feelings of disgust can impact moral judgements (Horberg et al., 2009; Moretti & Di Pellegrino, 2010; Ugazio et al., 2012). □

Of course, disgust is not the only emotion that can affect moral judgements and norms. As with moral disgust, research has shown that inducing anger can impact people's moral judgements. Interestingly, the impact of anger is in some cases different from the impact of disgust. To illustrate this distinction, it is useful to consider

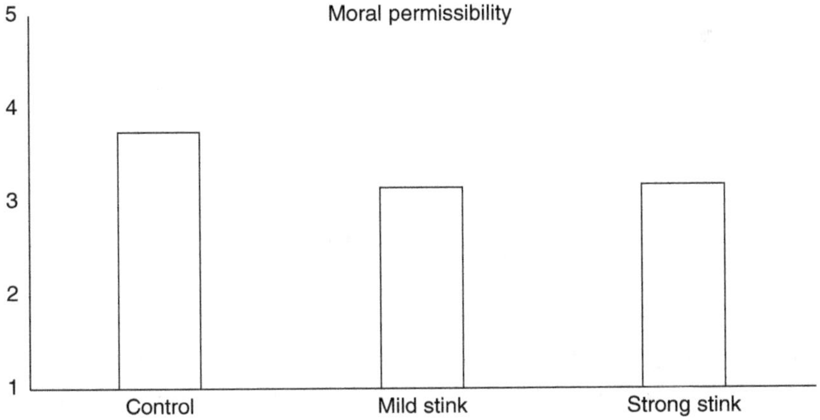

FIGURE 5.10 **Experimentally inducing disgust decreases moral permissibility**. Moral permissibility across conditions, averaged across the four moral violations. Moral violations did not interact with emotion induction. Figure based on Schnall et al. (2008).

a class of dilemmas introduced by moral philosophers that explore how people trade off two ethically justifiable courses of action: one that promotes overall well-being and one that respects certain rules and norms. A classic example of such a moral dilemma is the Trolley Problem, originally introduced by philosopher Philippa Foot (1967).

Definition (Trolley Problem). A runaway trolley is hurtling down a track towards five people who are unaware of the impending danger and cannot move out of the way. You are standing next to a lever that can switch the trolley onto an alternate track, but there is one person on this secondary track who would be killed if you pull the switch. Should you pull the lever to divert the trolley, sacrificing one person to save five others? See Figure 5.11. □

This dilemma forces individuals to weigh the consequences of action versus inaction and to consider whether it is morally permissible to actively cause a foreseeable harm to save more lives. Foot connected this dilemma to the problem of abortion by invoking the Doctrine of Double Effect, a principle in moral theology and ethics. This principle distinguishes between intended consequences

FIGURE 5.11 Graphical representation of the Trolley Problem.

and those that are merely foreseen but unintended. In the context of abortion, the Doctrine of Double Effect is used to evaluate whether it is morally acceptable to perform an action that has both good and bad effects, for instance, terminating a pregnancy to save the mother's life. By applying the Trolley Problem to abortion, Foot theoretically examined whether the moral permissibility of sacrificing one life for others depends on the intention behind the action or solely on its consequences. In both the Trolley Problem and certain abortion cases, the decision-maker faces a choice between causing a foreseen harm to prevent a greater harm or refraining from action and allowing a worse outcome to occur.

Thomson (1985) later introduced the Footbridge Dilemma, to include cases in which the decision-maker gets to decide whether to directly inflict a smaller harm to prevent a greater harm.

Definition (Footbridge Dilemma). In this variation, the same runaway trolley threatens five people's lives, but this time you are on a footbridge above the tracks next to a large man. The only way to stop the trolley is to push this man onto the tracks, where his substantial body mass would halt the trolley. However, doing so would result in his death. Is it acceptable to push the man to his death to save the five others? (See Figure 5.12.) □

Unlike the Trolley Problem, where harm is merely an unintended side effect, the Footbridge Dilemma requires a direct, personal action that results in someone's death, rendering the harm more direct.

FIGURE 5.12 Graphical representation of the Footbridge Dilemma.

These dilemmas illuminate the tension between consequentialist ethics, which focus on the outcomes of actions, and deontological ethics, which emphasise the inherent rightness or wrongness of actions regardless of their consequences. Although it is debated whether judgements in these dilemmas predict behaviour in real-life moral dilemmas (Bostyn et al., 2018; Evans & Brandt, 2019; Plunkett & Greene, 2019), these dilemmas represent one of the most commonly used ways to study people's moral decision-making.

Research has demonstrated that specific emotions significantly influence how individuals resolve moral dilemmas (e.g., Strohminger et al., 2011; Ugazio et al., 2012; Valdesolo & DeSteno, 2006). An interesting example is the following.

Experimental Result (Anger Amplifies Consequentialist Judgements, Disgust Amplifies Deontological Judgements). Ugazio et al. (2012) conducted a series of studies examining how anger and disgust affect decisions in both personal moral dilemmas (such as the Footbridge Dilemma) and impersonal moral dilemmas (such as the Trolley Problem).

In one experiment, disgust was induced by showing the experimental group a two-minute video clip featuring an actor interacting with human vomit, while the control group viewed a neutral two-minute video of someone describing a painting. In a separate experiment aimed at inducing anger, participants were asked to write an essay, which was then evaluated on four criteria: rationality, logic, interest, and intelligence. The feedback provided was either negative or neutral, depending on the condition.

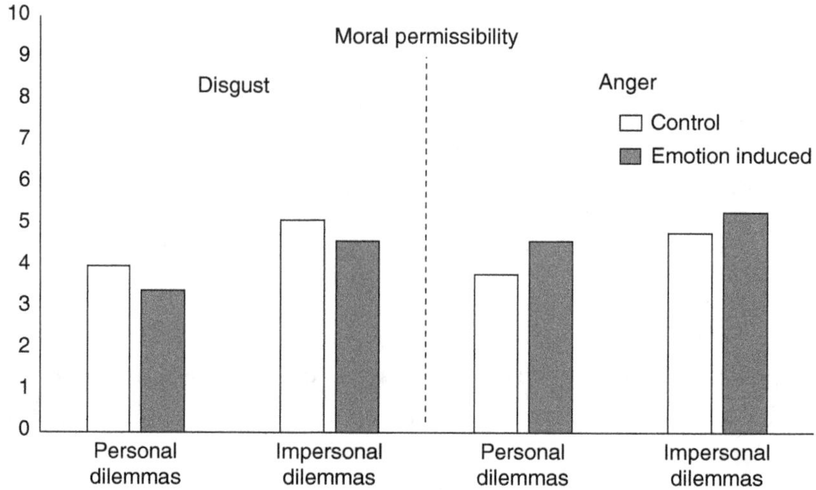

FIGURE 5.13 **Inducing anger or disgust has divergent effects on moral permissibility in personal and impersonal dilemmas.** Average moral permissibility of the utilitarian action in personal and impersonal dilemmas across conditions. Inducing disgust makes people more likely to make deontological judgements in both types of dilemmas. Inducing anger makes people more likely to make utilitarian judgements in both types of dilemmas. Figure based on Ugazio et al. (2012), Experiment 2.

The results revealed that participants in the disgust condition tended to make more deontological judgements in personal moral dilemmas compared to the control group. Conversely, participants in the anger condition were more likely to express consequentialist judgements compared to the control group. A similar trend was observed in impersonal moral dilemmas (Ugazio et al., 2012). See Figure 5.13. □

One possible explanation for these findings lies in the motivational orientations of these emotions. Anger is an action-oriented emotion that propels individuals towards approach behaviours. When people are angry, they are motivated to address and rectify the source of their anger, which can lead them to focus on outcomes and endorse consequentialist reasoning. This proactive stance encourages taking decisive actions to achieve desired results, even if it means bending certain ethical rules.

In contrast, disgust is an avoidance emotion that motivates individuals to distance themselves from offensive or contaminating stimuli. This aversive reaction may heighten sensitivity to moral violations and reinforce adherence to moral norms. The desire to avoid what is perceived as morally tainted may lead to deontological judgements, where actions are judged strictly based on their adherence to moral rules, irrespective of the consequences.

Some studies have also explored how generally relying on emotions, rather than reason, influences moral judgements. I collaborated with Everett and Earp to investigate how prompting individuals to rely on emotions versus reason affects moral judgements, employing the Oxford Utilitarianism Scale (OUS; Kahane et al., 2018). The OUS is a psychometric instrument designed to assess individual differences in utilitarian moral reasoning along two dimensions:

- **Instrumental harm:** This factor evaluates the extent to which a person endorses harming one individual if it leads to a greater overall good.
- **Impartial beneficence:** This factor measures the degree to which a person exhibits equal concern for the well-being of all individuals, valuing everyone's welfare without bias or preference.

Experimental Result (Relying on Emotions Decreases Instrumental Harm, while Having No Effect on Impartial Beneficence). We conducted three studies with American participants recruited through Amazon Mechanical Turk. Each study aimed to explore whether inducing reliance on emotion versus reason would differentially affect the two factors of the OUS. In the first experiment, we employed the original emotion induction priming used by Levine et al. (2018). Participants were randomly assigned to either the emotion condition or the reason condition. They were instructed to rely on emotions or reason when completing the OUS. In the second and third experiments, we introduced modifications to the priming instructions to test the generality of our findings and address potential concerns about the original wording.

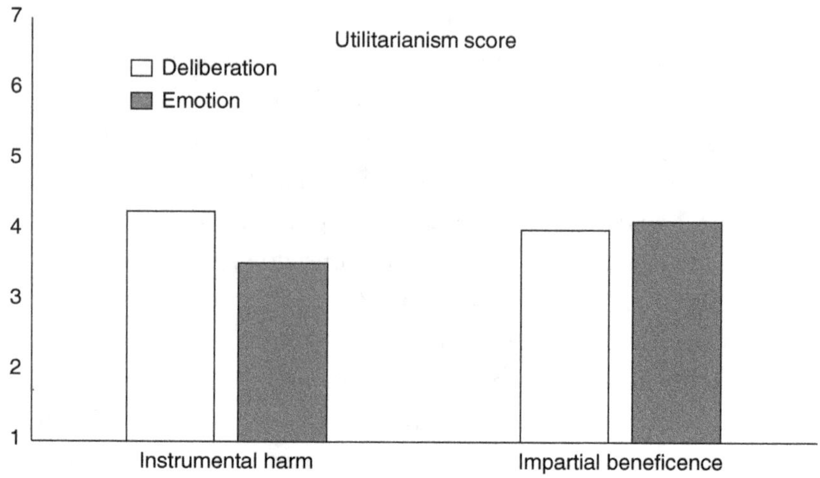

FIGURE 5.14 **People induced to rely on emotions tend to make more deontological judgements in the instrumental harm dimension, but not in the impartial beneficence dimension.** Average utilitarianism score in the Oxford Utilitarianism Scale split by utilitarianism dimension (instrumental harm vs impartial beneficence) and priming (relying on emotions vs reason). Figure based on Capraro et al. (2019a), Study 1.

Despite these variations, our results were consistent across all three studies. We found that promoting reliance on emotion made participants more likely to reject instrumental harm; that is, they were less willing to endorse actions that involved harming someone, even if it was for the greater good. In contrast, the factor of impartial beneficence remained unaffected by the emotion induction. Whether participants were instructed to rely on emotion or reason did not significantly affect their willingness to value everyone's welfare equally. See Figure 5.14. □

Another class of moral dilemmas where reliance on emotion versus reason influences judgement involves speciesism. Speciesism refers to the assignment of different moral values or rights to beings solely based on their species membership. It is a form of bias where humans prioritise their own species over others, often leading to the exploitation and mistreatment of non-human animals. Speciesism is analogous to other prejudices like racism or sexism but is directed towards different species rather than races or genders (Caviola et al., 2019).

Experimental Result (Relying on Emotions Increases Pet-Speciesism; Relying on Reason Increases Anthropocentric Speciesism). In research that I conducted with Caviola published in 2020, we aimed to determine whether inducing reliance on emotion would affect people's speciesist attitudes. We hypothesised that, on an emotional level, people generally have an affinity for animals. Conversely, when engaging in deliberate thought, they tend to assign a higher moral status to humans over animals.

We conducted an experiment with participants recruited from Amazon Mechanical Turk, involving several hundred American adults. Participants were randomly assigned to either the emotion induction condition or the reason induction condition, using the same methodology as in the previous studies. Subsequently, participants encountered a moral scenario where they had to choose to save one of two entities.

- In the **anthropocentric scenario**, the choice was between a human or a highly intelligent chimpanzee.
- In the **pet scenario**, the decision was between a dog or a pig.

Our findings indicated that the preference for humans over chimpanzees was more pronounced when participants based their decisions on reason rather than emotion. Conversely, the preference for dogs over pigs was stronger when decisions were emotionally driven rather than based on deliberation. See Figure 5.15.

These outcomes suggest that humans, when prompted to follow their emotions, are more likely to differentiate between animals based on likability, whereas they consider moral standing when using reason. Consequently, under emotional conditions, humans tended to exhibit 'pet-speciesism', where pets are preferred to non-pets, while under rational conditions, 'anthropocentric speciesism' prevailed, where humans are viewed as superior to other species. I refer to the original article for follow-up studies supporting this interpretation. □

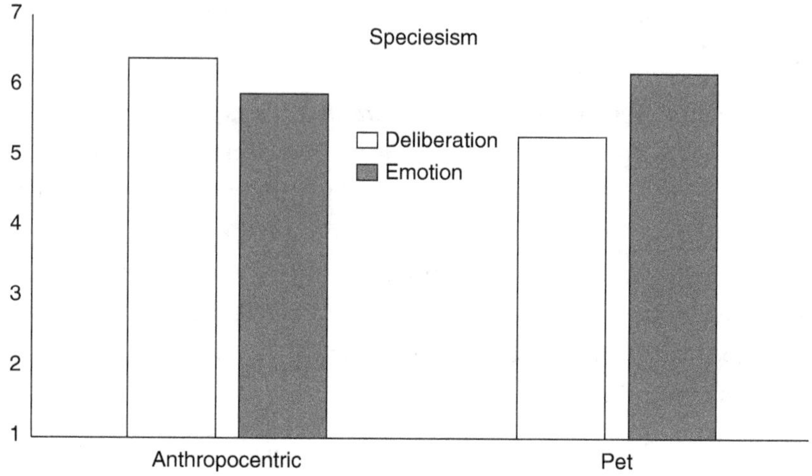

FIGURE 5.15 **Relying on emotion reduces anthropocentric speciesism and increases pet-speciesism**. Speciesism score (1 = definitely save chimpanzee/pig to 7 = definitely save human/dog) across conditions. Figure based on Caviola and Capraro (2020).

Of course, this research only scratches the surface. Other studies have also examined the effects of additional emotions, such as fear (Singh et al., 2013) and compassion (Condon & DeSteno, 2011), on moral judgements. Moreover, I have focused here on moral judgements, without exploring how these emotions can shape social norms regarding acceptable behaviour (Hareli et al., 2013; Heerdink et al., 2019; Lange et al., 2022).

The Causal Effect of Norm Violation on Emotion

In 2014 I moved to Amsterdam for a post-doc position at the Centre for Mathematics and Computer Science (CWI). A few days after my arrival, while I was taking a walk around the city, I suddenly heard an old Dutch woman yelling at me in a language I couldn't understand. My puzzled expression must have been evident because she quickly switched to English: 'Don't walk in the bike lane. Get out!' Coming from Rome, a famously chaotic Italian city, walking in the bike lane was never really an issue, but for Dutch people it is quite a serious norm violation. I felt very ashamed, especially because this happened in public, and I could feel the eyes of the passersby on me. This intense feeling of shame made me quickly learn and adapt to the new norm. During the two years that I lived in Amsterdam, I never again walked in the bike lane.

This story illustrates that breaching a norm can evoke emotions, which in turn reinforce the norm. This reinforcing cycle has been shown experimentally by Schaumberg and Skowronek (2022).

Experimental Result (Violating a Norm Can Cause Shame, Which in Turn Reinforces the Norm). The authors aimed to explore how witnessing another's display of shame after a norm violation influences observers' interpretations of social norms and their subsequent behaviour. They proposed that when someone expresses shame following a transgression, it sends a clear signal that the behaviour in question is socially disapproved of. In contrast, witnessing no emotion or another emotion (e.g., embarrassment or a neutral expression) would result in a weaker inference about the norm.

To test this, the researchers conducted a series of experiments, involving a total of 3,726 US-based adult participants. In each study, participants were randomly assigned to view a scenario in which a target individual had engaged in a questionable behaviour and then either displayed shame, no specific emotion, or an alternative discrete emotion. After observing the target's emotional response, participants were asked to infer the relevant social norm and then indicate how they would behave in a similar situation.

The results consistently showed that when the target expressed shame, participants made stronger norm inferences and were significantly more likely to choose behaviours that aligned with the perceived social norm. This pattern was not observed in the conditions where other emotions or no emotion was displayed. In short, the expression of shame functioned as an effective mechanism for broadcasting social norms and reinforcing conformity, suggesting that shame plays a positive role in promoting social cohesion by

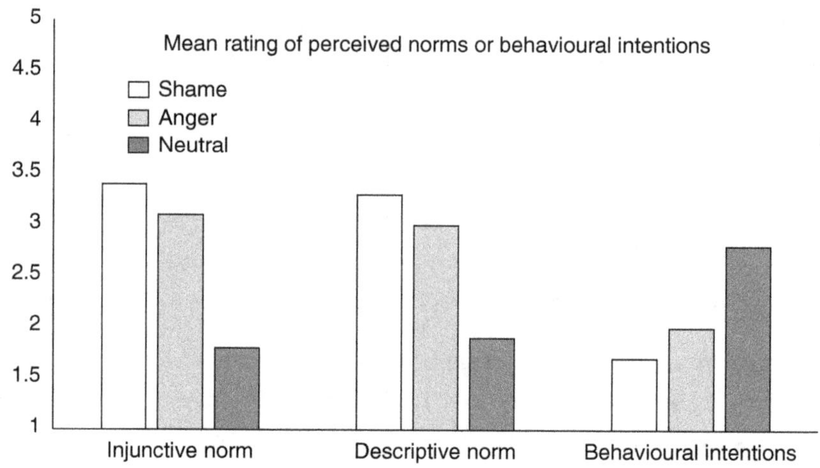

FIGURE 5.16 **Shame broadcasts social norms and influences behavioural intentions more than anger.** Mean rating of perceived injunctive norm, descriptive norm, and behavioural intentions, split by the emotional expression made by observers in Study 1 by Schaumberg and Skowronek (2022).

transmitting critical normative information. Figure 5.16 reports the comparison between shame and anger (Study 1). I refer to the original paper for many other emotions. □

Of course, shame is not the only emotion that we can experience when we violate a norm. Guilt is another prevalent response (Giguère et al., 2014; Tangney & Dearing, 2003; Van Kleef et al., 2015). Like shame, guilt can also motivate corrective actions and self-regulation, reinforcing socially acceptable norms (Carlsmith & Gross, 1969; Konecni, 1972).

Guilt and shame are the primary emotions we experience when we violate a norm. In contrast, when we observe norm violations in others, we most commonly feel anger and disgust.

Experimental Result (Observing a Norm Violation Can Cause Disgust). Simpson et al. (2006) showed each participant 16 images, 8 designed to activate physical disgust (e.g., vomit, urine) and 8 intended to represent moral violations without any explicit bodily reference (e.g., racism, betrayal, hypocrisy), each accompanied by a brief description. After each image, subjects were asked to evaluate the emotional experience elicited by each image. The emotional experience was measured in terms of anger, disgust, fear, happiness, and sadness. After 15 minutes, the subjects were shown the images again and asked to re-evaluate the intensities of the various emotions elicited. The same procedure was repeated after another 15 minutes.

Combining all three measurements, the results showed that after being exposed to the moral violations, participants reported high levels of disgust, anger, and, to a lower extent, sadness. The most interesting part of the results emerged when the authors analysed the

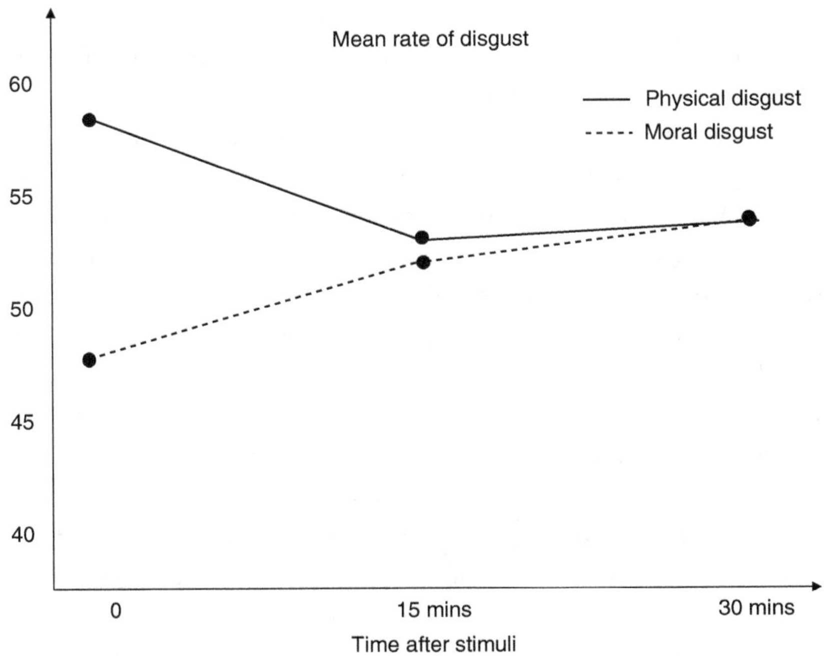

FIGURE 5.17 **Moral disgust increases over time, while physical disgust decreases over time.** Mean self-reported disgust ratings after exposure to physically disgusting stimuli versus moral violations, measured at three time points: immediately after exposure, 15 minutes later, and 30 minutes later. Figure based on Simpson et al. (2006).

evolution of the emotion of disgust over time. They noticed that in response to the disgusting images, the emotion of disgust decreased over time. In contrast, in response to the images of moral violations, the emotion of disgust increased over time. This interaction between time and stimulus was not statistically significant for any of the other emotions. See Figure 5.17.

The association between moral violations and disgust has been confirmed using different methodologies. For example, Chapman et al. (2009) recorded the movements of the 'levator labii superioris' muscles in subjects who participated as recipients in the Ultimatum Game. These muscles, which are responsible for both lifting the upper lip and wrinkling the nostrils, were observed to determine if moral transgressions produce a facial reaction typically associated with the emotion of disgust. The results showed that the upper lip was activated in the expected manner to a greater extent as the unfairness of the received proposal increased.

Another study by Zhong and Liljenquist (2006) asked participants to recall a time when they had committed a moral or immoral action. Afterwards, participants were required to complete word fragments, some of which could be completed using either cleanliness-related words or unrelated words. For example, S _ _ P could be completed with SOAP or SLIP. The authors observed that individuals asked to recall a moral transgression completed the fragments using words related to the concept of cleanliness more frequently than the control group. This suggests that exposure to immoral behaviours increases the accessibility of words and the adoption of cleanliness-related behaviours, likely cause by an increased feeling of disgust. □

The literature connecting norm violations and anger spans decades. For instance, Juvonen (1991) found that witnessing uncivil behaviour evokes anger towards the deviant, while Chaurand and Brauer (2008) reported that bystanders are more likely to speak out against norm violators when they experience higher levels of anger. I refer readers interested in this topic to the specialised literature.

6 Sentiment Analysis

MAIN CLASSIFICATIONS OF EMOTIONS

In Chapter 5, we saw that one of the primary channels through which language can influence decision-making is the emotional response it evokes. Therefore, to accurately quantify the effect of language on decision-making, it is essential to find ways to measure the emotional content of a text. This is precisely where sentiment analysis comes in. Developed by computational linguists, sentiment analysis involves a range of tools developed by computational linguists specifically to classify texts according to various emotions. This chapter introduces the fundamentals of these tools.

Sentiment-analysis tools vary in their approach based on two main factors: (i) the underlying classification of emotions they employ and (ii) the algorithms they use to determine how a text aligns with each identified emotion category. Before we explore the tools themselves, it is therefore important to understand how emotions can be classified.

The classification of emotions has been a subject of study in psychology and related disciplines for decades (Ekman, 1992; Frijda, 1986; Plutchik, 2001; Tomkins, 2008). Within the scope of this chapter, I will focus on two principal classifications. The first is a broader approach that simply categorises emotions into positive and negative. This dichotomy is useful for quickly assessing the general sentiment of textual data. The second approach offers a more granular classification by identifying a range of basic emotions.

Positive and Negative Emotions

The positive–negative dichotomy is primarily grounded in two-dimensional models of emotions (Barrett & Russell, 1999; Lang et al., 2013; Reisenzein, 1994). These models posit that all affective states can be described along two main dimensions: valence (positive or negative) and arousal (high or low).

Positive emotions are those that are generally perceived as pleasant by the individual experiencing them. These emotions are typically elicited by experiences that are desirable or beneficial, such as achieving a goal, enjoying social interactions, or engaging in pleasurable activities. Positive emotions help expand the range of thoughts and actions a person can have at any given moment, which in turn helps them build long-lasting personal strengths. These strengths can be physical, like better health; intellectual, like sharper thinking; or social and psychological, like stronger relationships and greater mental resilience (Fredrickson, 2001). Positive emotions contribute significantly to important life outcomes, including friendship development, marital satisfaction, higher incomes, and better physical health (Fredrickson, 1998; Lyubomirsky et al., 2005). Common examples of positive emotions include joy, serenity, amusement, pride, and love.

Negative emotions are generally associated with feelings of distress, discomfort, or displeasure, making them subjectively unpleasant experiences for individuals. These emotions include sadness, anger, fear, disgust, jealousy, and guilt. They typically arise in response to perceived threats, challenges, or obstacles, serving critical adaptive functions that influence behaviour and decision-making. Negative emotions often serve as a signal that something in the environment poses a threat or is harmful. For example, fear arises in response to immediate danger, prompting the fight-or-flight response, which prepares the body to either confront the threat or escape from it (LeDoux, 2003). Similarly, disgust acts as a protection mechanism against contamination, encouraging avoidance of potentially harmful substances or environments (Rozin & Fallon, 1987).

An important property for sentiment-analysis tools is that positive emotions are relatively independent of negative emotions. This means that feeling positive emotions is not merely the absence of negative emotions and vice versa. An individual can experience high levels of both positive and negative emotions simultaneously, or they may experience low levels of both (Watson et al., 1988). Concretely, this implies that if we aim to measure the 'positivity' and 'negativity' of a text through a sentiment-analysis tool, we need to measure them independently. The negativity of a text is not merely the opposite of positivity.

While the positive–negative dichotomy is useful, it obviously simplifies the richness of human emotional experience. As reviewed in Chapter 5, there are situations in which experiencing different negative emotions may drive people to different choices (e.g., feelings of disgust make people more deontological in the Trolley Problem and its variants, while feelings of anger make them more consequentialist). Consequently, to gain a more granular understanding of the relationship between emotion and behaviour, it is important to move beyond the simple positivity/negativity binary and consider a range of basic emotions.

Basic Emotions

What are the basic emotions? This fascinating and complex question has attracted generations of cognitive scientists, who have proposed widely varying views. For instance, Mowrer (1960) takes a minimalistic approach, positing only pleasure and pain as the fundamental emotional states. At the other end of the spectrum, Frijda (1986) identifies 18 basic emotions, ranging from commonly cited ones like anger and fear to less typical states such as arrogance, humility, and indifference.

This section does not attempt a comprehensive review of every theory. Instead, it will briefly outline two influential frameworks for basic emotions, since they provide the theoretical foundation for many sentiment-analysis tools.

Ekman's Theory of Emotions. One of the seminal works in the study of basic emotions comes from psychologist Paul Ekman, who, through cross-cultural studies, identified six basic emotions that he argued were universally recognised across different societies: anger, disgust, fear, happiness, sadness, and surprise. These emotions are not only universally recognisable through facial expressions but are also linked to specific biological processes (Ekman, 1992).

Ekman's theory posits that these basic emotions are hard-wired into our brains, having evolved to quickly respond to stimuli that posed survival threats or opportunities in our evolutionary past.

- **Anger** is a primal emotion that typically emerges in infancy when a child's goals are thwarted, such as when they are denied a toy or object (Lewis et al., 2006). Evolutionary theorists suggest that anger developed as a strategy to signal displeasure and to motivate individuals to confront and resolve conflicts. This emotion can mobilise energy and focus attention on fighting injustices or threats, thereby increasing the chances of rectifying a situation in one's favour (Sell et al., 2009).
- **Disgust** initially evolved to protect against disease and contamination (Rozin & Fallon, 1987). Over time, this emotion also came to play a role in moral and social judgements, deterring behaviours that are considered unethical or socially unacceptable (Chapman & Anderson, 2013). Disgust thus serves both a physical and a social regulatory function, helping maintain both health and norms.
- **Fear** is a critical survival mechanism that activates the fight-or-flight response, preparing individuals to either escape from danger or stand and fight. This emotion is triggered by perceived threats and can lead to physiological changes that enhance the ability to respond to hazardous or life-threatening situations (LeDoux, 1996). Fear's evolutionary purpose is to help organisms survive by avoiding or confronting danger.
- **Happiness** is associated with numerous evolutionary benefits. It not only promotes social bonds and cooperation by making individuals more approachable and agreeable but also enhances creativity and flexibility in thinking. These traits are advantageous for problem-solving and navigating complex social environments (Fredrickson, 1998). Additionally, happiness is linked to better health and longer life, suggesting its role in promoting reproductive success and longevity (Lyubomirsky et al., 2005).
- **Sadness** signals a need for help and elicits support and empathy from others. Evolutionary psychologists suggest that expressing sadness can strengthen social bonds by communicating vulnerability and the need

for assistance, thereby facilitating cooperative behaviour and communal support (Campos et al., 1989). Additionally, sadness can lead to improved problem-solving by promoting a more detail-oriented and analytical thinking approach, which is crucial during times of loss or failure (Andrews & Thomson Jr, 2009).

- **Surprise** functions to heighten awareness and pivot attention quickly to new and unexpected events. This rapid shift in focus can help individuals better adapt to sudden changes in their environment, making it a crucial component of survival in dynamic settings (Meyer et al., 1997). The ability to quickly assess new information can determine an organism's ability to cope with and adapt to new threats or opportunities. □

Plutchik's Theory of Emotions. Plutchik (1962, 1980, 1994) proposes eight basic emotions, which include the six identified by Ekman (joy, sadness, anger, fear, disgust, and surprise), as well as trust and anticipation. One of Plutchik's key contributions is the organisation of these emotions into what he called the 'Wheel of Emotions', where basic emotions are arranged into opposites. In particular:

- **Trust** reflects a feeling of safety and confidence in another person, group, or the environment. It arises when we perceive someone as reliable, benevolent, and competent, qualities that foster cooperation and social bonding. In Plutchik's model, trust sits opposite to disgust; where disgust drives us to reject and distance ourselves, trust pulls us closer, encouraging collaboration, intimacy, and mutual support.
- **Anticipation** captures the emotional state of looking forward to a future event, outcome, or experience. It combines elements of curiosity and eagerness, motivating us to prepare for what's coming next. In Plutchik's wheel, anticipation stands in contrast to surprise: whereas surprise is a reaction to the unexpected, anticipation is directed toward expected or desired developments, fuelling planning, hope, and goal-oriented behaviour.

Therefore, both these additional basic emotions serve adaptive functions. Trust facilitates social cohesion and cooperation. By enabling individuals to form stable alliances and share resources, trust enhances group protection and mutual aid, thereby increasing the chances of survival and reproductive success. Anticipation, on the other hand, equips organisms with the ability to prepare for future events. This forward-looking emotion encourages vigilance and proactive planning, allowing individuals to capitalise on opportunities and mitigate potential threats. Hence, Plutchik's framework, like Ekman's, is grounded in evolutionary theory.

Additionally, emotions are represented in the wheel in a way that corresponds to their intensity. Emotions located closer to the centre of the wheel are more intense, while those farther from the centre are less so. For example, ecstasy is a more intense form of joy, while serenity represents a less intense version.

Furthermore, Plutchik's wheel also introduces the concept of emotional combinations, which he termed primary dyads. These dyads are formed by blending two neighbouring basic emotions. For example, joy and trust combine to form love, while anticipation and joy blend to create optimism. See Figure 6.1. □

These theories of basic emotions have been highly influential, yet they have also faced significant criticism. While it is beyond the scope of this book to review the entire range of critiques, I will highlight two that are particularly relevant.

The first criticism concerns the completeness and categorisation of the basic emotions. Some argue that the commonly cited list of six emotions might be incomplete or even include states that do not qualify as emotions. Researchers have proposed additional candidates for basic emotions based on similar criteria of universal facial expressions and distinct physiological patterns. For instance, some have suggested that emotions such as pride, shame, or awe should also be considered basic because they are foundational to social interactions and have clear evolutionary significance (Deonna et al., 2012; Keltner & Haidt, 2003; Tracy & Robins, 2004). It has also been suggested that embarrassment, with its unique physiological marker of blushing, could be a basic emotion. This raises the issue that embarrassment is not included because it is not particularly prevalent in our society, while it is in others like the Balinese (Geertz, 1973), suggesting

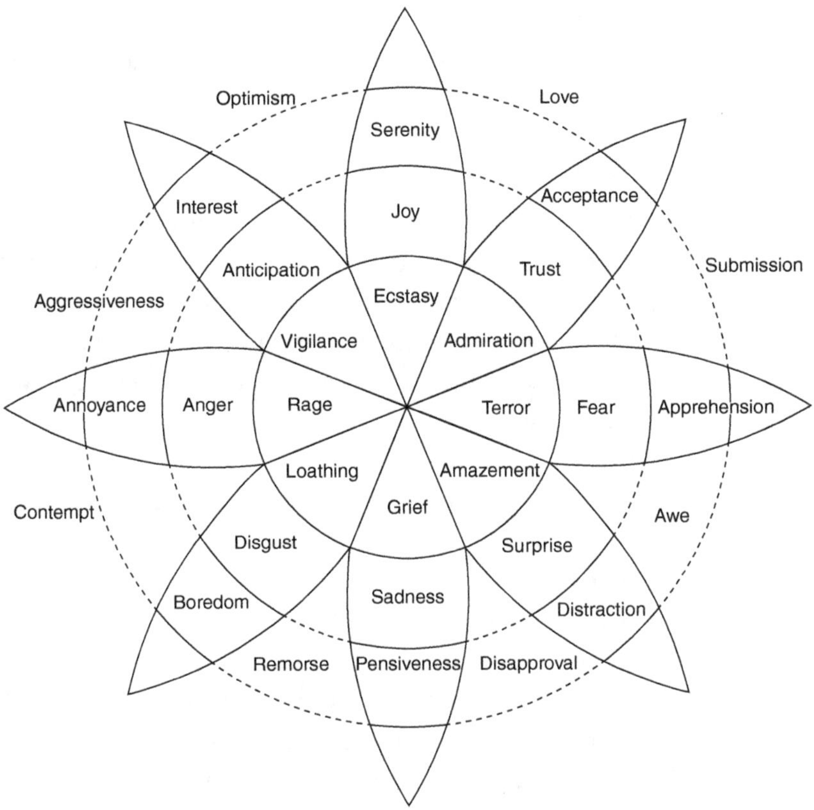

FIGURE 6.1 The Wheel of Emotions.

that theories of emotions may be Western-centric (Ortony & Turner, 1990). Additionally, it has been argued that surprise is not an emotion because it is neutrally valenced and is better described as a cognitive state rather than an affective one (Ortony et al., 1987).

The second criticism is even more fundamental and can be applied to any theory of basic emotions. These theories propose that more complex emotions emerge from combinations of basic emotions. Yet they fail to outline any rules for such combinations or explain the mechanisms by which these combinations occur. This oversight is particularly troubling given that these basic emotions are thought to have distinct physiological and neural characteristics, and it remains unclear how such distinct signatures could be merged without any theoretical framework being provided (Ortony & Turner, 1990).

BINARY SENTIMENT-ANALYSIS TOOLS

Numerous sentiment-analysis tools employ binary classification systems to evaluate emotions, categorising sentiments simply as either positive or negative. In this section we will see some key examples of such tools and their applications, highlighting both the domains in which they can be useful and their limitations, with a specific focus on behavioural economics.

There are three main approaches to sentiment analysis, the lexicon-based approach, the machine-learning approach, and the hybrid approach (Wankhade et al., 2022). To start, let us consider lexicon-based approaches.

A sentiment lexicon is a database of lexical features (e.g., words) that have been tagged according to specific criteria. At a macrolevel, there are two main ways to tag these features: semantic orientation and intensity. Sentiment-analysis tools based on semantic orientation assign a simple positive or negative score to each feature; those based on intensity assign a continuous number that can distinguish various levels of positivity or negativity.

Tools Based on Semantic Orientation

One of the earliest sentiment-analysis tools based on semantic orientation was introduced by Stone et al. (1966). This tool's lexicon comprises over 11,000 words, including 1,915 words labelled as positive and 2,291 labelled as negative. A more recent and highly used tool that employs semantic orientation is the Linguistic Inquiry and Word Count program (LIWC; Pennebaker et al., 2001).

Methodological Tool (LIWC). LIWC is a piece of text-analysis software tailored to examining emotional, cognitive, structural, and process components within text data. It uses a dictionary that features nearly

4,500 words categorised into one or more of 76 categories, including 905 words specifically labelled as either positive or negative. □

Applications of LIWC have varied widely, from analysing political sentiments in tweets (Tumasjan et al., 2010) to predicting the onset of depression from social media texts (De Choudhury et al., 2013b), assessing emotional changes in pregnant mothers through Twitter posts (De Choudhury et al., 2013a), measuring national happiness through Facebook updates (Kramer, 2010), and distinguishing between content and discontent romantic couples via instant messaging (Hancock et al., 2007). In the following, I describe two relevant applications in more detail.

Experimental Result (Association between LIWC Positivity/Negativity and Happiness/Unhappiness). Kramer (2010) studied a behavioural model of happiness by analysing the difference between positive and negative word usage in Facebook status updates. Over 1,000 participants provided these updates and completed a questionnaire on life satisfaction. The author calculated a positivity (percentage of positive words) and negativity score for each update. These metrics were then adjusted by normalising them against the mean and standard deviation, to account for the fact that the LIWC dictionary contains more negative than positive words. Finally, the difference between these normalised measures was considered as a potential behavioural measure of happiness.

After introducing its definition, the author studied convergent and face validity of this happiness measure. For convergent validity, the author explored whether the behavioural measure of happiness was correlated with self-reported life satisfaction, confirming that this association exists. For face validity, the author examined the broader temporal trends in these happiness measures. Peaks were typically noted on national and cultural holidays such as Christmas, Thanksgiving, Halloween, New Year's Day, and Independence Day. Conversely, significant dips were observed on days of national sorrow: notably 22 January 2008, which saw both the death of popular actor Heath Ledger and a significant Asian stock market crash, and 25 June 2009, the day pop-culture legend Michael Jackson passed away unexpectedly. Additionally, a consistent weekly cycle appeared, with Fridays showing a noticeable uplift in mood, being approximately 9.7% happier than the least happy day of the week, confirming the widespread sentiment that Friday is the most cheerful day. □

Experimental Result (LIWC Makes It Possible to Predict the Onset of Depressive Disorders from Twitter Posts). Another noteworthy study used LIWC and other text-analysis software programs to predict the onset of major depressive disorders from Twitter posts (De Choudhury et al., 2013b). The research was conducted on Amazon Mechanical Turk, where participants first completed the Center for Epidemiologic Studies Depression Scale to assess levels of depression. They were also asked to estimate the onset date of their depression if they had been clinically diagnosed. Participants were then invited to provide access to their Twitter accounts. The analysis focused on participants who agreed to share their social media account.

The researchers used the depression scale to categorise participants into two groups based on the severity of their depression: one group exhibited high levels of depression while the other showed little to no signs. For those in the depressed group, all Twitter posts from the year leading up to the reported onset of depression were collected. For example, for a user whose depression started on 17 July 2012, all posts from 17 July 2011 to 16 July 2012 were compiled. For non-depressed participants, posts from the year prior to the survey date were gathered.

The researchers then used the social media posts to build various measures, including positive and negative emotions, using LIWC. This process involved scanning each post through LIWC's dictionary to calculate the frequency of words tied to positive or negative emotional expressions, thus generating a post-level emotional score.

These scores were then aggregated for the entire year. Finally, scores among the depressed and non-depressed groups were compared.

One of the key results of this work was that using language more heavily laden with negative emotions could predict depression before its estimated onset. □

The significance of these findings is considerable. The researchers propose the future development of privacy-respecting software applications and services that could serve as early warning systems by providing personalised alerts and information to individuals, potentially helping to pre-empt the onset of depression.

While the potential applications of these tools are promising, it is important to recognise the limitations inherent in semantic orientation-based approaches like LIWC. One significant drawback is their inability to capture the intensity of sentiments expressed by words. For example, the statement 'The movie I watched yesterday was fantastic' implies a much stronger positive sentiment than 'The movie I watched yesterday was okay'. However, a tool like LIWC might score both sentences similarly, as each contains a single positive term. This lack of sensitivity to intensity can be especially problematic in contexts such as predicting the onset of depression. In mental health, the difference in emotional intensity can be critical: minor forms of depression, which many individuals may experience at some point, need to be distinguished from major forms of depression that can have severe consequences, including an increased risk of suicide.

This limitation points to the need for sentiment-analysis tools that can assess not only the binary polarity but also the magnitude of the sentiment expressed.

Tools Based on Sentiment Intensity

Several sentiment-analysis tools have been developed over the years to measure sentiment intensity.

Methodological Tool (ANEW). One of the earliest attempts was the Affective Norms for English Words (ANEW; Bradley & Lang, 1999) lexicon. This lexicon builds on previous work that analysed a wide range of verbal judgements and found that the variance in emotional assessments could be explained by three main dimensions: pleasure, arousal, and dominance (Osgood et al., 1957). The pleasure dimension measures the degree of positive affect a word evokes, ranging from 'happy' to 'unhappy'; the arousal dimension assesses the intensity of emotional activation a word induces, from 'excited' to 'calm'; and the dominance dimension captures the sense of control or empowerment associated with a word, ranging from 'controlled' to 'in control'. Thus, this tool goes beyond the binary classification of emotions as simply positive or negative, although it does not attempt to classify different emotions. The authors built a dictionary by collecting ratings for 1,034 English words, assessing their pleasure, arousal, and dominance levels on a scale from 1 to 9, with a neutral midpoint at 5. Words rated below 5 are considered negative, while those rated above 5 are deemed positive. □

The ANEW lexicon has been used in a variety of contexts across multiple fields over the years. For instance, Verona et al. (2012) conducted a study employing emotionally neutral and negative words to analyse the differences in reactions between offenders without personality disorders and those diagnosed with antisocial personality disorder. Their findings revealed that offenders with antisocial personality disorders exhibited heightened sensitivity to negative emotional words in both Go and No-Go tasks, indicating an inability to regulate emotional processing when inhibitory control was necessary. Another avenue of research explores how emotional properties influence word processing and memory. Kousta et al. (2009) observed that participants processed positive and negative words more quickly than neutral words.

This sentiment-analysis tool, as well as those presented in the previous section, is grounded in a lexicon that has been manually tagged. While this method offers certain advantages, such as maintaining control over the categorisation process, it also presents significant limitations: the manual tagging by humans restricts the scalability of the approach and is the primary reason for the relatively low number of features in the lexicon. A critical drawback is that if a word is not present in the lexicon, it will not be counted, which can be a significant oversight if that word is crucial for determining the sentiment of the text. For example, consider the word 'ghosted', a relatively modern slang term used to describe the sudden cessation of communication without explanation. If this term is absent from the lexicon, its significant negative connotation could be overlooked, leading to a misunderstanding of the sentiment in a text discussing social interactions. This omission could skew the analysis, especially in contexts where understanding emotional undertones is essential, such as in social media sentiment analysis or customer feedback on dating apps.

Another limitation of the previous tools is that the lexicon is composed of individual words, meaning each word is assigned a single, fixed sentiment score regardless of its usage or context. This is a major drawback because words can take on different meanings and potentially carry different sentiments, depending on the context in which they are used. For example, consider the word 'bright'. In the sentence 'The bright sun made the day feel cheerful', the word carries a positive sentiment, evoking happiness and warmth. However, in the sentence 'The bright light in the interrogation room was harsh and unsettling', the same word might convey a negative sentiment. Tools that rely solely on word-level sentiment scores would assign 'bright' the same positive value in both cases, completely missing the nuance that arises from context.

To overcome these shortcomings, newer tools employ advanced algorithms to determine sentiment by considering the contextual interpretation of words. One notable example is SentiWordNet, created by Baccianella et al. (2010).

Methodological Tool (SentiWordNet). This resource stems from the automated annotation of all synsets (i.e., synonym sets) in WordNet, a lexical database comprising 155,327 words organised into 175,979 synsets (Fellbaum, 1998; Miller, 1995). Words belonging to the same lexical category and bearing similar meanings are grouped into synsets. For polysemous words (those with multiple meanings) each sense is allocated to a separate synset. Thus, the same word can appear in several synsets. Each synset is further clarified through a brief gloss (definition) and, often, one or more usage examples. For example, the word 'steal' appears in the synset defined by the gloss 'Take without the owner's consent' and in the synset defined by the gloss 'A stolen base in baseball'.

SentiWordNet assigns each synset three numerical scores indicating its positivity, negativity, and objectivity (neutrality). These scores range from 0 to 1, with their combined total always equalling 1 for a given synset. Unlike earlier lexicons that relied solely on human compilation, SentiWordNet uses a combination of machine-learning algorithms alongside traditional lexicon-based methods. SentiWordNet's computational architecture operates through two main phases.

The first phase is broken down into four sub-steps.

1. **Seed set expansion**. Two small 'seed' sets are initialised, one containing all the synsets containing seven 'archetypically positive' terms and the other containing all the synsets containing seven 'archetypically negative' terms. These sets are then expanded by traversing various WordNet binary relations. Relations that preserve polarity add new synsets to the same seed set, while relations that invert polarity place the synsets into the opposite seed set. The process can be customised by adjusting the traversal radius, which defines the distance from the original seed set.
2. **Classifier training**. The expanded synsets from the previous step, along with a separate set of synsets assumed to exhibit objectivity (neutrality), are used to train a ternary classifier. This classifier categorises synsets into one of three categories: positive (Pos), negative (Neg), or objective (Obj). This process is repeated eight times, varying both the traversal radius and the learning algorithm used.

3. **Synset classification**. Using the trained classifiers from Step 2, all WordNet synsets are assigned to one of the three categories: Pos, Neg, or Obj.
4. **Classifier combination**. The final positivity, negativity, and objectivity scores for each synset are calculated as the average values assigned by the eight classifiers.

Therefore, at the end of the first phase, each synset is assigned initial positivity, negativity, and objectivity scores.

The second phase aims at smoothing these values through a random-walk phase over a graph built from WordNet definitions. The underlying network for this random walk is created by defining a link from one synset (s_1, the definiens) to another (s_2, the definiendum) if the gloss of s_1 contains at least a term in s_2. The random-walk approach assumes that positivity and negativity within WordNet flow dynamically through the network. This flow is guided by the lexical relationships and definitions, where if a term is predominantly defined using positively connotated terms, it is likely to be perceived as positive, and similarly for negative terms. Starting with initial values determined in a preceding step, these values are subject to potential modification in each iteration of the process. The random walk continues to iterate until a point of convergence is reached. I refer to Esuli and Sebastiani (2007) for the mathematical details of the model. □

Sentiment-analysis tools based on sentiment intensity are particularly useful for classifying a text in contexts where intensity plays a crucial role, such as in product reviews (Cernian et al., 2015; Hamouda & Rohaim, 2011; Singh et al., 2013).

Taking a step back towards behavioural economics, we might ask whether these tools could also be applied to explain the effects of linguistic variations in the experimental instructions of decision-making problems. In principle, this could be possible if we assume, following the LENS model, that the emotions evoked by the instructions can impact decisions.

THE LIMOLES UTILITY FUNCTION

In the experiment that I conducted with Vanzo, we demonstrated that altering the instructions of the Dictator Game can elicit a significant shift in altruistic behaviour (Capraro & Vanzo, 2019). Let us now examine whether such behavioural shifts can be rationalised by sentiment scores.

To briefly recapitulate the experimental design, participants were randomly assigned to one of six treatments of the Dictator Game, each involving a stake of 50 cents. The treatments differed solely in the lexical choice used to describe the key action. For instance, in the steal treatment, the self-serving action was labelled 'Steal from the other participant'. In contrast, the remaining treatments employed the terms 'take', 'demand', 'give', 'donate', and 'boost'. The empirical results indicated that the highest levels of altruistic behaviour were observed in the steal frame, whereas the lowest levels were associated with the boost frame.

To examine whether these results can be explained by sentiment scores, it is necessary to introduce a utility function that incorporates the impact of the sentiment elicited by the linguistic description of an action. The easiest such utility function is a linear combination of monetary utility and language-based sentiment utility. Hence, this utility function corresponds to the 'upper part' of the LENS model, combined with monetary utility. I will denote this utility function using the acronym LiMoLES, referring to the (Li) nearly separable combination of (Mo)netary utility and the LES part of the LENS model.

Since this utility function will play a critical role in the remainder of this book, rather than confining its introduction to the context of the extreme Dictator Game, I present it in the general framework of experimental economic decisions. Recall that an experimental economic decision is given by a set of individuals, I, potentially affected by the decision; a decision-maker, d; an action set for the decision-maker, A; an economic payoff map, π_d; and by a linguistic description of the decision problem. Abusing the notation somewhat, let us denote by a the linguistic description of action $a \in A$.

Definition (LiMoLES Utility Function). Given an experimental economic decision, the LiMoLES utility function of the decision-maker d is defined as:

$$u_d(a) = \pi_d(a) + \lambda_d s_d(a), \tag{6.1}$$

where $\pi_d(a)$ represents the monetary payoff that the decision-maker receives when implementing the action (with linguistic description) a, λ_d represents the sensitivity of the decision-maker to the emotional content of text, and $s_d(a)$ is the sentiment that the decision-maker experiences when reading the linguistic description of action a. □

It is important to emphasise that this utility function is independent of any specific sentiment-analysis tool. Tools such as SentiWordNet provide a means to estimate $s_d(a)$. For instance, when using SentiWordNet or similar lexicons that assess positivity and negativity, we define $s_d(a)$ as the difference between the positivity and negativity of a. For more complex approaches that use basic emotions, this definition can be generalised by summing the intensities of positive emotions and subtracting the intensities of negative emotions, as long as the basic emotions can be classified into positive and negative.

Throughout the remainder of this book, I will demonstrate that the LiMoLES utility function is consistent with a wide range of experimental results, provided that the sentiment $s_d(a)$ is accurately estimated using appropriate tools.

To illustrate the predictive power of the LiMoLES utility function, let us now derive general predictions within the context of the extreme Dictator Game. Recall that, in this game, the polarity of a frame is defined as the sentiment associated with the altruistic action minus the sentiment associated with the self-serving action. By identifying the frame with the linguistic description of the altruistic action (e.g., 'boost'), I denote the polarity of frame a as $Pol(a)$. My goal is to show that the rate of altruistic actions depends on $Pol(a)$.

The intuition is simple: the greater the polarity, the stronger the drive towards the altruistic action. Clearly, however, for this drive to effectively translate into a behavioural shift from the self-serving to the altruistic action, it is crucial that the distribution of λ_d (which measures sensitivity to the language framing) is continuous. We can formalise this intuition in the following proposition.

Proposition (Predictions in the Extreme Dictator Game). Consider a population of dictators with LiMoLES utility function and suppose that λ_d is continuously distributed. Let P be the probability of choosing the altruistic action in the extreme Dictator Game. Then, P is strictly increasing in $Pol(a)$.

Proof. Let A_a denote the altruistic action in frame a and S_a the self-serving action in that same frame. The difference in utility between the altruistic and self-serving actions is:

$$\Delta u_d = (\pi_d(A_a) - \pi_d(S_a)) + \lambda_d(s_d(A_a) - s_d(S_a)). \quad (6.2)$$

The altruistic action has a higher payoff than the self-serving action if $\Delta u_d > 0$, that is:

$$\lambda_d > \frac{\pi_d(S_a) - \pi_d(A_a)}{Pol(a)}. \quad (6.3)$$

Note that the numerator of this ratio is constant (across frames a) and always positive, therefore the condition becomes less stringent when $Pol(a)$ increases. To demonstrate that this implies that P is strictly increasing in $Pol(a)$, let us define the threshold sensitivity as follows:

$$\lambda_d^*(c) = \frac{\pi_d(S_a) - \pi_d(A_a)}{Pol(a)}. \quad (6.4)$$

Let F be the cumulative distribution function of λ_d. In that case:

$$P(altruistic) = \Pr(\lambda_d > \lambda_d^*) = 1 - F(\lambda_d^*(a)). \quad (6.5)$$

Now, F is a strictly increasing function, because it is the cumulative distribution of a continuous distribution. Moreover, in the above condition, the argument of F is strictly increasing in $Pol(a)$. It follows that $P(altruistic)$ is strictly increasing in $Pol(a)$. □

TESTING THE LIMOLES UTILITY FUNCTION USING SENTIWORDNET AND SENTIHUMAN

The proposition in the previous section makes testable predictions about the sentiment scores of the various frames in the extreme Dictator Game. In this section, I evaluate whether these predictions are verified using two ways to calculate sentiment scores. Let us start this evaluation using SentiWordNet.

Example (Explaining Behavioural Differences between the Steal and Boost Frames Using SentiWordNet). Consider the steal and boost frames, which produced the highest and lowest levels of altruistic behaviour in the extreme Dictator Game. According to the proposition, we expect that

$$Pol(steal) > Pol(boost). \tag{6.6}$$

To evaluate whether this condition is supported by SentiWordNet, let us examine the corresponding sentiment scores. For the word 'steal', defined by the gloss 'take without the owner's consent', SentiWordNet assigns a negativity score of 0.5, a positivity score of 0, and a neutrality score of 0.5. Defining the sentiment score as

$$s_d(steal) = Pos(steal) - Neg(steal), \tag{6.7}$$

we obtain $s_d(steal) = -0.5$.

Similarly, for the complementary expression 'don't steal' we derive

$$s_d(don't\ steal) = 0.5. \tag{6.8}$$

Thus, the polarity of the steal frame, defined as the difference between the sentiment of the altruistic action (here, 'don't steal') and the sentiment of the self-serving action (here, 'steal'), is given by

$$Pol(steal) = 1. \tag{6.9}$$

Turning to the boost frame, let us consider a relevant synset with the gloss 'be beneficial to', which is characterised by a positivity score of 0.25, a negativity score of 0, and a neutrality score of 0.75. Therefore, we obtain $s_d(boost) = 0.25$ and, consequently,

$$Pol(boost) = 0.5. \tag{6.10}$$

Thus, we have $Pol(steal) > Pol(boost)$, as expected. □

Therefore, it appears that the LiMoLES utility function, when employing sentiment scores derived from SentiWordNet, successfully predicts the behavioural patterns in the boost and steal frames, those providing the lowest and the highest rate of altruistic behaviour. However, difficulties emerge when we consider the intermediate frames.

Example (Failure to Explain Behavioural Differences across Frames Using SentiWordNet). Consider the donate frame. The most relevant WordNet synset for 'donate' is defined by the gloss 'give to a charity or good cause', to which SentiWordNet assigns a positivity score of 0.625, a negativity score of 0, and a neutrality score of 0.375. Consequently, if we define the sentiment score as

$$s_d(donate) - s_d(don't\ donate) = 1.25, \tag{6.11}$$

this value exceeds the corresponding measure for the steal frame, which was equal to 1. Under the LiMoLES utility function, the above proposition would therefore predict that altruistic behaviour in the donate frame should be more frequent than in the steal frame.

However, empirical findings contradict this prediction: in my study with Vanzo, we reported that altruistic behaviour occurs in approximately 29% of cases in the steal frame, compared to only about 12% in the donate frame, with this difference being statistically significant (Capraro & Vanzo, 2019). □

Is this mismatch between predictions and data attributable to limitations in SentiWordNet's ability to accurately capture the sentiment associated with specific words, or does it indicate a shortcoming in the utility function itself? Although it is conceivable that a simplistic utility function may not fully capture the complexities of decision-making, I contend that, at least in the context of the extreme Dictator Game, the primary issue lies in the measurement of sentiment rather than in the utility function per se.

Experimental Result (Explaining Behavioural Differences across Frames Using Human Sentiment Scores). To see this, consider data collected in a follow-up study in collaboration with Vanzo. Participants were recruited via Amazon Mechanical Turk and presented with all six frames of the Dictator Game in a randomised order. For each frame, participants provided ratings of the sentiment they would experience when making both the altruistic choice and the self-regarding choice, yielding a total of 12 sentiment ratings per participant (i.e., two per frame).

For each frame, we computed the difference between the sentiment rating for the altruistic option and that for the self-interested option (named 'polarity'). This human-derived difference can be compared with the analogous difference computed using SentiWordNet and actual altruistic behaviour, thereby allowing us to assess whether human sentiment polarities offer superior predictive validity relative to those generated by SentiWordNet.

Table 6.1 presents the resulting ratings. Specifically, the SentiWordNet polarity for a given frame is defined as the SentiWordNet sentiment score for the altruistic action minus the SentiWordNet sentiment score for the self-interested action. In parallel, the SentiHuman polarity for a frame is determined by subtracting the average sentiment score for the self-interested action from the average sentiment score for the altruistic action.

The findings are particularly noteworthy. Not only do the SentiHuman polarities exhibit substantially greater variability across frames compared to the SentiWordNet polarities, but the ordering of the SentiHuman polarities precisely reflects the observed ranking

Table 6.1 *Sentiment scores collected using a human sample explain behaviour in the Dictator Game.*

Frame	SentiWordNet polarity	SentiHuman polarity	Altruistic behaviour
Boost	0.50	0.295	0.05
Give	0	0.43	0.09
Donate	1.25	0.46	0.12
Demand	0.5	0.53	0.15
Take	0	0.53	0.15
Steal	1	0.815	0.30

For each frame of the extreme Dictator Game, the second column reports sentiment polarity (the sentiment score of the altruistic action minus that of the self-serving action) as estimated by SentiWordNet. The third column reports sentiment polarity estimated by a human sample, and the fourth column presents the average altruistic behaviour observed in an independent human sample.

of average altruistic behaviour, with all pairwise relationships being numerically preserved. □

These results suggest that, at least in the simple case of the extreme Dictator Game, the LiMoLES utility function

$$u_d(a) = \pi_d(a) + \lambda_d s_d(a) \tag{6.12}$$

effectively rationalises human behaviour, contingent upon the accurate estimation of the sentiment scores. While SentiWordNet is capable of capturing broad, extreme patterns (e.g., it correctly indicates that the boost frame generates lower altruistic behaviour than the steal frame), it fails to account for more nuanced details. These details can be captured by human-generated sentiment scores.

The superior precision of human ratings can be attributed, in part, to the methodology used in calculating sentiment scores. In SentiWordNet, sentiment scores are computed by selecting the synset that most closely matches the linguistic description of the action. However, this approach introduces two primary issues. First, the selection process is inherently subjective: it is not always clear which synset is the most appropriate match. In our case, this was relatively straightforward because the actions were described using a single, well-defined keyword; in more complex scenarios, however, this ambiguity could pose significant challenges. Second, the SentiWordNet approach does not take into account the broader context in which an action occurs. In experimental economic games, the contextual details provided by the experimental instructions can substantially influence the sentiment associated with a given action. For instance, while the word 'donate' is rated highly positive in SentiWordNet (likely reflecting a general association of donation with positive sentiment) the SentiHuman scores for 'donate' are considerably lower and more closely aligned with observed behaviour in the specific context of the Dictator Game.

Human ratings address these limitations by enabling participants to evaluate actions within the full context provided by the experimental instructions. Nevertheless, this method is not without its challenges. For example, it is not easily scalable, as it necessitates the collection of sentiment scores for each new context or experimental setting.

I will discuss the issue of scalability and context in depth in the next chapters. I conclude this chapter by observing that the LiMoLES utility function can be easily expanded to basic emotions, provided that they can be classified into positive and negative emotions, and with a description of some sentiment-analysis tools introduced to measure the sentiment tenor of a text according to various basic emotions.

EXTENDING THE LIMOLES UTILITY FUNCTION FROM BINARY SENTIMENT TO BASIC EMOTIONS

We have seen in the previous sections that behaviour can sometimes be influenced by the specific emotions experienced by the decision-maker. For example, eliciting disgust inclines individuals towards deontological judgements in personal moral dilemmas, whereas evoking anger encourages more utilitarian judgements (Ugazio et al., 2012). Although this effect was not directly caused by experimental manipulations of the linguistic description of the decision problem, it is plausible that instructions designed to evoke disgust may diminish the propensity to endorse utilitarian actions, while those eliciting anger may enhance such endorsements. This raised the question: is the LiMoLES utility function sufficiently flexible to accommodate these differential emotional effects?

As an initial step, let us note that the LiMoLES utility function can be straightforwardly extended to account for basic emotions, provided that these emotions can be dichotomised into positive and negative categories.

Definition (Extension of the LiMoLES Utility Function to Basic Emotions). Consider n basic emotions, partitioned into k positive emotions and $n-k$ negative emotions. The LiMoLES utility function is defined through

$$\begin{aligned} s_d(a) = w_{d,1}s_{d,1}(a) + \cdots + w_{d,k}s_{d,k}(a) \\ -w_{d,k+1}s_{d,k+1}(a) - \cdots - w_{d,n}s_{d,n}(a). \end{aligned} \tag{6.13}$$

The weights $w_{d,e}$ represent the extent to which the decision-maker d is sensitive to emotion e, whereas the sentiment scores $s_{d,e}(a)$ represent the intensity of the emotion e that the decision-maker experiences when contemplating the action expressed through the linguistic description a. □

It is important to note that these weights $w_{d,e}$ are not necessarily uniform across emotions. Moreover, the basic emotional responses $s_{d,e}(a)$ may vary over time. Some emotions may be particularly pronounced at the outset of the decision process but fade rapidly, whereas others may persist over a longer duration.

This extended formulation provides a finer-grained framework for understanding how discrete emotions contribute to decision-making. In particular, it allows us to rationalise the differential effect of different emotions on deontological judgements.

Example (Explaining the Differential Effects of Anger and Disgust on Deontological Judgements). Let us consider the two treatments separately:

- When disgust is induced, people are more likely to choose the deontological action. We could rationalise this using the previous utility function by assuming that the utilitarian action produces more disgust (a negative emotion) than the deontological action. Therefore, to decrease the negative emotion felt during the decision problem, participants turn to the deontological action.
- Conversely, when anger is induced, participants tend to favour the utilitarian option. This suggests that the utilitarian action may generate less anger (a negative emotion) than the deontological alternative, thereby rendering it more attractive because it can alleviate the negative affect.

This example indicates that the LiMoLES utility function is sufficiently flexible to account for the divergent influences of discrete negative emotions on moral decision-making. In other words, the fact that two negative emotions, disgust and anger, can lead to opposite behavioural outcomes does not contradict the utility framework; rather, it reflects that the option which minimises the negative emotional experience varies depending on the emotional context. This highlights that the sentiment associated with an action is not an invariant property inherent solely to the action itself but is contingent upon the broader framing. The primary objective of this book is to quantify one specific aspect of this phenomenon: the linguistic description of both the context in which an action occurs and the action itself.

Does this imply that considering discrete emotions is superfluous? On the contrary, incorporating discrete emotions is far from pointless; it offers a more refined and granular understanding of the decision-making process by decomposing the overall emotional component $s_d(a)$ into its constituent basic emotions.

However, it is important to recognise the limitations of the LiMoLES utility function. According to the LENS model, an alternative pathway through which linguistic descriptions of available actions can influence behaviour is via the evocation of norms. I devote Chapter 7 to this aspect of the model, the LiMoLNoS utility function. For now, having argued for the added value of incorporating basic emotions into the analysis of economic decision-making, I conclude this section by presenting several examples of sentiment-analysis tools designed to measure the emotional tenor of a text along various discrete emotional dimensions.

SENTIMENT-ANALYSIS TOOLS BASED ON DISCRETE EMOTIONS

Attempts to classify textual content into basic emotions date back to the late 1980s and early 1990s (Elliott, 1992; Ortony et al., 1988). These early tools were typically based on 'keyword spotting', meaning they started by classifying unambiguous emotional words (e.g., happy, sad) and then searched for those words in the text. While these tools represented an important starting point, they suffered from several limitations, primarily their reliance on surface characteristics of emotions. For example, the sentence 'I came home to find an empty closet, a note on the counter, and the ring left behind' carries a strong negative emotion. However, it does not contain any unambiguous emotional words, so tools based on keyword spotting would likely classify it as neutral or fail to classify it altogether.

One approach to overcoming this limitation is to classify entire sentences. The earliest large-scale sentiment-analysis tool that moved beyond binary classification into positive and negative emotions and classified entire sentences was developed by Liu et al. (2003).

Methodological Tool (Classifying Sentences Based on Ekman's Theory). The aim of this tool was to classify sentences into emotion categories based on Ekman's theory: happy, sad, angry, fearful, disgusted, and surprised. The tool used Open Mind Commonsense (Singh, 2002), a collection of 400,000 facts about the everyday world, and classified each of these facts into emotion categories using a combination of linguistic models. I will describe in some detail how this combination works, in line with this book's usual goal of providing an intuitive understanding of the techniques used in this field. Readers interested in further details are encouraged to consult the original reference.

The first step involved extracting sentences from the Open Mind Commonsense corpus that contain some prototypically emotional words (e.g., happy, angry). Since the affective valence of these prototypical words is fairly stable across contexts, these words were used as ground terms to build the following approach.

Then, the authors created four linguistic models that assign values to specific parts of these sentences. The first two models share the same input–output structure. When a sentence is inputted into the model, its output takes the form:

$$[a \text{ happiness}, b \text{ sadness}, c \text{ anger}, d \text{ fear}, e \text{ disgust}, f \text{ surprise}],$$

where *a*–*f* are positive real numbers representing the intensity of each emotion associated with the input sentence.

- The first model addresses sentences framed as subject–verb–object 1–object 2. Some of these categories can also be empty. For example, the authors consider the sentence 'getting into a car accident can be scary', where the subject is impersonal, the verb is 'getting into', object 1 is 'car accident', and object 2 is empty. Since the word 'scary', a prototypical fearful word, assigns an affective quality to this sentence, the model would return the output for the sentence 'getting into a car accident' as follows:

$$[0 \text{ happiness}, 0 \text{ sadness}, 0 \text{ anger}, 1 \text{ fear}, 0 \text{ disgust}, 0 \text{ surprise}].$$

- The second model focuses on extracting concepts and assigning values to them. For example, in the sentence 'car accidents can be scary', the model identifies the concept 'car accident' and assigns the same output:

$$[0 \text{ happiness}, 0 \text{ sadness}, 0 \text{ anger}, 1 \text{ fear}, 0 \text{ disgust}, 0 \text{ surprise}].$$

- The third model is also a concept-level model, designed to extract contexts. However, its output differs from the previous models in that it is not a 6-tuple but a single number ranging from –1 to 1, representing the extent to which a context has negative or positive connotations. This approach allows the model to assign valence to sentences containing negative verbs, such as 'I wrecked my car'.
- The fourth model assigns a 6-tuple of the same form to verbs and adverbial modifiers within a sentence, as they can sometimes be entirely responsible for conveying the emotion of the sentence. For example: 'Mouldy bread is disgusting/Fresh bread is delicious.'

Next, the authors took the following steps. First, they processed all the sentences in the Open Mind Commonsense corpus through these models. For each sentence, they extracted subsentences in the form of subject–verb–object 1–object 2, as well as concepts and modifiers, and assigned values using the prototypically emotional words.

After this annotation process, the authors applied smoothing techniques to ensure a more seamless transition between consecutive sentences. This approach is based on the idea that two consecutive sentences in a story typically exhibit some degree of continuous affectivity. Therefore, if two consecutive sentences have significantly different annotations, they need to be revised. The authors employed four methods for this purpose: decay, interpolation, global mood, and meta-emotion.

Decay is particularly useful when an emotional sentence is followed by a neutral sentence. In such cases, it is unlikely that the neutral sentence is entirely devoid of emotion. To account for this, a decay factor is applied to the emotions in the preceding sentence, and the second sentence is annotated according to this decayed value. Interpolation is employed when a neutral sentence appears between two sentences annotated with the same emotion, such as two angry sentences. In this scenario, the neutral sentence is re-annotated to reflect the same emotion, but with a discount factor. Global mood considers the overall mood of entire paragraphs and incorporates a memory of this mood into each sentence within the paragraph.

Meta-emotion enables the analysis of more complex emotional patterns, such as frustration, which can be defined as the repetition of low-intensity anger.

The authors tested the performance of this model by asking 20 participants to write engaging stories on an interface that automatically added emojis at the end of each sentence. For one group, the added emoji was a static neutral face; for another group, it was a random emotional face; and for the third group, the emoji was generated based on the model. Participants were then asked to evaluate the system across four dimensions: whether the program was entertaining, interactive, and intelligent, and whether they would use it again. The results revealed that the emotional faces generated by the model were rated as more interactive, more intelligent, and more likely to be adopted compared to the other conditions. □

Another relevant sentiment-analysis tool was developed by Mohammad and Turney (2013).

Methodological Tool (Classifying Phrases Based on Plutchik's Theory). Similar to the previous tool, this one does not merely classify words but also phrases. More specifically, it categorises term–sense pairs, where a term can be a word or an entire phrase, and the sense is a short explanation that helps disentangle the different meanings a term can have in various contexts.

This tool departs from the previous one in two dimensions. First, it is not based on Ekman's theory of six emotions, but on Plutchik's theory of eight basic emotions: joy, sadness, anger, fear, trust, disgust, surprise, and anticipation. Second, the methodological approach is different, as it is less based on automatic processes, and more on human annotations, which are crowdsourced on Amazon Mechanical Turk.

The crowdsourcing method has some inherent challenges. A primary obstacle involves the complexity of explaining semantic relationships to research participants. To mitigate this impediment, researchers initially presented participants with a linguistic choice problem, before soliciting emotional annotations. Specifically, participants received a quartet of potential senses and had to identify the most semantically proximate sense to the target word. Three alternatives functioned as deliberate unrelated options. The remaining selection represented a precise sense for one potential interpretation of the target term. Through this choice problem, researchers aimed to communicate the specific sense required for annotation without resorting to extensive definitional explanations.

These linguistic choice problems were automatically generated using the *Macquarie Thesaurus*, which segments linguistic resources into approximately 1,000 conceptual clusters, representing broad semantic domains. In practice, this means that for a prompt word, like 'startle', the authors asked, 'Which word is closest in meaning (most related) to *startle*?', with only one clearly correct answer, and the other three randomly drawn from their vocabulary. Then participants were asked various questions about this word, including the extent to which it is associated with each of the eight basic emotions.

Following this procedure, the authors obtained at least three annotations for 8,883 term–sense pairs. The different emotion annotations for a target term were consolidated by determining the majority class of emotion intensities. For a given term–sense pair, the majority class is the intensity level most frequently chosen by the participants to represent the degree of emotion evoked by the word. In the case of ties, the stronger intensity level was selected. □

TOWARDS NORMATIVE ANALYSIS

The sentiment-analysis tools introduced in previous sections have been shown to be useful in various applications. However, I would like to conclude this chapter by providing examples of situations where these tools (and emotions more generally) are insufficient to explain human decisions in economic problems. My approach will be qualitative rather than quantitative, meaning my goal is not to provide examples of quantitatively poor predictions of human behaviour.

Instead, I aim to argue that these tools are inherently limited in predicting human behaviour because behaviour is not merely driven by emotions.

Following the LENS model, people's behaviour also depends on the norms suggested by the text introducing a decision problem and describing available actions, and this influence often extends beyond emotions. The easiest case to illustrate this is the Footbridge Dilemma, where one person must decide whether to push a man off a bridge to stop an incoming trolley, thereby saving five people who would otherwise die. This and similar dilemmas involving causing direct harm for the greater good have been extensively studied by moral philosophers and psychologists. One classic finding is that many people experience an intense emotional response to the thought of pushing the man off the bridge (Greene et al., 2001). However, when given the opportunity to reflect, some switch their choice and decide to sacrifice one life for the greater good, resisting their initial emotional response (Greene et al., 2008). While these initial results have been debated, in a meta-analysis of over 100 studies manipulating cognitive processes during personal moral dilemmas, I found that promoting deliberation makes people more likely to opt for the utilitarian option (Capraro, 2024). So, why are people more likely to make utilitarian decisions under reflection?

One possibility is that the emotional value of the deontological option decreases, making the utilitarian alternative relatively more appealing. However, this explanation appears to be incomplete at closer scrutiny. In the Footbridge Dilemma, the decision-maker's payoff does not depend on their choice, therefore the LiMoLES utility function cannot predict a strict preference for the utilitarian option. At most, it would predict indifference with a chance-based selection of the utilitarian option. This is an implausible scenario, which contrasts with the empirical observation that some people do have preferences for utilitarian choices.

This limitation persists even if one considers any utility function that is monotonically increasing in both material payoff and the intensity of experienced emotions. Under the assumption that the deontological action is associated with a more positive emotional response than the utilitarian option, such a utility function could, at most, nullify the role of emotions, thereby rendering the decision-maker indifferent between the two alternatives. It will never make the utilitarian action preferable.

Consequently, it appears necessary for the utilitarian option to possess an additional subjective value that is independent of the emotional component. This value is likely normative in nature. That is, following deliberation, the utilitarian option may be perceived as more morally appropriate, even in the absence of a corresponding positive emotional reaction. In other words, the LiMoLES utility function, which incorporates the role of emotions, should be augmented with a LiMoLNoS utility function that accounts for the influence of norms, thereby integrating both emotional and normative determinants into the complete LENS model.

To be clear, I am not claiming the utilitarian option is universally more moral, nor that morality is always disconnected from emotions. Morality is often emotionally linked. However, in some cases, morality and emotion may diverge, potentially in the Footbridge Dilemma when actors can deliberate. Some people might come to see pushing the man off the bridge as the right action, despite feeling negative emotions about doing so.

We can build similar examples considering more realistic economic scenarios, too. For example, consider a pharmaceutical company which must decide whether to price a life-saving drug:

1. **At market rates (high price):** This choice allows continued research funding.
2. **At cost price (low price):** This choice enables wider access for low-income patients, but limits future research capabilities.

This scenario presents a normative decision where the 'moral' choice requires rational deliberation about complex ethical trade-offs. Sentiment analysis is unlikely to provide meaningful insights.

Instead, a 'normative-analysis' tool that can extract the normative tenor of a decision problem might be valuable.

Moreover, this example highlights the complexity of normative analysis. Similar to sentiment analysis, a binary approach that merely signals the perceived moral righteousness of an action is overly reductive. Morality is a multidimensional construct, and, as Chapter 7 will explore, many real-world situations are characterised by conflicts between competing moral principles.

7 Normative Analysis

MORAL FOUNDATIONS THEORY

I concluded Chapter 6 by noting that people's morality is multidimensional, spanning a variety of moral principles that may occasionally conflict, leading to both social and individual conflict. When distinct groups within a society become divided along moral lines, such divisions can precipitate significant social conflict; similarly, an individual may experience internal conflict when confronted with competing moral imperatives.

But what are these fundamental moral principles? The initial sections of this chapter are devoted to two principal theories that decompose human morality into foundational dimensions: moral foundations theory and morality-as-cooperation theory.

Moral foundations theory occupies a middle ground between two divergent approaches. On one end lies the empirical approach, which posits that moral values are primarily acquired during childhood and adolescence through socialisation processes. According to this view, the human mind does not come pre-equipped with specific moral content; rather, it possesses general learning mechanisms that facilitate knowledge acquisition. The cross-cultural similarities observed in moral domains are attributed not to genetic predispositions but to the universal challenges, such as resource allocation, child-rearing, and conflict resolution, that all societies confront, leading them to develop analogous moral solutions.

At the other extreme is the nativist approach, which asserts that moral concepts such as justice, harm, and respect are evolutionarily ingrained within the human mind. Proponents of this perspective argue that these moral values emerge in children regardless of formal instruction, and that any cultural variations in moral implementation stem from local adaptations of these universal principles.

Moral foundations theory contends that morality is both innate and learned. Specifically, the theory posits a link between certain inherent moral intuitions (i.e., immediate judgements that arise without conscious deliberation) and virtues that are predominantly social constructs.

In the article that initiated research on this topic, Haidt and Joseph (2004) sought to understand which moral principles could be internalised and integrated into the mind at an intuitive level. They argued that not all behaviours become intuitive through the internalisation of evolutionarily adaptive responses. For instance, while humans appear predisposed to fear certain stimuli, such as snakes or rats, that have posed genuine threats throughout evolutionary history, other fears are not innate but may be acquired through experience. For example, although potentially hazardous entities like knives or fire may evoke fear, this response is generally learned rather than preprogrammed.

To identify the fundamental moral intuitions, Haidt and Joseph examined social behaviours common to human evolutionary history and the evolutionary mechanisms that rendered such behaviours adaptive. The underlying premise is that morality functions to suppress or regulate selfish impulses in favour of cooperative living. In accordance with this rationale, the authors proposed four fundamental moral modules, each defined in terms of opposing forces.

- The **care/harm module** is rooted in the mammalian mother–child attachment system, whereby the rapid recognition of a child's signals of distress conferred significant evolutionary advantages by reducing child mortality. This module underlies the development of capacities to request and provide assistance, initially within the mother–child dyad and later extending to other social relationships. Compassion is the primary moral emotion associated with this module, from which virtues such as kindness and care emerge.

- The **authority/subversion module** reflects the evolution of social hierarchies, which emerged as a result of unequal distributions of strength, talent, and fortune. Cooperation within a hierarchical structure, where individuals adhere to their respective roles, can yield greater evolutionary success than rebellion, which often leads to social exclusion or even death. In this context, hierarchies are viewed as a form of cooperation, conferring protection on those who comply and power on those at the top. The moral emotions associated with this module include respect for authority and resentment towards those who undermine the social order, while virtues such as obedience, respect, and loyalty are derived from it.
- The **fairness/cheating module** originates from the evolutionary context of large, loosely connected social groups where kinship ties are often weak or absent. Fairness, as manifested in behaviours such as equitable sharing and reciprocal altruism, fosters long-term cooperation and enhances survival prospects. Marriage, perhaps the most ubiquitous form of non-kin cooperation, exemplifies this module. The emotions underpinning this domain include gratitude, anger, and guilt, and the associated virtues are justice, fairness, and trust.
- The **purity/degradation module** is based on the evolutionary adaptive strategy to avoid pathogens and parasites, which can pose significant threats to human survival. The immediate emotional response of disgust, elicited by cues such as corpses or excrement, can function as a protective mechanism. Over time, cultural norms have evolved to regulate bodily practices and safeguard public health. Disgust is the central moral emotion in this module, and the virtues associated with it include cleanliness, purity, and chastity.

In a footnote, Haidt and Joseph describe a potential fifth module:

- The **loyalty/betrayal module**, which is also rooted in our evolutionary history as social animals. Unlike the authority/subversion module, this dimension emphasises in-group loyalty and cooperation irrespective of hierarchical status, leading individuals to favour members of their own group over outsiders, who may be perceived as competitors. The fundamental emotions here include fear of strangers and resentment toward traitors, with the corresponding virtues being patriotism and self-sacrifice.

One of the principal achievements of moral foundations theory is its ability to explain political preferences. In subsequent research, Graham et al. (2009) classified the care/harm and fairness/cheating dimensions as 'individualising' dimensions, foundational to the liberal philosophical tradition that prioritises individual rights and freedoms. In contrast, the remaining three dimensions were grouped as 'binding' dimensions, which underpin the conservative tradition that emphasises social cohesion, tradition, and loyalty. Their findings demonstrate that American liberals and conservatives systematically differ in the relative importance they assign to these moral dimensions.

Experimental Result (Liberals Evaluate the Individualising Dimensions Higher than Conservatives, while Conservatives Evaluate the Binding Dimensions Higher than Liberals). In the first study, Graham et al. collected responses from 1,613 adults registered on the Project Implicit website. Upon registration, subjects reported their political orientation on a scale ranging from 1 ('strongly liberal') to 7 ('strongly conservative'). Additionally, participants were asked to respond to the prompt 'When you decide whether something is right or wrong, to what extent are the following considerations relevant to your thinking?' using a response scale from 0 ('never relevant') to 5 ('always relevant'). Fifteen considerations were presented, with three items corresponding to each of the five moral foundations. To give one example for each dimension:

- Whether or not someone suffered emotionally
- Whether or not some people were treated differently than others
- Whether or not someone did something to betray his or her group
- Whether or not someone showed a lack of respect for authority
- Whether or not someone did something disgusting

The authors carefully avoided overt political references; for example, an item such as 'Whether or not someone was denied his or her rights' was intended to capture moral relevance in a politically neutral manner, applicable to diverse ideological perspectives (e.g., LGBTQIA+ rights for liberals and gun ownership rights for conservatives).

The results revealed that among strongly liberal individuals, the two individualising dimensions, care/harm and fairness/cheating, are rated significantly higher than the three binding dimensions, loyalty/betrayal, authority/subversion, and purity/degradation. In contrast, among strongly conservative individuals, the ratings for the five moral dimensions tend to be more uniform. Thus, while conservatives do not necessarily rate the binding dimensions as exceptionally high in absolute terms, they do rate them relatively high compared with liberals; correspondingly, liberals place greater emphasis on the individualising dimensions than conservatives. See Figure 7.1. □

These empirical findings informed the development of a 30-item questionnaire. As of the time of writing, this questionnaire remains the most widely used instrument for measuring moral foundations and can be downloaded at https://moralfoundations.org/questionnaires/.

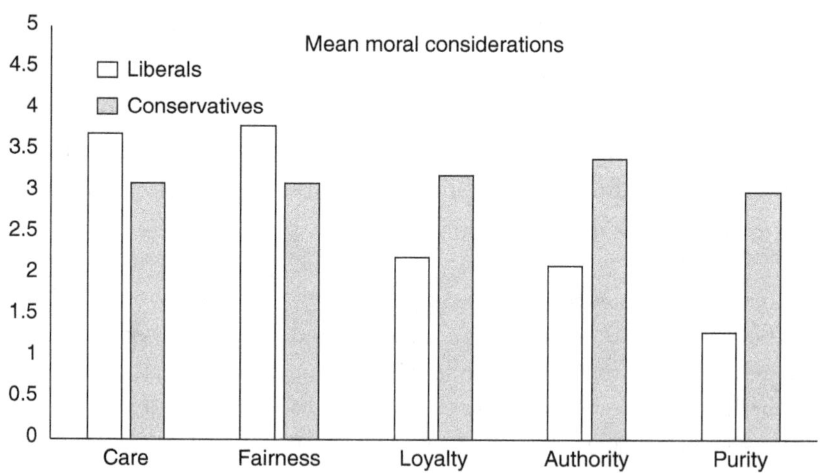

FIGURE 7.1 **Liberals score higher than conservatives in individualising dimensions, while conservatives score higher than liberals in the binding dimensions.** Self-reported mean considerations across moral foundations split according to political orientation. Figure based on Iyer et al. (2012).

Experimental Result (Mapping between Moral Foundations and Ethical Opinion). Moral foundations theory provides a useful lens for understanding ethical divisions on real-world issues. To illustrate this, I present preliminary findings from a sample of 574 American participants recruited via Amazon Mechanical Turk. In addition to completing the Moral Foundations Questionnaire, participants shared their views on 30 potentially divisive contemporary issues.

Table 7.1 summarises the results of a series of linear regressions predicting the moral acceptability of each issue based on participants' scores across the five moral foundations. In the table, entries labelled 'acceptable' indicate a positive and statistically significant regression coefficient ($p < 0.05$), while 'unacceptable' indicates a negative and significant coefficient. Given the modest sample size, these results should be interpreted with appropriate caution.

Still, the findings offer intriguing, albeit preliminary, insights. First, the vast majority of issues were moralised: at least one moral foundation was significantly associated with participants' evaluations. Second, distinctive 'splits' in moral judgement emerged. Often, one or more of the individualising foundations (care, fairness) predicted moral approval, while one or more of the binding foundations (loyalty, authority, purity) predicted disapproval, or vice versa. For instance, participants scoring high on care and fairness tended to find abortion to be morally acceptable, while those scoring high on purity tended to find it unacceptable. Similarly, those high in care tended to oppose the death penalty, whereas those high in authority were more likely to support it.

Interestingly, divergences sometimes arose within the same foundation cluster. For example, views on revenge revealed a split within the individualising foundations: individuals high in care generally found revenge unacceptable, while those high in fairness tended to view it as acceptable. Likewise, within the binding foundations, opinions on issues such as extramarital relationships and human cloning diverged; those high in in-group loyalty viewed these practices as acceptable, whereas those high in purity tended to disapprove. □

Table 7.1 *Opinions on ethical issues correspond to different moral foundations.*

Ethical issue	Moral foundation				
–	Care	Fairness	Loyalty	Authority	Purity
Abortion	Acceptable	Acceptable	–	–	Unacceptable
Death penalty	Unacceptable	–	–	Acceptable	–
Euthanasia	–	–	–	–	Unacceptable
Animal testing	Unacceptable	–	Acceptable	–	–
Use of animal furs	Unacceptable	–	–	–	–
Premarital sex	Acceptable	Acceptable	–	–	Unacceptable
Relationships between married people	–	–	Acceptable	–	Unacceptable
Divorce	Acceptable	–	–	–	Unacceptable
Animal cloning	–	–	–	Unacceptable	Unacceptable
Human cloning	–	–	Acceptable	–	Unacceptable
Stem cell research	–	Acceptable	–	–	Unacceptable
Suicide	–	–	–	–	Unacceptable
Having children out of wedlock	Acceptable	Acceptable	–	–	Unacceptable
Gambling	–	–	–	–	Unacceptable
Polygamy	–	–	–	Unacceptable	Unacceptable
Homosexual relationships	Acceptable	Acceptable	–	–	Unacceptable
Incest	Unacceptable	–	Acceptable	–	–
Revenge	Unacceptable	Acceptable	–	–	–

Stealing	Unacceptable	–	Acceptable	–	–
Flirting	–	–	–	–	Unacceptable
Smoking cigarettes	–	–	–	–	Unacceptable
Smoking marijuana	Acceptable	–	Unacceptable	–	Unacceptable
Drinking alcohol	Acceptable	–	–	–	Unacceptable
Drug use	–	–	–	–	Unacceptable
Rich taxed more than the poor	Acceptable	Acceptable	–	–	Unacceptable
Public healthcare system	Acceptable	Acceptable	–	–	Unacceptable
Open immigration	Acceptable	Acceptable	–	Unacceptable	–
Adoption by same-sex couples	Acceptable	Acceptable	–	Unacceptable	Unacceptable

Regression predicting the acceptability of each ethical issue as a function of the five moral foundations. The entries labelled 'acceptable' in the table indicate that the regression coefficient is positive and statistically significantly different from 0; the entries labelled 'unacceptable' indicate that the regression coefficient is negative and statistically significantly different from 0. The significance threshold is set at 0.05. Results are based on a sample of 574 American participants and should therefore be interpreted with caution, given the relatively small sample size.

There have been various attempts to expand the five moral foundations to include other foundations. Iyer et al. (2012) aimed to study a growing political ideology in the United States, libertarianism, which does not map onto the classic left/liberal–right/conservative dichotomy. For example, libertarians are typically conservative on economic matters (against government intervention to limit the free market), but liberal on social issues (against government intervention in matters like sex and drugs). Libertarian philosophy argues that the individual is the unit of value and that freedom is the precondition for individual flourishing. One of the main divergences of thought that led libertarianism to separate from liberalism in the early twentieth century is the rejection of the idea that the needy impose a moral duty on others. To study people belonging to this political ideology, Iyer et al. introduced two additional dimensions to the Moral Foundations Questionnaire: economic liberty and lifestyle liberty. Two sample items are:

- People who are successful in business have a right to enjoy their wealth as they see fit.
- I think everyone should be free to do as they choose, so long as they don't infringe upon the equal freedom of others.

The authors conducted an experiment measuring how liberals, conservatives, and libertarians score in the Moral Foundations Questionnaire and in these additional dimensions. Regarding liberals and conservatives, the results showed the usual tendency, with liberals scoring higher than conservatives on the two individualising dimensions and conservatives scoring higher than liberals on the three binding dimensions. On these five dimensions, libertarians scored lower than both liberals and conservatives. However, libertarians scored the highest on the two liberty dimensions. Here, liberals and conservatives showed the expected behaviour, with liberals higher on lifestyle liberty and conservatives higher on economic liberty.

The liberty dimensions are very useful for explaining some conflicts surrounding public health issues.

Experimental Result (Association between Liberty Scores and Vaccine Hesitancy). Amin et al. (2017) interviewed 1,007 parents residing in the United States, aged between 18 and 50, with at least one child under 13 years old. Parents were asked to fill out a validated scale measuring their hesitancy towards vaccinating their children. Based on the responses to this scale, the authors divided the parents into three categories: slightly hesitant, moderately hesitant, and very hesitant. Finally, the parents completed the Moral Foundations Questionnaire, including the liberty dimensions.

Comparing parents with high levels of hesitation with those with low levels of hesitation, the authors found that the former were characterised by significantly higher values of purity and liberty and significantly lower values of respect for authority. These low values in the authority dimension were interpreted as anti-science sentiments, where science is perceived as an authority against which to rebel. Figure 7.2. □

Experimental Result (Association between Liberty Dimensions and Attitudes towards Social Distancing). Another relevant study was conducted by Tarry et al. (2022). The authors collected observations from 209 participants in Canada and the United States during the COVID-19 pandemic. Participants were asked various questions regarding their attitudes towards social distancing and their intentions to practise it. Additionally, participants completed the expanded Moral Foundations Questionnaire, including two dimensions of liberty.

In both samples, the authors found that both the binding dimensions and the dimension of economic liberty were negatively associated with attitudes towards social distancing and with intentions to practise it. In the American sample, the authors found that the individualising dimensions were positively correlated with attitudes towards social distancing and with intentions to practise it. □

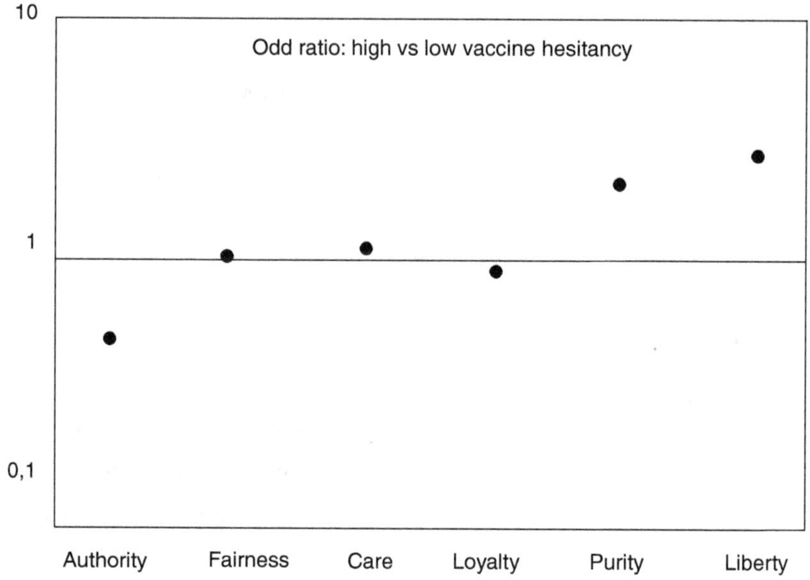

FIGURE 7.2 **Vaccine hesitancy is associated with higher values of purity and liberty and lower values of authority.** Odd ratios of a logistic regression predicting whether a participant is in the high vs low vaccine hesitancy group as a function of the scores in the moral dimensions of moral foundations theory. Figure based on Amin et al. (2017).

More recently, Atari et al. (2023) introduced a refinement to moral foundations theory by proposing an updated questionnaire (MFQ-2). The key innovation is the subdivision of the fairness foundation into two distinct dimensions: equality and proportionality. Equality refers to the principle that all individuals should receive the same treatment, resources, and opportunities, regardless of their individual characteristics or contributions. Proportionality refers to the concept that rewards, punishments, and resources should be distributed based on individual merit, effort, or contribution. The authors examined the MFQ-2 across 25 diverse societies worldwide, confirming that equality and proportionality are loosely correlated, which suggests they are related but distinct moral foundations.

MORALITY-AS-COOPERATION THEORY

Moral foundations theory posits that human morality emerged through the internalisation of behaviours that promote social cooperation, with distinct moral dimensions corresponding to the various challenges societies encounter. However, anthropologist Oliver Curry and his colleagues have critically examined the implementation of this approach, particularly in the construction of the Moral Foundations Questionnaire. Their central critique is that moral foundations theory lacks a coherent, systematic theory of cooperation; instead, it deduces certain moral dimensions ad hoc by reflecting on behaviours presumed to facilitate social cooperation, without exhaustively classifying all behaviours associated with cooperative interactions.

To provide explicit examples, one of the fundamental rules of cooperation is kin altruism, which guides cooperation between genetically related individuals according to Hamilton's rule (1964): if r is the genetic relatedness coefficient between two individuals, c is the cost of an individual's altruistic act towards another individual, and b is the benefit created by the altruistic action, then the altruistic action will be performed if $r > b / c$. This rule was also included in Nowak's (2006) five fundamental rules of cooperation. Moral foundations theory suggests that the care/harm foundation evolved from the mother–child bond, implying that kin altruism should fall within this dimension. Yet in the Moral Foundations Questionnaire, only two questions relate to family, and neither belongs to the care/harm dimension: one is categorised under fairness/cheating, the other under loyalty/betrayal.

Relatedly, according to moral foundations theory *direct reciprocity* (cooperation based on the principle 'I help you today; you help me tomorrow') is included in the fairness/cheating foundation. This is theoretically questionable, as reciprocity does not necessarily entail fairness concerns. Empirical evidence from Chapman et al. (2023) shows that trustee behaviour in the Trust Game is not significantly correlated with measures of inequality aversion, challenging the assumed connection.

Next, Curry turns his critique to cooperative behaviours that seem to be entirely neglected by moral foundations theory. The first such behaviour is the respect for private property and the concomitant moral proscription against stealing. This behaviour can be interpreted as a mechanism for resolving conflicts over contested resources. Nonetheless, the Moral Foundations Questionnaire does not directly address private property. The closest reference pertains to inheritance issues within the fairness/cheating domain. The second is related to competitive altruism, which includes costly signals of group membership such as heroism. Attributes such as courage and heroism, which are morally valorised by many societies and contribute to in-group cohesion. In principle, these qualities should be subsumed under the loyalty/betrayal dimension of moral foundations theory, but it is unclear to what extent this actually happens.

Then, Curry moves to arguing that certain dimensions included in moral foundations theory are not directly associated with particular forms of cooperation and, thus, should not be classified as foundational. For instance, the care/harm dimension is not uniquely linked to a single form of cooperative behaviour, as it may manifest in familial, communal, or broader social contexts. Likewise, the purity/degradation dimension, as originally conceived by Haidt et al., is more closely related to individual protection against pathogenic threats than to any cooperative process. Curry et al. maintain that while aspects of care and purity may influence moral behaviour, they do so primarily through their interaction with other moral dimensions, suggesting that these other dimensions should be regarded as the true foundations of morality.

Finally, Curry argues for an empirical limitation of moral foundations theory: although the theory posits five distinct dimensions, several experimental studies indicate that a two-dimensional model (dividing moral reasoning into individualising and binding dimensions) more accurately fits the data. While this statistical critique is understandable, it must be recognised that some ethical dilemmas reveal subdivisions within the individualising dimensions (e.g., the ethics of revenge) or within the binding dimensions (e.g., the ethics of animal experimentation), indicating that these dimensions do capture distinct and non-redundant aspects of morality.

With the aim of overcoming these limitations, Curry and his colleagues developed an alternative theoretical framework. While their model also rests on the premise that morality comprises a set of rules designed to facilitate social cooperation, it diverges from moral foundations theory in its operationalisation of this concept. By employing a game-theoretic argument, the authors identified seven fundamental cooperative behaviours. The first three directly stem from dyadic or group-level cooperation.

1. **Love for one's family (*family*)**. This dimension has its biological roots in kin altruism, whereby genes favour copies of themselves in other individuals, which allows cooperation among genetically related individuals.
2. **Help towards one's group (*group*)**. This dimension is associated with the mutualism that characterises social groups that succeed through group bonding and cooperation.
3. **Return of favours (*reciprocity*)**. This dimension draws from reciprocal altruism, which enables the evolution of cooperation among individuals with weak or absent kinship or group ties.

The other four represent conflict resolution strategies that can be understood as cooperative as they minimise conflict costs for all parties involved:

1. **Being brave (*bravery*)**. One way to resolve a conflict is through a symbolic hierarchy of winners and losers. In this perspective, symbols that project the image of being winners or losers are seen as morally positive. On the winners' side, these symbols are courage, ability, and heroism.
2. **Respecting superiors (*respect*)**. On the losers' side, these symbols are obedience, respecting superiors, and humility.
3. **Dividing contested resources (*fairness*)**. When a contested resource is divisible, a possible conflict resolution is resource division. This division

can be made in proportion to each party's bargaining power. In the generic case where bargaining power is identical, the resource should be divided equally.

4. **Recognition of property (*property*).** Another way to resolve conflicts is by recognising the ownership of a resource.

The main prediction of the theory is that these moral dimensions are universal worldwide, meaning they are positively evaluated from a moral viewpoint.

Experimental Result (These Moral Dimensions Are Universal Worldwide). To test this prediction, Curry et al. (2019b) conducted an experiment on 60 societies of varying complexity, from hunter-gatherer groups to modern kingdoms and states. They started with a digital archive called Human Relations Area Files, containing thousands of texts from different societies, and randomly generated 60 societies from all continents. For each of these societies, over 1,200 pages of cultural data were available. From this material, they extracted what was classified by other professional anthropologists as belonging to the domains 'ethics' or 'norms'. The authors completed the collection with additional research searching for relevant keywords within the archive. In this manner, they reached a final sample of 3,460 paragraphs from 603 different sources published over a period of 300 years.

To code the material, the authors looked at how each individual sentence could be included in each of the seven moral dimensions. For example, 'helping a brother' or 'caring for a fragile relative' were placed in the family dimension, 'working together' or 'adopting local conventions' were placed in the group dimension, and so on. Since an occurrence might have a negative moral valence, the next step was to measure the moral valence of each occurrence. The evaluation was carried out independently by the first two authors of the article and then subsequently by a third researcher unaware of the research hypotheses. This procedure resulted in a total of 962 paragraphs with moral valence.

Results show that of these 962 paragraphs, all but one positively evaluated the corresponding cooperative behaviour. The only exception came from a Micronesian population known as the Chuuk, for whom 'to steal openly from others is admirable in that it shows a person's dominance and demonstrates that he is not intimidated by the aggressive powers of others'. Thus, rather than describing the act of stealing as morally positive in absolute terms, it was overtaken in relative terms by another moral dimension, the bravery dimension. Further demonstrating this, in the other seven paragraphs where the Chuuk referred to respecting property, they always did so with a positive valence. □

Clearly, the uniform positive valuation of all seven moral dimensions across societies does not imply that these societies share identical moral frameworks. Cross-cultural heterogeneity in morality can be understood as arising from differences in the relative strength with which each moral dimension is evaluated. Indeed, in a comparative analysis, Curry et al. observed that while all seven moral dimensions received positive evaluations across various societies, there was significant variability in their frequency of occurrence. Additionally, some dimensions were more frequent than others. The property dimension was significantly more prevalent than the dimensions of bravery, respect, and fairness, with fairness being significantly less frequent than all other dimensions. The remaining differences among dimensions did not reach statistical significance.

The subsequent question Curry et al. posed was whether other moral values can be expressed as a combination of the seven fundamental values found in the first study, similar to how molecules can be expressed as combinations of elements. The underlying idea is that when societies confront complex challenges, they devise integrative solutions that amalgamate basic moral elements. To investigate this possibility, Curry et al. (2022) analysed pairs of moral 'elements' to determine whether their combination could be represented as a distinct composite moral value. Through this approach, they identified 21 unique 'moral molecules' (see Table 7.2).

Table 7.2 *Twenty-one moral molecules of order 2, identified by Curry et al. (2022).*

–	Group	Reciprocity	Bravery	Respect	Fairness	Property
Family	Fraternity	Blood revenge	Family pride	Filial piety	Gavelkind	Primogeniture
Group	–	Friendship	Patriotism	Tribute	Diplomacy	Common ownership
Reciprocity	–	–	Honour	Confession	Turn-taking	Restitution
Bravery	–	–	–	Modesty	Mercy	Munificence
Respect	–	–	–	–	Arbitration	Mendicancy
Fairness	–	–	–	–	–	Queuing

To illustrate how such combinations operate, consider the following examples.

Example (Fraternity). By integrating the value of helping one's group with that of supporting one's family, the principle of 'treating one's group like a family' is derived, which forms the basis of brotherhood. This involves extending the unique obligations a person has towards their family members to a broader community, regardless of genetic ties. The fraternity value is widely esteemed across numerous cultures and, for example, constitutes one of the three cardinal values espoused during the French Revolution.

Example (Blood Revenge). When the value of familial solidarity is combined with that of (negative) reciprocity, a moral imperative emerges regarding the retribution for negative actions committed against a family member. This synthesis gives rise to the notion of 'blood revenge', an ancient punitive practice observed in many human societies. Data from a study encompassing 168 societies reveal that in 38 societies, blood revenge is elevated to a moral imperative, while in 90 societies, it is deemed a legitimate response (Eriksen & Horton, 1992).

Furthermore, by incorporating three moral elements, an additional 35 moral molecules can be obtained. For instance, by integrating the elements of respect, family, and reciprocity, one can articulate the value of caring for one's aging parents. Similarly, by combining four moral elements, namely bravery, reciprocity, family, and group, one can construct the moral value of avenging wrongs against one's family and group, a construct that may be interpreted as 'mafia honour'. Progressing further, one can generate 21 molecules by combining 5 moral elements, 7 molecules by combining 6, and a single molecule by uniting all 7 moral elements.

Additionally, moral molecules may be constructed with varying numbers of elements. For example, starting from friendship, which can be derived from the combination of one atom of group with one atom of reciprocity, one can create a configuration of one atom of group and two atoms of reciprocity, yielding a group relationship that is more heavily based on reciprocity, which Curry et al. identify with collegiality. Conversely, combining two atoms of group with one atom of reciprocity results in a relationship predominantly based on group, one that surpasses friendship in strength, which might be characterised as camaraderie. This construction illustrates that the space of moral possibilities is virtually infinite, particularly when considering the various quantitative contributions of each fundamental element. Even when only relative values are considered, the combinatorial possibilities number in the millions. Both cultures and individuals may differ based on the weight they assign to each moral dimension. To empirically assess these valuations, Curry et al. (2019a) developed a questionnaire analogous to the Moral Foundations Questionnaire, which is provided in their paper's appendix.

Nonetheless, this theory too is not without its critics. Several shortcomings were raised in the 'Comments' section in the initial article proposing the theory (Curry et al., 2019b). For instance, Bloom observed that numerous behaviours are moralised despite lacking a direct effect on cooperation. The treatment of corpses, for example, is moralised in nearly every culture, and many cultures moralise specific sexual behaviours such as masturbation, promiscuity, sexual violence, and infidelity. Similarly, Smith and Kurzban noted that certain moral behaviours appear inefficient; for example, the prohibition against consuming cows in India, which some argue contributes to poverty and famine, or the moral interdiction on selling one's own organs, even though a person can survive with a single kidney. Moreover, critics have pointed out that individuals tend to modify their moral values in accordance with their self-interest, endorsing equality or equity depending on what is most beneficial (DeScioli et al., 2014).

In response, Curry et al. (2019b) have argued that the theory of morality as cooperation is not incompatible with these behaviours. They contend that the moralisation of corpse care, for instance, may be justified by its public health implications, thereby constituting a cooperative strategy. Similarly, certain sexual behaviours may be moralised due to their ultimate association with cooperative solutions. For example, incest may be morally condemned owing to its deleterious effects on offspring health, aligning with the family dimension; stable, long-term relationships may be moralised favourably in contrast to short-term, promiscuous encounters, as they facilitate joint child-rearing (reflecting the group or family dimensions); adultery may be deemed immoral because it violates the mutual exclusivity agreement inherent in reciprocal relationships; and masturbation might be considered immoral as it is related to the incapacity to find a sexual partner (relating to the bravery dimension), while monogamy might be valorised for ensuring the equitable distribution of sexual resources (fairness).

This same logic can address some of Smith and Kurzban's critiques. For example, cows in India are revered as 'mothers' and serve as potent symbols of group identity; thus, the prohibition against slaughtering and consuming them may be understood as being guided by the family and group dimensions. Curry and his collaborators maintain that these examples do not, in fact, contradict the theory of morality as cooperation, which posits that morality is ultimately self-interested. Therefore, it is unsurprising that, when faced with a choice between two moral principles, individuals tend to favour the one that most closely aligns with their self-interest. Moreover, the theory does not purport that moral rules are invariably cooperative; rather, it posits that they originate from cooperative strategies, which may occasionally yield adverse outcomes, particularly in contexts not encountered during earlier stages of evolution, such as the moral prohibition against selling one's own organs.

In sum, there is an ongoing debate about the precise nature and number of moral dimensions. Different theoretical frameworks propose alternative classifications, and there is room for disagreement about which dimensions are fundamental, how they should be operationalised, and how they relate to one another. While the exact taxonomy remains contested, there is broad consensus that morality is multidimensional: human moral reasoning cannot be reduced to a single axis. Building on this insight, the next sections shift focus from theorising about moral dimensions to examining how moral content is expressed in natural language. Specifically, I explore methods for measuring the normative content of text.

LEXICON-BASED NORMATIVE ANALYSIS

How can we measure the normative tenor of a text? The idea is analogous to sentiment analysis, with the obvious difference that, instead of measuring different emotions, the objective here is to assess different moral values. Like for sentiment analysis, the simplest method involves constructing a lexicon and then tallying the frequency of its constituent terms within a given text. Following this idea, the earliest attempt to create a moral lexicon was made in the seminal article by Graham et al. (2009).

Methodological Tool (Moral Foundations Dictionary). In their fourth study, Graham et al. aimed to analyse moral differences in sermons from liberal and conservative churches, with the goal of showing that liberal discourse is more based on individualising dimensions, while conservative discourse is more focused on binding dimensions.

To this end, the authors first identified two churches, one that is recognised as more liberal and one as more conservative, and downloaded all the public sermons given at them between 1994 and 2006. They then constructed a dictionary grounded in the five moral dimensions by generating an extensive list of synonyms and antonyms for each dimension. This 'expansive' phase was subsequently refined through a 'contractive' phase, during which synonyms that were frequently employed in a non-moral context were systematically excluded. For example, the word 'just' is more commonly used in the sense of 'only' rather than 'fair', and was therefore removed from the moral lexicon.

Following the construction of the dictionary, the authors extracted all sentences within the sermons that contained words from the lexicon. These sentences were compiled into a document and evaluated by a panel of independent researchers, who were blinded to the study's hypotheses and the origin of the sentences. Each sentence was rated as supporting (+1), opposing (–1), or being neutral/inconclusive (0) with respect to the moral dimension associated with the keyword. It is noteworthy that a sentence may include a term from a particular moral dimension yet convey an opposing moral stance. For instance, one sermon featured the sentence: 'Do not let some selfish ecclesiastic or governmental authority tell you what to believe, read the Bible with your own eyes and open your heart directly to Jesus.' Although this sentence contains the word 'authority', it explicitly repudiates the concept of deference to authority.

As predicted, liberal sermons were characterised by a stronger emphasis on the individualising dimensions, whereas conservative sermons demonstrated a greater focus on the binding dimensions. Beyond these results, the significance of this study lies in its first attempt to conduct a normative analysis. □

In recent years, this lexicon has undergone significant expansion. One aspect of this expansion relates to the size of the lexicon. Initially, it featured only 324 distinct words, which constrained its ability to capture variations in moral foundations within texts. The number of words has been expanded by several authors. One expansion was undertaken by Frimer et al. (2019), who included 204 words per moral foundation. However, this expansion has been shown to be a poor predictor of people's moral concerns, as demonstrated in a study involving over 2,000 participants who responded to the Moral Foundations Questionnaire and provided access to their Facebook posts: responses to the Moral Foundations Questionnaire were only loosely related to the occurrences of the expanded dictionary, and could be better predicted by other text-analysis tools (Kennedy et al., 2021). More details on this will be provided in Chapter 8.

Another expansion was developed by Rezapour and Diesner (2019), who catalogued over 4,000 words. A subsequent work by Rezapour et al. (2021) employed this augmented version to measure the moral content of a collection of tweets covering diverse viewpoints on political and ethical issues, including stances on atheism, climate change, abortion, Trump, Clinton, and feminism. The analysis revealed distinct moral signatures across different topics. For instance, discussions on feminism exhibited the highest values of fairness, while atheism displayed prominent levels of purity. Interestingly, high purity values appeared in tweets both supporting and opposing atheism, though it was more pronounced among those opposed.

A second dimension of expansion related to the number of moral foundations. The initial lexicon and subsequent expansions classified words only according to the five moral foundations of the original theory. An extension that adds the liberty foundation was developed by Araque et al. (2024).

Methodological Tool (The Morality-as-Cooperation Dictionary). In recent years, alternative lexicons grounded in morality-as-cooperation theory have emerged (Alfano et al., 2024; Malik et al., 2025). The latest and most comprehensive of these dictionaries was developed using input from a nationally representative sample of 1,070 US participants, balanced in terms of political affiliation and gender. This sampling strategy was intended to minimise the risk of moral annotations being skewed by the biases of a demographically uniform group of coders. Participants underwent online training designed to familiarise them with the seven moral dimensions posited by the morality-as-cooperation framework. Each individual was subsequently tasked with annotating 20 news articles, randomly drawn from a corpus of 5,594 texts. Collectively, they produced 56,125 annotations. These textual highlights were each labelled with one of the seven morality-as-cooperation categories.

Subsequently, the authors built a dictionary-based scoring tool aligned with the methodology outlined by Hopp et al. (2021). They computed the relative association between each word and morality-as-cooperation domain. This was done by counting how many times a word was tagged under a specific moral category and dividing that count by the total number of times the word appeared in documents coded by annotators working within that same morality-as-cooperation domain. For instance, if the word 'protect' appeared in 60 bravery-related annotations and occurred 100 times in texts handled by coders focused on bravery, its bravery score would be 0.6. The result of this procedure was a seven-dimensional vector for each word, where each dimension captured the word's average moral loading in relation to one of the morality-as-cooperation categories.

The authors then evaluated the empirical usefulness of this enhanced Morality-as-Cooperation Dictionary (eMACD) by conducting 10 distinct validation studies to test its reliability and value for moral content analysis. In one such test, they found that the right-leaning media outlet *Breitbart* consistently emphasised themes of reciprocity, heroism, and respect more than *The New York Times*. Conversely, the left-leaning *Huffington Post* gave greater weight to themes of fairness, reciprocity, and deference than *The New York Times*. In another validation, they observed that articles containing higher levels of moral language were more likely to be shared on social media platforms, corroborating earlier findings by Brady et al. (2019).

MEASURING THE PRESENCE OF PERSONAL AND SOCIAL NORMS

Moral foundations theory and morality-as-cooperation theory seek to decompose human morality into its fundamental dimensions. Using the classifications of norms introduced in Chapter 5, these theories aim to elucidate how personal norms may be dissected into distinct dimensions. However, as discussed in previous chapters, personal norms are not the sole normative influences on human decision-making. Although I have argued that behaviour in one-shot and anonymous economic decisions is primarily driven by personal norms, evidence also indicates that injunctive norms play a significant role in such contexts (Bašić & Verrina, 2024). Additionally, it is possible that descriptive norms also play a role in these contexts, although there has been little study of this role. Moreover, in economic games, the impact of social norms likely increases compared to economic decisions, given the greater salience of beliefs and expectations.

This observation raises a question: is it possible to develop a text-analysis tool that can distinguish the normative tenor of a text in terms of its emphasis on personal, injunctive, or descriptive norms? To the best of my knowledge, at the time of writing, no text-analysis tool has been specifically designed for this purpose. The most closely related tool is Delphi, developed by Jiang et al. (2021).

Delphi is trained on a large dataset including 1.7 million examples of judgements concerning everyday situations. It is designed to take a quotidian scenario as an input and produce a certain output. Delphi can operate in two modes.

- **In the yes/no mode**, Delphi returns a classification label based on whether the society generally agrees or disagrees with the action described in the input. This mode is intended to capture the injunctive norm, providing an assessment of whether a given action is deemed socially acceptable.
- **In its free-form mode**, Delphi outputs a classification label indicating whether the action described is morally positive, discretionary (i.e., falling into a neutral category where moral judgement is left to individual discretion), or negative. This approach appears to tap more directly into personal norms.

Delphi does not explicitly address descriptive norms, nor does it calculate distinct weights that represent the relative contributions of personal, injunctive, and descriptive norms to the overall normative tenor of a text. Such weights would be particularly valuable for integration into a utility function that incorporates all norms. Therefore, while Delphi represents a useful starting point for the evaluation of various norms present in a text, its limitations underscore the importance of future work on this topic.

THE LIMOLNOS UTILITY FUNCTION

The impact of language on behaviour via norms can be formalised using a utility function that is mathematically analogous to the LiMoLES utility function introduced in Chapter 6.

Definition (LiMoLNoS Utility Function). Given an experimental economic decision, the LiMoLNoS utility function of the decision-maker d is defined as:

$$u_d(a) = \pi_d(a) + v_d n_d(a), \tag{7.1}$$

where $\pi_d(a)$ represents the monetary payoff that the decision-maker receives upon implementing the action (with linguistic description) a, v_d denotes the sensitivity of the decision-maker to the normative content of a text, and $n_d(a)$ is the normative value that the decision-maker experiences when reading the linguistic description of action a. □

Although the LiMoLNoS utility function is mathematically analogous to the LiMoLES utility function, these two functions may differ substantially across individuals. For example, personality factors may differentially influence these functions. It is plausible that individuals with a highly emotional disposition exhibit a high λ_d, the parameter representing sensitivity to the emotional tenor of a text; however, such heightened sensitivity does not necessarily imply an equivalent sensitivity to the normative value of a text, v_d. Although these two parameters may be correlated for some individuals, in general they might differ significantly. It would be of considerable interest to conduct experiments to investigate the relationship between these parameters as a function of individual differences.

Moreover, the sentiment tenor of an action, $s_d(a)$, may differ from its normative value, $n_d(a)$. Some actions might evoke a strong emotional response without necessarily carrying significant normative weight, and, conversely, certain actions may have a pronounced normative value without eliciting a comparably strong emotional response.

Analogous to the refinement of the LiMoLES function, the LiMoLNoS function can be enhanced to yield a finer-grained explanation of human behaviour. We can obtain a first refinement by splitting the normative value $n_d(a)$ into its three principal components: personal norms, injunctive norms, and descriptive norms. This yields the function:

$$u_d(a) = \pi_d(a) + \nu_d(\mu_d M_d(a) + \iota_d I(a) + \delta_d D(a)). \tag{7.2}$$

Here, the personal (or moral) norm, $M_d(a)$, is understood to depend significantly on the individual, whereas the injunctive normative value, $I(a)$, and the descriptive normative value, $D(a)$, are more reflective of social values. Hence, they do not depend on the decision-maker. However, decision-makers may differ in their capacity to perceive these values, and this heterogeneity is captured by the sensitivity parameters, ι_d and δ_d.

Note that when $\mu_d = 0$ and $\delta_d = 0$, this function reduces to one that accounts solely for the injunctive norm, in a manner analogous to the function considered by Krupka and Weber (2013). Similarly, when $\iota_d = 0$ and $\delta_d = 0$, the function simplifies to one that incorporates only personal norms, which is mathematically akin to the model that Perc and I introduced in our paper 'Mathematical foundations of moral preferences' (2021). Furthermore, when $\delta_d = 0$, the function captures both personal and injunctive norms, similar to the function presented by Bašić and Verrina (2024). A mathematically similar function to the complete LiMoLNoS utility function has been introduced by Gavrilets (2021), who additionally considered compliance with authority. Therefore, this refinement of the LiMoLNoS utility function is connected to several other previous proposals, although it differs from them in a major conceptual point: The LiMoLNoS utility function is explicitly grounded as a language-based utility function, defined directly on the linguistic descriptions of available actions.

Another refinement of the LiMoLNoS utility function can be obtained by decomposing the personal norm $M_d(a)$ into fundamental dimensions. Specifically, if we consider a theory of morality in which an individual's moral considerations can be partitioned into n dimensions, $M_{i,d}(c)$, with corresponding weights $w_{i,d}$, then we have:

$$M_d(c) = w_{1,d}M_{1,d}(c) + \cdots + w_{n,d}M_{n,d}(c). \quad (7.3)$$

Finally, we can use the LENS model to combine the LiMoLES and LiMoLNoS utility functions to account for the interaction between emotions and norms. The simplest mathematical formulation of such an interaction is the product of the two variables, leading to the LiMoLENS utility function.

Definition (LiMoLENS Utility Function). Given an experimental economic decision, the LiMoLENS utility function of the decision-maker d is defined as:

$$u_d(a) = \pi_d(a) + \sigma_d s_d(a) + v_d n_d(a) + \rho_d s_d(a) n_d(a), \quad (7.4)$$

where ρ_d represents a measure of the degree of independence between the sentiment value and the normative value of the text for the decision-maker. □

Note that if ρ_d is large (in absolute terms), the extent to which a decision-maker's behaviour is influenced by the joint consideration of both emotional and normative aspects is not simply the sum of their separate influences, but these factors interact in a manner that could either reinforce or mitigate the other. Conversely, a ρ_d close to zero would imply that sentiment and normative evaluations influence behaviour largely independently of one another.

This represents arguably the simplest mathematical formalisation of the LENS model. I do not claim that this utility function fully captures the entirety of human behaviour; rather, I propose that this framework may explain several regularities observed in experimental economic decisions and games. I will discuss some of the foreseeable limitations of the LENS model and its mathematisation in Chapter 9.

We shall now transition to the final technical chapter of this book, Chapter 8, in which I employ large language models to conduct text analysis (primarily sentiment analysis) in a manner that can significantly explain human behaviour beyond the economic consequences of the available actions.

8 The Role of Large Language Models

Part 2

LIMITATIONS OF LEXICON-BASED TEXT-ANALYSIS TOOLS

In the previous chapters I explored a range of lexicon-based sentiment- and normative-analysis tools that can quantify the emotional and normative tenor in text. These tools rely on predefined lists of words or multi-word expressions that are associated with specific sentiment scores or normative values. On the positive side, these tools are extremely simple and interpretable. However, several limitations constrain their effectiveness in the domain of experimental economic decisions and games.

To develop an initial intuition regarding these limitations, recall that experimental economic decisions and games are characterised by a set of instructions that establish the contextual background, and by a set of available options, which are also described using individual words, phrases, or complete sentences. Consequently, two attributes appear crucial for a text-analysis tool to yield robust predictions about human behaviour: (i) context sensitivity and (ii) the ability to effectively process multi-word expressions.

However, achieving these capabilities with conventional lexicon-based approaches is challenging.

Context insensitivity: Lexicon-based methods assign a fixed sentiment or normative value to each word regardless of the context in which it appears. For instance, the word 'happy' is typically marked as positive, yet in a sentence such as 'I am not happy', the method might erroneously assign a positive value unless explicitly programmed to recognise negation. Although more advanced lexicon-based tools such as SentiWordNet can correctly process straightforward negations and other basic syntactic constructions, they remain largely context-free. This context-free assumption frequently leads to the misinterpretation of complex linguistic phenomena. As demonstrated in Chapter 6, SentiWordNet fails to assign appropriate sentiment to strategy descriptions like 'taking from the other participant', a discrepancy that is evident when comparing the tool's output with human annotations and observed behavioural outcomes.

Limited handling of multi-word expressions: Many sentiment expressions are not reducible to individual words but rather to phrases or idioms (e.g., 'over the moon'). Lexicon-based methods that consider only unigrams or fail to effectively process bigrams and trigrams can miss these subtleties, thereby distorting the overall sentiment or normative analysis. Although more advanced tools can process bigrams and trigrams and therefore overcome some of these limitations, it is difficult to scale these solutions. This limitation is particularly relevant in applications in behavioural economics, given that in many decision problems, strategies are described using entire phrases, such as 'taking from the other participant'. Therefore, it is important to have text-analysis tools that can handle multi-word expressions with precision.

Recent advances in LLMs offer a promising alternative. As reviewed in Chapter 4, LLMs are trained on vast corpora of data, enabling them to learn complex linguistic structures and, in principle, to achieve greater context sensitivity and improved processing of multi-word expressions compared to traditional lexicon-based methods. However, the fact that LLMs can theoretically provide context-dependent sentiment and normative assessments does not necessarily imply that their outputs will significantly enhance our understanding of human behaviour. In the following sections, I will demonstrate that the underlying phenomena are more complex than they might initially appear. This complexity becomes evident upon introducing BERT, one of the first widely adopted LLMs. Although BERT represents a significant advancement over traditional lexicon-based text-analysis tools, it remains insufficient for capturing the full linguistic content of an economic decision problem in a manner that explains human behaviour beyond the economic consequences of available actions. By contrast, more advanced models such as GPT-4 can conduct sentiment analysis in a way that better accounts for human behaviour than outcome-based preferences, at least in the relatively straightforward context of the Dictator Game. These findings suggest that advanced LLMs may offer a powerful means to transition from outcome-based to language-based preferences, enabling us to quantify the impact of language on decision-making.

BERT

One of the first examples of an LLM to see widespread use in sentiment and normative analysis is BERT, which stands for 'Bidirectional Encoder Representations from Transformers' (Devlin et al., 2018). The first keyword here is 'bidirectional', meaning that a peculiar characteristic of BERT is that it processes sentences in both directions, considering what comes before and after a given token. This technical trick allows the model to learn the full context of each word. For example, consider the word 'bat'. In the sentence 'He saw a bat hanging from the cave ceiling', the context 'hanging from the cave ceiling' indicates that the word 'bat' refers to the nocturnal mammal. However, in 'He grabbed his bat to hit the baseball', the context provided by 'grabbed' and 'to hit the baseball' makes it clear that the word 'bat' is used in the sense of sports equipment. By processing both the preceding and following words, BERT can accurately determine which meaning of 'bat' is intended.

The way BERT learns this bidirectionally is through a technique called Masked Language Modelling (MLM). During training, MLM randomly selects a fixed percentage (typically 15%) of tokens in an input sentence and replaces them with a special [MASK] token. The model is then tasked with predicting the original tokens that were masked, using the surrounding unmasked words as clues. This forces BERT to integrate context from both directions, before and after the masked word, to make an accurate prediction. For example, given the sentence 'He grabbed his [MASK] to hit the baseball', BERT must deduce from the words 'grabbed' and 'to hit the baseball' that the missing word is 'bat'. Similarly, if presented with 'He saw a [MASK] hanging from the cave ceiling', the context provided by 'hanging from the cave ceiling' leads the model to infer that the missing token is 'bat', referring to the animal rather than sports equipment.

The other keyword in BERT's name is 'transformer'. For any fixed word, BERT uses the transformer architecture to assign attention values to all the other words in the input sentence. More specifically, the transformer first decomposes a sentence into individual tokens and converts each token into three distinct vectors: queries, keys, and values. When processing a token, for example 'bank' in the sentence 'The bank can secure a loan because it has strong reserves', the transformer computes the dot product between the query vector of 'bank' and the key vectors of all tokens in the sentence. This dot product measures the 'closeness' between 'bank' and each other word, indicating how strongly they are related in the given context. Consequently, words like 'loan' and 'reserves' receive higher attention weights because they are contextually more relevant to 'bank', whereas less informative words like 'the' receive lower weights. These attention weights are continuously updated during the pretraining phase and provide a key process through which the neural network fine-tunes its parameters.

The BERT base model has been fine-tuned to perform specific tasks, particularly binary sentiment analysis using the SST-2 dataset, a collection of film reviews with annotated sentiment labels. This fine-tuning process adapts the pretrained model to distinguish between positive and negative sentiment, and the resulting model is freely available on Hugging Face. It outputs both a sentiment label and the associated probability score for each piece of text. This capability enables us to quantify the sentiment linked to various actions within decision-making scenarios. Building on this, we can investigate whether these sentiment measures help explain human behaviour.

To explore this idea, I examine the usual six Dictator Game frames introduced in my 2019 paper with Vanzo. These frames have been developed explicitly to study the effect of language on human behaviour and are characterised by minimal lexical variations in the description of available actions. Additionally, the instructions are extremely succinct. Consequently, if an LLM can conduct sentiment analysis in a manner that explains human behaviour, it is expected that such a model would exhibit particularly precise performance on these frames.

Example (Sentiment Analysis Using BERT Fails to Explain Human Behaviour in the Extreme Dictator Game). Let us start with the most extreme and arguably simplest case: the steal frame. Here, the actions available to the decision-maker were labelled 'steal from the other participant' and 'don't steal from the other participant'. Intuitively, it seems the first action should have negative sentiment, while the second action should have positive sentiment. In agreement with this intuition, BERT assigns a negative label with probability 0.94 to 'steal from the other participant' while it assigns a positive label with probability 0.91 to 'don't steal from the other participant'.

Now, consider the opposite extreme: the boost frame. This frame is characterised by eliciting the lowest amount of altruistic behaviour among human participants. Consequently, for the sentiment analysis to capture this pattern accurately, one would expect that the sentiment associated with the phrase 'boost the other participant' and its negated counterpart 'don't boost the other participant' would be nearly equivalent. However, when prompting BERT to compute the sentiment scores of these expressions, the language model assigns 'boost the other participant' a positive label with a probability of 0.99, while it assigns 'don't boost the other participant' a negative label with the same probability. Thus, somewhat surprisingly, BERT categorises the boost frame as being more polarising than the steal frame. Consequently, if we were to apply the LiMoLES utility function, we would predict a higher rate of altruistic behaviour in the boost frame than in the steal frame, an outcome that is diametrically opposed to the empirical observations of human behaviour.

Of course, this argument does not depend on the specific choice of the LiMoLES utility function, which merely provides the simplest means of formalising the sentiment expressed by the linguistic description of available actions using a utility function that linearly combines this sentiment with the monetary payoff. Any utility function that is monotonically increasing in sentiment would yield similar predictions: higher levels of altruism in the boost frame than in the steal frame. A prediction that is contradicted by the experimental evidence. This discrepancy suggests not that the LiMoLES utility function is inherently flawed, but rather that BERT may be limited in its ability to accurately estimate the sentiment of these actions in a manner that reliably reflects human behaviour. □

One potential explanation for this failure is that prompting BERT to compute the sentiment of 'boost the other participant' in isolation may lead the model to produce a relatively context-free sentiment estimate, one that does not accurately reflect the affective experience of human participants when considering that decision. After all, choices are not made in a vacuum, but are embedded within the specific contextual framework provided by the decision problem. Although BERT's bidirectional architecture permits the incorporation of contextual information more effectively than unidirectional models, its capacity is ultimately constrained by the input it receives.

In principle, we could try to overcome this limitation by supplying BERT with the full set of instructions for the decision problem in addition to the target phrase, aiming to signal to BERT that the sentiment of 'boost the other participant' should be assessed within the broader context delineated by an accompanying text describing the decision problem. However, this strategy introduces a new challenge, namely, how to efficiently communicate the extended context to BERT, given that the model does not permit the inclusion of a separate context window. One viable approach is to concatenate the decision instructions with the available actions and to prompt BERT to calculate the sentiment for the combined text. Let us then explore whether this approach yields more accurate sentiment estimates that better align with human behaviour.

Example (Testing the Inclusion of Experimental Instructions in BERT Input). As an initial attempt, I prompted BERT to evaluate the sentiment of the following text, which mechanically concatenates the original instructions with the target action:

> *There are $0.50 available. You have to choose between two possible actions: BOOST THE OTHER PARTICIPANT: In which case, you get 0 cents and the other participant gets $0.50; DON'T BOOST THE OTHER PARTICIPANT: In which case, you get $0.50 and the other participant gets 0 cents. The other participant has no choice and will be paid according to your decision. No deception is used. You and the other participant will be paid according to your decision. BOOST THE OTHER PARTICIPANT.*

BERT assigned a negative sentiment label to this text with a probability of 0.87. When the altruistic action was replaced with the self-interested option ('don't boost the other participant'), BERT returned a negative label with a probability of 0.95. Thus, both the altruistic and self-interested actions are perceived negatively, though the self-interested action is deemed slightly more negative than the altruistic one. In principle, such an outcome might be consistent with the experimental data, which indicate relatively low levels of altruistic behaviour for the boost frame.

However, complications emerge when examining other frames. Consider the steal frame. I prompted BERT to compute the sentiment of the self-interested action:

> *There are $0.50 available. You have to choose between two possible actions: STEAL FROM THE OTHER PARTICIPANT: In which case, you get $0.50 and the other participant gets 0 cents; DON'T STEAL FROM THE OTHER PARTICIPANT:*

> *In which case, you get 0 cents and the other participant gets $0.50. The other participant has no choice and will be paid according to your decision. No deception is used. You and the other participant will be paid according to your decision. STEAL FROM THE OTHER PARTICIPANT.*

BERT returned a negative label with a probability of 0.93, which is comparable to, and actually slightly lower than, the probability assigned to the self-interested action in the boost frame. Yet when queried regarding the sentiment of the altruistic action in the steal frame, BERT again returned a negative label, this time with a probability of 0.86. As with the boost frame, BERT perceives the self-interested action as more negative than the altruistic action, which aligns with experimental expectations. However, the difference in probabilities is strikingly similar across frames: in the boost frame, the difference is $0.95 - 0.87 = 0.08$, while in the steal frame, it is $0.93 - 0.86 = 0.07$. If these probability differentials were truly determinative of behaviour, we would anticipate similar rates of altruism across the two frames. In contrast, human experimental data reveal a marked discrepancy: the rate of altruistic behaviour in the steal frame is approximately 30%, whereas that in the boost frame is as low as 5% (Capraro & Vanzo, 2019).

Another possibility we might explore is that the impersonal nature of the initial prompt may have induced the model to produce inaccurate sentiment estimations. To test this hypothesis, we can reformulate the prompt in the first person:

> *There are $0.50 available. I have to choose between two possible actions: STEAL FROM THE OTHER PARTICIPANT: In which case, I get $0.50 and the other participant gets 0 cents; DON'T STEAL FROM THE OTHER PARTICIPANT: In which case, I get 0 cents and the other participant gets $0.50. The other participant has no choice and will be paid according to my decision. No deception is used. The other participant and I will be paid according to my decision. I CHOOSE TO STEAL FROM THE OTHER PARTICIPANT.*

In this instance, the model returned a negative sentiment label with a probability of 0.94, an outcome remarkably similar to that observed under the earlier impersonal formulation. Furthermore, when we replace the self-interested action with the altruistic alternative ('I choose to not steal from the other participant'), BERT produces a negative label with a probability of 0.92. Thus, the difference between the two actions appears even more attenuated than in the previous impersonal case.

These examples represent only some extreme cases. Table 8.1 reports the differences between the sentiment scores of the altruistic and self-interested actions across various prompt formulations. Specifically, column 2 reports scores obtained using only the action phrase; column 3, scores when the action is expressed in the first person; column 4, scores when the instructions and the action are combined; and column 5, scores when instructions and the action are combined in the first person. The sentiment score for an action is calculated by multiplying the associated label (+1 for positive or −1 for negative) by the probability assigned to that label by BERT. Although this method has its limitations (for instance, it ignores the probabilities of labels with lower likelihoods and does not account for potential neutral labels) it is evident that these sentiment scores offer a poor explanation for the actual altruistic behaviour observed in the experiment, as summarised in column 6 of Table 8.1.

To show this inability more formally, we can conduct a series of linear regressions predicting actual human altruistic behaviour as a function of the differences in sentiment scores across frames. Although each regression suffers from limited statistical power, it is apparent that the predictions are far from 'promising', regardless of how 'promising' is defined. The outputs of these regressions, reported in the final row of Table 8.1, indicate that the first two regression slopes are virtually flat, while the fourth regression slope actually trends in the opposite direction. The only regression that shows a slight positive trend is the third one; however, the standard error of the coefficient is excessively large relative to the coefficient itself, rendering it statistically indistinguishable from zero. □

Table 8.1 *Sentiment analysis conducted using BERT provides a poor explanation of human altruistic behaviour.*

Frame	Sentiment polarity				Actual human altruism in experiment
–	Only action (impersonal)	Only action (first-person)	Instructions + action (impersonal)	Instructions + action (first-person)	–
Boost	1.99	1.98	0.08	0.03	0.05
Give	1.32	0.20	0.01	0.02	0.09
Donate	1.52	0.39	0.05	0.03	0.12
Demand	1.53	1.72	0.01	-0.00	0.15
Take	-1.06	-1.31	-0.01	-0.01	0.15
Steal	1.85	1.93	0.07	0.02	0.30
Correlation with human behaviour	0.00 (0.04)	0.01 (0.03)	0.26 (1.16)	-1.11 (2.55)	–

For each frame of the extreme Dictator Game, the second column reports sentiment polarity (the difference between the sentiment of the altruistic action and that of the self-serving action) when BERT is prompted with the action expressed in impersonal form. The third column shows sentiment polarity when BERT is prompted with the action expressed in the first person. The fourth column reports sentiment polarity when BERT is prompted with the instruction plus action in impersonal form, while the fifth column presents sentiment polarity for the instruction plus action in personal form. The sixth column displays observed altruistic behaviour as measured in Capraro and Vanzo (2019). The final row reports the regression coefficients and standard errors for linear models predicting altruistic behaviour based on the sentiment polarity measures.

Looking at Table 8.1, we can draw some informal conclusions about why BERT (fine-tuned for sentiment analysis) might fail. In the first two columns (where BERT is queried using only the action phrase), there is considerable variability across frames. This pattern suggests that, absent context, BERT computes sentiment on a relatively context-independent version of each action, adding substantial noise and yielding highly heterogeneous scores. The take frame is particularly illustrative: BERT rates the altruistic action as more negative than the self-interested action, exactly opposite to intuitive and empirical expectations.

However, when we append the decision instructions to each action, the sentiment differentials all converge near zero. This likely occurs because the single-word difference between the two actions is drowned out within dozens of surrounding words; BERT's sentiment score appears to scale with text length, rendering small but behaviourally critical lexical variations negligible.

In sum, BERT, even when fine-tuned for sentiment analysis, does not reliably explain human behaviour in simple economic decisions, like extreme Dictator Games deliberately introduced to study language effects. One possible explanation is that its fine-tuning on film reviews does not generalise to economic decision contexts. A domain-specific fine-tuning regimen may perform better.

Recently, Preniqi et al. (2024) introduced MoralBERT, a BERT variant specifically refined to assess moral dimensions via moral foundations theory. MoralBERT is trained on three specialised corpora: the Moral Foundations Twitter Corpus (35,108 tweets annotated for five moral principles; Hoover et al., 2020), the Moral Foundations Reddit Corpus (13,995 posts; Trager et al., 2022), and 1,509 vaccine-debate Facebook posts (Beiró et al., 2023). When prompted, MoralBERT outputs 10 continuous scores corresponding to 5 virtues (care, fairness, loyalty, authority, purity) and 5 opposite vices (harm, cheating, betrayal, subversion, degradation). That raises the following question: can MoralBERT's 'normative analysis' better explain human behaviour across the six Dictator Game frames?

Example (MoralBERT's Normative Analysis Can Explain Human Behaviour in the Dictator Game, with a Caveat). Table 8.2 presents the differences between moral scores assigned by MoralBERT to the altruistic versus self-interested actions across the 10 dimensions (columns 2–11), along with an aggregate 'moral polarity' measure (column 12), defined as the sum of virtue scores minus the sum of vice scores for each treatment. Column 13 reports the observed rates of altruistic behaviour from Capraro and Vanzo (2019).

Overall, MoralBERT's normative scores align more closely with human behaviour than the generic sentiment scores produced by BERT. In particular, the boost frame exhibits a moral polarity near zero, indicating equivalent moral value assigned to both the altruistic and self-interested options, consistent with the low observed altruism rate (5%). Conversely, the steal frame yields a moral polarity of 0.81, reflecting a substantially higher moral valuation of the altruistic action compared to the self-serving action, concordant with the higher altruism rate (30%). A linear regression predicting altruism rate from moral polarity produces a statistically significant positive coefficient ($\beta = 0.207$, $t = 4.69$, $p = 0.009$).

From a formal perspective, this finding supports a simple, LiMoLNoS-like utility function of the shape:

$$u_d(c) = \pi_d(a) + \mu_d M_d(a), \tag{8.1}$$

where $\pi_d(a)$ is the monetary payoff received by the decision-maker when they choose action a, μ_d is an individual parameter representing the extent to which the decision-maker cares about doing the morally right thing, and $M_d(a)$ represents the extent to which the decision-maker believes that taking action a is the morally right thing to do. The significant regression suggests that this language-based utility function captures the aggregate patterns observed in Capraro and Vanzo (2019).

I emphasise 'aggregate' because closer scrutiny reveals limitations. In fact, MoralBERT assigns negative moral polarity to both the give and donate frames, implying that in these frames the

Table 8.2 *Moral polarity calculated using MoralBERT is associated with altruistic behaviour in the Dictator Game.*

Frame	Normative polarity										Moral polarity	Human altruism
–	Care	Harm	Fairness	Cheating	Loyalty	Betrayal	Authority	Subversion	Purity	Degradation	–	–
Boost	-0.00	0.01	0.00	-0.00	0.01	0.00	0.00	-0.00	0.00	0.00	0.00	0.05
Give	-0.12	-0.00	-0.00	-0.00	0.04	0.13	0.00	0.00	0.00	0.00	-0.22	0.09
Donate	-0.01	0.00	0.00	-0.00	0.09	0.17	0.00	-0.00	0.00	-0.00	-0.09	0.12
Demand	0.06	-0.19	-0.00	0.00	0.02	0.00	-0.00	-0.00	-0.00	-0.04	0.29	0.15
Take	0.21	-0.00	-0.00	0.00	-0.01	-0.01	-0.00	0.00	-0.00	-0.00	0.21	0.15
Steal	0.04	-0.81	-0.00	0.01	0.05	0.00	-0.00	-0.00	-0.04	-0.01	0.85	0.30

For each frame of the extreme Dictator Game and for each vice and virtue, columns 2–11 report sentiment polarity (the normative score of the altruistic action minus that of the self-serving action) computed using MoralBERT. Column 12 reports overall moral polarity, defined as the sum of the normative scores of the virtues minus the sum of the scores of the vices. Column 13 presents altruistic behaviour observed in human participants, as measured by Capraro and Vanzo (2019).

self-interested action is deemed morally superior to the altruistic action. According to the LiMoLNoS utility function (as well as to any utility function that is increasing in the moral component), such inequality would predict zero altruistic behaviour. Yet empirical data show non-zero rates of altruism in both frames. In fact, the donate frame elicits a significantly higher generosity rate than the boost frame, directly contradicting MoralBERT's predictions (Capraro & Vanzo, 2019). Thus, while MoralBERT's normative analysis improves upon BERT, it remains an imperfect predictor of human decision-making across all linguistic framings. □

SENTIMENT ANALYSIS USING LLM-BASED CHATBOTS

In the previous section, we saw that BERT and, especially, MoralBERT have enabled a significant step forward in the quantification of the language used to describe an economic decision problem in a way that can help explain human behaviour beyond the economic consequences of the available actions. The predictions are still relatively imprecise when seen in detail. However, the results are certainly promising and give us reason to explore this issue in more depth.

One limitation of both BERT and MoralBERT is their relative context independence, meaning that informing the model that the action is being taken within the context described by the decision problem is not straightforward. One can add a context window artificially, by combining the instructions and the decision problem, but in that case the difference between two actions will reduce to a handful of words in a relatively long text. Consequently, these two actions would have a very similar sentiment. Therefore, the capacity of the model to differentiate between actions is somewhat limited.

Ideally, we would like to instruct the language model to incorporate a context window directly. This brings us to the second reason why LLMs, and LLM-based chatbots in particular, may reshape behavioural economics: they make it easy to add a context window.

As we will see, this can enable explanations of human behaviour that go beyond the economic consequences of available actions, in a way that is more effective than earlier models.

In practice, this means we could ask an LLM-based chatbot like GPT-4: 'Please read the following decision problem', then present the details of the problem, and finally ask it to rate the sentiment associated with each available action. An example using the boost frame is as follows:

> *Please read the following decision problem.*
>
> *There are $0.50 available. You have to choose between two possible actions:*
>
> *BOOST THE OTHER PARTICIPANT: In which case, you get 0 cents and the other participant gets $0.50;*
>
> *DON'T BOOST THE OTHER PARTICIPANT: In which case, you get $0.50 and the other participant gets 0 cents.*
>
> *The other participant has no choice and will be paid according to your decision. No deception is used. You and the other participant will be paid according to your decision.*
>
> *Now imagine a population of people living in the USA. What do you think the average response to the following questions would be? (Please return an exact number with two decimal digits).*
>
> *How negative or positive is the action of 'not boosting the other participant' on a 1–7 scale? Answer only with a number, with 1 being 'very negative' and 7 being 'very positive'.*
>
> *How negative or positive is the action of 'boosting the other participant' on a 1–7 scale? Answer only with a number, with 1 being 'very negative' and 7 being 'very positive'.*

The specific wording for collecting sentiments is adapted from Rathje et al. (2024), who first studied the capability of GPT in conducting text analysis. When prompted in this way, GPT-4 simply responds with a context-based estimation of the sentiment:

This decision problem highlights a classic dilemma between self-interest and altruism. Since no empirical data specific to this scenario are available, we can make educated guesses based on general tendencies observed in studies of human behavior regarding altruism and selfishness.

1. ***Not Boosting the Other Participant**: This action, where the participant chooses to keep the money, might be viewed negatively by some as it shows a lack of altruism. However, given that many individuals prioritise their own interests, especially in financial matters where the sum is not negligible, this action might not be deemed extremely negative. It is likely perceived as somewhat negative to neutral, depending on individual beliefs about fairness and self-interest. An estimated average rating on a 1–7 scale (where 1 is 'very negative' and 7 is 'very positive') might be around **3.00**.*
2. ***Boosting the Other Participant**: This action represents a purely altruistic choice, as the participant gains nothing and gives all to another. In general, altruistic behaviors are viewed positively, especially in controlled settings where the context emphasises fairness or generosity. Therefore, this action is likely viewed quite positively, though not universally perfect since some may argue it's not rational economically. An estimated average rating might be around **6.00**.*

These estimates are hypothetical and would likely vary based on cultural, socio-economic, and individual differences in attitudes towards altruism and self-gain.

It then becomes an experimental question whether these scores can be used to accurately explain human behaviour in economic games. Therefore, let us try to do this for all six frames.

Example (GPT-4's Sentiment Analysis Allows Us to Explain Human Behaviour in the Extreme Dictator Game). Given the non-deterministic nature of GPT-4, I ran the above prompt 8 times for each frame. The number 8 was chosen simply because it results in a total of 48 prompts, which could be completed in two iterations, given that at the time of this experiment, there was a limit of 25 prompts every 3 hours on GPT-4. At the same time, 8 prompts per condition seems to be a reasonable starting point for some preliminary results. To avoid learning effects within a single conversation, I deleted the chat and started a new one for each prompt.

Table 8.3 presents the results of this analysis and reveals several interesting findings. First, the difference in sentiment between the altruistic action and the self-interested action strongly depends on the framing and is also quite heterogeneous across iterations within the same prompt. For example, the average sentiment score of 2.25 for the boost frame results from one score of 3, two scores of 3.5, and five scores of 2. This variability confirms that GPT-4 does not behave deterministically on this task. Only in one case, the demand frame, did GPT-4 return the same sentiment scores across all eight iterations (2 for 'demand from the other participant', 6 for 'don't demand from the other participant').

Most importantly, the difference in sentiment between the altruistic and self-interested actions, as estimated by GPT-4, is an exceptionally strong predictor of the actual rate of altruistic behaviour observed in the experiment. Not only are the two variables highly correlated across the six frames ($\beta = 0.077$, $t = 6.92$, $p = 0.002$), but even the finer details are well captured. This is evident in the ordering of the frames in Table 8.3: the ranking based on the sentiment difference between altruistic and self-interested actions exactly mirrors the ranking of altruistic behaviour rates, except for a minor discrepancy between the demand and take frames. According to GPT-4, these two frames show slightly different sentiment polarity, yet they yield the same rate of altruistic behaviour in the experiment.

One might wonder whether such precise predictions simply stem from GPT-4 having been trained on the results of Capraro and Vanzo (2019), and whether it is merely reproducing this knowledge.

Table 8.3 *Sentiment analysis conducted using GPT-4 allows us to explain altruistic behaviour in the Dictator Game.*

Frame	Sentiment polarity	Rate of altruistic behaviour
Boost	2.25	0.05
Give	2.81	0.09
Donate	3.19	0.12
Demand	4.00	0.15
Take	4.12	0.15
Steal	5.25	0.30

For each frame of the extreme Dictator Game, the second column shows the sentiment polarity (difference between the sentiment of the altruistic and self-interested actions), as estimated by GPT-4. The third column reports the actual rate of altruistic behaviour observed in the original experiment (Capraro & Vanzo, 2019).

To rule out this possibility, we can prompt GPT-4 to directly estimate actual human behaviour in each of the six frames from Capraro and Vanzo (2019). The prompt used in the demand frame was as follows:

> *Please read the following decision problem:*
>
> *There are $0.50 available. You have to choose between two possible actions:*
>
> *DEMAND FROM THE OTHER PARTICIPANT: In which case, you get $0.50 and the other participant gets 0 cents;*
>
> *DON'T DEMAND FROM THE OTHER PARTICIPANT: In which case, you get 0 cents and the other participant gets $0.50.*
>
> *The other participant has no choice and will be paid according to your decision. No deception is used. You and the other participant will be paid according to your decision.*
>
> *Now imagine that there is a population of 1,000 people living in the USA facing this decision problem. How would you estimate the distribution of their choices? Please, for each choice, report a result in the form X±Y, where X is the estimated number of people making their choice, and Y is the error.*

Table 8.4 *GPT-4 does not estimate human altruistic behaviour with precision.*

Frame	GPT-4's predicted altruistic behaviour	Actual altruistic behaviour
Boost	0.37	0.05
Give	0.32	0.09
Donate	0.34	0.12
Demand	0.37	0.15
Take	0.40	0.15
Steal	0.55	0.30

For each frame of the extreme Dictator Game, the second column reports the rate of altruistic behaviour predicted by GPT-4 and the third column reports the actual rate of altruistic behaviour in a human sample, as measured by Capraro and Vanzo (2019).

As with the sentiment scores, to account for the non-deterministic nature of GPT-4's outputs, I ran this prompt eight times for each frame. Table 8.4 reports the mean results. It is clear that GPT-4's predictions of actual human behaviour deviate substantially from the real data. While GPT-4 correctly predicts that the rate of altruistic behaviour in the steal frame would be higher than in other frames, the absolute values are greatly overestimated. For instance, in the boost frame, GPT-4 predicts that, on average, 37% of participants would act altruistically, whereas in reality, only 5% did. Even the ordering of frames is not accurately captured: according to GPT-4, the lowest rate of altruistic behaviour should occur in the give frame; in reality, the lowest rate was observed in the boost frame. Since GPT-4's estimations of actual behaviour are much less accurate than its sentiment-based predictions, it seems unlikely that the strong predictive power of the sentiment scores arises from GPT-4 having been trained on the results of Capraro and Vanzo (2019). □

FORMAL PREDICTIONS IN THE DICTATOR GAME

In the previous section, we saw preliminary results suggesting that sentiment scores computed using GPT-4 can help explain human behaviour in the extreme Dictator Game. In this section, I aim to take a step further and derive a general prediction that can be tested across a broader range of Dictator Games.

Consider a Dictator Game in which the dictator decides how to divide a fixed sum of money, normalised to 1, between themselves and the recipient. Assume the dictator's preferences follow the LiMoLES utility function:

$$u(a) = \pi(a) + \sigma S(a), \tag{8.2}$$

where $\pi(a)$ represents the dictator's monetary payoff when the dictator implements action a, σ represents the extent to which the dictator follows their emotions, and $S(a)$ represents the sentiment that the dictator feels when contemplating action a. As before, here we identify an action with its linguistic description.

The goal of this section is to estimate the expected rate of giving in a population of dictators as a function of sentiment scores, under a set of relatively natural assumptions. I will then test this prediction in a separate experiment.

To derive this estimation, I rely on four assumptions:

- **Action space**. The dictator considers only three possible actions: the self-serving action (s, keeping all the money), the equitable action (e, splitting the money equally), and the altruistic, other-regarding action (o, giving all the money to the recipient). Engel's (2011) meta-analysis of Dictator Game behaviour shows that approximately 60% of participants choose one of these three options, making this a reasonably realistic assumption.
- **Dictator's rationality**. The dictator is component-wise rational; that is, if an action a' dominates another action a in both the monetary payoff and the sentiment, then the dominated action a is eliminated from consideration. In other words, the dictator considers only actions that are not dominated by any other action.
- **Choice rule**. The probability that the dictator chooses action a depends on the utility of the action as calculated by the logit formula:

$$p(a) = \frac{e^{\lambda u(a)}}{\sum_{a'} e^{\lambda u(a')}}, \tag{8.3}$$

where $\lambda \geq 0$ is a precision parameter. For $\lambda = 0$, the formula degenerates to a purely random selection, as each action is chosen with equal probability. For $\lambda \to \infty$, the choice converges to a deterministic rule in which the action with the highest utility is always selected. This assumption captures decision noise and reflects the idea that agents are more likely to choose higher-utility options while still allowing for occasional suboptimal choices. This form of probabilistic choice has a long tradition in behavioural modelling (e.g., Luce, 1959; McKelvey & Palfrey, 1995; Pennycook et al., 2021).

- **Distribution of sensitivities**. The parameter σ, which determines the weight individuals place on emotional sentiment, is assumed to be distributed in the population according to a smooth, continuously differentiable density function $f(\sigma)$. This ensures that small changes in sentiment scores lead to smooth changes in behaviour, avoiding discontinuities. In other words, the population is 'well spread' with respect to σ, and individuals near any given threshold of emotional sensitivity are always present in the population.
- **Distribution of sentiment scores**. Finally, we assume that the sentiment scores $S(e)$ and $S(o)$ are distributed such that their linear combinations $S(o) - S(e)$ and $S(o) + S(e)$ are independent and have continuously differentiable densities. This technical assumption greatly simplifies the mathematical derivation of the expected giving rate. However, it is not essential and can be relaxed. I will return to this point at the end of the section.

Definition. Let

$$U = \begin{cases} S(e) - S(s), & \text{if } S(e) \geq S(o) \\ \dfrac{S(o) + S(e)}{2} - S(s), & \text{if } S(e) < S(o) \end{cases}. \tag{8.4}$$

Theorem. Under the assumptions above, the average rate of giving in a population of dictators is strictly increasing with U.

Proof. The first case is simple. If $S(e) \geq S(o)$, then the equitable strategy dominates the altruistic strategy in terms of both monetary payoff and sentiment. Therefore, we can eliminate the altruistic strategy from the analysis. The choice between the self-interested and the equitable action will then depend on the difference between their utilities, which is

$$\begin{aligned} u(e) - u(s) &= (0.5 + \sigma S(e)) - (1 + \sigma S(s)) \\ &= -0.5 + \sigma(S(e) - S(s)) \end{aligned} \tag{8.5}$$

and depends linearly on $S(e) - S(s)$.

The case $S(e) < S(o)$ is technical but conceptually not difficult. Consider an individual with sensitivity parameter σ. Let $p(a|\sigma)$ be the probability that this individual chooses action a. The expected giving of this individual is:

$$G(\sigma) = 0 \cdot p(s|\sigma) + \frac{1}{2} p(e|\sigma) + p(o|\sigma) = \frac{1}{2} p(e|\sigma) + p(o|\sigma). \tag{8.6}$$

As a first goal, I shall show that this function is increasing in the variable U, by demonstrating that $\frac{\partial G}{\partial U} > 0$.

With this aim in mind, it is useful to introduce some notation that will simplify the computation of the various partial derivatives. First, let us set:

$$\Delta_e = S(e) - S(s), \tag{8.7}$$

$$\Delta_o = S(o) - S(s). \tag{8.8}$$

Observe that:

$$U = \frac{\Delta_e + \Delta_o}{2}. \tag{8.9}$$

Define also:

$$\delta = \frac{\Delta_o - \Delta_e}{2} = \frac{S(o) - S(e)}{2}. \tag{8.10}$$

And observe that:

$$\Delta_e = U - \delta \qquad \Delta_o = U + \delta. \tag{8.11}$$

Note also that the utilities corresponding to the various options can be rewritten as:

$$u(s) = 1 + \sigma S(s) \tag{8.12}$$

$$u(e) = 0.5 + \sigma S(e) = 0.5 + \sigma S(s) + \sigma \Delta_e \tag{8.13}$$

$$u(o) = \sigma S(o) = \sigma S(s) + \sigma \Delta_o. \tag{8.14}$$

We can now rewrite the probabilities that a dictator with sensitivity parameter σ chooses each available action as:

$$p(s \mid \sigma) = \frac{e^{\lambda(1+\sigma S(s))}}{e^{\lambda(1+\sigma S(s))} + e^{\lambda(0.5+\sigma S(s)+\sigma\Delta_e)} + e^{\lambda(\sigma S(s)+\sigma\Delta_o)}} = \frac{e^{\lambda}}{e^{\lambda} + e^{0.5\lambda} \cdot e^{\lambda\sigma\Delta_e} + e^{\lambda\sigma\Delta_o}} \tag{8.15}$$

$$p(e \mid \sigma) = \frac{e^{0.5\lambda} \cdot e^{\lambda\sigma\Delta_e}}{e^{\lambda} + e^{0.5\lambda} \cdot e^{\lambda\sigma\Delta_e} + e^{\lambda\sigma\Delta_o}} \tag{8.16}$$

$$p(o \mid \sigma) = \frac{e^{\lambda\sigma\Delta_o}}{e^{\lambda} + e^{0.5\lambda} \cdot e^{\lambda\sigma\Delta_e} + e^{\lambda\sigma\Delta_o}}. \tag{8.17}$$

Now, let us introduce the following additional notation:

$$A = e^{\lambda}, B = e^{0.5\lambda}, E_1 = e^{\lambda\sigma\Delta_e} = e^{\lambda\sigma(U-\delta)}, \quad E_2 = e^{\lambda\sigma\Delta_o} = e^{\lambda\sigma(U+\delta)}, D = A + BE_1 + E_2. \tag{8.18}$$

With this notation, the various probabilities can be rewritten as:

$$p(s|\sigma) = \frac{A}{D} \tag{8.19}$$

$$p(e|\sigma) = \frac{BE_1}{D} \tag{8.20}$$

$$p(o|\sigma) = \frac{E_2}{D}. \tag{8.21}$$

Now, we need to compute the derivative, with respect to U, of the probabilities $p(e|\sigma)$ and $p(o|\sigma)$. Since these functions depend on E_1 and E_2, it is convenient to first compute the derivatives of these functions.

Now, in what follows, let us treat U as a variable and keep δ constant. (We move beyond this limitation in the next step of the proof.)

We have:

$$\frac{\partial E_1}{\partial U} = \frac{\partial(e^{\lambda\sigma(U-\delta)})}{\partial U} = \lambda\sigma e^{\lambda\sigma(U-\delta)} = \lambda\sigma E_1 \tag{8.22}$$

$$\frac{\partial E_2}{\partial U} = \frac{\partial(e^{\lambda\sigma(U+\delta)})}{\partial U} = \lambda\sigma e^{\lambda\sigma(U+\delta)} = \lambda\sigma E_2. \tag{8.23}$$

Note that the denominator $D = A + BE_1 + E_2$ also depends on E_1 and E_2. Its derivative with respect to U is:

$$\frac{\partial D}{\partial U} = B\frac{\partial E_1}{\partial U} + \frac{\partial E_2}{\partial U} = \lambda\sigma(BE_1 + E_2). \tag{8.24}$$

We are now ready to compute $\frac{\partial p(e|\sigma)}{\partial U}$ and $\frac{\partial p(o|\sigma)}{\partial U}$. Starting from the first one, we have:

$$\begin{aligned}\frac{\partial p(e|\sigma)}{\partial U} &= \frac{\partial\left(\frac{BE_1}{D}\right)}{\partial U} \\ &= \frac{\frac{\partial(BE_1)}{\partial U}\cdot D - \frac{\partial D}{\partial U}\cdot BE_1}{D^2} \\ &= \frac{B\lambda\sigma E_1 D - BE_1\lambda\sigma(BE_1 + E_2)}{D^2} \\ &= \frac{B\lambda\sigma E_1(D - BE_1 - E_2)}{D^2}.\end{aligned} \tag{8.25}$$

Now, notice that $D - BE_1 - E_2 = A$. Therefore,

$$\frac{\partial p(e|\sigma)}{\partial U} = \frac{B\lambda\sigma E_1 A}{D^2}. \tag{8.26}$$

Note now that all factors $A, B, \lambda, \sigma, E_1, D^2$ are positive. Hence

$$\frac{\partial p(e|\sigma)}{\partial U} > 0. \tag{8.27}$$

Similarly, we have:

$$\begin{aligned}\frac{\partial p(o|\sigma)}{\partial U} &= \frac{\partial\left(\frac{E_2}{D}\right)}{\partial U} \\ &= \frac{\frac{\partial E_2}{\partial U}\cdot D - \frac{\partial D}{\partial U}\cdot E_2}{D^2} \\ &= \frac{\lambda\sigma E_2 D - E_2\lambda\sigma(BE_1 + E_2)}{D^2} \\ &= \frac{\lambda\sigma E_2(D - BE_1 - E_2)}{D^2} \\ &= \frac{\lambda\sigma E_2 A}{D^2} > 0.\end{aligned} \tag{8.28}$$

Given that both $\frac{\partial p(e|\sigma)}{\partial U} > 0$ and $\frac{\partial p(o|\sigma)}{\partial U} > 0$, it follows that

$$\frac{\partial G}{\partial U} = 0.5 \cdot \frac{\partial p(e|\sigma)}{\partial U} + \frac{\partial p(o|\sigma)}{\partial U} > 0. \tag{8.29}$$

Therefore, the function G, which represents the expected giving of an individual with sensitivity parameter σ, is increasing in U. Importantly, this holds when δ is kept constant.

Now, for fixed U and δ, the average (with respect to σ) population giving can be computed as

$$H(U,\delta) = \int_0^\infty G(U,\delta,\sigma) f(\sigma) d\sigma. \tag{8.30}$$

The regularity hypothesis on the distribution f allows us to interchange integration and differentiation (using the standard dominated convergence theorem). Therefore, we have

$$\frac{\partial H(U,\delta)}{\partial U} = \int_0^\infty \frac{\partial G(U,\delta,\sigma)}{\partial U} f(\sigma) d\sigma > 0. \tag{8.31}$$

Therefore, when δ is fixed, the average giving in the population is increasing in U.

Now, we use our fourth assumption (that U and δ are independently distributed) to show that the average giving in the population of dictators continues to increase in U, even when δ is allowed to vary. The overall population average giving, which we denote by $\bar{G}$, is obtained by averaging H over δ:

$$\bar{G}(U) = \int_\delta H(U,\delta) g(\delta) d\delta. \tag{8.32}$$

Here $g(\delta)$ is the density distribution of δ. This distribution is assumed to be independent of U. Therefore, when we differentiate $\bar{G}$ with respect to U, we obtain:

$$\frac{\partial \bar{G}}{\partial U} = \int_\delta \frac{\partial H(U,\delta)}{\partial U} g(\delta) d\delta. \tag{8.33}$$

Now, both $\frac{\partial H(U,\delta)}{\partial U}$ and $g(\delta)$ are positive: the former because of what I have shown before, and the latter because it is a density. It follows that the integral of their product is positive as well. Therefore, $\bar{G}$ is strictly increasing in U. This concludes the proof. □

I have proven this theorem under a specific set of assumptions. However, the same conclusion holds under alternative assumptions. For instance, a key assumption is that the probability of a dictator choosing a particular action is governed by a logit rule based on utility. One might ask whether the result still holds for dictators who are perfect utility-maximisers, those who always choose the action that maximises their utility with probability 1, and all other actions with probability 0. In this case, the proof requires some modifications, since the probability function is no longer continuous and some steps from the original derivation cannot be directly applied. Nonetheless, the core result still holds. Similarly, although the proof has been developed using the LiMoLES utility function, the result can be extended to more general utility functions that do not necessarily combine monetary payoffs and sentiment in a linear fashion. In fact, it is sufficient that the utility function is strictly increasing in the sentiment component. The proofs of these more general results are reported in a research article co-authored with Di Paolo and Pizziol, where we also test the prediction (Capraro et al., 2025b).

TESTING THE PREDICTION

The aim of this section is to test the prediction derived in the previous section, namely that the average giving in a population of dictators should increase with

$$U = \begin{cases} S(e) - S(s), & \text{if } S(e) \geq S(o) \\ \dfrac{S(o) + S(e)}{2} - S(s), & \text{if } S(e) < S(o) \end{cases}. \tag{8.34}$$

Experimental Result (GPT-4's Sentiment Analysis Allows Us to Explain Human Behaviour in the Dictator Game). To test this prediction, we collected as many Dictator Game experimental instructions as possible and prompted GPT-4 to estimate the sentiment of the linguistic descriptions of each strategy. We issued a public call for instructions on relevant forums (the Economic Science Association and the Society for Judgment and Decision Making) and solicited colleagues' contributions, which we supplemented with a manual literature search.

In an initial data collection phase, we obtained instructions from 61 Dictator Game treatments (Capraro et al., 2024c). We have since expanded this to 107 experimental instructions. The results reported here pertain to this full dataset (results for the initial subset are virtually identical and are detailed in the original paper).

Like in the previous example, for each experimental instruction, we prompted GPT-4 to 'please read this decision problem', followed by the experimental instruction. After the experimental instruction, in the same prompt, we asked:

> Now imagine that there is a population of people living in [country]. What do you think the average response to the following questions would be? (Please return an exact number with two decimal digits). How negative or positive is the action of [action referring to 'keeping all/keeping half/giving all the endowment'] on a 1–7 scale, with 1 being 'very negative' and 7 being 'very positive'?

In this prompt, [action referring to...] was replaced with the exact words used by the authors in the specific experimental instruction, and [country] with the country where the experiment was conducted.

Next, we normalised the sentiment scores and average giving between 0 and 1, so that we could more easily interpret effect sizes. From GPT-4's output we built our independent variable of interest U. Then we conducted a linear regression, with fixed effects at the study level, predicting average giving as a function of U.

In line with the prediction, the results show that the coefficient of U is positive and significantly different from 0 ($\beta = 0.349$, $t = 4.39$, $p < 0.001$). See Figure 8.1.

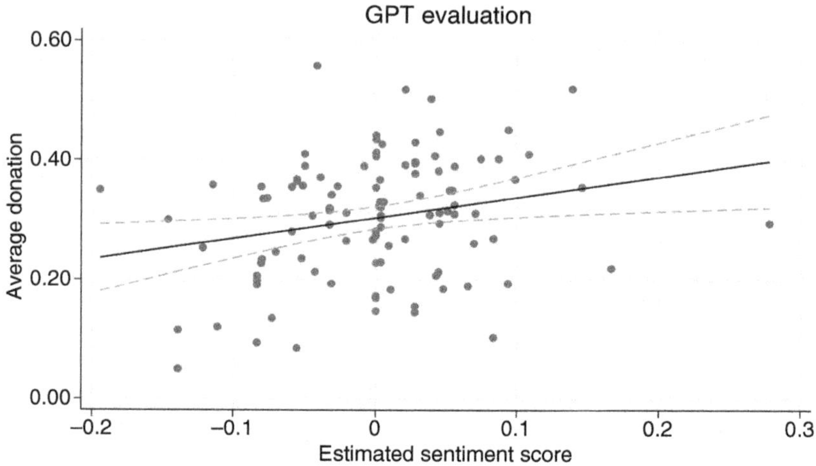

FIGURE 8.1 **Sentiment scores computed using GPT-4 are associated with altruistic behaviour in the Dictator Game.** Each dot represents a study for which we have collected experimental instructions. The x-axis corresponds to the U value calculated using GPT-4; the y-axis corresponds to the average donation in the study.

One might worry that GPT-4 simply memorised human experimental results. To address this, we prompted GPT-4 to predict average giving directly, without sentiment scores. GPT-4's direct behavioural predictions were, on average, 12 percentage points higher than the true giving rates, reflecting a systematic overestimation of altruism and underestimation of self-interested and equitable choices (Capraro et al., 2025). This provides initial evidence that GPT-4 did not merely recall human behaviour from these specific situations. A second, and arguably stronger, piece of evidence is that GPT-4's predictions were not significantly correlated with actual behaviour (Capraro et al., 2025). This discrepancy confirms that our sentiment-based regression is not an artefact of GPT-4's exposure to the data. □

TESTING PREDICTIONS IN OTHER GAMES

I would like to conclude this chapter by deriving analogous predictions for other games in which language has been shown to influence behaviour, and by examining whether sentiment analysis via GPT-4 can explain human behaviour in these contexts. The choice of GPT-4 reflects its prominence among current chatbots; comparable results likely hold with other advanced LLM-based chatbots. Evaluating multiple chatbots' sentiment-analysis capabilities lies beyond this book's scope. Rather, my aim is to demonstrate that such tools can be leveraged to explain human behaviour beyond the economic consequences of available actions.

Experimental Result (GPT-4's Sentiment Analysis Allows Us to Explain Human Behaviour in the Equity–Efficiency Trade-Off Game). In Chapter 3, I noted that behaviour in the Equity–Efficiency Trade-Off Game depends critically on how the two options are framed. When the equitable option is labelled 'nice', participants overwhelmingly choose the equitable option; when the efficient option is labelled 'nice', they overwhelmingly choose the efficient option. Can we account for this switch of preferences using the LiMoLES language-based utility function, with GPT-4 sentiment scores?

Because the Equity–Efficiency Trade-Off Game presents only two options, the prediction is straightforward: the proportion of participants choosing the efficient option should increase with the difference between its sentiment score and that of the equitable option.

To test this hypothesis, I shall analyse each study my research group conducted on the Trade-Off Game. Rather than aggregate across studies, I aim to show that in every individual experiment, the sentiment score of the positively framed option exceeds that of the negatively framed option, regardless of the economic payoffs.

Using the original instructions for both frames of the Trade-Off Game (as published in the appendix of Capraro & Rand, 2018), I prompted GPT-4 to estimate the sentiment of each action exactly as in the Dictator Game analysis. To account for GPT-4's non-deterministic outputs, I repeated each prompt 10 times, deleting and restarting the chat before each run.

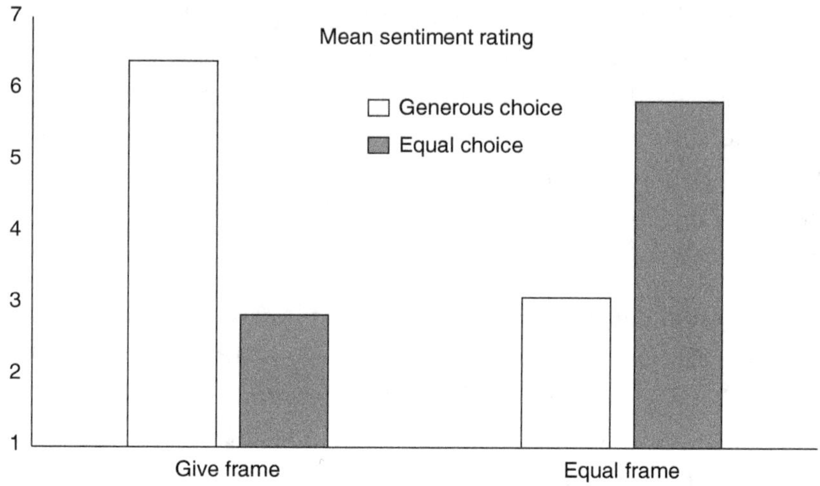

FIGURE 8.2 **GPT-4's sentiment scores are sensitive to linguistic framing in the Trade-Off Game**. Mean sentiment ratings of the available actions in the Equity–Efficiency Trade-Off Game, divided by frame. In both the give frame and the equal frame, the positively framed option has higher ratings than the negatively framed option.

For the give frame, the mean sentiment rating for the 'to be nice' action was 6.4 ($SE = 0.07$), whereas 'not to be nice' averaged 2.85 ($SE = 0.08$). Thus, in this frame, the positively labelled option yields a much higher sentiment score than its counterpart.

Repeating the procedure in the equal frame, where the 'nice' and 'not nice' labels swap, we again observe that the 'nice' action (now monetarily the less generous option) receives a higher sentiment rating (5.85 ± 0.08) than the 'not nice' action (3.10 ± 0.07). Hence, GPT-4's sentiment scores are highly sensitive to linguistic framing in a manner that mirrors the actual behavioural outcomes. See Figure 8.2.

Similar patterns emerge in other variants of the Equity–Efficiency Trade-Off Game. In Study 3 of the same 2018 article, we employed the labels 'more generous' versus 'less generous' to frame the efficient and equitable allocations, and 'more fair' versus 'less fair' to frame the equitable and efficient allocations. Participants were markedly more likely to choose the positively framed option in each case. In line with these behavioural results, eliciting sentiment scores from GPT-4, the 'more generous' label consistently scored 6.50 across 10 trials, much higher than the score obtained by 'less generous' (2.55 ± 0.09). Likewise, the sentiment score obtained by the 'more fair' option (5.90 ± 0.07) was much higher than the sentiment score obtained by the 'less fair' option (2.75 ± 0.11).

In a subsequent 2018 work with Tappin, we introduced frames where one option was positively or negatively labelled (e.g., 'be generous') and the other remained neutral ('Option 2'). Behavioural data again revealed strong framing effects, and GPT-4's sentiment scores reflected the same hierarchy: positively framed > neutrally framed > negatively framed. Comparable results were observed in a 2021 work with Jordan and Tappin.

In conclusion, across multiple experimental variants, the Equity–Efficiency Trade-Off Game exhibits framing effects that align with predictions from the LiMoLES utility function when employing sentiment scores generated by GPT-4. □

Experimental Result (GPT-4's Sentiment Analysis Allows Us to Explain Human Behaviour in the Bribery Game). As an additional application, I shall now show that GPT-4 can also account for the framing effects observed in the Bribery Game reported in the 2022 experiment that I conducted with Ścigała, Zettler, and Pfattheicher. In this experiment, citizens could bribe public officials to bypass a formal procedure. There were two treatments. In the bribe frame, citizens chose between 'offer the bribe' and 'do not offer the bribe', while officials chose between 'accept the bribe' and 'do not accept the bribe'. In the cooperation frame, the bribe was relabelled as a 'cooperation offer', so citizens chose between 'cooperate with the public official' and 'do not cooperate with the public official', and officials chose between 'accept the cooperation offer' and 'do not accept the cooperation offer'.

Results showed that citizens were more likely to make a cooperation offer than to offer a bribe, and officials were more likely to accept a cooperation offer than to accept a bribe. Can this pattern be explained by the LiMoLES utility function, using sentiment scores from GPT-4?

Since the Bribery Game involves only two strategies per role, the LiMoLES utility function predicts that the proportion of citizens offering a bribe (or making a cooperation offer) should increase with the sentiment difference between this action and its negation. An analogous prediction holds for public officials. Moreover, the sentiment associated with offering a bribe should be more negative than that associated with making a cooperation offer; likewise, accepting a bribe should score more negatively than accepting a cooperation offer.

To evaluate these predictions, I repeated the GPT-4 sentiment prompts 10 times for each frame and role. The results align perfectly with the theoretical predictions:

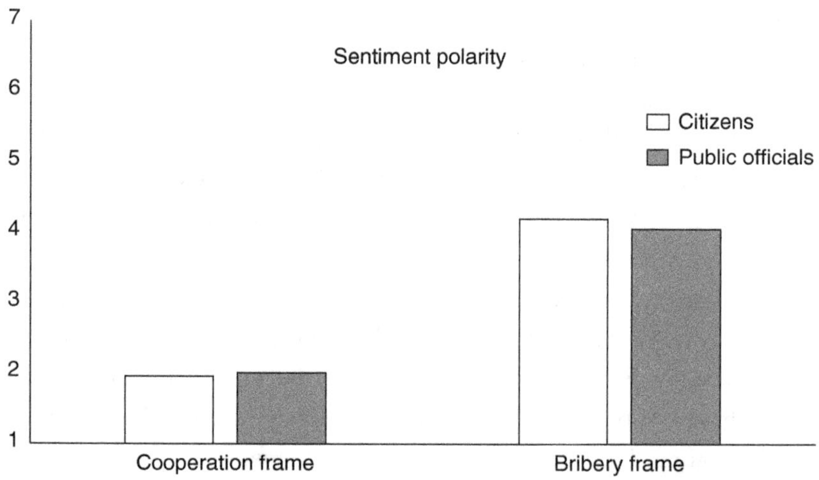

FIGURE 8.3 **GPT-4's sentiment scores are sensitive to linguistic framing in the Corruption Game**. Sentiment polarity (sentiment score of the non-self-serving action minus the sentiment score of the self-serving action) for citizens and public officials in the two frames of the Corruption Game. In the bribery frame this polarity is much higher than in the cooperation frame.

- Offer a bribe: mean = 1.90 (*SE* = 0.07)
- Accept a bribe: mean = 2.00 (*SE* = 0.07)
- Make a cooperation offer: mean = 3.27 (*SE* = 0.21)
- Accept a cooperation offer: mean = 2.92 (*SE* = 0.14)

Thus, both offering and accepting a bribe receive very negative ratings, whereas making or accepting a cooperation offer, though still rated slightly negative, score significantly higher.

Conversely, the negated actions yield positive sentiment:

- Do not offer a bribe: mean = 6.10 (*SE* = 0.07)
- Do not accept a bribe: mean = 6.05 (*SE* = 0.05)
- Do not make a cooperation offer: mean = 5.22 (*SE* = 0.12)
- Do not accept a cooperation offer: mean = 4.92 (*SE* = 0.14)

These sentiment differentials mirror the empirical behaviour: citizens and officials are more likely to engage in the corrupt act when it is framed as an act of cooperation than when it is explicitly labelled a bribe. Therefore, the LiMoLES utility function with GPT-4 sentiment scores successfully explains the framing effects in the Bribery Game. See Figure 8.3.

9 Broader Implications and Future Directions

SUMMARY OF THE BOOK

Understanding why we make the choices we do has likely fascinated thinkers ever since humans first became aware that decision-making itself is a distinct mental act. In the earliest moments of metacognition, when our ancestors realised not only that they could act, but that they chose among alternatives, they must have wondered what drives us towards one option rather than another. This question lies at the very heart of philosophy, economics, sociology, psychology, neuroscience, and artificial intelligence. The search for explanations of human behaviour is, in many ways, the origin story of these disciplines.

Human behaviour, however, is profoundly complex. In real life, the factors that influence our actions are numerous and often interact in dynamic and difficult-to-predict ways. We are affected by our internal states as well as by external circumstances. We are influenced by the presence or absence of others, by the framing of choices, by past experiences, and by imagined futures. Biology, culture, language, and context all shape what we do.

Against this backdrop of complexity, the study of decision-making in one-shot and anonymous economic decisions and games might seem almost trivial. And yet it is precisely because of their simplicity that such scenarios have proven to be a powerful entry point into the study of human behaviour. These scenarios, such as the Dictator Game, the Ultimatum Game, the Public Good Game, and many others, strip away the messiness of everyday life to isolate specific economic and psychological mechanisms. They allow us to test cleanly whether, for example, people will act selfishly when no one is watching, or whether they will punish unfairness even at a cost to themselves. While clearly limited in ecological validity, these experimental paradigms provide a controlled environment in which to explore foundational questions about why we do what we do.

Over the past five decades, researchers have discovered that even within these highly simplified contexts, human behaviour remains far more intricate than classical economic theory once assumed. Initially, it was believed that individuals in these games would simply maximise their own monetary payoff. However, empirical results quickly undermined this view. Participants routinely give money away in Dictator Games, reject unfair offers in Ultimatum Games, and contribute to public goods even when free riding is the more profitable option.

The next theoretical move was to assume that individuals do not merely maximise raw monetary payoffs, but rather a broader utility function, one that incorporates the monetary outcomes received by others, allows for subjective distortions of probability, and accounts for psychological phenomena such as loss aversion, where losses are weighted more heavily than equivalent gains. These consequentialist utility models, which consider all the economic outcomes, their timing, and their perceived likelihood, helped account for several deviations from strict self-interest observed in experiments. However, even these enriched models have proven insufficient. Human behaviour often resists rationalisation within the framework of economic consequentialism. It has become increasingly evident that, if individuals are maximising a utility function at all, it must be more complex than these models suggest and not economically consequentialist.

One important dimension of this complexity, which I have explored in this book, is language. The way decisions are framed linguistically can have a significant impact on the choices people make. That is, even when the underlying economic structure of a decision problem remains identical, people may behave differently depending on how the options are described. For instance, calling a transfer of money a 'donation' rather than a 'boost' can change how much people give. Referring to a choice as 'stealing' rather than 'taking' can influence how much people take. Labelling a choice as 'bribing' or 'cooperating' can impact whether people engage in unethical behaviour or not. These effects are not merely superficial; they tap into deep emotions and norms that are triggered by language.

The insight that linguistic framing matters is not new. Experimental economists have long recognised that the words used to describe a decision problem can affect behaviour. However, rather than studying these effects as phenomena in their own right, many researchers have treated them as 'demand effects' to be minimised or eliminated in order to preserve the purity of the experimental design. But this attitude misses something crucial: language is not noise. It is a core part of human interaction. Most real-world decisions are not made in silence or isolation, but through conversation, persuasion, negotiation, and narrative. Humans make *demands* of each other all the time, requesting that we do certain things, and how we phrase those requests matters.

One reason economists may have historically neglected the role of language is its inherently qualitative nature. Unlike incentives or probabilities, linguistic effects used to be difficult to quantify with precision, making them resistant to traditional analytical tools. But this limitation may no longer hold. Today, advances in LLMs such as GPT-4 offer a powerful new approach to measuring the influence of language on decision-making.

Sentiment analysis conducted with GPT-4 sheds new light on well-known language-based framing effects across several economic games. In the Dictator Game, for instance, the average between the sentiment of the altruistic and the equitable action minus the sentiment of the self-interested option predicts average giving across over 100 experiments with human subjects. Similar patterns emerge in the Trade-Off Game and the Bribery Game, pointing to a systematic and generalisable way to measure the effect of language on decision-making.

The use of LLMs to model human decision-making is still in its early stages, but it offers exciting opportunities as well as important ethical challenges (Feuerriegel et al., 2025). In this final chapter, I will outline what I see as the most promising directions for future research, and I will reflect on the broader ethical and societal implications that must be taken into account as this line of inquiry continues to develop.

LIMITATIONS AND FUTURE RESEARCH

I will highlight four main limitations and corresponding directions for future research, beginning with the most immediate. All the examples discussed thus far, in which sentiment analysis using LLMs helps explain human behaviour, pertain to one-shot economic decisions. While these results are promising, they raise an important question: what happens in strategic games or in iterated contexts?

Beyond One-Shot Economic Decisions

In Chapter 8, we saw that LLMs can effectively explain human behaviour in several well-known economic games, including the Dictator Game, the Trade-Off Game, and the Bribery Game. However, it is important to note that two of these, the Dictator Game and Trade-Off Game, are not actually economic games in the strict sense, but economic decisions where only one player makes a choice. The Bribery Game, while technically a two-player interaction, is still relatively simple: strategic uncertainty is present only for the citizen, who must act without knowing how the public official will respond. The official, by contrast, makes their decision after observing the citizen's move. This asymmetry keeps the game relatively tractable.

These examples raise a natural next question: what happens in more complex, truly interactive games where both players face uncertainty, and where strategic interdependence plays a stronger role? A paradigmatic example is the one-shot Prisoner's Dilemma, where both players must choose simultaneously without knowing the other's action. The complexity here lies not only in the preference structure of the players but also in their beliefs about what the other will do. This introduces a methodological question: do language-based framing effects operate primarily through preferences, through beliefs, or through some interaction of the two?

There is emerging evidence that beliefs may play a central role. For instance, as discussed in Chapter 3, Dufwenberg et al. (2011) showed that changing the frame of the Prisoner's Dilemma from a neutral condition to the 'Community Game' alters expectations about what others will do, which in turn shifts behaviour. This suggests that at least part of the framing effect is mediated by beliefs. Similarly, other studies have found that framing the options as 'give' versus 'take' affects cooperation in one-shot Prisoner's Dilemmas, but these effects vanish in iterated games or in non-strategic settings like the Dictator Game (Dreber et al., 2013; Ellingsen et al., 2012). This again points towards the idea that framing effects in strategic settings may be transmitted primarily through changes in beliefs about others' behaviour.

If linguistic framing affects not only preferences but also beliefs about others' actions, then the proposed formalisations of language-based utility functions (i.e., the LiMoLES and LiMoLNoS utility functions) may be incomplete. The LiMoLES utility function is defined solely over the focal player's own actions, modulated by the sentiment associated with linguistic framing, but it does not incorporate the player's expectations about how others are likely to behave. LiMoLNoS takes a step further by incorporating beliefs in the form of descriptive norms: what people think others typically do. While this is a meaningful extension, it remains an open question whether this limited treatment of beliefs is sufficient to capture the full extent of language-based framing effects in strategic contexts. Addressing this limitation is essential if we aim to develop a more complete and predictive model of how language shapes behaviour in strategic interactions.

The incorporation of beliefs into utility functions has a rich tradition, going back at least to Harsanyi's foundational work on games with incomplete information (1967), where utility is maximised over subjective beliefs about others' types and actions. Later developments pushed this idea further. Rabin (1993) proposed a fairness equilibrium in which utility depends on beliefs about the intentions of others, specifically how kind or unkind their choices seem given available alternatives. Geanakoplos et al. (1989) developed a formal framework for psychological games, where utility depends not just on outcomes, but also on higher-order beliefs (what I believe about what you believe I will do). More recently, Battigalli and Dufwenberg (2022) elaborated the concept of belief-dependent motivations, emphasising how various emotions, including guilt and shame, can emerge from players' beliefs about others' expectations.

These frameworks offer promising starting points for integrating beliefs into language-based utility models. What is missing so far in the LiMoLES and LiMoLNoS utility functions is an explicit formalisation of how linguistic cues shape not only an individual's own preferences, but also their expectations about others' behaviour.

Beyond One-Shot Interactions

A second compelling direction for future research concerns what happens *beyond* one-shot interactions. Specifically, how do linguistic interactions shape behaviour over time, and how might this dynamic influence both the evolution of behaviour and, reciprocally, the evolution of language itself? This question invites us to explore the intersection of evolutionary game theory and the study of linguistic framing.

Evolutionary game theory examines how strategies evolve across generations in populations, shaped by their relative success. It has long been applied to study the emergence and stability of cooperative behaviours (Perc et al., 2017), as well as other social behaviours such as honesty (Capraro et al., 2019c), altruistic punishment (Szolnoki et al., 2012), and trust (Kumar et al., 2020). In parallel, researchers have also used evolutionary models to investigate the development and stabilisation of language (Baronchelli et al., 2006;

Danovski & Brede, 2022; Puglisi et al., 2008). However, these two research strands, evolution of behaviour and evolution of language, have often proceeded in isolation. In reality, it is highly plausible that language and behaviour co-evolve, shaping and being shaped by one another over time.

Consider a situation in which two agents engage in a brief verbal exchange before making a decision. Through this interaction, each agent can influence the other's perception of the decision problem, for example by highlighting certain aspects of the payoffs, framing the options in moral terms, or signalling social norms. As a result, the agents' final decisions are shaped not only by the economic structure of the interaction but also by the preceding conversation. When such interactions occur repeatedly, whether between the same individuals or across a larger population, the effects of language and decision-making may begin to reinforce one another. Over time, certain linguistic patterns may become associated with specific behavioural outcomes, and vice versa. This sets the stage for co-evolutionary dynamics between language and social behaviour.

While the study of such co-evolutionary processes is fascinating in its own right, and largely independent of LLMs, I believe LLMs can play a major role in exploring this domain. In particular, they open up two methodological possibilities that were previously unavailable.

First, LLMs can serve as powerful virtual laboratories for studying the co-evolution of language and behaviour. Imagine a simulated environment in which a population of LLM agents interacts repeatedly through verbal communication, then makes decisions in economic games. These interactions can be structured to reflect different economic games, such as cooperative games, like the Public Good Game and the Prisoner's Dilemma, or competitive, zero-sum games. Through LLMs we could simulate how language evolves across interactions, depending on the interaction type. Because LLMs can be trained, modified, and iterated much more quickly than human populations, such simulations could offer rapid insights into evolutionary processes that would take centuries or millennia to observe in natural human settings.

For instance, in positive-sum environments, we might observe the emergence of linguistic conventions that efficiently signal cooperative intent. Over time, these signals could become ritualised into moral norms or cooperative narratives, potentially mirroring how human cultures developed shared ethical frameworks that promote prosocial behaviour (Curry et al., 2019b; Joseph & Haidt, 2004). Conversely, in zero-sum contexts, language may become more strategic or deceptive. Agents might begin to use the same words with different intentions, reflecting the ambiguity and manipulation often observed in competitive negotiations or adversarial interactions.

Second, LLMs can offer a novel way to investigate the cognitive mechanisms that link language to behaviour. Traditional evolutionary models usually focus on how strategies spread in populations over time, using abstract representations of behaviour (e.g., 'cooperate' vs 'defect') and assuming very simple, fixed rules of interaction. While these models are valuable for capturing macrolevel patterns, they often ignore or oversimplify the microlevel psychological processes that drive actual decisions.

LLMs, by contrast, can simulate realistic, context-sensitive reasoning. This allows them to act not just as tools for predicting text, but as models of how people process and respond to different linguistic framings. For example, by analysing how small variations in wording influence the emotional valence or perceived norms associated with a choice, LLMs can mimic the subtle ways in which language shapes human judgement and behaviour.

In this sense, LLMs may allow researchers to move beyond simply observing that a framing effect exists, and instead probe into *why* it occurs: what features of the language trigger the change in behaviour? What emotions are elicited? What implicit assumptions about others' actions are activated? These insights can then be used to build more psychologically realistic models of decision-making.

Taken together, these directions suggest a fertile new research agenda at the intersection of behavioural science, computational linguistics, artificial intelligence, and evolutionary theory. Understanding how language and behaviour evolve together could shed light on foundational questions about human cooperation, morality, and culture. And with the advent of LLMs, we now have the computational tools to simulate, test, and refine these theories at a scale and speed that would have been unimaginable just a few years ago.

The Mathematisation of the LENS Model

According to the LENS model, the linguistic description of a decision problem may evoke emotions and suggest norms of behaviour in the decision-maker, which then interact to shape strategic choices. This qualitative framework can account for several experimental regularities related to linguistic framing effects, as described in Chapter 5.

However, transforming this qualitative model into a quantitative, predictive utility function presents a significant challenge. There are, in principle, infinitely many ways to formalise the LENS model mathematically. The LiMoLES, LiMoLNoS, and LiMoLENS utility functions represent arguably the simplest and most tractable formalisations, each expressing utility as a linear combination of relevant factors:

- **LiMoLES** linearly combines monetary payoff and emotions;
- **LiMoLNoS** linearly combines monetary payoff and norms;
- **LiMoLENS** combines all three, payoff, emotions, and norms, plus the product of sentiment and norms, which formalises the interaction between these two factors in the simplest way.

This approach offers empirical tractability, especially in early-stage modelling. However, this formal simplification comes at a cost: it may oversimplify the complexity of human decision-making.

First, it is possible that the economically consequentialist component of the utility function (which, in all these utility functions, is simply reduced to the decision-maker's own economic payoff) is actually more complex. For example, social preferences may also influence the utility function, relatively independently of personal and social norms (Gächter et al., 2025).

Second, both emotions and moral norms are multidimensional constructs, not scalar quantities. In theory, one could extend these functions to account for multiple emotional and normative dimensions by expanding the vector space and maintaining linearity. But this assumes that complex emotions and norms are just weighted sums of more 'basic' building blocks. This assumption is theoretically questionable. As mentioned in Chapter 6, one of the long-standing critiques of basic emotion theories is the lack of a convincing account for how complex emotions arise: whether they can be decomposed into linear combinations, or whether they involve emergent properties that require non-linear representations.

For example, we may construct a situation where two emotions, shame and guilt, are likely to interact in a non-additive way. Imagine a taxpayer deciding whether to evade taxes. Guilt may arise from the internalised understanding that tax evasion is morally wrong, reflecting a personal failure to contribute to the public good. Shame, in contrast, is more social, reflecting the anticipated judgement by others if the evasion is discovered. Now consider the following three scenarios:

- **High guilt, low shame:** The person feels strongly that tax evasion is wrong, but believes they will never be caught. Guilt dominates, and this may push them toward compliance out of internal moral discomfort.
- **Low guilt, high shame:** The person doesn't feel morally conflicted about evasion itself, but fears social exposure and reputational damage. Again, this may lead to compliance, but for entirely different reasons, avoiding public disapproval rather than internal moral regret.
- **High guilt, high shame:** This is where non-additivity becomes evident. The interaction of both emotions doesn't necessarily lead to stronger compliance. Instead, the person may experience emotional overload, leading to paralysis, indecision, or even a defensive reaction

(e.g., rationalising evasion or shifting blame). The joint presence of both emotions might not sum linearly to 'double compliance pressure'; rather, their combined intensity could induce avoidance or suppression behaviours, emergent effects not predictable from linear models.

This kind of non-linear interplay, where combinations of emotions give rise to qualitatively new psychological states or coping strategies, suggests that even basic extensions of the LiMoLES-type utility functions might fail to capture the complexity of real emotional influences on decision-making. Modelling these effects may require incorporating interaction terms, thresholds, or even system-dynamics-style feedback loops between cognitive and affective components.

Third, there is good reason to believe that, even if emotions and norms were scalar, the impact they have on behaviour is not always linear. That is, increasing the intensity of an emotion or the strength of a perceived norm does not always produce a proportional change in behaviour. Instead, behavioural responses may exhibit threshold effects, saturation, or even reversals, depending on the context.

Take, for example, moral outrage in the context of collective action. Suppose an individual observes increasing levels of corporate wrongdoing, such as pollution or tax evasion. As the emotion of outrage intensifies, one might expect a gradual increase in the individual's willingness to act, for instance by signing petitions, attending protests, or boycotting the company.

But this increase is not necessarily linear. Initially, as outrage rises from low to moderate levels, people may become more likely to take action: they move from apathy to engagement. However, beyond a certain point, further increases in outrage may not translate into more action. Instead, they may trigger disillusionment or learned helplessness, especially if the individual perceives their actions as ineffective or if institutional mechanisms seem unresponsive. In this case, very high levels of outrage can paradoxically lead to withdrawal or inertia, rather than heightened engagement. The relationship between emotion intensity and behaviour thus may follow in some cases an inverted-U shape.

A similar effect can be seen with perceived social norms. Imagine a social norm against tax evasion. When the perceived norm against evasion is low to moderate, increases in this norm lead to higher compliance: individuals feel social pressure to pay taxes honestly, and compliance rates increase steadily. However, once the norm becomes very strong and people feel intense moral pressure or fear of social judgement, this can paradoxically backfire for some. The norm may trigger reactance: individuals may feel their autonomy is threatened and respond by deliberately evading taxes to assert control, even if they know it is socially disapproved. Here, very strong norms may not increase compliance linearly; instead, they may produce a non-linear response where some people actually comply less.

These examples illustrate that scalar inputs (emotions or norms) can give rise to non-linear output functions in behaviour. Recognising this kind of structure is essential if we want utility models to reflect human behaviour more precisely.

Finally, this book presents a practical framework for quantifying how linguistic framing influences economic decision-making. However, alternative, more abstract, approaches have also been developed. The emerging theory of language-based decisions (Bjorndahl & Halpern, 2021, 2023) and games (Bjorndahl et al., 2013) provides a formal foundation for modelling how linguistic descriptions shape strategies. For example. Bjorndahl et al. introduce mild conditions under which rationalisable strategies are guaranteed to exist. While these theoretical models provide deep formal insights, the approach in this book offers empirical tools for measuring language effects in economic contexts. Future research could explore bridges between these methodologies, combining formal rigour with empirical applicability.

Beyond the LENS Model

The LENS model represents a useful framework for understanding how language influences decision-making. Its strength lies in focusing on two key pathways, emotions and norms, which we are beginning to measure with increasing precision. This focus makes the model a practical starting point for formalising the role of language in economic behaviour. However, as with any simplification, the LENS model inevitably omits certain complexities inherent to linguistic effects on human decisions.

For instance, in Chapter 5, I referenced the model introduced by Farrow et al. (2018), which offers a somewhat more nuanced perspective by identifying four distinct pathways through which language can shape behaviour: emotions, identity, spontaneous associations, and fluency.

This model is not mutually exclusive with the LENS model; rather, it can be seen as complementary. Emotions are a core component in both models, while moral norms in the LENS model correspond closely to the identity-related processes described by Farrow et al. Looking at the differences, the model by Farrow et al. does not explicitly consider social norms, but includes spontaneous associations and fluency, two linguistic mechanisms not explicitly addressed by the LENS model.

Spontaneous associations refer to the automatic, often unconscious, connections people make between concepts that shape their perceptions and decisions. For example, Nelson and Simmons (2009) demonstrated that people tend to believe that travelling north takes longer than travelling south, likely because they associate 'north' with 'uphill' and 'south' with 'downhill'.

Fluency is defined as the ease with which information is processed. Alter and Oppenheimer (2006) found that stocks with easy-to-pronounce names tend to outperform those with difficult-to-pronounce names, suggesting that fluency can affect economic choices, presumably because fluent information feels more familiar or trustworthy.

The LENS model primarily emphasises emotional and normative pathways. As such, it does not explicitly capture these effects of spontaneous association and fluency. In some cases, these effects might be indirectly subsumed under emotional reactions (such as negative emotions triggered by difficult-to-pronounce words leading to avoidance behaviours) but it is unlikely that all such linguistic influences can be fully quantified within the current LENS framework without substantial expansion.

Spontaneous associations and fluency may fundamentally alter how decision problems are mentally represented. For example, a complex decision might be simplified through heuristic reasoning triggered by fluency, or a decision problem that activates certain associations might be mentally recoded as a different decision problem altogether. In other words, individuals might not be optimising over the original decision problem (D1) but rather over a cognitively transformed version (D2) shaped by language-driven mental representations.

This kind of transformation is deeper than what is captured by formalisations like the LiMoLES and LiMoLNoS utility functions, which adjust the utility function by incorporating the sentiments and the norms evoked by the linguistic descriptions but leave the underlying structure of the decision intact. In contrast, spontaneous associations and fluency may lead to a reframing of the decision context itself, changing not just how individuals evaluate options, but what they believe the decision is about. This suggests that language can influence decision-making not only by modulating preferences, but also by altering the perceived nature of the problem to be solved.

This insight opens an intriguing line of inquiry into the cognitive representation of decision problems and the interplay between language and mental models of decision problems. Currently, quantitative tools for capturing these dynamic, representation-level effects are, to my knowledge, absent. However, exploring these questions is crucial for advancing our understanding of how language shapes economic behaviour and decision-making more broadly.

Beyond Language

While language is a central component of human decision-making, and has been the primary focus of this book, it is certainly not the only factor that shapes how we make decisions. Linguistic framings are powerful, but they are embedded in a much broader ecology of cues that influence human behaviour, often in subtle and underappreciated ways.

Consider the case of online experiments or e-commerce interfaces. In such contexts, visual elements like the colour used to highlight options can have measurable effects on choices. Red may signal danger or loss, green may signal safety or gain. These colour associations can activate affective heuristics, which in turn affect behaviour. Companies often exploit default effects by preselecting certain options, such as travel insurance or seat upgrades. Many users, not wanting to expend cognitive effort to change the default, go along with it, despite potentially incurring higher costs.

Moving beyond the digital domain, real-life interactions also demonstrate the power of non-linguistic cues. In face-to-face communication, the tone of voice, cadence, and even the physical attractiveness of the interlocutor can influence how information is received and acted upon. These features, while non-verbal, are often processed automatically and can shape our decisions.

Some of these effects could, in principle, be integrated into the LENS model, if we stretch the definition of 'language' to include a broader notion of mental representation. In this abstract sense, any perceptual cue (visual, auditory, tactile) might be internally 'translated' into a form of *mentalese*, a cognitive language of thought. From this perspective, one could argue that even colour or voice tone becomes part of a language-like system that evokes emotions and norms, thus influencing strategy selection.

However, this abstract approach comes at a cost: operationalisability. One of the strengths of the LENS model, as developed in this book, is its empirical tractability. When the 'language' in question is an actual language, such as English, Italian, or Chinese, we can apply LLMs to quantify its influence. But when we shift to a broader definition of language as any mental representation, we lose this methodological clarity. How do we measure *mentalese*? How do

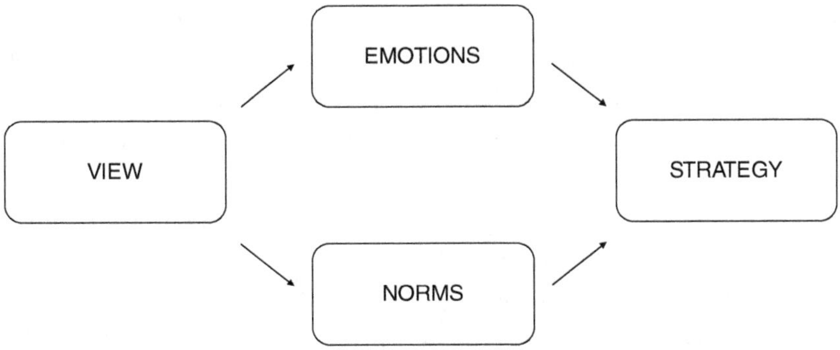

FIGURE 9.1 Visual representation of the VENS model.

we quantify the internal transformation from visual input to emotions and norms?

A promising direction for future research is to develop a VENS model, a visual analogue of the LENS model. In this framework, the Visual representation of the decision problem evokes Emotions and activates perceived Norms, which in turn influence Strategy choice (see Figure 9.1). This would be particularly relevant in digital contexts such as online marketplaces, app interfaces, or virtual environments, where visual stimuli dominate and language plays only a partial role.

Operationalising the VENS model could leverage multimodal AI systems. In addition to LLMs, there are now powerful vision-language models (e.g., CLIP, Flamingo, Gemini, GPT-4 with vision capabilities) that can process images and text jointly. These models could be prompted with screenshots of online decision environments to assess the affective and normative content perceived by a 'simulated observer'. The extracted emotional and normative predictions could then be tested for their predictive power over actual human behaviour.

Of course, visual input is not the only remaining frontier. Smell, touch, kinaesthetic feedback, and even internal physiological states can all modulate decision-making. If you get too close to a fire, you withdraw your hand, not because you reasoned based on a cost–benefit analysis, but because of deeply embedded sensorimotor circuits. Capturing such responses may require a new generation of AI systems, not based on next-word prediction, but on *next-action prediction*: agents that, given a multimodal stream of past decision problems and actions, infer the most likely next action.

Ultimately, the broader goal of behavioural economics remains unchanged: to understand how humans behave in economic interactions. If factors like colour, layout, auditory cues, or even tactile feedback systematically affect decision-making, then they fall squarely within the domain of behavioural economics. Thus, we must eventually expand our methodological toolkit to measure these factors. But recognising the limitations of current models is not a weakness; it is a signpost pointing towards the next horizon of behavioural economics.

ETHICAL CONSIDERATIONS

I have been searching for a utility function that can describe human behaviour for more than a decade, beginning with my early *model of human cooperation* (Capraro, 2013). Throughout this search, I have often asked myself: *why do we care?* Suppose we succeed in identifying a utility function that accurately explains human behaviour: what could we actually do with it? What are the potential benefits and risks? In this final section of the book, I aim to reflect on these questions.

BENEFITS IN MODELLING HUMAN UTILITY

Improving Policy Effectiveness through Precision Modelling

One of the most immediate and compelling positive applications lies in the domain of public policy. By incorporating a more realistic utility function, policymakers can design interventions that are more effective.

Take, for instance, tax compliance. Classic deterrence models focus on enforcement and penalty structures (Allingham & Sandmo,

1972). But real-world behaviour is also driven by guilt, shame, trust, and fairness norms (Grasmick & Bursik, 1990; Kirchler et al., 2008). If a utility function captures the relative weights individuals assign to these sentiments and norms, policies can be designed to activate intrinsic motivations rather than relying solely on extrinsic deterrents. This could result in higher compliance at a lower enforcement cost (Dwenger et al., 2016).

This can also be applied to global cooperation. Different societies place different weights on norms, emotions, and monetary incentives, which can lead to misunderstandings in diplomacy, global trade, or development interventions. A utility function that accounts for culturally specific weights can improve international cooperation.

Diagnosing and Addressing Behavioural Pathologies

Beyond enhancing social welfare, personalised utility functions hold significant promise for improving individual welfare. We can imagine many different applications in economic interactions, but their potential extends well beyond economics. For example, individuals with depression often exhibit greater impulsivity and inconsistency in intertemporal choices, often preferring immediate, smaller rewards over larger, delayed ones, indicating a steeper discounting of future benefits (Takahashi et al., 2008). Similarly, individuals with antisocial personality disorder frequently engage in behaviours that are deceitful, impulsive, and aggressive, often lacking remorse for their actions. These patterns can lead to criminal activities and other forms of unethical conduct (Black, 2015). A utility function that integrates affective and normative components could be used to quantify these distortions, providing both diagnostic insights and therapeutic targets.

To be more specific, consider a depressed individual who routinely declines social invitations, avoids pleasurable activities, or fails to pursue rewarding goals, not because these outcomes lack subjective value, but because that individual's internal valuation system underweights future rewards or excessively weights feelings of shame or unworthiness. A personalised utility function could model this distorted valuation pattern by assigning disproportionately low utility to potential gains and high disutility to normative emotions like shame. Once these imbalances are formally captured, clinicians can use them to guide targeted interventions. For example, cognitive-behavioural therapy could be employed to challenge and reframe the maladaptive beliefs underlying these utility weights (Beck, 1979). In this context, the utility function becomes not merely a descriptive tool but a clinically generative one: it reveals the structure of dysfunctional preferences and guides efforts to reshape them in ways that promote well-being.

Enabling Personalised, Ethical Choice Architectures

In the private sector, utility functions can guide the design of choice architectures that more transparently reflect the heterogeneity of human preferences, thereby optimising the user experience in a transparent manner. While digital platforms already use machine learning to predict and shape behaviour, these systems often operate as opaque black boxes, optimised primarily for commercial goals such as engagement, conversion, or time-on-site. As a result, they are frequently aligned more with the platform's profit incentives than with users' actual interests (Pasquale, 2015; O'Reilly et al., 2024).

In contrast, explicit utility functions can lead to a transparent framework for behavioural prediction, making it possible to not only enhance accuracy, but also ensure that predictions are aligned with individual well-being. Transparent models allow users to understand how their preferences are being represented and why specific options are offered. Making the modelling process visible constrains platforms to align with user goals, if only to maintain public legitimacy and avoid backlash. Rather than maximising engagement at all costs, utility-based systems could be designed to help users pursue their own long-term objectives, such as saving money, improving mental health, or making sustainable and ethical choices. In this sense, utility functions may serve not only as technical tools but as instruments for shaping digital environments that empower rather than exploit.

Designing Norm-Sensitive AI Systems

As AI systems are increasingly tasked with interacting with humans in a variety of domains, they will need to incorporate utility functions that reflect human-like priorities. A utility function that includes emotional and normative dimensions provides a foundation for building artificial agents that are better attuned to human preferences.

In applications like autonomous vehicles, negotiation bots, and AI-assisted legal reasoning, the incorporation of emotions and norms into AI decision-making processes is essential. For instance, autonomous vehicles must make split-second decisions that balance efficiency with ethical considerations, such as the well-being of passengers and pedestrians (Awad et al., 2018). Similarly, negotiation bots should understand and respect human emotions and cooperative norms to facilitate effective negotiations (Chawla et al., 2023; Kramár et al., 2022). In the legal domain, AI systems assisting in legal reasoning must consider the multifaceted structure of norms and laws (Ashley, 2017). By embedding these human-centric considerations into their utility functions, AI systems can augment human decision-making in complex environments.

RISKS IN MODELLING HUMAN UTILITY

Greater explanatory power comes with greater ethical responsibility. In this section, I discuss some of the most salient ethical concerns that arise from the development, dissemination, and application of utility functions.

Manipulative Applications

Perhaps the most immediate and pressing ethical risk associated with the development of a utility function that accurately predicts human behaviour lies in its potential for manipulative applications.

If such a function enables precise prediction of individual decisions across a wide range of economic contexts, it can just as easily be deployed to steer behaviour, not necessarily to benefit the decision-maker, but rather to serve the goals of those who control the choice architecture.

This is not a hypothetical concern. Commercial actors, political entities, and platform designers already rely on behavioural insights to influence users, often in subtle ways that bypass conscious awareness. With a refined utility function at their disposal, actors could exploit predictable patterns to frame decisions in ways that systematically nudge individuals towards outcomes aligned with third-party interests, even when these diverge from the individual's long-term well-being.

Similar concerns have already been raised in the literature on dark patterns (Mathur et al., 2019) and sludges (Sunstein, 2019). These concepts describe deliberate manipulations of decision environments, such as prechecked boxes for paid add-ons, obscured opt-out options, or emotionally manipulative messaging. These manipulations exploit cognitive heuristics without the user's informed consent. Importantly, these manipulations are often justified as 'choice-preserving' because the agent retains formal autonomy, despite being functionally steered in predictable directions.

A predictive utility function would radically amplify the effectiveness of such techniques. Where current nudging is based on probabilistic population-level tendencies, utility-based manipulation would offer individual-level precision, optimising interventions based on each person's decision profile. This represents a shift from generic behavioural influence to personalised behavioural engineering.

Surveillance and Privacy Invasion

The development of a highly refined utility function capable of accurately predicting human behaviour is likely to require granular, personalised behavioural data, including not only observable decisions but also internal states such as emotions, moral intuitions, and possibly even neural or physiological signals. This need for intimate data raises immediate concerns regarding surveillance and privacy.

Companies and governments already collect massive quantities of behavioural data, from online clicks, dwell time, and purchasing habits to biometric inputs like voice patterns and heart rate variability, leading to what has been named 'the age of surveillance capitalism' (Zuboff, 2019). A utility function that aspires to include emotional or normative dimensions would likely demand even more intimate sources of information. This might include facial-expression analysis, sentiment detection in language, gaze tracking, or even electrophysiological data collected through wearable devices or neurotechnology (Burwell et al., 2017).

There are many associated ethical risks. For example, there is the danger of coercive, opaque, or non-consensual data collection, especially among vulnerable populations such as children, individuals with low digital literacy, or politically marginalised groups. These populations may lack the ability to meaningfully consent or resist invasive surveillance mechanisms embedded in everyday technologies. Once data is collected, it can feed into opaque profiling systems where individuals are labelled, scored, or segmented into behavioural types, possibly influencing the opportunities, prices, or treatments they receive, without their knowledge or ability to contest such classifications (Mühlhoff, 2021).

Discrimination and Algorithmic Bias

Relatedly, utility functions might replicate or even exacerbate social inequalities. If parameters are estimated using biased datasets or fail to account for structural injustices, they can embed these biases in prediction and decision-making processes (Eubanks, 2018).

For instance, consider an employer who aims to maximise productivity. In this case, the utility function will depend on the expected productivity of employees. However, expected productivity is often estimated using observable attributes and historical data. If that data reflects a long-standing underrepresentation of (e.g.) women or minorities in certain fields due to systemic bias, the utility function may 'learn' that being male or from a dominant ethnic group is a predictor of higher utility. In this way, the function does not merely mirror past inequalities, it actively reinforces them by guiding future decisions based on flawed premises (Mehrabi et al., 2021).

The same issue arises when predicting economic behaviour. If the parameters of the utility function are estimated through a set that overrepresents certain socioeconomic or cultural groups, such as WEIRD populations (Western, Educated, Industrialised, Rich, and Democratic; Henrich et al., 2010), the utility function may mischaracterise behaviours typical of underrepresented groups. This can lead to erroneous conclusions about who is more or less cooperative, generous, or rational, thereby feeding into discriminatory stereotypes or unfair treatment.

Moral Responsibility and Predictive Determinism

A utility function that accurately predicts human behaviour raises profound ethical and philosophical questions about free will, agency, and responsibility. If we can model a person's actions with high precision, then this predictive power may be misinterpreted as a form of behavioural determinism. In such a world, knowing the utility function could be seen as equivalent to knowing what a person *will* do, rather than what they *choose* to do.

Consider, for instance, an individual who commits a heinous crime, such as murder. Suppose the utility function correctly predicts this behaviour based on a low internalisation of social norms and a strong preference for short-term rewards. Can we still hold them morally responsible for their actions? Or are they merely following a trajectory shaped by their utility parameters, parameters that may, in many cases, be influenced by genetics, early life experiences, or the surrounding social environment?

This question touches on long-standing debates in moral and legal philosophy. Concepts of moral responsibility and legal culpability often rest on the idea of counterfactual agency, the notion that individuals could have acted differently under the same circumstances (Fischer & Ravizza, 1998; Frankfurt, 1969). If utility functions undermine this idea, by presenting behaviour as predictable and determined by a utility function, then we risk eroding the foundations of praise, blame, and accountability.

CONCLUSION

For thousands of years, the search for an explanation of human behaviour has been a central focus of philosophical inquiry and scientific investigation. From ancient moral philosophy to modern neuroscience, thinkers have grappled with the question: why do we do what we do?

This pursuit may be deeply tied to the emergence of metacognition, the ability to reflect on our own thoughts and actions. Once we became aware of our own behaviour and its consequences, the desire to understand and improve it may have followed naturally. Perhaps this impulse is even linked to the uniquely human awareness of our own mortality (Becker, 1974; Pyszczynski et al., 2015; Suddendorf & Corballis, 2007). If our time is finite, the urgency to make better choices, both individually and collectively, becomes more pressing. The desire to understand human behaviour might be part of a broader existential project linked to our ambition to delay death and extend the duration of life for as long as possible.

In this broader intellectual and existential context, developing a utility function for economic interactions represents one small, yet meaningful, step forward. It offers a formal, testable way to describe what people value and how they make decisions in economic contexts. Though narrow in scope, such a model can have far-reaching implications, helping us design better policies, develop more ethical technologies, and even support mental health.

Yet this promising path must be pursued with caution. The same tools that help us understand human preferences can be used to manipulate or exploit them. If we are to use utility functions not just to describe but to influence behaviour, then ethical safeguards must be embedded at every stage, ensuring transparency, accountability, and respect for human dignity.

As we build utility functions, we must remain aware that they are part of a larger project: the age-old human aspiration not merely to understand ourselves, but to become better versions of who we are.

References

Abeler, J., Nosenzo, D., & Raymond, C. (2019). Preferences for truth-telling. *Econometrica, 87*(4), 1115–1153.

Afriat, S. N. (1967). The construction of utility functions from expenditure data. *International Economic Review, 8*(1), 67–77.

Afriat, S. N. (1972). Efficiency estimation of production functions. *International Economic Review, 13*, 568–598.

Aldrovandi, S., Brown, G. D., & Wood, A. M. (2015). Social norms and rank-based nudging: Changing willingness to pay for healthy food. *Journal of Experimental Psychology: Applied, 21*(3), 242.

Alempaki, D., Doğan, G., & Yang, Y. (2021). Lying in a foreign language? *Journal of Economic Behavior & Organisation, 185*, 946–961.

Alfano, M., Cheong, M., & Curry, O. S. (2024). Moral universals: A machine-reading analysis of 256 societies. *Heliyon, 10*(6), e25940.

Allingham, M. G., & Sandmo, A. (1972). Income tax evasion: A theoretical analysis. *Journal of Public Economics, 1*(3–4), 323–338.

Alter, A. L., & Oppenheimer, D. M. (2006). Predicting short-term stock fluctuations by using processing fluency. *Proceedings of the National Academy of Sciences, 103*(24), 9369–9372.

Amin, A. B., Bednarczyk, R. A., Ray, C. E., Melchiori, K. J., Graham, J., Huntsinger, J. R., & Omer, S. B. (2017). Association of moral values with vaccine hesitancy. *Nature Human Behaviour, 1*(12), 873–880.

Andersen, S., Harrison, G. W., Lau, M. I., & Rutström, E. E. (2008). Eliciting risk and time preferences. *Econometrica, 76*(3), 583–618.

Andrade, E. B., & Ariely, D. (2009). The enduring impact of transient emotions on decision making. *Organisational Behavior and Human Decision Processes, 109*(1), 1–8.

Andreoni, J., & Miller, J. (2002). Giving according to GARP: An experimental test of the consistency of preferences for altruism. *Econometrica, 70*, 737–753.

Andreoni, J., & Petrie, R. (2004). Public goods experiments without confidentiality: A glimpse into fund-raising. *Journal of Public Economics, 88*(7–8), 1605–1623.

Andrews, P. W., & Thomson Jr, J. A. (2009). The bright side of being blue: Depression as an adaptation for analysing complex problems. *Psychological Review, 116*(3), 620.

Araque, O., Gatti, L., Consoli, S., & Kalimeri, K. (2024). A Novel Lexicon for the moral foundation of liberty. *arXiv preprint arXiv:2407.11862.*

Ashley, K. D. (2017). *Artificial intelligence and legal analytics: New tools for law practice in the digital age.* Cambridge University Press.

Ashton, M. C., Lee, K., Perugini, M., Szarota, P., De Vries, R. E., Di Blas, L., ... De Raad, B. (2004). A six-factor structure of personality-descriptive adjectives: Solutions from psycholexical studies in seven languages. *Journal of Personality and Social Psychology, 86*(2), 356–366.

Atari, M., Haidt, J., Graham, J., Koleva, S., Stevens, S. T., & Dehghani, M. (2023). Morality beyond the WEIRD: How the nomological network of morality varies across cultures. *Journal of Personality and Social Psychology, 125,* 1157–1188.

Awad, E., Dsouza, S., Kim, R., Schulz, J., Henrich, J., Shariff, A., ... Rahwan, I. (2018). The moral machine experiment. *Nature, 563*(7729), 59–64.

Axelrod, R. (1984). *The evolution of cooperation.* Basic Books.

Ayers, J. W., Poliak, A., Dredze, M., Leas, E. C., Zhu, Z., Kelley, J. B., ... Smith, D. M. (2023). Comparing physician and artificial intelligence chatbot responses to patient questions posted to a public social media forum. *JAMA Internal Medicine, 183*(6), 589–596.

Baccianella, S., Esuli, A., & Sebastiani, F. (2010, May). Sentiwordnet 3.0: An enhanced lexical resource for sentiment analysis and opinion mining. In *Lrec* (Vol. 10, No. 2010, pp. 2200–2204).

Bagozzi, R. P., Gopinath, M., & Nyer, P. U. (1999). The role of emotions in marketing. *Journal of the Academy of Marketing Science, 27*(2), 184–206.

Barcelo, H., & Capraro, V. (2015). Group size effect on cooperation in one-shot social dilemmas. *Scientific Reports, 5*(1), 7937.

Baronchelli, A., Dall'Asta, L., Barrat, A., & Loreto, V. (2006). Topology-induced coarsening in language games. *Physical Review E – Statistical, Nonlinear, and Soft Matter Physics, 73*(1), 015102.

Barrett, L. F., & Russell, J. A. (1999). The structure of current affect: Controversies and emerging consensus. *Current Directions in Psychological Science, 8*(1), 10–14.

Bašić, Z., & Verrina, E. (2024). Personal norms – and not only social norms – shape economic behavior. *Journal of Public Economics, 239,* 105255.

Basu, K. (1994). The traveler's dilemma: Paradoxes of rationality in game theory. *The American Economic Review, 84*(2), 391–395.

Battigalli, P., & Dufwenberg, M. (2022). Belief-dependent motivations and psychological game theory. *Journal of Economic Literature, 60*(3), 833–882.

Bearden, J. N., Rapoport, A., & Murphy, R. O. (2006). Sequential observation and selection with rank-dependent payoffs: An experimental study. *Management Science, 52*(9), 1437–1449.

Beck, A. T. (1979). *Cognitive therapy and the emotional disorders.* Penguin.

Becker, E. (1974). *The denial of death.* Free Press.

Beiró, M. G., D'Ignazi, J., Perez Bustos, V., Prado, M. F., & Kalimeri, K. (2023, April). Moral narratives around the vaccination debate on facebook. In *Proceedings of the ACM Web Conference 2023* (pp. 4134–4141).

Benartzi, S., & Thaler, R. H. (2001). Naive diversification strategies in defined contribution saving plans. *American Economic Review, 91*(1), 79–98.

Bentham, J. (1789). *An introduction to the principles of morals and legislation.* T. Payne and Son.

Berg, J., Dickhaut, J., & McCabe, K. (1995). Trust, reciprocity, and social history. *Games and Economic Behavior, 10*(1), 122–142.

Bertrand, J. (1883). Review of 'Theorie mathematique de la richesse sociale' and 'Recherche sur les principes mathematiques de la theorie des richesses'. *Journal des Savants*, 499–508.

Bicchieri, C. (2005). *The grammar of society: The nature and dynamics of social norms.* Cambridge University Press.

Bicchieri, C. (2016). *Norms in the wild: How to diagnose, measure, and change social norms.* Oxford University Press.

Binmore, K. (1987). Modeling rational players: Part I. *Economics & Philosophy, 3*(2), 179–214.

Biziou-van-Pol, L., Haenen, J., Novaro, A., Liberman, A. O., & Capraro, V. (2015). Does telling white lies signal pro-social preferences? *Judgment and Decision Making, 10*(6), 538–548.

Bjorndahl, A., & Halpern, J. Y. (2021). Language-based decisions. Proceedings of the 18th Conference on Theoretical Aspects of Rationality and Knowledge, TARK 2023.

Bjorndahl, A., & Halpern, J. Y. (2023). Sequential language-based decisions. Proceedings of the 19th Conference on Theoretical Aspects of Rationality and Knowledge, TARK 2023.

Bjorndahl, A., Halpern, J. Y., & Pass, R. (2013). Language-based games. Proceedings of the 14th Conference on Theoretical Aspects of Rationality and Knowledge, TARK 2013, pp. 39–48.

Black, D. W. (2015). The natural history of antisocial personality disorder. *The Canadian Journal of Psychiatry, 60*(7), 309–314.

Blazquiz-Pulido, J. F., Polonio, L., & Bilancini, E. (2024). Who's the deceiver? Identifying deceptive intentions in communication. *Games and Economic Behavior, 145*, 451–466.

Blount, S. (1995). When social outcomes aren't fair: The effect of causal attributions on preferences. *Organisational Behavior and Human Decision Processes, 63*(2), 131–144.

Bolton, G. E., & Ockenfels, A. (2000). ERC: A theory of equity, reciprocity, and competition. *American Economic Review, 90*, 166–193.

Bolukbasi, T., Chang, K. W., Zou, J. Y., Saligrama, V., & Kalai, A. T. (2016). Man is to computer programmer as woman is to homemaker? Debiasing word embeddings. *NIPS'16: Proceedings of the 30th International Conference on Neural Information Processing Systems, 29*, 4356–4364.

Bostyn, D. H., Sevenhant, S., & Roets, A. (2018). Of mice, men, and trolleys: Hypothetical judgment versus real-life behavior in trolley-style moral dilemmas. *Psychological Science, 29*(7), 1084–1093.

Bracha, A., & Brown, D. J. (2012). Affective decision making: A theory of optimism bias. *Games and Economic Behavior, 75*(1), 67–80.

Bradley, M. M., & Lang, P. J. (1999). Affective Norms for English Words (ANEW): Instruction manual and affective ratings. Technical Report C-1, The Center for Research in Psychophysiology, University of Florida.

Brady, W. J., Wills, J. A., Burkart, D., Jost, J. T., & Van Bavel, J. J. (2019). An ideological asymmetry in the diffusion of moralised content on social media among political leaders. *Journal of Experimental Psychology: General, 148*(10), 1802.

Brañas-Garza, P. (2007). Promoting helping behavior with framing in Dictator Games. *Journal of Economic Psychology, 28*(4), 477–486.

Brañas-Garza, P., Capraro, V., & Rascon-Ramirez, E. (2018). Gender differences in altruism on Mechanical Turk: Expectations and actual behaviour. *Economics Letters, 170*, 19–23.

Brañas-Garza, P., Espín, A. M., Exadaktylos, F., & Herrmann, B. (2014). Fair and unfair punishers coexist in the Ultimatum Game. *Scientific Reports, 4*(1), 6025.

Brown, J. R., Kling, J. R., Mullainathan, S., & Wrobel, M. V. (2008). Why don't people insure late life consumption? A framing explanation of the under-annuitisation puzzle. *American Economic Review, 98*(2), 304–309.

Brynjolfsson, E., Li, D., & Raymond, L. R. (2025). Generative AI at work. *The Quarterly Journal of Economics, 140*(2), 889–942.

Burwell, S., Sample, M., & Racine, E. (2017). Ethical aspects of brain computer interfaces: A scoping review. *BMC Medical Ethics, 18*, 1–11.

Cadsby, C. B., & Maynes, E. (1998). Gender and free riding in a threshold Public Good Game: Experimental evidence. *Journal of Economic Behavior & Organisation, 34*(4), 603–620.

Camerer, C. F. (2011). *Behavioral game theory: Experiments in strategic interaction*. Princeton University Press.

Camerer, C. F., Ho, T. H., & Chong, J. K. (2004). A cognitive hierarchy model of games. *The Quarterly Journal of Economics, 119*(3), 861–898.

Campos, J. J., Campos, R. G., & Barrett, K. C. (1989). Emergent themes in the study of emotional development and emotion regulation. *Developmental Psychology, 25*(3), 394.

Cappelen, A. W., Sørensen, E. Ø., & Tungodden, B. (2013). When do we lie? *Journal of Economic Behavior & Organisation, 93*, 258–265.

Capraro, V. (2013). A model of human cooperation in social dilemmas. *PloS One, 8*(8), e72427.

Capraro, V. (2024). The dual-process approach to human sociality: Meta-analytic evidence for a theory of internalised heuristics for self-preservation. *Journal of Personality and Social Psychology, 126*(5), 719.

Capraro, V. (2025). Human behaviour through a LENS: How Linguistic content triggers Emotions and Norms and determines Strategy choices. *Current Opinion in Psychology, 64*, 102024.

Capraro, V., & Barcelo, H. (2015). Group size effect on cooperation in one-shot social dilemmas II: Curvilinear effect. *PloS One, 10*(7), e0131419.

Capraro, V., & Barcelo, H. (2021). Telling people to 'rely on their reasoning' increases intentions to wear a face covering to slow down COVID-19 transmission. *Applied Cognitive Psychology, 35*(3), 693–699.

Capraro, V., Di Paolo, R., Perc, M., & Pizziol, V. (2024c). Language-based game theory in the age of artificial intelligence. *Journal of the Royal Society Interface, 21*(212), 20230720.

Capraro, V., Di Paolo, R., & Pizziol, V. (2025). A publicly available benchmark for assessing large language models' ability to predict how humans balance self-interest and the interest of others. *Scientific Reports, 15*(1), 21428.

Capraro, V., Di Paolo, R., & Pizziol, V. (2025b). Language and economic decisions *Available at SSRN*: https://papers.ssrn.com/sol3/papers.cfm?abstract_id=5549386.

Capraro, V., Everett, J. A., & Earp, B. D. (2019a). Priming intuition disfavors instrumental harm but not impartial beneficence. *Journal of Experimental Social Psychology, 83*, 142–149.

Capraro, V., Halpern, J. Y., & Perc, M. (2024a). From outcome-based to language-based preferences. *Journal of Economic Literature, 62*(1), 115–154.

Capraro, V., Jagfeld, G., Klein, R., Mul, M., & de Pol, I. V. (2019b). Increasing altruistic and cooperative behaviour with simple moral nudges. *Scientific Reports, 9*(1), 11880.

Capraro, V., Jordan, J. J., & Rand, D. G. (2014a). Heuristics guide the implementation of social preferences in one-shot Prisoner's Dilemma experiments. *Scientific Reports, 4*(1), 6790.

Capraro, V., Jordan, J. J., & Tappin, B. M. (2021). Does observability amplify sensitivity to moral frames? Evaluating a reputation-based account of moral preferences. *Journal of Experimental Social Psychology, 94*, 104103.

Capraro, V., Lentsch, A., Acemoglu, D., Akgun, S., Akhmedova, A., Bilancini, E., … Viale, R. (2024b). The impact of generative artificial intelligence on socioeconomic inequalities and policy making. *PNAS Nexus, 3*(6), page191.

Capraro, V., & Perc, M. (2021). Mathematical foundations of moral preferences. *Journal of the Royal Society Interface 18*(175), 20200880. https://royalsocietypublishing.org/doi/10.1098/rsif.2020.0880.

Capraro, V., Perc, M., & Vilone, D. (2019c). The evolution of lying in well-mixed populations. *Journal of the Royal Society Interface, 16*(156), 20190211.

Capraro, V., & Rand, D. G. (2018). Do the right thing: Experimental evidence that preferences for moral behavior, rather than equity or efficiency per se, drive human prosociality. *Judgment and Decision Making, 13*(1), 99–111.

Capraro, V., Smyth, C., Mylona, K., & Niblo, G. A. (2014b). Benevolent characteristics promote cooperative behaviour among humans. *PloS One, 9*(8), e102881.

Capraro, V., & Vanzo, A. (2019). The power of moral words: Loaded language generates framing effects in the extreme Dictator Game. *Judgment and Decision Making, 14*(3), 309–317.

Capraro, V., Vanzo, A., & Cabrales, A. (2022). Playing with words: Do people exploit loaded language to affectothers' decisions for their own benefit? *Judgment and Decision Making, 17*(1), 50–69.

Carlsmith, J. M., & Gross, A. E. (1969). Some effects of guilt on compliance. *Journal of Personality and Social Psychology, 11*(3), 232.

Castagnetti, A., Proto, E., & Sofianos, A. (2023). Anger impairs strategic behavior: A beauty-contest based analysis. *Journal of Economic Behavior & Organisation, 213*, 128–141.

Castagnetti, S. A., Massaro, S., & Proto, E. (2018). The influence of anger on strategic cooperative interactions. In *Academy of management proceedings* (p. 14162). Academy of Management 10510.

Catola, M., D'Alessandro, S., Guarnieri, P., & Pizziol, V. (2021). Personal norms in the online public good game. *Economics Letters, 207*, 110024.

Caviola, L., & Capraro, V. (2020). Liking but devaluing animals: Emotional and deliberative paths to speciesism. *Social Psychological and Personality Science, 11*, 1080–1088.

Caviola, L., Everett, J. A., & Faber, N. S. (2019). The moral standing of animals: Towards a psychology of speciesism. *Journal of Personality and Social Psychology, 116*(6), 1011.

Cernian, A., Sgarciu, V., & Martin, B. (2015, June). Sentiment analysis from product reviews using SentiWordNet as lexical resource. In *2015 7th international conference on electronics, computers and artificial intelligence (ECAI)* (pp. WE-15). IEEE.

Chang, D., Chen, R., & Krupka, E. (2019). Rhetoric matters: A social norms explanation for the anomaly of framing. *Games and Economic Behavior, 116*, 158–178.

Chapman, H. A., & Anderson, A. K. (2013). Things rank and gross in nature: A review and synthesis of moral disgust. *Psychological Bulletin, 139*(2), 300.

Chapman, H. A., Kim, D. A., Susskind, J. M., & Anderson, A. K. (2009). In bad taste: Evidence for the oral origins of moral disgust. *Science, 323*(5918), 1222–1226.

Chapman, J., Dean, M., Ortoleva, P., Snowberg, E., & Camerer, C. (2023). Econographics. *Journal of Political Economy Microeconomics, 1*(1), 115–161.

Charness, G., & Grosskopf, B. (2001). Relative payoffs and happiness: An experimental study. *Journal of Economic Behavior & Organisation, 45*, 301–328.

Charness, G., & Rabin, M. (2002). Understanding social preferences with simple tests. *The Quarterly Journal of Economics, 117*(3), 817–869.

Chaurand, N., & Brauer, M. (2008). What determines social control? People's reactions to counternormative behaviors in urban environments. *Journal of Applied Social Psychology, 38*(7), 1689–1715.

Chawla, K., Clever, R., Ramirez, J., Lucas, G. M., & Gratch, J. (2023). Towards emotion-aware agents for improved user satisfaction and partner perception in negotiation dialogues. *IEEE Transactions on Affective Computing, 15*, 433–444.

Chen, Y., Liu, T. X., Shan, Y., & Zhong, S. (2023). The emergence of economic rationality of GPT. *Proceedings of the National Academy of Sciences, 120*(51), e2316205120.

Choshen-Hillel, S., & Yaniv, I. (2011). Agency and the construction of social preference: Between inequality aversion and prosocial behavior. *Journal of Personality and Social Psychology, 101*(6), 1253.

Cialdini, R. B., Kallgren, C. A., & Reno, R. R. (1991). A focus theory of normative conduct: A theoretical refinement and reevaluation of the role of norms in human behavior. In *Advances in experimental social psychology* (Vol. 24, pp. 201–234). Academic Press. www.sciencedirect.com/science/article/abs/pii/S0065260108603305.

Cialdini, R. B., Reno, R. R., & Kallgren, C. A. (1990). A focus theory of normative conduct: Recycling the concept of norms to reduce littering in public places. *Journal of Personality and Social Psychology, 58*(6), 1015.

Circi, R., Gatti, D., Russo, V., & Vecchi, T. (2021). The foreign language effect on decision-making: A meta-analysis. *Psychonomic Bulletin & Review, 28*, 1–11.

Clark, R. (2023). *Meaningful games: Exploring language with game theory*. MIT Press.

Clot, S., Grolleau, G., & Méral, P. (2017). Payment vs. compensation for ecosystem services: Do words have a voice in the design of environmental conservation programs? *Ecological Economics, 135*, 299–303.

Condon, P., & DeSteno, D. (2011). Compassion for one reduces punishment for another. *Journal of Experimental Social Psychology, 47*(3), 698–701.

Costa, A., Foucart, A., Arnon, I., Aparici, M., & Apesteguia, J. (2014). 'Piensa' twice: On the foreign language effect in decision making. *Cognition, 130*(2), 236–254.

Costa-Gomes, M., Crawford, V. P., & Broseta, B. (2001). Cognition and behavior in normal-form games: An experimental study. *Econometrica, 69*(5), 1193–1235.

Costello, T. H., Pennycook, G., & Rand, D. G. (2024). Durably reducing conspiracy beliefs through dialogues with AI. *Science, 385*(6714), eadq1814.

Crosetto, P., & Filippin, A. (2013). The 'bomb' risk elicitation task. *Journal of Risk and Uncertainty, 47*, 31–65.

Curry, O. S., Alfano, M., Brandt, M. J., & Pelican, C. (2022). Moral molecules: Morality as a combinatorial system. *Review of Philosophy and Psychology, 13*(4), 1039–1058.

Curry, O. S., Chesters, M. J., & Van Lissa, C. J. (2019a). Mapping morality with a compass: Testing the theory of 'morality-as-cooperation' with a new questionnaire. *Journal of Research in Personality, 78*, 106–124.

Curry, O. S., Mullins, D. A., & Whitehouse, H. (2019b). Is it good to cooperate? Testing the theory of morality-as-cooperation in 60 societies. *Current Anthropology, 60*(1), 47–69.

Dal Bó, E., & Dal Bó, P. (2014). 'Do the right thing:' The effects of moral suasion on cooperation. *Journal of Public Economics, 117*, 28–38.

Danovski, K., & Brede, M. (2022). On the evolutionary language game in structured and adaptive populations. *Plos One, 17*(8), e0273608.

De Choudhury, M., Counts, S., & Horvitz, E. (2013a). Predicting postpartum changes in emotion and behavior via social media. In *Proceedings of the SIGCHI conference on human factors in computing systems* (pp. 3267–3276).

De Choudhury, M., Gamon, M., Counts, S., & Horvitz, E. (2013b). Predicting depression via social media. In *Proceedings of the international AAAI conference on web and social media* (Vol. 7, No. 1, pp. 128–137).

Dell'Acqua, F., McFowland III, E., Mollick, E. R., Lifshitz-Assaf, H., Kellogg, K., Rajendran, S., ... Lakhani, K. R. (2023). Navigating the jagged technological frontier: Field experimental evidence of the effects of AI on knowledge worker productivity and quality. *Harvard Business School Technology & Operations Management Unit Working Paper*, (24-013).

Deonna, J. A., Rodogno, R., & Teroni, F. (2012). *In defense of shame: The faces of an emotion*. Oxford University Press.

DeScioli, P., Massenkoff, M., Shaw, A., Petersen, M. B., & Kurzban, R. (2014). Equity or equality? Moral judgments follow the money. *Proceedings of the Royal Society B: Biological Sciences, 281*(1797), 20142112.

Devlin, J., Chang, M.-W., Lee, K., & Toutanova, K. (2018). Bert: Pre-training of deep bidirectional transformers for language understanding. *arXiv preprint arXiv:1810.04805*.

Dillard, J. P., & Shen, L. (2005). On the nature of reactance and its role in persuasive health communication. *Communication Monographs, 72*(2), 144–168.

Dreber, A., Ellingsen, T., Johannesson, M., & Rand, D. G. (2013). Do people care about social context? Framing effects in dictator games. *Experimental Economics, 16*, 349–371.

Dufwenberg, M., Gächter, S., & Hennig-Schmidt, H. (2011). The framing of games and the psychology of play. *Games and Economic Behavior, 73*(2), 459–478.

Dwenger, N., Kleven, H., Rasul, I., & Rincke, J. (2016). Extrinsic and intrinsic motivations for tax compliance: Evidence from a field experiment in Germany. *American Economic Journal: Economic Policy, 8*(3), 203–232.

The Economist. (2024). www.economist.com/united-states/2024/02/28/is-googles-gemini-chatbot-woke-by-accident-or-design

Ekman, P. (1973). Cross-cultural studies of facial expression. In P. Ekman (Ed.), *Darwin and facial expression: A century of research in review/Academic* (pp. 169–222). Academic Press.

Ekman, P. (1992). An argument for basic emotions. *Cognition & Emotion, 6*(3–4), 169–200.

Ellingsen, T., Johannesson, M., Mollerstrom, J., & Munkhammar, S. (2012). Social framing effects: Preferences or beliefs? *Games and Economic Behavior, 76*(1), 117–130.

Elliott, C. D. (1992). *The affective reasoner: A process model of emotions in a multiagent system*. Northwestern University.

Engel, C. (2011). Dictator games: A meta study. *Experimental Economics, 14*(4), 583–610.

Engel, C., & Zhurakhovska, L. (2016). When is the risk of cooperation worth taking? The Prisoner's Dilemma as a game of multiple motives. *Applied Economics Letters, 23*(16), 1157–1161.

Engelmann, D., & Strobel, M. (2004). Inequality aversion, efficiency, and maximin preferences in simple distribution experiments. *American Economic Review, 94*(4), 857–869.

Erat, S., & Gneezy, U. (2012). White lies. *Management Science, 58*(4), 723–733.

Ericksen, K. P., & Horton, H. (1992). 'Blood Feuds': Cross-cultural variations in Kin group vengeance. *Behavior Science Research, 26*(1–4), 57–85.

Eriksson, K., Strimling, P., Andersson, P. A., & Lindholm, T. (2017). Costly punishment in the Ultimatum Game evokes moral concern, in particular when framed as payoff reduction. *Journal of Experimental Social Psychology, 69,* 59–64.

Esuli, A., & Sebastiani, F. (2007). Pageranking wordnet synsets: An application to opinion mining. In *Proceedings of the 45th Annual Meeting of the Association of Computational Linguistics* (pp. 424–431).

Eubanks, V. (2018). *Automating inequality: How high-tech tools profile, police, and punish the poor.* St. Martin's Press.

Evans, A. M., & Brandt, M. J. (2019). Comparing the effects of hypothetical moral preferences on real-life and hypothetical behavior: Commentary on Bostyn, Sevenhant, and Roets (2018). *Psychological Science, 30,* 1380–1382.

Falk, A., Fehr, E., & Fischbacher, U. (2003). On the nature of fair behavior. *Economic Inquiry, 41*(1), 20–26.

Farrow, K., Grolleau, G., & Mzoughi, N. (2018). What in the word! The scope for the effect of word choice on economic behavior. *Kyklos, 71*(4), 557–580.

Fazio, R. H. (2001). On the automatic activation of associated evaluations: An overview. *Cognition & Emotion, 15*(2), 115–141.

Fehr, E., & Schmidt, K. M. (1999). A theory of fairness, competition, and cooperation. *The Quarterly Journal of Economics, 114,* 817–868.

Fellbaum, C. (1998). WordNet: An electronic lexical database. *MIT Press Google Scholar, 2,* 678–686.

Fellner, C. H., & Schwartz, S. H. (1971). Altruism in disrepute: Medical versus public attitudes toward the living organ donor. *New England Journal of Medicine, 284*(11), 582–585.

Feuerriegel, S., Maarouf, A., Bär, D., Geissler, D., Schweisthal, J., Pröllochs, N., ... Van Bavel, J. J. (2025). Using natural language processing to analyse text data in behavioural science. *Nature Reviews Psychology, 4,* 1–16.

Fischbacher, U., & Föllmi-Heusi, F. (2013). Lies in disguise – An experimental study on cheating. *Journal of the European Economic Association, 11*(3), 525–547.

Fischer, J. M., & Ravizza, M. (1998). *Responsibility and control: A theory of moral responsibility*. Cambridge University Press.

Flusberg, S. J., Holmes, K. J., Thibodeau, P. H., Nabi, R. L., & Matlock, T. (2024). The psychology of framing: How everyday language shapes the way we think, feel, and act. *Psychological Science in the Public Interest, 25*(3), 105–161.

Foot, P. (1967). The problem of abortion and the doctrine of double effect. *Oxford, 5*, 5–15.

Forsythe, R., Horowitz, J. L., Savin, N. E., & Sefton, M. (1994). Fairness in simple bargaining experiments. *Games and Economic Behavior, 6*(3), 347–369.

Frankfurt, H. (2018). Alternate possibilities and moral responsibility. In D. Widerker & M. McKenna (Eds.), *Moral responsibility and alternative possibilities: Essays on the importance of alternative possibilities* (pp. 17–25). Routledge.

Frankfurt, H. G. (1969). Alternate possibilities and moral responsibility. *Journal of Philosophy, 66*, 829–839. Reprinted in Frankfurt 1988, pp. 1–10.

Fredrickson, B. L. (1998). What good are positive emotions? *Review of General Psychology, 2*(3), 300–319.

Fredrickson, B. L. (2001). The role of positive emotions in positive psychology: The broaden-and-build theory of positive emotions. *American Psychologist, 56*(3), 218.

Frijda, N. H. (1986). *The emotions*. Cambridge University Press.

Frimer, J. A., Boghrati, R., Haidt, J., Graham, J., & Dehgani, M. (2019). Moral foundations dictionary for linguistic analyses 2.0. https://osf.io/ezn37/overview.

Fulgu, R. A., & Capraro, V. (2024). Surprising gender biases in GPT. *Computers in Human Behavior Reports*.

Gächter, S., Molleman, L., & Nosenzo, D. (2025). Why people follow rules. *Nature Human Behaviour, 9*, 1342–1354. https://doi.org/10.1038/s41562-025-02196-4.

Gaffal, M., & Padilla Gálvez, J. (2024). Negotiation, game theory and language games. In M. Gaffal & J. Padilla Gálvez (Eds.), *Dynamics of rational negotiation: Game theory, language games and forms of life* (pp. 11–40). Springer Nature Switzerland.

Garcia, J., & Hankins, W. (1975, January). The evolution of bitter and the acquisition of toxiphobia. In D. A. Denton & J. P. Coghlan (Eds.), *Olfaction and Taste: V. Proceedings of the 5th International Symposium on Olfaction and Taste* (pp. 39–45). Academic Press.

Gärtner, M., Andersson, D., Västfjäll, D., & Tinghög, G. (2022). Affect and prosocial behavior: The role of decision mode and individual processing style. *Judgment and Decision Making*, 17(1), 1–13.

Gavrilets, S. (2021). Coevolution of actions, personal norms and beliefs about others in social dilemmas. *Evolutionary Human Sciences, 3*, e44.

Geanakoplos, J., Pearce, D., & Stacchetti, E. (1989). Psychological games and sequential rationality. *Games and Economic Behavior, 1*(1), 60–79.

Geertz, C. (1973). Person, time, and conduct in Bali. In C. Geertz (Ed.), *The interpretation of cultures: Selected essays* (pp. 360–411). Basic Books.

Giguère, B., Lalonde, R. N., & Taylor, D. M. (2014). Drinking too much and feeling bad about it? How group identification moderates experiences of guilt and shame following norm transgression. *Personality and Social Psychology Bulletin, 40*(5), 617–632.

Gilovich, T. (2002). *Heuristics and biases: The psychology of intuitive judgment*. Cambridge University Press.

Gneezy, U. (2005). Deception: The role of consequences. *American Economic Review, 95*(1), 384–394.

Gneezy, U., & Imas, A. (2014). Materazzi effect and the strategic use of anger in competitive interactions. *Proceedings of the National Academy of Sciences, 111*(4), 1334–1337.

Goh, E., Bunning, B., Khoong, E., Gallo, R., Milstein, A., Centola, D., & Chen, J. H. (2023). ChatGPT influence on medical decision-making, Bias, and equity: A randomised study of clinicians evaluating clinical vignettes. Available at: www.ncbi.nlm.nih.gov/pmc/articles/PMC10705632/.

Goldstein, J. A., Chao, J., Grossman, S., Stamos, A., & Tomz, M. (2024). How persuasive is AI-generated propaganda? *PNAS Nexus, 3*(2), page034.

Goli, A., & Singh, A. (2024). Frontiers: Can large language models capture human preferences? *Marketing Science, 43*(4), 709–722.

Graham, J., Haidt, J., & Nosek, B. A. (2009). Liberals and conservatives rely on different sets of moral foundations. *Journal of Personality and Social Psychology, 96*(5), 1029.

Grasmick, H. G., & Bursik, R. J. (1990). Conscience, significant others, and rational choice: Extending the deterrence model. *Law & Society Review, 24*(3), 837–861.

Green, L., Fristoe, N., & Myerson, J. (1994). Temporal discounting and preference reversals in choice between delayed outcomes. *Psychonomic Bulletin & Review, 1*, 383–389.

Greene, J. D., Morelli, S. A., Lowenberg, K., Nystrom, L. E., & Cohen, J. D. (2008). Cognitive load selectively interferes with utilitarian moral judgment. *Cognition, 107*(3), 1144–1154.

Greene, J. D., Sommerville, R. B., Nystrom, L. E., Darley, J. M., & Cohen, J. D. (2001). An fMRI investigation of emotional engagement in moral judgment. *Science, 293*(5537), 2105–2108.

Güth, W., Schmittberger, R., & Schwarze, B. (1982). An experimental analysis of ultimatum bargaining. *Journal of Economic Behavior & Organisation, 3*(4), 367–388.

Haidt, J., & Joseph, C. (2004). Intuitive ethics: How innately prepared intuitions generate culturally variable virtues. *Daedalus, 133*(4), 55–66.

Hamilton, W. D. (1964). The genetical evolution of social behaviour. II. *Journal of Theoretical Biology, 7*(1), 17–52.

Hamouda, A., & Rohaim, M. (2011, January). Reviews classification using sentiwordnet lexicon. In *World congress on computer science and information technology* (Vol. 23, pp. 104–105). sn.

Hancock, J. T., Landrigan, C., & Silver, C. (2007, April). Expressing emotion in text-based communication. In *Proceedings of the SIGCHI conference on Human factors in computing systems* (pp. 929–932).

Hareli, S., Moran-Amir, O., David, S., & Hess, U. (2013). Emotions as signals of normative conduct. *Cognition & Emotion, 27*(8), 1395–1404.

Harlé, K. M., & Sanfey, A. G. (2007). Incidental sadness biases social economic decisions in the Ultimatum Game. *Emotion, 7*(4), 876.

Harsanyi, J. C. (1967). Games with incomplete information played by 'Bayesian' players, I–III Part I. The basic model. *Management Science, 14*(3), 159–182.

Hayakawa, S., Lau, B. K. Y., Holtzmann, S., Costa, A., & Keysar, B. (2019). On the reliability of the foreign language effect on risk-taking. *Quarterly Journal of Experimental Psychology, 72*(1), 29–40.

Heberlein, T. A., & Black, J. S. (1976). Attitudinal specificity and the prediction of behavior in a field setting. *Journal of Personality and Social Psychology, 33*(4), 474.

Heerdink, M. W., Koning, L. F., Van Doorn, E. A., & Van Kleef, G. A. (2019). Emotions as guardians of group norms: Expressions of anger and disgust drive inferences about autonomy and purity violations. *Cognition and Emotion, 33*(3), 563–578.

Henrich, J., Boyd, R., Bowles, S., Camerer, C., Fehr, E., Gintis, H., & McElreath, R. (2001). In search of homo economicus: Behavioral experiments in 15 small-scale societies. *American Economic Review, 91*(2), 73–78.

Henrich, J., Heine, S. J., & Norenzayan, A. (2010). The weirdest people in the world? *Behavioral and Brain Sciences, 33*(2–3), 61–83.

Hinojosa, J. A., Moreno, E. M., & Ferré, P. (2020). Affective neurolinguistics: Towards a framework for reconciling language and emotion. *Language, Cognition and Neuroscience, 35*(7), 813–839.

Hoffman, E., McCabe, K., Shachat, K., & Smith, V. (1994). Preferences, property rights, and anonymity in bargaining games. *Games and Economic Behavior, 7*(3), 346–380.

Holt, C. A., & Laury, S. K. (2002). Risk aversion and incentive effects. *American Economic Review, 92*(5), 1644–1655.

Hoover, J., Portillo-Wightman, G., Yeh, L., Havaldar, S., Davani, A. M., Lin, Y., ... Dehghani, M. (2020). Moral foundations twitter corpus: A collection of 35k tweets annotated for moral sentiment. *Social Psychological and Personality Science, 11*(8), 1057–1071.

Hopp, F. R., Fisher, J. T., Cornell, D., Huskey, R., & Weber, R. (2021). The extended Moral Foundations Dictionary (eMFD): Development and applications of a crowd-sourced approach to extracting moral intuitions from text. *Behavior Research Methods, 53*, 232–246.

Horberg, E. J., Oveis, C., Keltner, D., & Cohen, A. B. (2009). Disgust and the moralisation of purity. *Journal of Personality and Social Psychology, 97*(6), 963.

Hsu, M., Anen, C., & Quartz, S. R. (2008). The right and the good: Distributive justice and neural encoding of equity and efficiency. *Science, 320*(5879), 1092–1095.

Huang, L., Lei, W., Xu, F., Liu, H., Yu, L., Shi, F., & Wang, L. (2020). Maxims nudge equitable or efficient choices in a Trade-Off game. *Plos One, 15*(6), e0235443.

Huang, L., Lei, W., Xu, F., Yu, L., & Shi, F. (2019). Choosing an equitable or efficient option: A distribution dilemma. *Social Behavior and Personality: An International Journal, 47*(10), 1–10.

Ibanez, L., Moureau, N., & Roussel, S. (2017). How do incidental emotions impact pro-environmental behavior? Evidence from the Dictator Game. *Journal of Behavioral and Experimental Economics, 66*, 150–155.

Isaac, R. M., Walker, J. M., & Williams, A. W. (1994). Group size and the voluntary provision of public goods: Experimental evidence utilising large groups. *Journal of Public Economics, 54*(1), 1–36.

Iyengar, S. S., & Lepper, M. R. (2000). When choice is demotivating: Can one desire too much of a good thing? *Journal of Personality and Social Psychology, 79*(6), 995–1006.

Iyer, R., Koleva, S., Graham, J., Ditto, P. H., & Haidt, J. (2010). Understanding libertarian morality: The psychological roots of an individualist ideology. *Available at SSRN 1665934.*

Jaffé, M. E., & Greifeneder, R. (2019). Less than I expected and oh so true? On the interplay between expectations and framing effects in judgments of truth. *Journal of Language and Social Psychology, 38*(5–6), 735–755.

Jiang, L., Hwang, J. D., Bhagavatula, C., Bras, R. L., Liang, J., Dodge, J., ... Choi, Y. (2025). Investigating machine moral judgement through the Delphi experiment. Nature Machine Intelligence, 7, 145–160.

Johnson, E. J., & Goldstein, D. G. (2003). Do defaults save lives? *Science, 302*(5649), 1338–1339.

Johnson, S. B., King, A. J., Warner, E. L., Aneja, S., Kann, B. H., & Bylund, C. L. (2023). Using ChatGPT to evaluate cancer myths and misconceptions: Artificial intelligence and cancer information. *JNCI Cancer Spectrum*, *7*(2), pkad015.

Juvonen, J. (1991). Deviance, perceived responsibility, and negative peer reactions. *Developmental Psychology*, *27*(4), 672.

Kahane, G., Everett, J. A., Earp, B. D., Caviola, L., Faber, N. S., Crockett, M. J., & Savulescu, J. (2018). Beyond sacrificial harm: A two-dimensional model of utilitarian psychology. *Psychological Review*, *125*(2), 131.

Kahneman, D. (2011). *Thinking fast and slow.* Farrar, Straus and Giroux.

Kahneman, D., Knetsch, J. L., & Thaler, R. H. (1986). Fairness and the assumptions of economics. *Journal of Business*, *59*(4, Part 2), S285–S300.

Kahneman, D., Knetsch, J. L., & Thaler, R. H. (1990). Experimental tests of the endowment effect and the Coase theorem. *Journal of Political Economy*, *98*(6), 1325–1348.

Kahneman, D., & Tversky, A. (1979). Prospect theory: An analysis of decision under risk. *Econometrica*, *47*(2), 263–291.

Karataş, M. (2020). Making decisions in foreign languages: Weaker senses of ownership attenuate the endowment effect. *Journal of Consumer Psychology*, *30*(2), 296–303.

Kay, A. C., & Ross, L. (2003). The perceptual push: The interplay of implicit cues and explicit situational construals on behavioral intentions in the Prisoner's Dilemma. *Journal of Experimental Social Psychology*, *39*(6), 634–643.

Keltner, D., & Haidt, J. (2003). Approaching awe, a moral, spiritual, and aesthetic emotion. *Cognition and Emotion*, *17*(2), 297–314.

Kennedy, B., Atari, M., Davani, A. M., Hoover, J., Omrani, A., Graham, J., & Dehghani, M. (2021). Moral concerns are differentially observable in language. *Cognition*, *212*, 104696.

Kipnis, D. (1972). Does power corrupt? *Journal of Personality and Social Psychology*, *24*(1), 33.

Kirchler, E., Hoelzl, E., & Wahl, I. (2008). Enforced versus voluntary tax compliance: The 'slippery slope' framework. *Journal of Economic Psychology*, *29*(2), 210–225.

Kissler, J., & Herbert, C. (2013). Emotion, Etmnooi, or Emitoon?–Faster lexical access to emotional than to neutral words during reading. *Biological Psychology*, *92*(3), 464–479.

Klauer, K. C., & Musch, J. (2003). Affective priming: Findings and theories. *The Psychology of Evaluation: Affective Processes in Cognition and Emotion, 7*, 49.

Konecni, V. J. (1972). Some effects of guilt on compliance: A field replication. *Journal of Personality and Social Psychology, 23*(1), 30–32.

Kőszegi, B. (2006). Emotional agency. *The Quarterly Journal of Economics, 121*(1), 121–155.

Kousta, S. T., Vinson, D. P., & Vigliocco, G. (2009). Emotion words, regardless of polarity, have a processing advantage over neutral words. *Cognition, 112*(3), 473–481.

Kramár, J., Eccles, T., Gemp, I., Tacchetti, A., McKee, K. R., Malinowski, M., ... Bachrach, Y. (2022). Negotiation and honesty in artificial intelligence methods for the board game of Diplomacy. *Nature Communications, 13*(1), 7214.

Kramer, A. D. (2010, April). An unobtrusive behavioral model of 'gross national happiness'. In *Proceedings of the SIGCHI conference on human factors in computing systems* (pp. 287–290).

Kreps, D. M. (1990). Corporate culture and economic theory. *Perspectives on Positive Political Economy, 90*(109–110), 8.

Kreps, S., McCain, R. M., & Brundage, M. (2022). All the news that's fit to fabricate: AI-generated text as a tool of media misinformation. *Journal of Experimental Political Science, 9*(1), 104–117.

Krupka, E. L., & Weber, R. A. (2013). Identifying social norms using coordination games: Why does Dictator Game sharing vary? *Journal of the European Economic Association, 11*(3), 495–524.

Kuang, J., & Bicchieri, C. (2024a). Language matters: How normative expressions shape norm perception and affect norm compliance. *Philosophical Transactions of the Royal Society B, 379*(1897), 20230037.

Kuang, J., & Bicchieri, C. (2024b). How language framing shapes the perception of social norms. *Current Opinion in Psychology, 60*, 101886.

Kuang, J., & Bicchieri, C. (2024c). How do people interpret social norm messages? Semantic ambiguity and pragmatic inferences. Available at: https://osf.io/preprints/psyarxiv/zmgjn.

Kuchinke, L., Jacobs, A. M., Grubich, C., Vo, M. L. H., Conrad, M., & Herrmann, M. (2005). Incidental effects of emotional valence in single word processing: An fMRI study. *NeuroImage, 28*(4), 1022–1032.

Kuhn, T. (1962). *The structure of scientific revolutions*. University of Chicago Press.

Kumar, A., Capraro, V., & Perc, M. (2020). The evolution of trust and trustworthiness. *Journal of the Royal Society Interface, 17*(169), 20200491.

Lammers, J., Stapel, D. A., & Galinsky, A. D. (2010). Power increases hypocrisy: Moralising in reasoning, immorality in behavior. *Psychological Science, 21*(5), 737–744.

Lang, P. J., Bradley, M. M., & Cuthbert, B. N. (2013). Motivated attention: Affect, activation, and action. In P. J. Lang, R. F. Simons, & M. T. Balaban (Eds.), *Attention and orienting* (pp. 97–135). Psychology Press.

Lange, J., Heerdink, M. W., & Van Kleef, G. A. (2022). Reading emotions, reading people: Emotion perception and inferences drawn from perceived emotions. *Current Opinion in Psychology, 43*, 85–90.

LeDoux, J. (1996). *The emotional brain: The mysterious underpinnings of emotional life*. Simon and Schuster.

LeDoux, J. (2003). The emotional brain, fear, and the amygdala. *Cellular and Molecular Neurobiology, 23*, 727–738.

Ledyard, J. O. (1995). Public goods: A survey of experimental research. In J. Kagel & A. Roth (Eds.), *Handbook of experimental economics* (pp. 111–194). Princeton University Press.

Levin, I. P., & Gaeth, G. J. (1988). How consumers are affected by the framing of attribute information before and after consuming the product. *Journal of Consumer Research, 15*(3), 374–378.

Levine, D. K. (1998). Modeling altruism and spitefulness in experiments. *Review of Economic Dynamics, 1*, 593–622.

Levine, E. E., Barasch, A., Rand, D., Berman, J. Z., & Small, D. A. (2018). Signaling emotion and reason in cooperation. *Journal of Experimental Psychology: General, 147*, 702.

Lewis, M., Ramsay, D. S., & Sullivan, M. W. (2006). The relation of ANS and HPA activation to infant anger and sadness response to goal blockage. *Developmental Psychobiology: The Journal of the International Society for Developmental Psychobiology, 48*(5), 397–405.

Liberman, V., Samuels, S. M., & Ross, L. (2004). The name of the game: Predictive power of reputations versus situational labels in determining Prisoner's Dilemma game moves. *Personality and Social Psychology Bulletin, 30*(9), 1175–1185.

Lin, H., & Sunder, S. (2002). Using experimental data to model bargaining behavior in Ultimatum Games. In R. Zwick & A. Rapoport (Eds.), *Experimental business research* (pp. 373–397). Springer US.

List, J. A. (2003). Does market experience eliminate market anomalies? *Quarterly Journal of Economics, 118*(1), 41–71.

Liu, H., Lieberman, H., & Selker, T. (2003). A model of textual affect sensing using real-world knowledge. In *Proceedings of the 8th international conference on Intelligent user interfaces* (pp. 125–132).

Loewenstein, G. (2000). Emotions in economic theory and economic behavior. *American Economic Review, 90*(2), 426–432.

Loewenstein, G. F., Hsee, C. K., Weber, E. U., & Welch, N. (2001). Risk as feelings. *Psychological Bulletin, 127*(2), 267–286.

Luce, R. D. (1959). *Individual choice behavior* (Vol. 4). Wiley.

Lyubomirsky, S., King, L., & Diener, E. (2005). The benefits of frequent positive affect: Does happiness lead to success? *Psychological Bulletin, 131*(6), 803.

Macy, M. W., & Flache, A. (2002). Learning dynamics in social dilemmas. *Proceedings of the National Academy of Sciences, 99*(suppl_3), 7229–7236.

Madan, R., & Ashok, M. (2023). AI adoption and diffusion in public administration: A systematic literature review and future research agenda. *Government Information Quarterly, 40*(1), 101774.

Madrian, B. C., & Shea, D. F. (2001). The power of suggestion: Inertia in 401(k) participation and savings behavior. *Quarterly Journal of Economics, 116*(4), 1149–1187.

Malik, M., Youk, S., Hopp, F. R., Curry, O. S., Cheong, M., Alfano, M., & Weber, R. (2025). The Extended Morality as Cooperation Dictionary (eMACD): A crowd-sourced approach via the moral narrative analyzer platform. *Communication Methods and Measures, 19*, 201–231.

Mathur, A., Acar, G., Friedman, M. J., Lucherini, E., Mayer, J., Chetty, M., & Narayanan, A. (2019). Dark patterns at scale: Findings from a crawl of 11K shopping websites. *Proceedings of the ACM on Human-Computer Interaction, 3*(CSCW), 1–32.

McKelvey, R. D., & Palfrey, T. R. (1995). Quantal response equilibria for normal form games. *Games and Economic Behavior, 10*(1), 6–38.

Mehrabi, N., Morstatter, F., Saxena, N., Lerman, K., & Galstyan, A. (2021). A survey on bias and fairness in machine learning. *ACM Computing Surveys (CSUR), 54*(6), 1–35.

Mei, Q., Xie, Y., Yuan, W., & Jackson, M. O. (2024). A turing test of whether AI chatbots are behaviorally similar to humans. *Proceedings of the National Academy of Sciences, 121*(9), e2313925121.

Meyer, W. U., Reisenzein, R., & Schützwohl, A. (1997). Toward a process analysis of emotions: The case of surprise. *Motivation and Emotion, 21*, 251–274.

Mieth, L., Buchner, A., & Bell, R. (2021). Moral labels increase cooperation and costly punishment in a Prisoner's Dilemma game with punishment option. *Scientific Reports, 11*, 10221.

Mill, J. S. (1863). *Utilitarianism*. Parker, Son, and Bourn, West Strand.

Miller, G. A. (1995). WordNet: A lexical database for English. *Communications of the ACM, 38*(11), 39–41.

Minsky, M., & Papert, S. (1969). *Perceptrons: An introduction to computational geometry*. The MIT Press.

Mohammad, S. M., & Turney, P. D. (2013). Crowdsourcing a word–emotion association lexicon. *Computational Intelligence*, *29*(3), 436–465.

Moretti, L., & Di Pellegrino, G. (2010). Disgust selectively modulates reciprocal fairness in economic interactions. *Emotion*, *10*(2), 169.

Motro, D., Ordóñez, L. D., Pittarello, A., & Welsh, D. T. (2018). Investigating the effects of anger and guilt on unethical behavior: A dual-process approach. *Journal of Business Ethics*, *152*, 133–148.

Mowrer, O. H. (1960). *Learning theory and behavior*. Wiley & Sons.

Mühlhoff, R. (2021). Predictive privacy: Towards an applied ethics of data analytics. *Ethics and Information Technology*, *23*(4), 675–690.

Nash Jr, J. F. (1950). Equilibrium points in n-person games. *Proceedings of the National Academy of Sciences*, *36*(1), 48–49.

Neilson, W. S. (2009). A theory of kindness, reluctance, and shame for social preferences. *Games and Economic Behavior*, *66*(1), 394–403.

Nelson, L. D., & Simmons, J. P. (2009). On southbound ease and northbound fees: Literal consequences of the metaphoric link between vertical position and cardinal direction. *Journal of Marketing Research*, *46*(6), 715–724.

von Neumann, J., & Morgenstern, O. (1944). *Theory of games and economic behavior*. Princeton University Press.

Nowak, M. A. (2006). Five rules for the evolution of cooperation. *Science*, *314*(5805), 1560–1563.

Noy, S., & Zhang, W. (2023). Experimental evidence on the productivity effects of generative artificial intelligence. *Science*, *381*(6654), 187–192.

Okun, A. M. (2010). *Equality and efficiency: The big tradeoff*. Brookings Institution Press.

O'Reilly, T., Strauss, I., & Mazzucato, M. (2024). Algorithmic attention rents: A theory of digital platform market power. *Data & Policy*, *6*, e6.

Ortony, A., Clore, G. L., & Collins, A. (1988). *The cognitive structure of emotions*. Cambridge University Press.

Ortony, A., Clore, G. L., & Foss, M. A. (1987). The referential structure of the affective lexicon. *Cognitive Science*, *11*(3), 341–364.

Ortony, A., & Turner, T. J. (1990). What's basic about basic emotions? *Psychological Review*, *97*(3), 315.

Osgood, C. E., Suci, G. J., & Tannenbaum, P. H. (1957). *The measurement of meaning*. University of Illinois.

Pasquale, F. (2015). *The black box society: The secret algorithms that control money and information*. Harvard University Press.

Patterson, I., & Pegg, S. (2013). Marketing the leisure experience to baby boomers and older tourists. In M. Sotiriadis & D. Gursoy (Eds.), *Marketing of tourism experiences* (pp. 156–174). Routledge.

Peng, S., Kalliamvakou, E., Cihon, P., & Demirer, M. (2023). The impact of AI on developer productivity: Evidence from github copilot. *arXiv preprint arXiv:2302.06590*.

Pennebaker, J. W., Francis, M., & Booth, R. (2001). *Linguistic inquiry and word count: LIWC 2001*. Erlbaum.

Pennycook, G., Epstein, Z., Mosleh, M., Arechar, A. A., Eckles, D., & Rand, D. G. (2021). Shifting attention to accuracy can reduce misinformation online. *Nature, 592*(7855), 590–595.

Perc, M., Jordan, J. J., Rand, D. G., Wang, Z., Boccaletti, S., & Szolnoki, A. (2017). Statistical physics of human cooperation. *Physics Reports, 687*, 1–51.

Pereda, M., Sánchez, A., & Capraro, V. (2021). *Personal norms, social norms, and intertemporal decisions*. Mimeo.

Plunkett, D., & Greene, J. D. (2019). Overlooked evidence and a misunderstanding of what trolley dilemmas do best: Commentary on Bostyn, Sevenhant, and Roets (2018). *Psychological Science, 30*(9), 1389–1391.

Plutchik, R. (1962). *The emotions: Facts, theories and a new model*. Crown Publishing Group/Random House.

Plutchik, R. (1980). A general psychoevolutionary theory of emotion. In R. Plutchik & H. Kellerman (Eds.), *Emotion: Theory, research, and experience* (Vol. 1, pp. 3–33). Academic Press.

Plutchik, R. (1994). *The psychology and biology of emotion*. HarperCollins College Publishers.

Plutchik, R. (2001). The nature of emotions: Human emotions have deep evolutionary roots, a fact that may explain their complexity and provide tools for clinical practice. *American Scientist, 89*(4), 344–350.

Pomazal, R. J. (1974). *Attitudes, normative beliefs, and altruism: Help for helping behavior*. University of Illinois at Urbana-Champaign.

Popper, K. R. (1959). *The logic of scientific discovery*. Hutchinson.

Preniqi, V., Ghinassi, I., Ive, J., Saitis, C., & Kalimeri, K. (2024, September). MoralBERT: A fine-tuned language model for capturing moral values in social discussions. In *Proceedings of the 2024 International Conference on Information Technology for Social Good* (pp. 433–442).

Puglisi, A., Baronchelli, A., & Loreto, V. (2008). Cultural route to the emergence of linguistic categories. *Proceedings of the National Academy of Sciences, 105*(23), 7936–7940.

Puntoni, S., De Langhe, B., & Van Osselaer, S. M. (2009). Bilingualism and the emotional intensity of advertising language. *Journal of Consumer Research, 35*(6), 1012–1025.

Pyszczynski, T., Solomon, S., & Greenberg, J. (2015). Thirty years of terror management theory: From genesis to revelation. In J. M. Olson & M. P. Zanna (Eds.), *Advances in experimental social psychology* (Vol. 52, pp. 1–70). Academic Press.

Rabb, N., Bowers, J., Glick, D., Wilson, K. H., & Yokum, D. (2022). The influence of social norms varies with 'others' groups: Evidence from COVID-19 vaccination intentions. *Proceedings of the National Academy of Sciences, 119*(29), e2118770119.

Rabin, M. (1993). Incorporating fairness into game theory and economics. *American Economic Review, 83*(5), 1281–1302.

Raghavan, P. (2024). https://blog.google/products/gemini/gemini-image-generation-issue/.

Rapoport, A., & Chammah, A. M. (1965). *Prisoner's dilemma: A study in conflict and cooperation* (Vol. 165). University of Michigan Press.

Rathje, S., Mirea, D. M., Sucholutsky, I., Marjieh, R., Robertson, C. E., & Van Bavel, J. J. (2024). GPT is an effective tool for multilingual psychological text analysis. *Proceedings of the National Academy of Sciences, 121*(34), e2308950121.

Rawls, J. (2017). A theory of justice. In: A. I. Cohen & C. H. Wellman (Eds.), *Applied ethics* (pp. 21–29). Routledge.

Reisenzein, R. (1994). Pleasure-arousal theory and the intensity of emotions. *Journal of Personality and Social Psychology, 67*(3), 525.

Ren, F., & Zhou, Y. (2020). CGMVQA: A new classification and generative model for medical visual question answering. *IEEE Access, 8*, 50626–50636.

Rezapour, R., & Diesner, J. (2019). Expanded morality lexicon. *University of Illinois Urbana-Champaign*. https://doi.org/10.13012/B2IDB-3805242_V1.1.

Rezapour, R., Dinh, L., & Diesner, J. (2021, August). Incorporating the measurement of moral foundations theory into analysing stances on controversial topics. In *Proceedings of the 32nd ACM conference on hypertext and social media* (pp. 177–188).

Rhoads, S. A., Vekaria, K. M., O'Connell, K., Elizabeth, H. S., Rand, D. G., Kozak Williams, M. N., & Marsh, A. A. (2023). Unselfish traits and social decision-making patterns characterize six populations of real-world extraordinary altruists. *Nature Communications, 14*(1), 1807.

Richards, G., & Wilson, J. (2004). The international student travel market: Travelstyle, motivations, and activities. *Tourism Review International, 8*(2), 57–67.

Rosenblatt, F. (1958). The perceptron: A probabilistic model for information storage and organisation in the brain. *Psychological Review, 65*(6), 386.

Ross, L., & Samuels, S. M. (1993). The predictive power of personal reputation vs. labels and construal in the Prisoner's Dilemma game. Unpublished manuscript, Stanford University, Palo Alto, CA.

Rozin, P., & Fallon, A. E. (1987). A perspective on disgust. *Psychological Review, 94*(1), 23.

Rubinstein, A. (2000). *Economics and language: Five essays.* Cambridge University Press.

Rumelhart, D. E., Hinton, G. E., & Williams, R. J. (1986). Learning representations by back-propagating errors. *Nature, 323*(6088), 533–536.

Samuelson, W., & Zeckhauser, R. (1988). Status quo bias in decision making. *Journal of Risk and Uncertainty, 1*(1), 7–59.

Sargın, A. E., Özdel, K., & Türkçapar, M. H. (2017). Cognitive-behavioral theory and treatment of antisocial personality disorder. In *Psychopathy-new updates on an old phenomenon* (Chapter 5). InTech Open. www.intechopen.com/chapters/55712.

Savage, L. J. (1951). The theory of statistical decision. *Journal of the American Statistical Association, 46*(253), 55–67.

Schaumberg, R. L., & Skowronek, S. E. (2022). Shame broadcasts social norms: The positive social effects of shame on norm acquisition and normative behavior. *Psychological Science, 33*(8), 1257–1277.

Schnall, S., Haidt, J., Clore, G. L., & Jordan, A. H. (2008). Disgust as embodied moral judgment. *Personality and Social Psychology Bulletin, 34*(8), 1096–1109.

Schotter, A., Weigelt, K., & Wilson, C. (1994). A laboratory investigation of multiperson rationality and presentation effects. *Games and Economic Behavior, 6*(3), 445–468.

Schwartz, S. H. (1977). Normative influences on altruism. In L. Berkowitz (Ed.), *Advances in experimental social psychology* (Vol. 10, pp. 221–279). Academic Press.

Ścigała, K. A., Zettler, I., Pfattheicher, S., & Capraro, V. (2022). Registered report: Does cooperation framing increase bribery engagement of prosocial individuals? https://doi.org/10.31234/osf.io/gfah8.

Sell, A., Tooby, J., & Cosmides, L. (2009). Formidability and the logic of human anger. *Proceedings of the National Academy of Sciences, 106*(35), 15073–15078.

Selten, R. (1998). Aspiration adaptation theory. *Journal of Mathematical Psychology, 42*(2–3), 191–214.

Simchon, A., Edwards, M., & Lewandowsky, S. (2024). The persuasive effects of political microtargeting in the age of generative artificial intelligence. *PNAS Nexus*, *3*(2), page035.

Simon, H. A. (1955). A behavioral model of rational choice. *The Quarterly Journal of Economics*, *69*(1), 99–118.

Simon, H. A. (1957). *Models of man: Social and rational.* John Wiley & Sons.

Simpson, J., Carter, S., Anthony, S. H., & Overton, P. G. (2006). Is disgust a homogeneous emotion? *Motivation and Emotion*, *30*, 31–41.

Singh, J. J., Garg, N., Govind, R., & Vitell, S. J. (2018). Anger strays, fear refrains: The differential effect of negative emotions on consumers' ethical judgments. *Journal of Business Ethics*, *151*, 235–248.

Singh, P. (2002). The public acquisition of commonsense knowledge. In *Proceedings of AAAI Spring Symposium: Acquiring (and Using) Linguistic (and World) Knowledge for Information Access* (Vol. 3).

Singh, V. K., Piryani, R., Uddin, A., & Waila, P. (2013). Sentiment analysis of movie reviews and blog posts. In *2013 3rd IEEE International Advance Computing Conference (IACC)* (pp. 893–898). IEEE.

Solnick, J. V., Kannenberg, C. H., Eckerman, D. A., & Waller, M. B. (1980). An experimental analysis of impulsivity and impulse control in humans. *Learning and Motivation*, *11*(1), 61–77.

Sparkman, G., & Walton, G. M. (2017). Dynamic norms promote sustainable behavior, even if it is counternormative. *Psychological Science*, *28*(11), 1663–1674.

Spitale, G., Biller-Andorno, N., & Germani, F. (2023). AI model GPT-3 (dis) informs us better than humans. *Science Advances*, *9*(26), eadh1850.

Spruyt, A., De Houwer, J., Hermans, D., & Eelen, P. (2007). Affective priming of nonaffective semantic categorisation responses. *Experimental Psychology*, *54*(1), 44–53.

Stahl II, D. O., & Wilson, P. W. (1994). Experimental evidence on players' models of other players. *Journal of Economic Behavior & Organisation*, *25*(3), 309–327.

Steiner, J. E. (1973). The gustofacial response: Observation on normal and anencephalic newborn infants. In *Symp Oral Sens Percept* (Vol. 4, No. 4, pp. 254–278).

Stone, P. J., Dunphy, D. C., Smith, M. S., & Ogilvie, D. M. (1966). *The general inquirer: A computer approach to content analysis in the behavioral sciences.* MIT Press.

Strohminger, N., Lewis, R. L., & Meyer, D. E. (2011). Divergent effects of different positive emotions on moral judgment. *Cognition*, *119*, 295–300.

Suddendorf, T., & Corballis, M. C. (2007). The evolution of foresight: What is mental time travel, and is it unique to humans? *Behavioral and Brain Sciences, 30*(3), 299–313.

Sunstein, C. R. (2019). Sludge and ordeals. *Duke Law Journal, 68*(8), 1843–1883.

Suri, G., Slater, L. R., Ziaee, A., & Nguyen, M. (2024). Do large language models show decision heuristics similar to humans? A case study using GPT-3.5. *Journal of Experimental Psychology: General, 163*, 1066–1075.

Susskind, J. M., Lee, D. H., Cusi, A., Feiman, R., Grabski, W., & Anderson, A. K. (2008). Expressing fear enhances sensory acquisition. *Nature Neuroscience, 11*(7), 843–850.

Sutter, M. (2009). Deception through telling the truth?! Experimental evidence from individuals and teams. *The Economic Journal, 119*(534), 47–60.

Szolnoki, A., Perc, M., & Szabó, G. (2012). Defense mechanisms of empathetic players in the spatial ultimatum game. *Physical Review Letters, 109*(7), 078701.

Takahashi, T., Oono, H., Inoue, T., Boku, S., Kako, Y., Kitaichi, Y., … Radford, M. H. (2008). Depressive patients are more impulsive and inconsistent in intertemporal choice behavior for monetary gain and loss than healthy subjects – An analysis based on Tsallis' statistics. *Neuroendocrinology Letters, 29*(3), 351–358.

Tan, H. B., & Forgas, J. P. (2010). When happiness makes us selfish, but sadness makes us fair: Affective influences on interpersonal strategies in the Dictator Game. *Journal of Experimental Social Psychology, 46*(3), 571–576.

Tangney, J. P., & Dearing, R. L. (2003). *Shame and guilt*. Guilford Press.

Tappin, B. M., & Capraro, V. (2018). Doing good vs. avoiding bad in prosocial choice: A refined test and extension of the morality preference hypothesis. *Journal of Experimental Social Psychology, 79*, 64–70.

Tarry, H., Vézina, V., Bailey, J., & Lopes, L. (2022). Political orientation, moral foundations, and COVID-19 social distancing. *PloS One, 17*(6), e0267136.

Tavits, M., & Pérez, E. O. (2019). Language influences mass opinion toward gender and LGBT equality. *Proceedings of the National Academy of Sciences, 116*(34), 16781–16786.

Taylor, M. J., Vlaev, I., Maltby, J., Brown, G. D., & Wood, A. M. (2015). Improving social norms interventions: Rank-framing increases excessive alcohol drinkers' information-seeking. *Health Psychology, 34*(12), 1200.

Thaler, R. H. (1994). *Quasi rational economics*. Russell Sage Foundation.

Thaler, R. H., & Benartzi, S. (2004). Save more tomorrow: Using behavioral economics to increase employee saving. *Journal of Political Economy, 112*(S1), S164–S187.

Thaler, R. H., & Sunstein, C. R. (2008). *Nudge: Improving decisions about health, wealth, and happiness*. Yale University Press.

Thielmann, I., Spadaro, G., & Balliet, D. (2020). Personality and prosocial behavior: A theoretical framework and meta-analysis. *Psychological Bulletin, 146*(1), 30–90.

Thomson, J. J. (1985). The trolley problem. *Yale Law Journal, 94*(6), 1395–1415.

Tomkins, S. S. (2008). *Affect imagery consciousness: The complete edition: Two volumes*. Springer Publishing Company.

Tracy, J. L., & Robins, R. W. (2004). Show your pride: Evidence for a discrete emotion expression. *Psychological Science, 15*(3), 194–197.

Trager, J., Ziabari, A. S., Davani, A. M., Golazizian, P., Karimi-Malekabadi, F., Omrani, A., ... Dehghani, M. (2022). The moral foundations reddit corpus. *arXiv preprint arXiv:2208.05545*.

Tumasjan, A., Sprenger, T., Sandner, P., & Welpe, I. (2010, May). Predicting elections with twitter: What 140 characters reveal about political sentiment. In *Proceedings of the international AAAI conference on web and social media* (Vol. 4, No. 1, pp. 178–185).

Tversky, A., & Kahneman, D. (1974). Judgment under uncertainty: Heuristics and Biases. *Science, 185*(4157), 1124–1131.

Tversky, A., & Kahneman, D. (1981). The framing of decisions and the psychology of choice. *Science, 211*(4481), 453–458.

Tversky, A., & Kahneman, D. (1992). Advances in prospect theory: Cumulative representation of uncertainty. *Journal of Risk and Uncertainty, 5*, 297–323.

Ugazio, G., Lamm, C., & Singer, T. (2012). The role of emotions for moral judgments depends on the type of emotion and moral scenario. *Emotion, 12*, 579.

Valdesolo, P., & DeSteno, D. (2006). Manipulations of emotional context shape moral judgment. *Psychological Science, 17*(6), 476–477.

Van Kleef, G. A., Wanders, F., Stamkou, E., & Homan, A. C. (2015). The social dynamics of breaking the rules: Antecedents and consequences of norm-violating behavior. *Current Opinion in Psychology, 6*, 25–31.

Vaswani, A., Shazeer, N., Parmar, N., Uszkoreit, J., Jones, L., Gomez, A. N., Kaiser, Ł., & Polosukhin, I. (2017). Attention is all you need. *Advances in Neural Information Processing Systems, 30*.

Verona, E., Sprague, J., & Sadeh, N. (2012). Inhibitory control and negative emotional processing in psychopathy and antisocial personality disorder. *Journal of Abnormal Psychology, 121*(2), 498.

Wald, A. (1949). Statistical decision functions. *The Annals of Mathematical Statistics, 20*(2), 165–205.

Wankhade, M., Rao, A. C. S., & Kulkarni, C. (2022). A survey on sentiment analysis methods, applications, and challenges. *Artificial Intelligence Review, 55*(7), 5731–5780.

Watson, D., Clark, L. A., & Tellegen, A. (1988). Development and validation of brief measures of positive and negative affect: The PANAS scales. *Journal of Personality and Social Psychology, 54*(6), 1063.

Wedekind, C., & Milinski, M. (2000). Cooperation through image scoring in humans. *Science, 288*(5467), 850–852.

Werbos, P. (1974). *Beyond regression: New tools for prediction and analysis in the behavioral sciences*. PhD thesis, Committee on Applied Mathematics, Harvard University, Cambridge, MA.

Wirtz, B. W., Weyerer, J. C., & Geyer, C. (2019). Artificial intelligence and the public sector – Applications and challenges. *International Journal of Public Administration, 42*(7), 596–615.

Yap, M. J., & Seow, C. S. (2014). The influence of emotion on lexical processing: Insights from RT distributional analysis. *Psychonomic Bulletin & Review, 21*, 526–533.

Zelmer, J. (2003). Linear public goods experiments: A meta-analysis. *Experimental Economics, 6*, 299–310.

Zhong, C. B., & Liljenquist, K. (2006). Washing away your sins: Threatened morality and physical cleansing. *Science, 313*(5792), 1451–1452.

Zuboff, S. (2019). *The age of surveillance capitalism: The fight for a human future at the new frontier of power*. PublicAffairs.

Index

www.ingramcontent.com/pod-product-compliance
Lightning Source LLC
LaVergne TN
LVHW011703200926
848484LV00004B/1050

* 9 7 8 1 0 0 9 7 3 3 0 4 5 *